D1396529

The Psychology of
Teaching

W. Lambert Gardiner

The Psychology of Teaching

Brooks/Cole Publishing Company, Monterey, California
A Division of Wadsworth, Inc.

Consulting Editor: Edward L. Walker

Printed in the United States of America

10 9 8 7 6 5 4 3 2 1

Library of Congress Cataloging in Publication Data
Gardiner, W. Lambert.
  The psychology of teaching.

  Bibliography: p. 361
  Includes index.
  1. Educational psychology. I. Title.
LB1051.G223   371.1'02   78-32090
ISBN 0-8185-0290-8

Acquisition Editor: *Todd Lueders*
Manuscript Editor: *Beth Luey*
Production Editor: *Micky Lawler*
Interior and Cover Design: *Katherine Minerva*
Caricatures and Technical Illustrations: *Kevin East*
Chapter-Opening Photos: *Creative Associates*
Typesetting: *Graphic Typesetting Service, Los Angeles, California*

To
Jennifer

Preface

This is yet another textbook on educational psychology. Ho hum. It is not, however, that traditional potpourri of this and that from here and there that psychologists have, until now, dragged out when asked by educators what they have to offer. What is presented here is not one discipline applied (like a Band-Aid?) to another—as suggested by such previous titles as *Psychology* and *Teaching*, *Psychology* in *Teaching*, *Psychology* for *Teaching*, *Psychology* Applied to *Teaching*—but a distinct discipline on its own, *The Psychology* of *Teaching*.

The book consists of three sections—Knowing the Subject, Knowing the Student, and Teaching the Subject to the Student—focusing, in turn, on the teacher's three major sets of skills. Within the second section, behaviorism is presented as the theoretical basis for teaching as an outside-in process (Chapter 3); humanism as the theoretical basis for teaching as an inside-out process (Chapter 4); and the interactionism of Jean Piaget as the theoretical basis for an optimal orchestration of inside-out developing and outside-in learning (Chapter 5). The other chapters expand on this basic thesis-antithesis-synthesis. Some practical implications of the interactionist theory are considered under the topics of readiness and critical period (Chapter 6). Individual differences are discussed from the outside-in and inside-out points of view, respectively, under intelligence (Chapter 7) and creativity (Chapter 8). Within the third section, the outside-in view of teaching is presented in terms of explaining and understanding (Chapter 9) and the inside-out view in terms of the discovery approach (Chapter 10). Education as viewed by this interactionist is considered, somewhat whimsically, as acquiring an operating manual for species *Homo sapiens* (Chapter 11). A close-up shot of the teaching process focuses on observer effects (Chapter 12), and a long-range shot provides various views of the classroom (Chapter 13).

Comprehensiveness is sacrificed somewhat at the altar of coherence. I tested my structure for stress by reading voraciously in the literature of educational psychology and found nothing that stretched it in any unseemly manner. However, although this text hits every major traditional topic in the field, it hits some with only a glancing blow. Since it is a relatively slim and inexpensive volume (my publisher will not let me call it "thin" and "cheap"), you can supplement it with the many excellent paperbacks available on educational technology, research methodology, cognitive psychology, or whatever topic you feel has been slighted.

This textbook is designed to be a basic text in educational psychology. It may also serve to remind students in courses on social, cultural, or philosophical foundations of education and other such general courses that teaching is the central process in the educational enterprise. Since we are all teachers (one can hardly talk without teaching), this book will be of interest to the general reader. The street is also a classroom, and the person in the street is also a teacher.

A textbook writer is a teacher, too. Indeed, I would prefer to call this a teaching book to avoid the authoritarian tone of *text*. Some structural features are designed to practice what I teach. Pre-exercises and post-exercises are provided to integrate the content of each chapter with the prior and subsequent experience of the reader. An outline at the beginning of each chapter presents the hierarchical structure underlying the sequential presentation. Marginal comments (in the form of caricatures with quotations from other authors and footnotes from this author) recognize that students should be inspired as well as informed.

In this era of textbooks "managed" by publishers, written by committees, and rewritten by "ghosts," it would be satisfying to say that I built this book myself. Certainly, I wrote it myself. I researched it myself. I typed it myself. I indexed it myself. I made all the mistakes myself. However, no person is an island, or even a peninsula. I had more than a little help from my friends.

Students helped. I class-tested this textbook at the University of Alberta in the winter term of 1977 and the summer session of 1978 and at the University of California at Santa Cruz in the fall quarter of 1977. Every member of those classes helped in some way—even if only with an embarrassing question or a quizzical expression that drove me back to the drawing board. Students usually appear in textbooks simply as "a student" (someone should erect a monument to The Unknown Student). However, some of my students should be singled out by name for services beyond the call of student duty. Dave Clyburn, Jackie Gall, Alice Killackey, Charlotte Rekken, and Al Stamp read the manuscript and, through their suggestions, improved the book.

Reviewers helped. Larry Goulet of the University of Illinois, Gary Garfield of California State Polytechnic University, Arthur Pearl of the University of California at Santa Cruz, and John E. M. Young of McGill University were encouragingly outspoken and never insultingly indifferent. Their negative comments improved the quality of this book, and their positive comments improved the morale of its author. Some friends and colleagues (two categories that are not mutually exclusive)—Bill Hague of the University of Alberta, Susan Lederman of Queen's University, Ann McGinty of the University of California at Los Angeles, Beth Moore-Milroy of the University of British Columbia, Berna Skrypnek of the University of Minnesota, and Jennifer Welsh of Ryerson Polytechnical Institute—provided informal, inspiring, and informative reviews. Guy Lefrancois didn't read my manuscript (he had the good sense to focus on writing his own), but he chivalrously arranged for places for me to live and work while I was writing a competing textbook.

Artists helped. Kevin East drew the caricatures, and Jamie Brooks, the Brooks/Cole Art Director, performed the no-less-artistic function of orchestrating the creative contributions to build a beautiful book.

Editors helped. I would like to have printed, bound, and delivered this book to you myself. However, I lack the vast expertise involved in transforming that messy manuscript I handed my publisher into this handsome book they handed on to you. Acquisition editor Todd Lueders, consulting editor Ed Walker, permissions editor Dick Verduin, production editor Micky Lawler, and manuscript editor Beth Luey performed their professional parts with their usual professional competence. Todd went way beyond the call of professional duty. The lonely life of the writer is best expressed in the anguished cry "Is there anyone out there?" Throughout the three years I was buried in this book, Todd assured and reassured me that there was, indeed, someone out there.

W. Lambert Gardiner

Contents

Prologue 1

1 PROLOGUE

PRE-EXERCISES

1. Previewing the First Class Meeting

It is the first moment of the first meeting with your first class on the first day of your teaching career. Thirty pairs of eyes gaze intently and expectantly at their new teacher. What do you think they will be thinking? What will you be thinking? How will each of those children differ at the end of the school year? Will you have much to do with those changes, or is your 9-to-4, Monday-to-Friday influence a minor variable in their lives? Are there any potential Albert Einsteins or Margaret Meads out there, or are they all going to settle into the miscellaneous category of "ordinary folks"? Does an Einstein become an Einstein because of teachers or despite them? What am I doing here anyway?

Now to more immediate questions.

How will I be different at that first moment than I am at this moment? What can I do in the interval between now and then to prepare myself for that challenge? How can I ensure that I will thrive as a teacher and not merely survive?

As I write this book, I will try to focus on that first terrifying yet exhilarating moment. I urge you to try to do so as you read it. It is designed to provide you with the skills that will prepare you for that challenge.

2. Two Views of Education

Read the following quotations.

Have these various thinkers reached the same conclusion about the two basic views of education? If so, what is that distinction? Add your own quotation stating this distinction in your words. Do you sense any preference for one view over the other? What is your preference? What implications does this preference have for your teaching?

"To come to a more fundamental cleavage: there can be no agreement between those who regard education as a means of instilling certain definite beliefs and those that think it should produce the power of independent judgment."—Bertrand Russell, *Education and the Good Life*

"Nothing can depart more from the Scottish idea, which I take to be to educate our men and women primarily not for their country's good but for their own, not so much to teach them what to think as how to think, not preparing them to give as little trouble as possible in the future but sending them into it in the hope that they will give trouble."—Sir James Barrie

"In teaching it is the method and not the content that is the message—the drawing out, not the pumping in."—R. Buckminster Fuller

"Here there are at least two irreconcilable possibilities: one, that man should be educated to become what he is; the other, that he should be educated to become what he is not. The first view assumes that each individual is born with certain potentialities which have a positive value for that individual and that it is his proper destiny to develop those potentialities within the framework of a society liberal enough to allow for an infinite variation of types. The second view assumes that whatever idiosyncrasies the individual may possess at birth, it is the duty of the teacher to eradicate them unless they conform to a certain ideal of character determined by the traditions of the society of which the individual has involuntarily become a member."—Herbert Read, *Education through Art*

"Our aim in education in general is two-fold, biological and social. From the biological side we wish to help the natural development of the individual, from the social standpoint it is our aim to prepare the individual for the environment."—Maria Montessori, *The Montessori Method*

"The history of educational theory is marked by opposition between the idea that education is development from within and that it is formation from without; that it is based upon natural endowments and that education is a process of overcoming natural inclinations and substituting in its place habits acquired under external pressures."—John Dewey, *Education and Experience*

"Education either functions as an instrument which is used to facilitate the integration of the younger generation into the logic of the present system and bring about conformity to it, or it becomes 'the practice of freedom,' the means by which men and women deal critically and creatively with reality and discover how to participate in the transformation of their world."—Paulo Freire, *Pedagogy of the Oppressed*

"Education can be regarded as socialization, to make the young conform harmoniously to society—and this can be a base or noble purpose, depending on the quality of the society. Or it may be regarded as the effort to perfect people as such, perhaps giving them defenses against the existing, or any, society, in the interest of liberty."—Paul Goodman, *The Community of Scholars*

"Education derives from the Latin verb *educare,* to train, to instruct, to put in, or from the verb *educere,* to draw out, to lead forth."—Mary Greer and Bonnie Rubinstein, *Will the Real Teacher Please Stand Up?*

"We talk about education—leading forth the natural intelligence of a child. But ours is just the opposite of leading forth. It is a ramming in of brain facts through the head, and a consequent distortion, suffocation and starvation of the primary centres of consciousness."—D. H. Lawrence, *Lawrence on Education*

"Teaching means creating situations where structures can be discovered; it does not mean transmitting structures which may be assimilated at nothing other than a verbal level."—Jean Piaget

"We must create new models for adults who can teach their children not what to learn, but how to learn and not what they should be committed to, but the value of commitment."—Margaret Mead, *Culture and Commitment*

1.1   ON TEACHING TEACHING

When teaching teaching, we tend to forget that the principles that apply to the second *teaching* also apply to the first. We often violate our own principles in the process of teaching them. We preach that "active learning is more effective than passive learning," and rows of students passively record our message to play it back to us at the end of the year. We fail students for forgetting that "reward is more effective than punishment." In this textbook, I will try to *demonstrate* rather than violate the principles I teach in the process of teaching them. * I hope to practice what I teach. Here are some of the features of the book's format and the principles of teaching that they illustrate.

1.11   Pre-exercises

Each chapter is preceded by some pre-exercises, which are designed to elicit any prior experience you may have had that is relevant to the content of the chapter. These pre-exercises could be considered as intellectual warm-up exercises. I hope they will muster whatever you already know on the topic and prime you to think about it. In some cases, these pre-exercises will not only elicit but will provide prior experience. Informal classroom experiments and

---

* A textbook writer is, of course, a teacher—unfortunately, a very limited teacher, because of being confined to a frustrating one-way visual channel of communication and restricted somewhat by the conventions of the textbook. In Section 9.2, I'll suggest ways in which we may perhaps overcome the first limitation and, in footnotes such as this throughout the textbook, I'll try to counter the second limitation.

STUDENTS PLANNING TO BECOME TEACHERS, ON THE OTHER HAND, "APPROACH THEIR EDUCATION WITH A <u>RELATIVELY</u> ACCURATE PICTURE OF WHAT TEACHERS DO." THEIR PICTURE IS RELATIVELY ACCURATE BECAUSE THEY HAVE SPENT SOME 10,000 HOURS IN DIRECT CONTACT WITH ELEMENTARY AND SECONDARY SCHOOL TEACHERS BY THE TIME THEY BEGIN THEIR FIRST YEAR OF COLLEGE. THE PREPARATION OF TEACHERS BEGINS NOT IN COLLEGE BUT IN KINDERGARTEN OR FIRST GRADE.

CHARLES E. SILBERMAN
CRISIS IN THE CLASSROOM

exercises, readings and writings may provide experiences common to all members of the class.* In those few cases in which there are definite answers, they are contained in the chapter (a fiendish device to encourage you to read it).

Such priming devices would be appropriate in any subject but are particularly appropriate to a course in educational psychology. Teaching is probably the only profession about which a teacher can assume that every one of his or her students has some previous experience. You can live your entire life without ever seeing a lawyer, doctor, physicist, or engineer in action. However, everyone using this textbook has not only seen a teacher in action but has *been* a teacher. You can hardly talk without teaching. If you have ever shown a younger sister how to tie her shoelaces, helped a friend with homework, given directions or advice, criticized someone's behavior or poetry, then you have been a teacher. You have also obviously been a student. It is this vast source of

---

* Teachers of teachers may like to use these exercises as class exercises. Another alternative is to offer them as opportunities. While teaching a course at the University of Alberta and the University of California at Santa Cruz out of which this book evolved, I found that students responded well to my laying out a huge smorgasbord of opportunities, which included many of these exercises, and evaluating them on the basis of the extent to which they took advantage of those opportunities.

previous experience as a teacher and as a student that I am trying to tap through the pre-exercises. You are already a teacher; this book aims only to help you become a better teacher. You already have a theory of teaching (whether you know it or not); this book aims only to help you develop a more explicit, articulate, consistent, and practical theory.

Teaching principle: New information should be integrated with old information.

1.12   *Post-exercises*

Each chapter is followed by some post-exercises, which are designed to integrate the theoretical content of the chapter with its practical implications for teaching. Whereas the pre-exercises tie the content of the chapter to the past, the post-exercises tie the content of the chapter to the future. These post-exercises are not designed, as are many end-of-chapter questions in textbooks, to check whether you have assimilated the content of the chapter. They are invitations, not inquisitions. There are no Gardiner-ordained "correct" answers at the back of the book or at the back of my mind,* although there are Gardiner opinions in the text. Feel free to disagree. The pre-exercises are designed to help you sketch your own subjective map of that aspect of the objective world considered in the chapter, and the post-exercises are designed to help you assimilate the content of the chapter into this subjective map. Keep only that part of the content which contributes to a clarification and sophistication of your subjective map.

Sometimes the same exercise will be included as both a pre-exercise and a post-exercise. In the light (if I may be so presumptuous) of the intervening chapter, how would you *now* answer such-and-such a question posed as a pre-exercise? This pre-and-post testing technique may show you how the intervening content affected your theory of teaching. However, post-exercises will typically pose "better" questions than pre-exercises. For example, a pre-exercise for this chapter invites you to consider your future role as a teacher by previewing your first meeting with your first class, whereas a post-exercise for this chapter invites you to consider your future role as a teacher in more precise terms by placing yourself on a dimension ranging from an extreme outside-in teacher to an extreme inside-out teacher. The function of the intervening content in the chapter is not so much to provide answers but to permit the asking of better questions.

The traditional view of educational psychology as the theory of the psychologist applied to the practice of the educator should be reexamined. The major criterion of theory is rigor, and the major criterion of practice is relevance. Rigor times relevance tends to be constant. That is, as rigor increases,

---

*I'm lying to you a little. A few exercises involve definite answers. In those cases, the answers are at the end of the chapter.

relevance tends to decrease, and, as relevance increases, rigor tends to decrease. Psychologists are high in rigor but low in relevance, whereas educators are high in relevance but low in rigor. Both their rigor × relevance constants are low. Zero times anything is still zero. Nor does pooling their resources help much. Zero *plus* zero is still zero. We need neither psychologists, who try to maximize rigor (until at times rigor mortis sets in), nor educators, who try to maximize relevance, but educational psychologists, who try to optimize the balance between rigor and relevance. I will try to be both rigorous and relevant to help you increase your personal rigor × relevance constant.

Teaching principle: Theory should be integrated with practice.

1.13   Hierarchical Outline

Information presented in a textbook should be integrated not only with the past experience of the student (as attempted in the pre-exercises) and with the future practice of the student (as attempted in the post-exercises) but also internally. A chapter is necessarily written sequentially—that is, as one word after another. One of the limitations of "linear literacy," says Marshall McLuhan, is that words must be strung "like beads on a string." However, underlying this sequential presentation there is, if it is an organized presentation, a hierarchical structure. I will try to overcome the limitation of linear literacy by presenting this hierarchical structure at the beginning of each chapter as a framework for the sequential presentation. You can use this outline as you are reading a chapter to check where you are, where you have been, and where you are going. You can also use it *after* you have read the chapter to see whether you can retrace the trip on your own. Check each distinction within the hierarchy to make sure you understand the basis for it. Try to reconstruct the content under each of the smallest subheadings, and check your reconstruction against the text.

Teaching principle: Structured information is easier to learn and remember than unstructured information.

1.14   References

Education seems to have changed little in essence throughout our recorded history. The Egyptian child copying a teacher's words with quill on papyrus in 6 B.C. is very much like the American child copying a teacher's words with a ball-point pen in a three-holed, loose-leaf binder. Innovation is merely in materials rather than in methods. The teaching machine appears new, but it merely conducts a very mechanical Socratic dialogue with the student. However, in relatively recent times, a new element has been introduced into human history. We have invented a way of thinking—involving careful observation and clear reasoning—that we call science. This way of thinking has greatly expanded our understanding of our world and of ourselves and has tremendous potential for improving our methods of communicating this understanding. This textbook could be viewed as an attempt to realize this potential. The clear reasoning of science will be presented in the text and the careful observation in the References, mentioned in the text and collected at the end of the book.

A textbook could be considered as a tertiary source based on primary sources (descriptions of experiments) and secondary sources (collation and discussion of a number of related experiments). The References contain the primary and secondary sources on which this tertiary source is based. This organization will permit you to study educational psychology at three levels, corresponding roughly to tertiary, secondary, and primary sources. You can read the text, which will provide an uncluttered overview of the field, or you can read the text and the secondary sources, or you can read the text and the secondary and primary sources to which the References direct you. You may want to study the subject first at the tertiary level, then at the secondary level, and then at the primary level—that is, sketch the subject and then fill in the details. Or you may want to survey the field and dig deeper only in the areas that interest you.

Teaching principle: A subject can be presented to provide understanding at various levels of sophistication.

1.15 Marginal Comments

Scientists have established conventions for presenting empirical material in journals but not for presenting theoretical material in textbooks. A description of an experiment in a journal article presents a review of the relevant prior experiments, an account of the procedure used in the experiment, an analysis of the results, and a discussion of the results with suggestions for further research. There are no such careful conventions in tertiary sources. Any paragraph of a textbook may contain a confusing mélange of statements of different types—theoretical and empirical, fact and opinion, opinion of author and of others.

I would like to establish some conventions with the readers of this textbook to disentangle these different types of statements. The References help disentangle empirical and theoretical statements—empirical material in references and theoretical material in text. Facts and opinions will be disentangled by presenting the more subjective material in a marginal way: statements of the author will appear as footnotes, and statements of others will appear as quotations. I believe that the academic world is ready for less pedantic and more personal textbooks, for less formal and more friendly textbook writers. Some people disagree. I will compromise by pushing my personal comments—anecdotes and jokes, half-baked ideas, and preposterous opinions—to the bottom of the page but not right off the page (as often recom-

mended). Personal comments by others will appear in balloons above caricatures of the person. Some readers may object to this "comic-strip" style. However, this device may give you a better feeling for the great conversation about
education than the traditional quotations. You are invited to join this conversation by adding your own comments in the wide margins provided to enable
you to talk back to me.

Teaching principle: Students must be inspired as well as informed.

1.16 Teaching Tools

A major distinction between our species and other animals is that we
have learned to use tools. This skill has enabled such a puny creature to
become (fortunately or unfortunately) the King of the Jungle. Each chapter is
designed to provide you with a tool for teaching. Not hardware tools (audio
aids, visual aids, Band-Aids, and so on), but software tools—the kind you can
carry around for the rest of your life in that handy, portable toolbox between
your ears. Your sensory tools (eyes, ears, and so on) enable you to build a
perceptual map of the world. Your most powerful tool—language—enables you

A COMPETENT EDUCATOR, LIKE AN ACCOMPLISHED
MUSICIAN, DEVOTES YEARS AND EFFORT TO ACQUIRING
TECHNIQUES. ONCE ACQUIRED, THEY ARE UNSEEN. THE
VIOLINIST PLAYS HIS MUSIC AS THOUGH PROBLEMS OF
FINGERING, BOWING AND DOUBLE STOPPING NEVER EXIS-
TED. A PRINCIPAL, A TEACHER, OR A PARENT CAN
RESPOND HELPFULLY, AS THOUGH CONGRUENT COMMU-
NICATION WERE HIS NATIVE TONGUE.

HAIM G. GINOTT
TEACHER AND CHILD

to group percepts, label them as concepts, and thus build a conceptual map of the world. Development of new concepts and consideration of new relationships between concepts allow you to think about the world in new ways.

Each chapter will attempt to offer a fruitful way of thinking about teaching. The tool may be a theory (such as the theory of Jean Piaget, Chapter 5), or a paradigm (such as behaviorism, Chapter 3), or a concept (such as intelligence, Chapter 7) or a pair of related concepts (such as explaining and understanding, Chapter 9). As you assimilate such tools, they become skills. The teacher is the primary teaching tool. Technique is not the only aspect of teaching (or even the most important), but it is the only aspect that can be taught. You must first have the technique in order to transcend it to that aspect of teaching which is caught (by infection, like a cold) rather than taught. The art of teaching can emerge only after the science of teaching is learned.

Teaching principle: Education is the process, not of accumulating information, but of acquiring tools for handling information.

1.2   ON SUBJECTS AND STUDENTS

An endless debate in education revolves around—and around and around—the question "Do we teach subjects or do we teach students?" The answer, as in so many such debates, is "Both!" We teach subjects to students. In order to do so, we must know the subject, we must know the student, and we must know how best to teach the subject to the student. The teacher must, therefore, possess all three sets of skills. The three major parts of this textbook focus, in turn, on each of those sets of skills—Chapter 2 on "Knowing the Subject," Chapters 3 through 8 on "Knowing the Student," and Chapters 9 through 13 on "Teaching the Subject to the Student." Let us take a broad look at each of those sets of skills in turn.

1.21   Knowing the Subject

Even a limited survey of the myriad subjects that can be taught would be beyond the scope of this textbook and way beyond the scope of this textbook writer's competence. I will assume that you have come to know your subject in other courses or from other sources. However, in Chapter 2, we will explore what is meant by "knowing the subject," whatever the subject.

The set of skills that constitutes knowing the subject is necessary but not sufficient for good teaching. Many Nobel Prize winners are notoriously poor teachers, despite the fact that they know their subject intimately—indeed, often *because* they know their subject intimately. The subject has become so integral a part of them that they can no longer empathize with the student who, by definition, has not yet integrated it within himself. A good player is not necessarily a good coach. University teachers are hired on the assumption that knowing the subject is a sufficient condition for teaching it, for an expert on a subject is automatically assumed to be competent as a teacher of that subject. I will argue in this textbook that, in addition to knowing the subject, a teacher must also know the student and know how best to teach the subject to the student.

The assumption that knowing a subject is sufficient for teaching it is unwarranted at any level of teaching. However, it is more justified at the university level. As the student gets older, the balance in relative importance of skills shifts from knowing the student to knowing the subject. Responsibility for knowing the student can be shifted more and more from the teacher to the student. In contrast, it is easy for the elementary school teacher to know all the arithmetic taught in grade 3 but not so easy for the university mathematics teacher to know all the esoteric branches of mathematics taught in graduate courses. This shift in importance is reflected in the fact that elementary school teachers tend to be "student" specialists (for example, a grade 3 teacher), whereas university teachers tend to be "subject" specialists (for example, a professor of differential calculus). Despite this shift in balance, all teachers must know the subject *and* the student in order to know how best to teach the subject to the student. Even a professor of mathematics who knew all the branches of the subject intimately would only be what Bertrand Russell calls "halfway clever" if he or she could not also communicate that knowledge to students. Neither should the need to know the subject be neglected by the grade 3 teacher. A mechanical understanding of the processes and products of the basic operations of arithmetic (addition, subtraction, multiplication, and division) is not enough to teach arithmetic even if that is all that one is required to teach in grade 3. While explicitly teaching those operations, you will be implicitly teaching a mechanical understanding of arithmetic. The utility and elegance of arithmetic become clear only when you understand the principles underlying the procedures. The history of the theory of numbers, the arbitrariness of the base 10, the relationship of arithmetic to everyday English and logic, and other such understandings about arithmetic would appear superficially irrelevant to teaching arithmetic in grade 3, since they are not specifically in the curriculum. However, a teacher with such a deeper understanding of the subject would be better able to provide inspiration as well as information and would have better insights into how best to teach arithmetic to grade 3 students.

1.22 Knowing the Student

The set of skills involved in knowing the student—the province of psychology—is presented in Chapters 3 through 8. Psychology is to education as physics is to engineering: it is the theory underlying the practice. I will argue later that the only system within the student that can be "taught" is the nervous system and that psychology is the study of the function of the nervous system.* This second major section of the book could be considered somewhat whimsically as a State of the Science message from a psychologist to a teacher.

The message is slanted. It focuses only on those aspects of knowing the student which are relevant to knowing how best to teach the student. Thus, it will consider maturation, since instruction must be dovetailed to maturation. It will not, however, provide a capsule course in genetics, which underlies maturation, as if to make an embryo geneticist of you. It will consider the typical educational setting, since this is the context in which teaching must usually take place. The aim of this textbook is to optimize teaching. However, most of us must teach under less than optimal conditions and must know how best to teach under those conditions. It will not, however, present a capsule history of education, as if to make a historian of you. Such a history might help explain why the traditional educational setting is as it is, but it bears only a very tenuous link to the immediate problem of teaching here and now.

The message is simplified. In sharing the relevant information generated by my colleagues, I present it without the careful qualifications they may perhaps prefer. When psychologists talk to one another, they invariably add, on every empirical issue, that "further research is necessary" and, on every theoretical issue, that "there is much to be said on both sides." Such scientific reticence is indeed appropriate and commendable within the community of scientists. It may not, however, be appropriate in offering our expertise as a basis for practical action. Teachers must act on the best information currently available, and psychologists should try to offer this information to them. We should compare what we have to offer with the alternatives available now rather than with some future ideal. By being so tentative and squeamish about correct form, psychologists may be relinquishing their responsibility. Pseudo-scientists rush in where scientists fear to tread. Psychology has, as yet, taken only a first few fumbling steps toward the understanding of the person, but its contribution is certainly already superior to the vague noises one usually hears in rap sessions about education. Here, for what it is worth, is what we have to offer.

Those who argue that we teach subjects tend to view teaching as an outside-in process, in which the teacher "passes on" the subject to the student; whereas those who argue that we teach students tend to view teaching as an inside-out process, in which the teacher facilitates the student's growth. A history of education could be written as an extended debate between advocates of those two basic views, which I will call outside-in teaching and inside-out teaching. In "Behaviorism and Outside-In Teaching" (Chapter 3), I will present the behavioristic theory of the person and argue that this theory is the basis of outside-in teaching, which is, in turn, the basis of traditional education. In "Humanism and Inside-Out Teaching" (Chapter 4), I will present the humanis-

---

* This definition of psychology does not imply that those chapters will deal only with neurons, hypothalami, and other mushy topics. One approach to understanding the function of a system is to study its structure, but this is only one of many approaches.

tic theory of the person and argue that this theory is the basis of inside-out teaching, which is, in turn, the basis of various proposed alternative systems of education. "The Theory of Jean Piaget" (Chapter 5) is then presented as the basis for an optimal balance between outside-in and inside-out teaching, which is, in turn, the basis for a new educational system. Chapters 3, 4, and 5 will be presented as thesis, antithesis, and synthesis. The dovetailing of outside-in and inside-out processes involves two important concepts: "Readiness and Critical Period" (Chapter 6). To that point in the section "Knowing the Student," all students will have been considered equal. Outside-in teachers view individual differences in terms of the capacity to benefit from instruction—"Intelligence" (Chapter 7)—whereas inside-out teachers view individual differences in terms of the extent to which the potential growth of the student is realized— "Creativity" (Chapter 8).

1.23   *Teaching the Subject to the Student*

The teacher shares the first set of skills—knowing the subject—with the expert in the given discipline and the second set of skills—knowing the student—with the psychologist. These two sets of skills are prerequisite to a third set of skills—knowing how best to teach the subject to the student— which is the special province of the teacher. That is, in order to know how best to teach the subject to the student, you must first know the subject *and* the student. They are preliminary skills to teaching just as skating and stick-handling are preliminary skills to playing hockey. Good hockey players have assimilated their skating and stick-handling skills so thoroughly that they have become automatic, and they can thus concentrate on playing hockey. Likewise, good teachers know the subject and the student so well that those skills have become part of them, and they can thus concentrate on teaching. This third set of skills is the focus of Chapters 9 through 13. Whereas the first two major sections are descriptive, this section is prescriptive; that is, it is concerned with how things should be rather than with how things are. You describe the subject and you describe the student, but you *pre*scribe how best to teach the subject to the student.

The various teaching specialists could be placed within a matrix with subjects on the rows and students on the columns. Thus, a tennis instructor would fall along the "tennis" row, a teacher of the blind down the "blind" column, and a junior high school mathematics teacher at the intersection of the "mathematics" row and the "junior high school" column. Although differences from subject to subject and from student to student will be considered, I will focus on general principles of teaching that apply throughout the matrix. I will argue that subjects are structured in surprisingly similar ways and that students, being members of the same species, operate according to essentially the same principles. I will argue further that these principles are not restricted to the limited and artificial setting of the classroom but apply equally well to giving guests directions to your home and teaching your child to have temper tantrums.

"Teaching the Subject to the Student" involves certain explaining skills of the teacher and certain understanding skills of the student. Those will be considered in "Explaining and Understanding" (Chapter 9). However, explaining is only one of the roads to understanding; another road will be considered in "The Discovery Approach" (Chapter 10). Bruner suggests that what is discovered is not information per se but tools for acquiring and organizing information. Your most important tool is your nervous system, and you and your students may learn how to use this tool better by consulting "An Operating Manual for Species *Homo sapiens*" (Chapter 11). Some recent studies with profound implications for the teacher-student relationship will be discussed in "Observer Effects" (Chapter 12). "Various Views of the Classroom" (Chapter 13) will take you beyond the psychology of teaching—the discipline I try to delineate in this book—to the social psychology and sociology of teaching.

1.3   ON PSYCHOLOGY AND EDUCATION

These three sets of skills—knowing the subject, knowing the student, and teaching the subject to the student—could be roughly considered as the provinces of education, psychology, and educational psychology, respectively. There are current changes within each of these disciplines that may best be described within the framework provided by Kuhn in his book *The Structure of Scientific Revolutions.*[117]* Kuhn argues that the development of a science is not characterized by a gradual evolution, as we tend to assume, but by a series of revolutions. The content of a particular science is organized within a framework into which the isolated bits of information more or less fit. As more and more information that does not fit within this framework accumulates, a new framework emerges within which this information fits more comfortably. There has been a revolution. The science is now organized within this new framework until it, in turn, is replaced by yet another framework. Thus, the history of astronomy can best be described in terms of a shift from the framework of Ptolemy to that of Copernicus to that of Newton to that of Einstein. Much recent evidence does not fit within Einstein's framework, and it will eventually be replaced by a more adequate framework developed by someone else—perhaps that red-headed boy in your grade 3 class, or that quiet girl in your physics class, or a child still waiting to be born within that pregnant woman you saw in the supermarket.

---

* Superscript numbers refer to items in the References, at the end of the book.

1.31 *Revolution in Psychology*

The science of psychology is in the throes of such a shift in framework just now. The behavioristic framework based on extrinsic motivation (Chapter 3) is being replaced by the humanistic framework based on intrinsic motivation (Chapter 4).

Psychology has been organized within the behavioristic framework since early in the century. Behaviorists argue that behavior is determined by the environment or, more precisely, that responses (the elements of behavior) are elicited by stimuli (the elements of environment). The nervous system is a mere mediator between stimuli and responses—a sort of telephone switchboard for linking incoming stimuli with outgoing responses. More and more evidence is accumulating that does not fit within this framework. The nervous system is intrinsically motivated. It has needs of its own. It initiates responses and adjusts its responses on the basis of the feedback from them. Such evidence is forcing a shift from the stimulus-response (S-R) framework of the behaviorist, based on the reflex arc, to the response-stimulus framework of the humanist, based on the feedback loop.

Postbehaviorists are trying to salvage the S-R framework by introducing lower-case *s*'s and *r*'s representing implicit stimuli and implicit responses within the nervous system to explain intrinsic motivation. Both Watson, the founder of behaviorism, and Skinner, its foremost modern exponent, pride themselves on studying observable stimuli and responses without recourse to unobservable (and hence inaccessible to science) processes mediating between the stimulus and the response. Those new models, teeming with little *s*'s and *r*'s, would make Skinner shudder and Watson whirl in his grave. These additions to the basic model are reminiscent of the epicycles Ptolemy kept adding to his model of the universe until it collapsed of its own weight and was traded for Copernicus's more streamlined model.

1.32 *Revolution in Education*

This shift from the extrinsic framework of behaviorism to the intrinsic framework of humanism in psychology is paralleled by an equivalent shift from outside-in teaching to inside-out teaching in education. If a person is extrinsically motivated, then education must occur from the outside in; if a person is intrinsically motivated, then education can occur from the inside out.

The outside-in teacher views education as the process of transmitting the culture (that is, the information accumulated by the group) from one generation to the next. The teacher, as a representative of the group, is entrusted with the acculturation process by which a child becomes a member of the society.

> WE ARE, IN MY VIEW, FACED WITH AN ENTIRELY NEW SITUATION IN EDUCATION WHERE THE GOAL OF EDUCATION, IF WE ARE TO SURVIVE, IS THE FACILITATION OF CHANGE AND LEARNING. THE ONLY MAN WHO IS EDUCATED IS THE MAN WHO HAS LEARNED HOW TO LEARN; THE MAN WHO HAS LEARNED TO ADAPT AND CHANGE; THE MAN WHO HAS REALIZED THAT NO KNOWLEDGE IS SECURE, THAT ONLY THE PROCESS OF SEEKING KNOWLEDGE GIVES A BASIS FOR SECURITY. CHANGINGNESS, A RELIANCE ON PROCESS RATHER THAN UPON STATIC KNOWLEDGE, IS THE ONLY THING THAT MAKES ANY SENSE AS A GOAL FOR EDUCATION IN THE MODERN WORLD.

CARL R. ROGERS
FREEDOM TO LEARN

Children born in different cultures have the same potential, but a Hottentot teacher makes Hottentots of them and an Eskimo teacher makes Eskimos of them.

Much recent criticism has been directed at this relay-race view of education. Kuhn's theory, which was described earlier, implies that the development of a society may parallel the development of a science.[117] The body of information that constitutes a culture may go through a series of revolutions. As a science meanders from framework to framework, those still working within an old framework are stuck up some stagnant bayou without a paddle. Their contributions to the science become part of the archive of back journal articles. Likewise, information within an old cultural framework is often obsolete and should not be forced on the next generation for whose new world it is no longer appropriate. In his *Learning for Tomorrow,* Toffler future-shocks us into the realization that these shifts in framework are occurring so rapidly that the information accumulated by one generation is becoming less and less relevant to the next.[220] In *Culture and Commitment,* Mead argues that we have moved from a society in which the old teach the young to one in which the young teach the old.[149]

An alternative view of education is emerging that emphasizes the development of the person from the inside out over the instruction of the person from the outside in. Inside-out teachers view education as the process of encouraging the realization of the person's potential. They argue that the inside-out maturational process is much more important than the outside-in instructional process. Maturation represents the wisdom that our species has accumulated over billions of years of survival in the harshest arena, whereas instruction represents the paltry cultural modifications each of us can acquire in his or her short life. The Hottentot child will indeed learn that houses are made of grass and the Eskimo child will learn that houses are made of ice, but those are minor cultural variations on the basic biological theme shared by all members of our species that we must protect ourselves from the extremes of heat and cold in order to survive. Throughout our history, a number of innovative individuals have tried to turn education inside out—Socrates in ancient Greece, Rousseau in France, Montessori in Italy, Tolstoi in Russia, Neill in Great Britain, and many others. However, today we may have the critical mass of educators with the inside-out attitude necessary to change the educational system.

As on most issues, there are extremists on both sides. The extreme outside-inners see the student as an empty bucket to be filled or a clean slate to be written on. The extreme inside-outers see maturation as such a wondrous process that we should merely sit back in awe and admire it. However, nothing grows in a vacuum. Even plants need outside-in influences like soil, sun, and

MARGARET MEAD
CULTURE AND COMMITMENT

water. We must create congenial environments for growth. Outside-inners emphasize our first set of teaching skills—knowing the subject; inside-outers emphasize our second set of skills—knowing the student. Just as we recognized that we must know the subject *and* the student in order to teach the subject to the student, so we recognize that education involves both outside-in and inside-out processes. In Chapter 5, we will consider the theory of Jean Piaget, which suggests how the outside-in process of learning is dovetailed to the inside-out process of development.

1.33 Revolution in Educational Psychology

The discipline that ostensibly focuses on our third set of skills—teaching the subject to the student—is educational psychology. It has, so far, failed to fulfill the promise of teaching those teaching skills. As a young science, psychology has been very apprehensive about its shaky scientific status among the older sciences. When invited to offer theory relevant to the practice of education, we have laid out a smorgasbord of statistics, genetics, experimental methodology, therapy, tests and measurements, instruction on operating audiovisual equipment, and so on and so on. Like an insecure child eager to impress a visitor, we have dragged out all our toys—including some pirated from the other kids in the neighborhood. A little knowledge may be a dangerous thing, but a potpourri of "little knowledges" is certainly a confusing thing. A teacher may indeed be a statistician, a geneticist, an experimental psychologist, a clinical psychologist, a psychometrician, and an engineer, but only in the trivial sense that a wife may be a chemist, a chef, a chauffeur, and a courtesan. Those skills do not constitute the essence of being a teacher. This textbook aims to teach those skills which define the teacher.

Educational psychology is beginning to struggle out of its adolescence and is becoming confident enough to assert itself as a separate discipline. It still depends somewhat on its parents—on education for knowing the subject and on psychology for knowing the student—but it has a life of its own in its focus on teaching the subject to the student. It has become assured enough to make prescriptive rather than descriptive statements, to say what should be rather than what is. The theory of instruction Bruner called for a decade ago and toward which he has contributed so much is beginning to emerge.[26] The last four reviewers of educational psychology in the *Annual Review of Psychology* were so impressed by the changes in the field that they renamed it "instructional psychology" to differentiate it clearly from its previous self.[67, 79, 146, 234] I follow their lead. However, I prefer to call this exciting, emerging field "the psychology of teaching," since instruction carries connotations of training rather than educating. By delineating this field, I hope to make explicit what was implicit in those reviews and to contribute toward Bruner's theory of

EDUCATION IS INDEED THE DULLEST OF SUBJECTS, AND I INTEND TO SAY AS LITTLE ABOUT IT AS I CAN. —THE BUSINESS OF THE PARENT AND THE TEACHER IS NOT EDUCATION BUT TEACHING. TEACHING IS SOMETHING THAT CAN BE PROVIDED FOR, CHANGED OR STOPPED. IT IS GOOD OR BAD, BRILLIANT OR STUPID, PLENTIFUL OR SCARCE. BESET AS IT IS WITH DIFFICULTIES AND ARMED WITH DEVICES, TEACHING HAS A THEORY, TOO, BUT IT IS ONE THAT CAN BE TALKED ABOUT SIMPLY AND DIRECTLY, FOR IT CONCERNS THE MANY MATTERS OF HUMAN KNOWLEDGE WHICH AFFECT OUR LIVES, FROM THE THREE R'S TO ELECTRONICS. TO DEAL WITH IT IN THAT FASHION IS IN FACT WHAT I AM GOING TO DO IN THIS BOOK: VERY SIMPLY AND LITERALLY I AM GOING TO TELL TALES OUT OF SCHOOL.

JACQUES BARZUN
TEACHER IN AMERICA

instruction. The psychology of teaching is the same field as educational psychology (all the familiar topics are here) but seen from the point of view of the teacher, which is the best point of view for a textbook for teachers.

Members of other professions often take a condescending attitude toward teaching as a profession. This attitude is best exemplified by George Bernard Shaw's comment "Those who can, do; those who can't, teach," to which more recent wags have added "Those who can't teach, teach teachers; those who can't teach teachers, write textbooks on the psychology of teaching." There is some justification for this attitude. Teachers have no set of skills uniquely their own which they can present as the basis for their professional compe-

THIS IS A BOOK ON CHILDHOOD. ONE MAY SCAN WORK AFTER WORK ON HISTORY, SOCIETY, AND MORALITY AND FIND LITTLE REFERENCE TO THE FACT THAT ALL PEOPLE START AS CHILDREN AND THAT ALL PEOPLE BEGIN IN THEIR NURSERIES. IT IS HUMAN TO HAVE A LONG CHILDHOOD, IT IS CIVILIZED TO HAVE AN EVEN LONGER CHILDHOOD. LONG CHILD-HOOD MAKES A TECHNICAL AND MENTAL VIRTUOSO OUT OF MAN, BUT IT ALSO LEAVES A LIFELONG RESI-DUE OF EMOTIONAL IMMATURITY IN HIM.

ERIK H. ERIKSON
CHILDHOOD AND SOCIETY

tence. This textbook is a modest step toward suggesting such a set of skills. The put-down of teachers is further justified by the fact that teachers often put themselves down. "I'm just a teacher." There is nothing "mere" about teachers, just as there is nothing "mere" about mothers. Child-bearing and child-rearing are the most important functions in any society. The young have a conspiracy against the old. They are planning to outlive us. It would be pointless to build a beautiful world and leave it in ugly hands. The function of teachers is to help those inheritors of our world realize their full human potential. Or, alternatively, the function of teachers is to plan their own obsolescence. I hope that, in this textbook, I can contribute to a more positive self-image of the teacher by pointing out that the teacher must not only know the subject (as does the expert on that subject) and know the student (as does the psychologist) but must also know how best to teach the subject to the student (a set of additional skills that are the unique competence of the teacher).

POST-EXERCISES

1. Models of the Teacher-Student Relationship

Think through each of the following models of the teacher-student relationship and then consider the questions below.

Teacher is to student as parent is to child
clerk is to customer
entertainer is to audience
coach is to player
programmer is to computer
guide is to traveler
therapist is to client
guard is to prisoner
guru is to follower
master is to apprentice
teapot is to teacup
Professor Higgins is to Eliza Doolittle
ventriloquist is to puppet
conductor is to orchestra
Svengali is to Trilby
cook is to diner
writer is to reader
babysitter is to baby
Don Juan is to Carlos Castañeda

Which of these models reflect an outside-in view of education?
an inside-out view of education?
some balance between the two views?

Which of these models best reflects the type of teacher you would like to be?

How do these models help you clarify your role as a teacher?

Do you agree that your function as a teacher is to help your students to "realize their full human potential" and/or to "plan your own obsolescence"?

(This textbook will contain many such arguable but questionable generalizations. From time to time, in the post-exercises, I will single out such preposterous propositions and invite you to challenge them. One function of a teacher is to set up straw men so that students can get intellectual exercise from knocking them down. Or is this yet another preposterous proposition?)

2. Outside-In and Inside-Out Attitudes to Education

Of the following statements, which reflect an outside-in attitude to education and which reflect an inside-out attitude?

"Give me a dozen healthy infants, well formed, and my own special world to bring them up in, and I'll guarantee to take any one at random and train him to become any type of specialist I might select—doctor, lawyer, artist, merchant-chief and, yes, even beggerman and thief, regardless of his talents, penchants, tendencies, abilities, vocations, and race of his ancestry."—J. B. Watson, *Behaviorism*

"No man can reveal to you aught but that which already lies half asleep in the dawning of your knowledge."

"The teacher who walks in the shadow of the temple, among his followers, gives not of his wisdom but rather of his faith and his livingness. If he is indeed wise, he does not bid you enter the house of his wisdom, but rather leads you to the threshold of your own mind."—Kahlil Gibran, *The Prophet*

"Anything which could be found out by thinking I never was told, until I had exhausted my efforts to find it out for myself."—John Stuart Mill, "Unwasted Years"

"There can be no learning (except in trivial, autistic instances) without teaching."—S. and T. Englemann, *Give Your Child a Superior Mind*

"Every time you teach a child something, you keep him from reinventing it."—Jean Piaget, lecture at New York University, March 21, 1967 (quoting a friend with approval)

"Give me a child until he is seven; after that, you may have him."—St. Ignatius of Loyola

"Don't let them go to dances—they may get sexy ideas."—Aunt Maud

"Thomas Gradgrind now presented Thomas Gradgrind to the little pitchers before him, who were to be filled so full of facts . . . he seemed a kind of cannon loaded to the muzzle with facts, and prepared to blow them clean out of the regions of childhood at one discharge."—Charles Dickens, "M'Choakumchild's Schoolroom"

"What a dangerous activity reading is, teaching is. All this plastering on of foreign stuff. Why plaster on at all when there's so much inside already?"—Sylvia Ashton-Warner, *Spinster*

"The adult judges them by his own measure: he thinks that the child's wish is to obtain some tangible object, and lovingly helps him to do this: whereas the child as a rule has for his unconscious desire, his own self-development. Hence he despises everything already attained, and yearns for that which is still to be sought for. For instance, he prefers the action of dressing himself to the state of being dressed, even finally dressed."—Maria Montessori, *The Montessori Method*

"The job of the psychotherapist (or the teacher) is to help a person find out what's already in him rather than to reinforce him or shape or teach him into a pre-arranged form, which someone else has decided upon in advance, a priori."—Abraham Maslow, "Some Educational Implications of the Humanistic Psychologies"

"The right kind of education consists in understanding the child as he is without imposing upon him an ideal of what we think he should be. To enclose him in the framework of an ideal is to encourage him to conform, which breeds fear and produces in him a constant conflict between what he is and what he should be; and all inward conflicts have their outward man-ifestations in society. Ideals are an actual hindrance to our understanding of the child and to the child's understanding of himself."—J. Krishnamurti, *Education and the Significance of Life*

"What happens in the schools is not unlike what happens in society at large when the penalties for improvidence, laziness or ignorance are not just softened but removed. When there is no such thing as failure, there is no such thing as success either. Motivation, the desire to excel, the urge to accomplishment—all these disappear."—S. I. Hayakawa

"I ought to have seen that I could never get what I wanted from someone like Miranda, with all her la-di-da ideas and clever tricks. I ought to have got someone who would respect me more. Someone ordinary I could teach."—John Fowles, *The Collector*

"Nobody can teach anyone anything."—W. R. Wees, *Nobody Can Teach Anyone Anything*

"If they've got nothing in their heads, you might as well fill them with something nice."—Martin Mayer, *The Schools* (quoting poetry teacher)*

"Better for each one is his own law of action, even if it be imperfect, than the law of another, even well applied. It is better to perish in one's own law; it is perilous to follow the law of another."—*Bhagavad Gita*

"The mind is not a vessel to be filled but a fire to be lighted."—Plutarch

"If you can read this, thank a teacher."—bumper sticker

"Where the public school conceives of itself merely as a place of instruction, and puts severe restraints on the relationships between persons, we conceived of ourselves as an environment for growth, and accepted the relationships between the children and ourselves as being the very heart of the school."—George Dennison, *The Lives of Children*

"We think of the mind as a storehouse to be filled when we should be thinking of it as an instrument to be used."—John W. Gardner, *Self-Renewal*

"The kids in my classes are helpful as I can use them as sounding boards and let their responses be a means of progressing with the lesson, but I could handle these matters differently if there were no students present. I could still teach chemistry."—Theodore W. Hipple, *Teaching in a Vacuum*, quoting a fellow teacher

"It seems to me that anything that can be taught to another is relatively inconsequential and has little or no significant influence on behavior."—Carl R. Rogers, *Freedom to Learn*

"FREE. Every Monday through Friday. Knowledge. Bring your own containers."—Notice on school bulletin board (quoted in *Reader's Digest*, October 1969)

"I taught them that material, all right, but they didn't learn it."—remark overheard in a teachers' lounge

* This and all other quotations from this source are from *The Schools*, by M. Mayer. Copyright 1963 by Doubleday Publishing Company. Reprinted by permission.

Part One

Knowing the Subject

Knowing 2
the Subject

2   KNOWING THE SUBJECT

PRE-EXERCISES

1. What Does "Knowing the Subject" Mean?

Presumably you know your subject (whether it be the grade 3 curriculum, grade 10 American history, or educational psychology) or you will know it when you begin to teach. But what do you mean when you say "I know my subject"?

Do you mean that you are aware of a particular set of problems and are competent in handling a set of tools for solving those problems? Do you mean that you can ask yourself a set of questions and evaluate various tentative answers to those questions? Do you mean that you know a set of facts and how those facts are organized? Do you mean that you understand a set of principles and can follow a set of procedures based on those principles? Do you mean that you can use a language—English, Spanish, algebra, Fortran? Do you mean that you have acquired a set of perceptual and motor skills? Do you mean that you have assimilated a particular point of view from which to survey the world?

Think through each of those possible answers with respect to your own subject. Think through each answer with respect to sciences, arts, languages, sports, and so on.

Does "I know my subject" perhaps mean different things with respect to different subjects?

2. Organizing Technical Terms

Here is a strategy for checking how well you know your subject and for getting to know it better.

a. Get a standard textbook on your subject and some packages of 3 × 5 index cards.
b. Go through the index and copy each of the technical terms on a 3 × 5 card.

c. Organize the cards into piles representing different sets. For example, if your subject is geometry, one of your sets would be *triangle,* and this pile of cards would contain the elements *right triangle, isosceles triangle,* and so forth. This procedure may require that you read the appropriate sections of the textbook to learn the meaning of the unfamiliar technical terms. If possible, organize those sets, in turn, into larger sets. For example, the set *triangle* will fit, along with *quadrilateral, polygon,* and so on, under the set *plane figure.*
d. Make a list of appropriate questions for each set of technical terms. For example, what is the definition of the term? How do the elements within the set differ? In what sense are they the same?
e. Ask yourself each question with respect to each element within each set. Read the relevant section of the textbook to check your answer, when you have one, and to provide your answer, when you don't have one.

I used this strategy with my own introductory textbook in psychology (*Psychology: A Story of a Search,* Second Edition. Monterey, Calif.: Brooks/Cole, 1974). The procedure not only helped me better understand the technical terms in my subject (the mere fact that I had written the book did not mean that I fully understood the technical terms it contained) but revealed the structure of my subject more clearly.

The technical terms fitted into 12 categories that turned out to be necessary because of the structure of psychology. Psychology involves a relationship between *experimenter* and *subject* in which the experimenter presents *stimuli* and the subject emits *responses.* The presentation of the stimuli and the measurement of the responses may require certain *tools* and *techniques.* The responses are transformed, through statistical analysis, into *facts,* and the facts are, in turn, further organized into *theories.* The facts may be expressed in terms of *numbers* or *pictures.* The theories may be expressed in terms of *functions* or *structures* of the nervous system.

The same 12 categories emerge from the organization of the technical terms in the index of *this* textbook—which is not surprising, since the psychology of teaching is a subdiscipline within psychology.

Perhaps you would like to repeat this exercise using this textbook to check and extend your understanding of educational psychology. The technical terms are in **boldface** in the text, so that you may find them easily.

I assume that you have learned, are learning, and will continue to learn your subject in other courses and from other sources. Helping you get to know your subject is beyond the scope of this textbook and way beyond the capacity of its author. The function of this chapter is not to help you learn your subject but to help you know better what you mean when you say "I know my subject."

Pre-exercise 1 for Chapter 1, in which you were invited to preview your first meeting with your first class, included the crucial question "What am I doing here?" Pre-exercise 1 for Chapter 2, in which you were invited to consider what you mean when you say "I know my subject," may provide a more precise answer to this question. The quick and easy answer is "I am teaching subject *X* to students *Y*." Let us say, to be more concrete, "I am teaching algebra to grade 10c." Presumably, then, you know grade 10 algebra, the students in grade 10c do not know grade 10 algebra, but, at the end of the course, as a result of your "teaching," they *will* know grade 10 algebra. You will have a clearer conception of what you are doing if you know what you mean by saying "I know my subject" and of *how* you are doing if you know how to check the validity of the statement when a student says, at the end of the course, "I too know the subject."

The question "What am I doing here?" triggers the further questions "How am I doing it?" and "How well am I doing it?" These questions focus, respectively, on ends, on means, and on the extent to which the ends are satisfied by the means. In the context of the psychology of teaching, these questions focus, respectively, on objectives, methods, and evaluation. This chapter will consider, in turn, objectives as ends (Section 2.1), methods as means (Section 2.2), and evaluation as means-ends (Section 2.3).

2.1 OBJECTIVES AS ENDS

Your answers to the question "What am I doing here?" are your instructional objectives. The quick and easy answer just given—I am teaching *X* to *Y*—is not much help. One obvious refinement is the recognition that "knowing the subject" is not an all-or-nothing matter. At the beginning of the course, everyone in the classroom, including you, knows "some" algebra and, at the end of the course, everyone in the classroom (including you, since teachers are not exempt from learning) knows "more" algebra. It is necessary to analyze the subject into elements to replace the vague terms "some" and "more" with precise statements about those aspects of the subject known by the students before and after the course. Let us look at three contributions toward a more precise answer to the question "What am I doing here?"—Mager's behaviorial objectives (Section 2.11), Bloom's taxonomy of educational objectives (Section 2.12), and Gagné's categories of learning (Section 2.13).

"THE SEARCH FOR MEANING IS NOT A SEARCH FOR AN AB-
STRACT BODY OF KNOWLEDGE, OR EVEN A CONCRETE
BODY OF KNOWLEDGE. IT IS A DISTINCTLY PERSONAL
SEARCH. THE ONE WHO MAKES IT RAISES INTIMATE PER-
SONAL QUESTIONS: WHAT REALLY COUNTS, FOR ME?
WHAT VALUES AM I SEEKING? WHAT, IN MY EXISTENCE
AS A PERSON, IN MY RELATIONS WITH OTHERS, IN MY
WORK AS A TEACHER, IS OF REAL CONCERN, PERHAPS OF
ULTIMATE CONCERN, TO ME?"

ARTHUR T. JERSILD
WHEN TEACHERS FACE THEMSELVES

2.11   Behavioral Objectives: Mager

Mager recommends that you state your instructional objectives in terms of **behavioral objectives.**[129] That is, rather than state what your students will *know* at the end of the course, the unit, or the lesson, you should state what they can *do.* Thus, for example, an instructional objective for Chapter 1 of this textbook would be "Student can classify the attitude underlying a series of statements about education as outside-in or inside-out" rather than "Student understands the distinction between outside-in and inside-out education." Mager continues to recommend even more precision by specifying the conditions of performance. An example would be "Student can classify the attitude underlying the following series of statements (listing statements in Postexercise 2 for Chapter 1) as outside-in or inside-out and get at least 20 out of the 25 items correct."

Stating your objectives in such precise terms clarifies what you are doing, not only to yourself but to your students. They should be involved, as much as possible, in formulating those objectives. We tend to assume that young children do not know what they need to know. However, if you invite them to contribute, they may surprise you. First-grade students surprised Ojemann and Pritchett,[161] and inner-city slum students surprised Finder.[56] Students should, at least, be given your list of behavioral objectives. Mager argues that "if you give your written objectives to your students, you may not have to do much else."[129]

2.12   Taxonomy of Educational Objectives: Bloom

If you were to ask a large number of teachers "What are you doing here?" they would provide a bewildering variety of answers. Biologists provide some order to the bewildering variety of flora and fauna by organizing them into a taxonomy—that is, by putting each plant and animal into an appropriate category, based on some characteristic they share, and putting those categories into larger and larger categories. In the same way, Bloom, Engelhart, Furst, Hill, and Krathwohl have provided some order to the bewildering variety of educational objectives by organizing them into a taxonomy.[21] They have provided taxonomies of cognitive, affective, and motor objectives. Let us focus on cognitive objectives, since those are most emphasized in schools and best developed by Bloom and his colleagues. The major categories within the cognitive domain are listed below.

> *Knowledge:* Those objectives that require remembering but not thinking.
> *Comprehension:* Those objectives that require not only knowing but understanding.
> *Application:* The ability to apply principles to actual situations.

Analysis: The ability to break a system into its elements and consider the relationships among those elements.

Synthesis: The ability to combine elements to create new systems.

Evaluation: The ability to make judgments based on internal evidence and/or external criteria.

Each major category, in turn, is divided into subcategories. Thus, for example, *knowledge* is divided into *knowledge of specifics, knowledge of ways and means of dealing with specifics,* and *knowledge of universals and abstractions.*

2.13   Categories of Learning: Gagné

Psychologists seldom talk about the process of knowing. Knowledge is the province of epistemology, a branch of philosophy, and psychology has cut the umbilical cord from mother philosophy. Psychologists talk instead about the processes of learning and remembering. Since "I have learned" and "I

LEARNING TO BE SKILLFUL WITH A BODY OF KNOWLEDGE IS MUCH LIKE LEARNING A LANGUAGE, ITS RULES FOR FORMING AND TRANSFORMING SENTENCES, ITS VOCABULARY, ITS SEMANTIC MARKERS, ETC. AS WITH LANGUAGE, THERE IS ALSO THE INTERESTING FEATURE IN ALL SUCH LEARNING THAT WHAT IS LEARNED IS INITIALLY "OUTSIDE" THE LEARNER — AS A DISCIPLINE OF LEARNING, AS A SUBJECT MATTER, AS A NOTATIONAL SYSTEM.

JEROME S. BRUNER
THE RELEVANCE OF EDUCATION

know" and "I will remember" are essentially equivalent statements in the past, present, and future tenses, respectively, psychologists can talk about knowing indirectly by talking about learning and remembering. Let us look at one psychologist's discussion of "knowing the subject" in terms of "having learned the subject."

Robert Gagné reviewed the various types of learning discovered by psychologists.[66] He observed that each theorist described a type of learning in one set of conditions and then generalized this type of learning to all conditions. Thus, Watson described classical conditioning and then "explained" all behavior in terms of classical conditioning (see Section 3.212); Skinner described instrumental conditioning and then "explained" all behavior in terms of instrumental conditioning (see Section 3.222); Kohler described insight learning in one set of conditions and then got involved in a debate over whether learning is *either* insight learning *or* trial-and-error learning (see Section 10.1). Gagné concluded that learning may be both insight learning and trial-and-error learning, depending on the conditions that lead to it. There are *many* types of learning, each characterized by a different set of conditions. Gagné classified the various types of learning described by the various psychologists into eight categories, as listed below. The conditions of learning that characterize each of those categories are not just environmental but organismic; that is, this type of learning is possible only when the person is in a certain state. This state is defined in terms of the acquisition of previous learning. The eight **categories of learning** are organized in a hierarchy from simple to complex learning, in which each type of learning is a prerequisite to the next.

Signal Learning: A stimulus, previously neutral, comes to elicit a response, because the stimulus is presented together with another stimulus which already elicits that response. This is the process of classical conditioning described in Section 3.21.

Stimulus-Response Learning: A stimulus, previously neutral, comes to elicit a response, because the response permits access to a stimulus which already elicits a satisfying response. This is the process of instrumental conditioning described in Section 3.22.

Chaining: A series of responses become linked as each response is classically conditioned to the feedback from the previous response. The series of responses permits access to a stimulus which already elicits a satisfying response. This category of learning is, thus, a combination of the first two categories.

Verbal Association: A chain in which the stimuli and responses are words. Since the link between words involves an arbitrary agreement among members of a language community, reinforcement is often mediated by another person or some coded connection between the stimulus word and response word. For example, the stimulus *match* may produce the response *alumette* because the French teacher assures the student this is correct or because the student has the mnemonic "A match is used to illuminate, so the word for match is *alumette.*"

Discrimination Learning: Variation of verbal responses to verbal stimuli as the student's store of verbal associations becomes more numerous and complex. For example, *match* may elicit not only *alumette* but the French equivalents of the various other meanings of *match*.

Concept Learning: Response to stimuli as a class. Whereas discrimination learning involves responding to differences among stimuli, concept learning involves responding to similarities. This category of learning requires the student to internalize various stimuli with elements in common as a concept, and enables the student to generalize from one stimulus to another.

Rule Learning: Combining two or more concepts to form a rule. Thus, the rule "The square of the hypotenuse is equal to the sum of the squares of the other two sides" requires understanding of the concepts *square, hypotenuse, equality, side,* and other concepts, like *triangle,* not even mentioned in the rule.

Problem-Solving: Combining two or more rules to solve a problem. Thus, the rule just given plus rules about the appropriate dimensions may be combined to solve the problem of laying out a baseball diamond.

2.2 METHODS AS MEANS

A clear statement of your instructional objectives helps you choose appropriate instructional methods as means to those ends. Since "knowing the subject" means different things for different subjects, different methods may be most appropriate for different subjects. Let us look at two broad implications of this statement—different subjects are characterized by different structures (Section 2.21) and subjects may be made artificially difficult because of inappropriate presentation (Section 2.22).

2.21 Natural Structures

Different subjects lend themselves naturally to different bases of organization and, hence, different methods of presentation. Bruner argues that knowing a subject means knowing the structure of the subject.[25] It is useful, then, to clarify the basic structure of your subject so that you may better know what you know when you know your subject and what your students will know when you have taught it to them. The basic structure of mathematics is obviously logical, and the basic structure of history is obviously chronological. It is not so obvious that the presentation of those subjects must be psychologically sound as well as logically and chronologically sound. A creative teacher of mathematics may get students involved in the theorem of Pythagoras by presenting it as a practical solution to laying right-angle corners in a playing field rather than as a conclusion deduced from a set of axioms. A creative teacher of history may capture the attention of a class by reading an item from that morning's newspaper, presenting the sequence of events that led to the current news, and encouraging the class to follow the story as it unfolds day by day in

A FIELD OF KNOWLEDGE, WHETHER IT BE MATH, HISTORY, SCIENCE, MUSIC, OR WHATEVER, IS A TERRITORY, AND KNOWING IT IS NOT JUST A MATTER OF KNOWING ALL THE ITEMS IN THE TERRITORY, BUT OF KNOWING HOW THEY RELATE TO, COMPARE WITH, AND FIT IN WITH EACH OTHER.

JOHN HOLT
HOW CHILDREN FAIL

the instant history of the newspaper. In each case, the logical and chronological structures of mathematics and history are respected, but they are taught upside down and backward because of certain overriding psychological considerations. However, it is necessary to know your subject upside down and backward in order to be able to focus on the psychological aspects of presenting it. We will see, in Chapter 10, that certain subjects in which the relationships between the elements tend to be necessary (like mathematics and physics) lend themselves more easily to the discovery method of teaching than subjects in which the relationships between the elements tend to be arbitrary (like history or geography).

2.22 Artificial Difficulty

Subjects are often made artificially difficult by being inappropriately presented. This is obvious in some cases. Tennis should not be taught by correspondence. Motor skills are better taught by showing in context than by telling out of context. It is not so obvious that showing is not enough, as I discovered when I eavesdropped on a friend's tennis lesson. It is not at all obvious that a science should not be taught in the same way during its early stage of development as during its late stage of development. For example, the apparent difficulty of psychology, as it is traditionally taught, is due to the fact that it is in its early stage of development but is being taught in a manner more appropriate to a science in its late stage of development. It is certainly difficult to memorize masses of unrelated facts—but only in the sense that it is difficult to eat consommé with chopsticks. The nervous system, like the chopsticks, is not designed for the function it is required to perform. It is certainly difficult to organize the unrelated facts available in the early stage of a science—but only in the sense that it is difficult to complete a jigsaw puzzle when most pieces are missing and many pieces from other puzzles are mixed in. In the early stage of a science, the disorderly product makes sense only in terms of the orderly process. Bruner argues, as stated earlier, that knowing a subject means knowing the structure of the subject. Psychology as process has a solid structure, but psychology as product has, as yet, only a very sketchy and superficial structure. Thus, we should be telling the story of the search rather than providing the miscellaneous catalog of findings generated so far by the search. We should be inviting students to look over our shoulders to see what we are doing rather than to grub around among the pile of debris at our feet.

2.3 EVALUATION AS MEANS-ENDS

Having formulated your objectives and chosen teaching methods to attain those objectives, it is necessary to evaluate the extent to which you have attained your chosen ends by your chosen means. Let us consider four important distinctions involved in this process of evaluation. It is useful to distinguish between evaluating and grading (Section 2.31); grading may be either norm-referenced or criterion-referenced (Section 2.32); tests, the major instrument of grading, may be either standardized or teacher-made (Section 2.33); questions on tests may be either objective or essay (Section 2.34).

2.31 Evaluating and Grading

Evaluation is the process of determining the extent to which *your* methods were effective in attaining *your* objectives. There is a tendency, however, for the emphasis to shift from evaluating the teacher to grading the students. The performance of the teacher should, indeed, be measured in terms of the performance of the students, since the objective of the teacher is that the

"IN MOST JOBS, IF A MAN DOES NOT DO WHAT HE IS PAID TO DO, HE IS CONSIDERED A FAILURE. IN TEACHING, WHEN THAT HAPPENS, THE STUDENT IS CONSIDERED A FAILURE."

NEIL POSTMAN AND **CHARLES WEINGARTNER**
THE SOFT REVOLUTION

students learn. It is important to keep in mind that this performance reflects not only their learning but your teaching. One positive effect of the recent pressure for **accountability** is that teachers may become more fully aware that their relationship with their students is synergetic; that is, the objectives of the teacher and the students are compatible. The relationship between the teacher and the class may become more like that between the coach and the team. In the traditional classroom, we get only an occasional glimpse of cooperation between teacher and class, as between coach and team, when the teacher is "coaching" the class for an external examination. If the teacher were hired or fired like the coach, on the basis of the performance of the "team," then this sense of cooperation might become more pervasive. Evaluation in the case of the coach is, of course, much easier: it is right up there on the scoreboard. When a teacher coaches a class for the game of life, the rules are less clear, the skills are more complex, and it is much more difficult to assess who is winning and by how many points.

The typical negative reaction to being "graded" may be further reduced by pointing out that this procedure is designed to provide each student with information about his or her learning. People feed dimes into machines in

GRADING DESTROYS THE USE OF TESTING, WHICH IS A GOOD METHOD OF TEACHING IF ONE CORRECTS THE TEST BUT DOES NOT GRADE IT. STUDENTS LIKE TO BE TESTED, TO GIVE STRUCTURE TO THEIR STUDYING AND TO KNOW WHERE THEY ARE; IF TESTED BUT NOT GRADED, THEY ARE EAGER TO LEARN THE RIGHT ANSWERS AND THEY ASK HOW TO SOLVE THE PROBLEM.

PAUL GOODMAN
THE COMMUNITY OF SCHOLARS

Greyhound bus stations for the opportunity to answer multiple-choice questions testing their general knowledge. Why, then, does your class groan when you offer them $10 worth of multiple-choice questions absolutely free? Perhaps it is because they know that, in the context of the classroom, the questions are not provided as a valuable service to assess how well the teacher has taught and how well each of them has learned. They are being judged. It is this subsidiary role of judge that distorts the teacher-student relationship.

2.32 Norm- and Criterion-Referenced Grading

Traditional tests tend to be **norm-referenced;** that is, a student's performance is judged with respect to the performance of other students who have previously or are concurrently taking the same test. Formulating the objectives of a course facilitates a shift to **criterion-referenced tests,** in which a student's performance is judged with respect to some criterion. Whereas a norm-referenced test indicates how well a student does in comparison to peers, a criterion-referenced test indicates how well she or he met the objectives of the course. In stating behavioral objectives, you can establish a standard by which you judge whether a student has attained those objectives. A student passes the course when he or she meets this criterion. Advocates of norm-

WE COULD LEARN NOTHING ABOUT MAXINE BY TESTING ELENA. AND SO THERE WAS NO COMPARATIVE TESTING AT ALL. THE CHILDREN NEVER MISSED THOSE INVIDIOUS COMPARISONS, AND THE TEACHERS WERE SPARED THE ABSURDITY OF RANKING DOZENS OF PERSONALITIES ON ONE UNIFORM SCALE.

GEORGE DENNISON
THE LIVES OF CHILDREN

referenced tests argue that they are a valuable preparation for "real-life" situations in which students will be competing with their peers. However, it could be argued that criterion-referenced tests are more like real-life tests. A pregnancy test indicates whether you are or are not pregnant; it does not give you a "B" in Pregnancy 101 or tell you that you are 78% pregnant.

Another way of viewing criterion-referenced tests is that they permit students to compete with their former selves rather than with other students. You can provide your students with an opportunity to know what they know by offering your test at the beginning of the course as well as at the end. The difference between their performance on the pretest (**entering behavior**) and their performance on the posttest (**terminal behavior**) would show them what they gained from the course. Whereas every student can win in this competition with his or her former self, and you, as teacher, also win when all your students win, norm-referenced testing requires that there must be losers.

2.33 *Standardized and Teacher-Made Tests*

Grading is usually accomplished by means of **paper-and-pencil tests.** You may want to combine them with a variety of other devices. For example, you could lay out a smorgasbord of relevant opportunities and provide credit to those students who take advantage of them. Those opportunities could include reading and reviewing books, attending and reviewing movies, writing papers, designing educational toys and games, presenting a paper in class, creating a slide-and-tape show, interviewing local authorities, and so on.

Paper-and-pencil tests may be either standardized or teacher-made. **Standardized tests** have been carefully constructed by experts, provide norms for large groups and technical information about validity and reliability, and come equipped with precise instructions for administration. You and your students may find them a useful source of information about how your students compare with a large group of peers. You can obtain information about such standardized tests from the test itself and its accompanying manual (write to test publishers for their catalogs), from the *Mental Measurements Yearbook*[28] (a sort of consumer's guide to tests), and a series of test evaluations published by the Center for the Study of Evaluation.

Teacher-made tests, like homemade clothes, can be custom-designed to fit your particular class. You can design them to measure precisely what you teach and what your students learn. You can personalize them by including the names of your students and reminding them of experiences you have shared. Your test should cover a representative sample of your behavioral objectives across a representative sample of content areas in your course. One way to ensure a representative sample is to construct a **table of specifications.**[65] This is a matrix with the various behaviors in your behavioral objectives on one axis and the various content areas of your course on the other axis. In each cell of this matrix, indicate the percentage of questions you think should test each combination of behavior and content. Figure 2-1 is an illustration of a

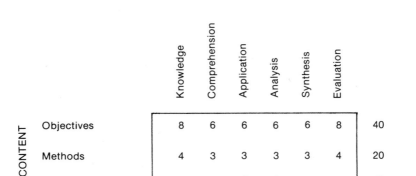

Figure 2-1.   Table of specifications: behavior-content matrix

behavior-content matrix, with Bloom's categories in the "behavior" columns and the subsections of this chapter in the "content" rows. A test constructed in this way can be used for diagnostic purposes. Poor performance by a particular student in a particular content area or on a particular behavior would suggest where further work is required. Poor performance by the class as a whole in particular content areas or particular behaviors would suggest where further work is required by the teacher. We tend to think of unfair tests as being unrepresentative with respect to content areas. The table of specifications suggests that they may also be unrepresentative with respect to behaviors. Teachers often state their objectives in terms of some sets of behaviors (let us say, application, synthesis, evaluation), use teaching methods that encourage another set of behaviors (let us say, analysis and comprehension), and evaluate on the basis of yet another set (let us say, knowledge). Students are, understandably, confused by and resentful of such inconsistencies.

2.34 Objective and Essay Questions

Test questions may be either **objective** or **essay.** Post-exercise 1 contains one example of each of the major forms within each category of question, based on the content of this chapter. We tend to assume that objective questions measure low-level skills and essay questions measure high-level skills. However, with imagination, all behaviors can be measured in all ways. The assumption that objective questions measure lower-level behaviors than essay questions may be due to the fact that they measure **recognition,** whereas essay questions measure **recall.** (We can, indeed, recognize more than we can recall. How many of your high school classmates can you recall? Now look at your high school graduation photograph and see how many more you can recognize that you were not able to recall.) Objective questions take longer to prepare and less time to correct than essay questions; the total time spent on an objective test is less for a large class and more for a small class. Objective tests are more reliable than essay tests. Studies reveal wide variability from judge to judge in evaluating essays.[45] Some sources of subjective bias which have been identified are the quality of the previous paper read, the quality of the early answers within a set of answers, the identity of the student who wrote the examination, and the characteristic mean and variability of scores by the teacher. However, essay questions may be more valid than objective questions. We usually claim to be measuring higher-order behaviors, and those behaviors may, indeed, be better measured by essay questions. The respective merits of each may, perhaps, be best optimized by a test containing a combination of objective and essay questions. Such a test would also be fairer, since students often prefer one over the other. One useful combination of the two forms includes the following statement among the instructions for multiple-choice items:

> If you think the question is ambiguous, write your best of all possible answers anyway but put (Ambiguous) after your choice. Explain on the back of the last page why it is ambiguous. If your guess is correct, you get the point anyway. However, even if your guess is "wrong," you may earn the point if your explanation illustrates that you understand the concept being tested.

This procedure defuses some of the negative reaction by some students to objective questions and helps you build less ambiguous examinations.

POST-EXERCISES

1. Objective Questions and Essay Questions

Objective Questions

a. **Completion**
   In the psychology of teaching, ends can be associated with ———— , means with ———— , and the relationship between means and ends with ———— .
b. **Matching**

Behavioral objectives	Bloom
Taxonomy of educational objectives	Gagné
Categories of learning	Mager

c. **Multiple-choice**
The following four distinctions are made within the section on evaluation. Which of these distinctions is most intimately related to the attempt to replace competition among students by cooperation among students?

1. Evaluating and grading
2. Norm-referenced and criterion-referenced grading
3. Standardized and teacher-made tests
4. Objective and essay questions

d. **True-false**
"Student understands the distinction between outside-in and inside-out education" is a behavioral objective.   T   F

Essay Questions

a. **Short-answer**
What is the distinction between norm-referenced and criterion-referenced grading? State two implications of this distinction.

b. **Long-answer**
Those who view teaching as an outside-in process tend to emphasize "knowing the subject," whereas those who view teaching as an inside-out process tend to emphasize "knowing the student." This chapter implies an outside-in attitude and is of interest only to outside-inners. Discuss.

2. Organizing Technical Terms—Again

Here is *my* organization of the technical terms in this textbook. You may like to compare it with *your* organization, if you took advantage of the opportunity offered in Pre-exercise 2. Sorry for not telling you I was going to do it for you before you did it yourself. I didn't tell you because the process is more important than the product. You will learn much more about the structure of *The Psychology of Teaching* by discovering it yourself (see Chapter 10).

Your organization may not be the same as mine. It is difficult to place all the technical terms clearly into those 12 categories. Each "difficulty," however, provides some insight into the structure of the new discipline being presented here.

First, two differences between the category systems for general psychology and the psychology of teaching are illuminating. The first two categories here are *teacher* and *student* rather than *experimenter* and *subject,* suggesting that the major focus of the psychology of teaching is the teacher-student relationship, with the experimenter-subject relationship secondary. There were so few items in the categories *number* and *picture* here that I placed them under *tool.* This suggests that the psychology of teaching is less concerned with the statistical analysis and representation of data than general psychology—a further symptom of the shift from the experimenter-subject relationship.

Second, there are some "difficulties" in placing the technical terms within this category system. I placed *source* under *teacher* and *destination* under *student,* but both terms could appear in both categories. This difficulty anticipates my argument in Chapter 9 that communication between teacher and student is a two-way process. I placed *conditioning* under *function,* but I could have placed it under *technique.* Behavioristic concepts tend to be techniques of the experimenter, whereas humanistic concepts tend to be functions of the subject. This reflects the outside-in emphasis of behaviorism and the inside-out emphasis of humanism. I

placed *intimate relationship* and *synergetic society* under *structure,* but I could have introduced a new category, *relationship,* since those terms do not refer to structures within the
student but relationships between the teacher and the student. General psychology, in aspiring
to objectivity, has not been concerned, until very recently, with the relationship between the
experimenter and the subject, whereas the psychology of teaching is intimately concerned
with the relationship between the teacher and the student.

You may find the following list useful for reviewing your understanding of the technical
terms in the text. You may also like to ask yourself appropriate questions with respect to each
item in each category. For example, with respect to each theory, you may ask "What facts does
it explain?" "What facts does it not explain?" "Are there any alternative theories?" "What are
their relative merits?"

TEACHER

authoritarian
democratic
laissez-faire

benevolent dictator
malevolent democrat

behaviorist
humanist
interactionist

discovery
expository

ecologist

environmentalist
hereditarian

Gestalt psychologist
neobehaviorist

inside-out
outside-in

psychologist
social psychologist
sociologist

source

STUDENT

destination

feral child
force-fed child

participant observer

teleophile
teleophobe

STIMULUS

conditioned stimulus
unconditioned stimulus

contact comfort

arousal function
cue function

goal

spiral curriculum
hidden curriculum

RESPONSE

behavior

  coping
  defending

  detour

  entering
  terminal

  prosocial

  verbal

circular reactions

  primary

secondary
tertiary

conditioned reflex
unconditioned reflex

echoic response
mand
tact

habit

TOOL

auditory channel
visual channel

basal age
ceiling age

communication unit
communication system
  centralized
  decentralized

cuisenaire rods

cumulative record

definition
  operational
  analytical
  practical

heuristics
mnemonics

initial teaching alphabet

intelligence quotient
mental age

inverse operation

language

  phoneme
  morpheme
  sentence
  discourse

  kernel sentence
  rules of transformation

  grapheme

programmed text
  linear
  branching
teaching machine

puzzle box
Skinner box

reasoning
  class
  ordinal
  propositional

reliability
validity

schedules of reinforcement
  fixed
  variable
  interval
  ratio

talking typewriter

taxonomy of educational objectives

test

  criterion-referenced
  norm-referenced

  essay
  objective
    completion
    matching
    multiple-choice
    true-false

  group
  individual

  intelligence
    Flanagan's test of mental ability
    primary mental abilities
    Stanford-Binet

  paper-and-pencil

  standardized
  teacher-made

  thematic apperception

variable
  independent
  dependent

extraneous
intervening

TECHNIQUE

affective education
confluent education

behavioral objectives

biofeedback
meditation

brainstorming

buzz group

clinical method
experimental method

computer-assisted instruction

demonstration

developmental discussion

dream deprivation
sensory deprivation

discovery teaching
expository teaching

factor analysis

jigsaw method

lecture
seminar
tutorial

organic method
phonetic method
whole-word method

method of successive approximations

reinforcement
  total
  partial

shaping

table of specifications

FACT

accountability

adultocentrism

aha phenomenon
eureka effect

critical period
sensitive period
readiness

cultural deprivation

destiny control

Eichmann effect

entropy

functional autonomy

gradient of reinforcement
law of effect

homeostasis

object concept
object constancy

observer effect
  Hawthorne effect
  self-fulfilling prophecy
  self-denying prophecy
  experimenter-bias effect
  Pygmalion effect
  Rosenthal sensitization effect

serendipity
zeitgeist

transfer

THEORY

activation theory
need-reduction theory
theory of evolution

cognitive dissonance

damaged culture

guided growth
natural readiness

hierarchy of needs

Jensenism

paradigm

structure of intellect

STRUCTURE

autonomic nervous system
central nervous system

old brain
new brain

left hemisphere
right hemisphere

association area
projection area
    sensory
    motor

intrinsic neurons
extrinsic neurons

sensory neurons
motor neurons
internuncial neurons

endocrine system

hypothalamus
reticular activating system

receptor

antagonistic society
synergetic society

contractual relationship
intimate relationship

abstract belief system
concrete belief system

deep structure
surface structure

enactive representation
iconic representation
symbolic representation

stage
    sensorimotor
    concrete-operations
        preoperational
        operational
        formal-operations

subjective map
    perceptual map
    conceptual map

self-esteem

FUNCTION

adaptation
    assimilation
    accommodation

categories of learning

conditioning
    classical
    instrumental
extinction
generalization
discrimination

convergent production skills
divergent production skills

creativity
    preparation
    incubation
    illumination
    verification

intelligence
    primary mental abilities

drive
    primary
    secondary

need
    biological
    sociological
    psychological

evaluation

expectation
    self-expectation

id
ego
superego

imprinting

learning
   trial-and-error
   insight

development
   ontogenetic
   phylogenetic

meaning

motivation

deficiency
growth

extrinsic
intrinsic

rationality
veridicality

recognition
recall

role
   sex role

socialization

symbolic function

Part Two

Knowing the Student

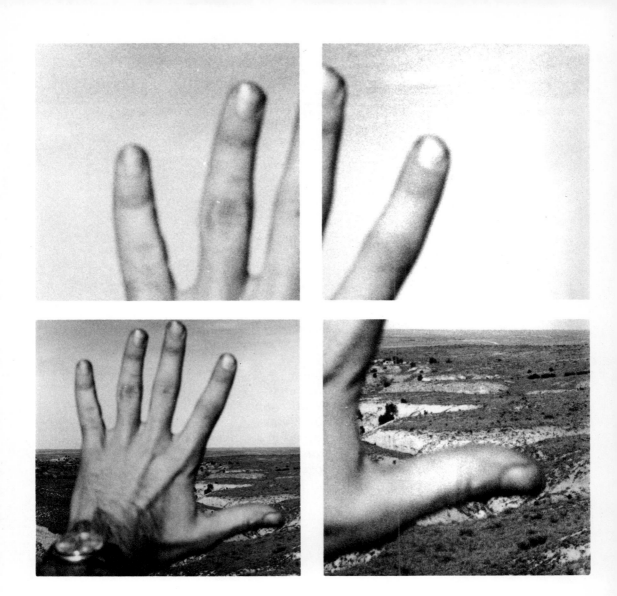

Behaviorism and Outside-In Teaching

3 BEHAVIORISM AND OUTSIDE-IN TEACHING

PRE-EXERCISES

1. Programmed Textbooks

Have you ever used a teaching machine or a programmed textbook? Here is a short program to give you a feel for programmed instruction.* Cover the answers on the right. Write your answers in the space provided and check them by uncovering the corresponding answer.

1. Each side of this square, *ABCD*, is two feet long. Then the size of the square is ——— square feet.

4

* From "Programmed Learning and the Socratic Dialogue," by I. S. Cohen, *American Psychologist*, 1962, 17, 772–775. Copyright 1962 by the American Psychological Association. Reprinted by permission.

2. Here we have another square, *DCFE*, equal to it in ——— .

area

3. And here a third square, *CHGF*, ——— in size to each of the others.

equal

4. Now we can fill up the space in the corner by adding another ——— of ——— size.

square, equal

5. All four squares, *ABCD, CDEF, CHGF, BIHC,* are ——— .

equal

6. How many times larger is this whole space, *AEGI,* than the square *ABCD?*
———

4

7. The lines *BD, DF, FH, HB,* drawn from corner to corner in each of the squares, cuts each square in ——— .

half

8. The four lines containing the space *BDFH* are of ——— length.

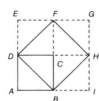

equal

9. Has each of the inside lines *(BD, DF, FH, HB)* cut off half of each of the squares? (yes/no) ——— .

yes

10. How many spaces of that size (for example, *DCF* or *BCH*) are there in *BDFH?*
———

4

11. How many in the square *ABCD?* ———

2

12. Four is how many times two? ———

2

13. If our original square *ABCD* contained four square feet, then how many square feet does this square *BDFH* contain?
———

8

14. From what line do we get this figure?
    _____   BD

15. From the line *BD* drawn cornerwise across
    our original four-foot figure *(ABCD),* a
    square can be drawn which is _____ as
    large as the original square.   twice

16. Such a line as *BD* is called the *diagonal.* To
    double the size of the square, you may
    draw a square from the _____ .   diagonal

This program is based on the Socratic dialogue presented in Pre-exercise 3 in Chapter 10. The programmer argues that "Socrates' sequencing of the material could easily be construed as the first draft of a teaching machine program." Do you agree?

How did your experiences with programmed learning differ from learning by more conventional methods? What kind of theory do you think underlies such devices as teaching machines and programmed textbooks? What principles are being applied?

Here are some programmed texts that cover much of the material presented in this chapter:

Barlow, J. A. *Stimulus and response.* New York: Harper & Row, 1968.
Geis, G. L., Stebbins, W. C., & Lundin, R. W. *Reflex and operant conditioning.* New York: Appleton-Century-Crofts, 1965.
Holland, J. G., & Skinner, B. F. *The analysis of behavior.* New York: McGraw-Hill, 1961.
Smith, W. I., & Moore, J. W. *Conditioning and instrumental learning.* New York: McGraw-Hill, 1966.

How does the programmed instruction in these textbooks differ from the more or less conventional instruction in this textbook?

Devotees of teaching machines assured us that they would revolutionize education. Have they? If not, why not?

Some teachers were concerned that teaching machines would replace them. Did they? If not, why not? What are the advantages of teaching machines over teachers? Of teachers over teaching machines?

2. Teacher Is to Student as Therapist Is to Client?

The three main "forces" in psychology today are behaviorism, Freudianism, and humanism. Representatives of each of these positions have written on education. For example:

behaviorism—Skinner, B. F. *The technology of teaching.* New York: Appleton-Century-Crofts, 1968.
Freudianism—Jones, R. *Fantasy and feeling in education.* New York: New York University Press, 1968.
humanism—Rogers, C. R. *Freedom to learn.* Columbus, Ohio: Merrill, 1969.

From what you know about each of these positions, what attitudes do you think they would have toward education? Would they tend to be outside-inners or inside-outers?

Representatives of each of these positions have, of course, also written on the application of their theories to therapy. From what you know about behavior therapy, psychoanalysis, and humanistic therapy, what insights does each offer into teaching? To what extent do you think the analogy of "teacher is to student as therapist is to client" holds? Think of some aspect of either relationship and then consider what would be equivalent in the other relationship. For example, what would be the equivalent in the therapist-client relationship of homework in the teacher-student relationship? What would be the equivalent in the teacher-student relationship of transference in the therapist-client relationship?

3. Black Boxes

The theory presented in this chapter is based on the concept of you as a "black box." That is, the behaviorist just observes what goes in and what comes out and the relationship between those inputs and outputs. This may seem like a very esoteric approach to understanding. However, you deal with black boxes every day.

Which black boxes did you deal with today? Here is a list of possible answers:

vending machine	car
elevator	telephone system
stove	typewriter
refrigerator	watch
washing machine	dog
radio	yourself
television set	other people

The last three systems (dog, yourself, other people) are essentially different from all the others. They are organisms, whereas the others are mechanisms. What is the essential difference? Is there any advantage to studying mechanisms in order to help understand organisms? What are the input and the output for each of the mechanisms? For each of the organisms? Can the output be predicted from the input in the case of the mechanisms? In the case of the organisms? If not, why not?

You put a quarter into a vending machine and press a certain button (input) and predict that you will get a cup of coffee and a nickel change (output). If your prediction is not confirmed, then it is reasonable to assume some malfunction in the system. Is it reasonable to make the same assumption in the case of an organism, such as a child in your class?

When a vending machine "misbehaves" by not giving you your change or your coffee, or by scalding your hand as you reach in and discover that it has run out of cups, you fix it or arrange to have it fixed by an expert. Do you do the same in the case of a child in your class? Is misbehavior not doing what one is supposed to do?

You come to distrust a certain vending machine because, on a number of occasions, it has not done what it is designed to do. Do we come to distrust people in the same way?

Some of you may not deal with some of these systems as black boxes. What are the alternatives? What are the relative advantages of the black-box approach and those alternative approaches?

Behaviorism is presented here in the form of six propositions: the person has only extrinsic needs, the person is conditioned from the outside in, the person is not responsible for behavior, the person has only extrinsic worth, the person is an interchangeable part, and the person has contractual relationships. Each proposition implies the next, and this system of propositions will be defined here as the behavioristic theory of the person.

The typical exposition of behaviorism considers only the first two propositions—"the person has only extrinsic needs" under the topic of motivation, and "the person is conditioned from the outside in" under the topic of learning. However, I have continued with a short presentation of four more propositions implied by those first two. I do so for two reasons. The fuller implications of the theory may help you better evaluate it, and the set of six propositions provides a useful contrast to the humanistic theory of the person, which will be presented in the next chapter.

Each of the first two propositions is followed by a statement about the practical implications of this proposition for teaching. I will argue that traditional education is largely based on a concept of teaching as an outside-in process and that outside-in teaching is based, in turn, on this behavioristic theory of the person.

3.1   THE PERSON HAS ONLY EXTRINSIC NEEDS

3.11   Theory of Evolution

The broad question in psychology is "What is the function of the nervous system?" and the broad answer provided by the theory of evolution is "to enable the organism to survive." The theory of evolution can thus be considered the basic theory in psychology. The next question is "*How* does the nervous system enable the organism to survive?" and the classic answer is "It ensures that the organism will approach things that are good for it (for example, things it eats) and that the organism will avoid things that are bad for it (for example, things that eat it)." The need-reduction theory describes the former mechanism and the activation theory describes the latter mechanism. The need-reduction theory and the activation theory can thus be considered as the means of fitting psychology within the basic framework of the **theory of evolution.** Let us look at each theory in turn.

3.12   Need-Reduction Theory

You are alive. You are in a precarious state. Life is a narrow tightrope with death on either side. To stay alive, you must maintain yourself within a narrow range of temperature, blood-sugar concentration, metabolic rate, and so on. Let us focus on temperature. You have been set by the great temperature-setter in the sky at 98.6° Fahrenheit (or 37° Centigrade if God has gone metric). You are allowed to vary a little about this optimal temperature. But a bit too high or a bit too low—and you die. Certain physiological mechanisms help you maintain your optimal temperature despite variation in the temperature of your environment. If your environment gets too cold, you shiver; if your environment gets too hot, you sweat. Consider, however, the alligator. It shivers not, neither does it sweat. Yet all alligators are not frozen alligators or boiled alligators. A group of alligatorologists organized an expedition to Africa to find out why. A few thousand miles and several thousand dollars later, they discovered that, when an alligator gets too warm, it slides into the cool water and, when an alligator gets too cold, it climbs onto a hot rock. Thus, the alligator maintains its optimal temperature by adjusting the environment to itself rather than by adjusting itself to the environment. It behaves. The process by which an organism maintains itself in its optimal state is called **homeostasis.** When it deviates from this optimal state, it may return to it either by adjusting itself to the environment or by adjusting the environment to itself. Our species, of course, uses both mechanisms. We shiver and sweat *and* we build furnaces and air conditioners. Adjusting ourselves to the environment is the province of physiology; adjusting the environment to ourselves is the province of psychology.

Let us take a closer look at the psychological mechanism. Imagine the hypothetical contented organism which has just been wined and dined. It is in its optimal state. However, it can't remain thus for long. The mere passage of time conspires against its bliss. It gets thirsty. It gets hungry. This physiological state of deprivation is called a **need.** The need can be satisfied by appropriate behavior with respect to some appropriate thing in the environment—by drinking water in the case of thirst and by eating bread in the case of hunger. Since the nervous system is the only system within the organism that "knows" the environment, the physiological need of the digestive system must be transformed into some psychological counterpart in the nervous system. This psychological counterpart, called the **drive,** orients the organism to the appropriate thing in the environment, called the **goal.** By making the appropriate response with respect to the goal, the drive is removed, the need is satisfied, and the optimal state is regained.

For a need in the digestive system to be transformed into a drive in the nervous system, there must be some mediator. A number of studies suggested that the mediator is the bloodstream acting on a structure in the brain stem called the **hypothalamus.** Following those clues, Teitelbaum stumbled on the strange case of the fat rats.[215] He destroyed a part of the hypothalamus in rats and observed that they got fat. They got fat, he noticed, by overeating. They overate by eating more at each meal rather than by eating more meals, and they overate until they reached a particular body weight and then ate only enough to maintain it. The fat rats were more finicky about their food than ordinary rats; that is, they began to refuse food with a lower concentration of impurities. As long as Teitelbaum continued to ask the obvious question "Why did the fat rats continue to eat?" he could not explain this strange set of facts. However, it suddenly struck him that the fruitful question was "Why did the fat rats stop eating?" and his answer soon began to emerge. Both normal and fat rats stop eating. The only difference is that fat rats stop later. Could it be, then, that some chemical in the bloodstream, whose concentration is correlated with body weight, acts on a part of the hypothalamus responsible for switching off eating behavior? The mechanism is turned off by a certain amount of this chemical. The smaller the area, the greater the concentration required to turn it off, and the greater the body weight. Teitelbaum now varied the amount of hypothalamus removed and found, indeed, that the more he removed, the greater the body weight of the rat before it stopped eating. The apparently incongruous fact that fat rats are finicky eaters now makes sense. The greater the concentration of this chemical in the bloodstream, the greater the concentration also of any impurity, and the greater awareness of it. The only missing link is the exact nature of this chemical. Teitelbaum doesn't know what it is, I don't know what it is, nobody yet knows what it is. Perhaps you can find out.

3.13   Activation Theory

Let us turn now from the positive to the negative drives, from the tendency to approach things that are good for us to the tendency to avoid things that are bad for us, from the need-reduction theory to the activation theory.

There are two ways in which we can avoid things that are bad for us. We can remove the thing or we can remove ourselves. The first involves fight, and the second involves flight. The emotion underlying the first is rage, and the emotion underlying the second is fear. Such primitive emotions must have played a dominant role in the early history of our species. Consider one of our remote ancestors confronted by a saber-toothed tiger. He has a tiger in his subjective map. He can remove it or remove himself. He can kill it or run away. The only good tiger is a dead tiger or a distant tiger.

An emotion-arousing stimulus has three broad effects—experiential (we feel angry or afraid), physiological (there are certain changes in our bodies), and behavioral (we fight or flee). Discovery of a structure in the brain called the **reticular activating system (RAS)** has clarified the interaction among these three effects. It has long been known that the emotion-arousing stimulus, like all stimuli, acts directly on the cortex. The stimulus is transformed at the appropriate **receptor** (a set of cells specialized for that purpose) into nerve impulses, which are transformed at the appropriate **projection area** of the cortex (a set of cells specialized for that purpose) into a perception. This is the **cue function** of the stimulus. It has recently been discovered that the emotion-arousing stimulus also acts *indirectly* on the cortex through the RAS. Nerve impulses, passing along tributaries of the nerve leading directly to the cortex, switch on the RAS, which projects diffusely onto the cortex. This is the **arousal function** of the stimulus. The arousal function is to alert you that *something* is happening in your environment (the RAS responds in the same way to sights, sounds, tastes, smells, and touches), whereas the cue function is to tell you precisely *what* is happening. The arousal function prepares you for an emergency, whether it is necessary for you to fight or flee. When the RAS is triggered, it acts upward on the cortex, producing the experiential effects, and downward on the **autonomic nervous system** and the **endocrine system** (responsible, respectively, for the physical and chemical aspects of your internal environment), producing the physiological effects. The action on the cortex alerts you to the emergency, and the action on the autonomic nervous system and the endocrine system provides you with the energy to meet the emergency. The cue function informs you whether there is indeed an emergency. Most stimuli are not worth getting emotional about. In those cases, the cortex acts down on the RAS to inhibit the arousal function. Animals without a cortex get mad at every little thing. The cue function also informs you of the nature of the emergency so that you can respond appropriately. Otherwise, you might attack tigers and run away from rabbits.

The need-reduction theory and the activation theory are diagramed together in Figure 3-1 to clarify the similarities and differences between them. Both theories involve a negative feedback loop to maintain the organism in its optimal state. Both theories describe the nervous system as a mediator between the internal environment (that is, the other subsystems of the organism) and the external environment. According to the **need-reduction theory,** the function of the nervous system is to mediate between a state of deprivation in the internal environment (a need) and a thing in the external environment that will satisfy the need (positive goal), so that the organism will approach that thing. According to the **activation theory,** the function of the nervous system is to mediate between a thing in the external environment (negative goal) and a state of the internal environment (an emotion), so that the organism will avoid that thing.

Since the nervous system is merely a mediator between internal and external environments, the person is extrinsically motivated.* The person is pushed and pulled by outside forces—pushed by needs and pulled by satisfiers of those needs, pushed by threatening things and pulled by the emotions generated by those things. Behaviorists argue that all human motivation is indeed determined by those extrinsic needs. **Secondary drives** are established through association with those primary drives. Thus, monkeys will work for tokens if

---

* When we refer to a person, we refer, more precisely, to the nervous system of the person. Our uniqueness lies in our nervous system. We talk to the eyes of a person rather than to the ears or the elbows because that is the only place where the nervous system is exposed. A brain transplant would differ dramatically from a heart transplant—it is the donor rather than the recipient who would survive in the recipient's body. *Extrinsic* thus means "from outside the nervous system"— that is, from the internal as well as the external environment.

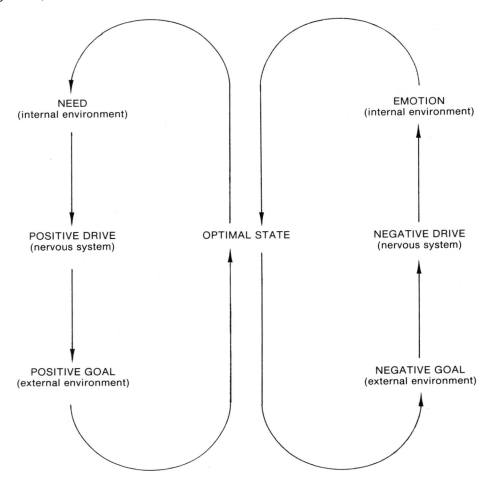

Figure 3-1. Need-reduction theory (left) and activation theory (right)

those tokens may be exchanged for food. Capitalism is established by making money the means to the end of satisfying basic biological needs. The behaviorist would explain your present behavior of reading this textbook by saying that you are reading this textbook in order to pass a course in order to get a degree in order to get a job in order to get money in order to buy food in order to satisfy your hunger in order to survive.

3.14 *Extrinsic Motivation*

Traditional education is based on **extrinsic motivation**—that is, on this first proposition of behaviorism that "the person has only extrinsic needs." Although lip service is paid to intrinsic motivation in school catalogs delivered to students at the beginning and in commencement addresses delivered at the end, for all practical purposes, the schooling in between is based on extrinsic motivation. It is assumed that learning is not an end in itself but a means to some other end. That "other end" is the hedonistic end of seeking pleasure and avoiding pain. Hence the elaborate superstructure of rewards (stars, points, grades, degrees, medals, smiles, jobs) and punishments (strappings, dunce caps, scowls, scoldings, detentions) that we associate with traditional schools. The grading system survives almost intact, despite its many recent critics, because it is an important element in this superstructure of extrinsic motivation. Even when teachers are advised to "motivate" students, they are being asked to provide extrinsic motivation rather than to trigger intrinsic motivation. "Interest" is added to the content like sugar coating to make the bitter pill of learning more palatable. Behaviorists have made a positive contribution by demonstrating that reward is more effective than punishment. Skinner argues convincingly that many of the discipline problems in the traditional classroom are side effects of punishment.[205] However, the motivational system is still extrinsic; behaviorists simply recommend a shift from the stick to the carrot. Both stick and carrot are still outside the donkey, which is being pushed by one and pulled by the other.

3.2 THE PERSON IS CONDITIONED FROM THE OUTSIDE IN

If the person has only extrinsic needs, then any change in behavior (that is, learning) must result from conditioning from the outside in. According to the behaviorist, there are two types of conditioning—classical and instrumental. Let us look at classical conditioning, focusing on the basic model of the pioneer, Pavlov, and the deluxe model of a more modern exponent, Watson; then look at instrumental conditioning, focusing on the basic model of the pioneer, Thorndike, and the deluxe model of a modern exponent, Skinner; and finally at classical and instrumental conditioning, in contrast and in combination.

3.21 Classical Conditioning

3.211 The Work of Pavlov

It all began—so the story goes—when a great Russian physiologist walked into his laboratory and a dog salivated. Most of us would merely have been flattered and continued with our physiology. But Ivan Petrovich Pavlov was not like most of us. He recognized this reaction as an important phenomenon. Pavlov had already won a Nobel Prize for physiology. Most of us would have been content. But Ivan Petrovich Pavlov was not like most of us. He began a 40-year investigation of this phenomenon and thus laid a cornerstone of modern psychology.[165] Have you ever heard of Twitmyer? He was an

American graduate student who stumbled on the same phenomenon before Pavlov, considered it footnoteworthy to his doctoral thesis, and went no further. Twitmyer was like most of us.

Environment affects behavior. This statement is true but vague. Pavlov suggested how it might be made more precise. Representing the organism as a rather unflattering empty box, we could consider environment as the set of stimuli acting on it and behavior as the set of responses produced by it. Now we can substitute the precise statement "stimulus x elicits response y" for the vague statement "environment affects behavior," as indicated in Figure 3-2a.

a. The transformation of the vague statement "environment affects behavior" to the precise statement "stimulus x elicits response y"

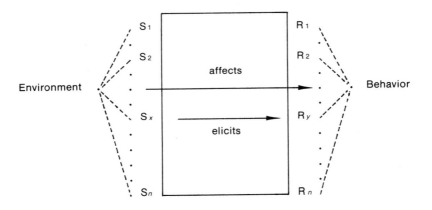

b. The creation of a conditioned reflex by presenting a CS and a UCS together

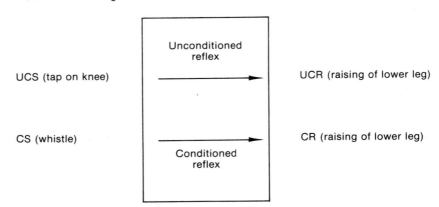

Figure 3-2. The basic model of classical conditioning

As we all know, an organism can come to behave differently in the same environment; that is, it can learn. How does it learn? Or, more precisely, how can stimulus *x*, which was previously neutral, come to elicit response *y?* Pavlov begins his answer by pointing out that certain stimuli are already capable of eliciting certain responses at birth. If I tap sharply below your knee, you will raise your lower leg. The tap (stimulus) is prewired to the raising of the lower leg (response). No experience necessary. Such a prewired link between a stimulus and a response is called an **unconditioned reflex (UCR).** If I blow a whistle, you will not raise your lower leg. However, if I were to blow a whistle, tap below your knee, blow a whistle, tap below your knee, and so on and so on, then eventually you would raise your lower leg to the whistle alone. Such an acquired link is called a **conditioned reflex (CR).** It is acquired by presenting a stimulus that was originally neutral—a **conditioned stimulus (CS)**—together with a stimulus that is already wired to a response—an **unconditioned stimulus (UCS).** This operation, called **classical conditioning,** is diagramed in Figure 3-2b.

Unconditioned reflexes are wired in at birth and typically persist until death. Conditioned reflexes are created and may also be destroyed. They may be destroyed by presenting the CS without the UCS a number of times. Thus, if I were to blow the whistle without tapping you below the knee, you would eventually, after a number of repetitions, cease to raise your lower leg to the whistle. This operation is called **extinction.** Neither the acquisition nor the extinction of a conditioned reflex is exactly specific to the original CS. That is, if my whistle had a frequency of 360 cycles per second (cps), you would still raise your leg to a whistle of 330 cps or 400 cps. This tendency for conditioning to spread to stimuli similar to the original stimulus is called **generalization.** Pavlov found that he could teach a dog to respond to one stimulus (say, a tone of 360 cps) and not to respond to another stimulus (say, a tone of 400 cps). That is, a dog is capable of **discrimination.** This effect was achieved by presenting the tone of 360 cps followed by meat powder and the tone of 400 cps followed by nothing.

3.212   *The Work of Watson*

Psychology was originally the study of consciousness, but a dynamic young man swept onto the psychological stage and transformed it into the study of behavior. He left as abruptly as he had arrived—into the world of commerce where he worked as a door-to-door salesman and eventually became vice-president of his company. As a psychologist, he was a good salesman. In his foray into psychology, John B. Watson left a permanent mark. He wrote the manifesto of **behaviorism,** and much of psychology since has been an extended debate about his thesis.[229] Most psychologists even today could be described as behaviorists or postbehaviorists or neopostbehaviorists or antibehaviorists. Watson argued that consciousness is unobservable and thus not amenable to scientific study. We must focus on observables—stimuli impinging on the organism and responses elicited from the organism—and find the functional relationships among them. He had to demonstrate how certain stimuli came to elicit certain responses, and he stumbled upon the work of Pavlov. Thus Pavlov was adopted as a rather reluctant grandfather of behaviorism.*

Watson demonstrated that classical conditioning can be used to explain not only simple, local responses like salivation but complex, whole-body responses like fear. We have many fears, ranging from specific things, like the number 13 (triskaidekaphobia) or getting stuck in chimney pots (Santa Claus-trophobia), to general things, like fear itself (phobophobia) or everything (panaphobia). How do we learn these fears? By classical conditioning, said Watson, and proceeded to demonstrate just how.[230] He introduced an 11-month-old infant named Albert to a white rat. When Albert first met the white rat, he reached for it and cooed at it and cuddled it. Albert liked white rats. Then Watson presented the rat a number of times, fiendishly arranging for his assistant, Rosalie Rayner (later to become Mrs. Watson, for those who like some romance in the story), to make a terrifying noise behind Albert each time. The noise scared Albert and made him cry. After a number of repetitions, Albert began to cry at the appearance of the white rat alone. Albert no longer liked white rats. Indeed, Albert did not like white rabbits, or balls of cotton wool, or beards, or men with beards, or men accompanying men with beards. That is, he did not like anything white and fluffy or anything associated with anything white and fluffy. Since this experiment was conducted in 1920, Albert may still be alive today. Do you happen to know a twitchy middle-aged man called Albert?

However, behavior does not consist of isolated responses, whether small or large, but of a stream of responses. Watson described that stream of responses we call a **habit** as a chain of conditioned reflexes. As each response is made, a stimulus is fed back to the brain to inform it that the response has been made. The links in the chain are formed as each such feedback stimulus becomes classically conditioned to the next response.† A certain subset of such habits, involving the muscles of the larynx and throat, is the basis for speech. Talking is the moving of the muscles of the throat, just as walking is the moving of the muscles of the leg. As children, we talk to ourselves but, since this is frowned upon, we learn, as adults, to talk to ourselves quietly. Thinking is simply talking to oneself so that no one else can hear. Thus Watson attempted to explain all behavior in terms of learning and all learning in terms of classical conditioning.

---

* It is rumored that, when Watson first stumbled onto Pavlov's work, he cried "Eureka!" but later denied it, since, according to his theory, he did not believe in insight.

† Superficially, this theory sounds farfetched. However, many of our habits are very mechanical. I once went into my bedroom to change my shoes and ended up in bed—much to the surprise of my guests. I can never type *ratio* without putting an *n* at the end. Damn it, I did it again while typing this.

3.22 Instrumental Conditioning

3.221 The Work of Thorndike

The theory of evolution placed our species firmly where it belongs, with the other animals. This has two broad implications: humans are seen as more animal-like and animals are seen as more human-like. The violent repercussions of the first implication are very familiar—Professor Huxley versus Bishop Wilberforce, Scopes versus State of Tennessee, raised apes versus fallen angels. Let us briefly consider the less familiar repercussions of the second implication. Certain scholars began to attribute human qualities to animals. They soberly collected anecdotes from retired colonels, vicars' wives, and other animal lovers that demonstrated how ingenious animals were in solving problems. A typical anecdote describes how a fieldmouse got honey out of a narrow-rimmed jar by squatting on the rim, dipping its tail into the honey, and licking its tail. Romanes—the leader of this movement, the father of comparative psychology, the Rona Barrett of the animal world—collected those stories in his book *Animal Intelligence*.[185] He concluded, on the basis of this anecdotal evidence, that animals are very intelligent.

The stage is now set for the next character in our cast. Enter Edward Thorndike, a poverty-stricken graduate student at Harvard University, arguing that "such anecdotes describe the behavior of an animal *after* it has learned. If one were to study the process of learning rather than the product, then perhaps the animals would not appear so intelligent." Thorndike set out to study the process of learning in animals. He collected a motley menagerie in his squalid room in a run-down rooming house. Enter his landlady. Exit Thorndike and his menagerie. Enter William James, one of the greatest and kindest characters in the cast of psychology. James housed the animals in the basement of his own home and arranged for Thorndike to continue his research at Columbia University.

The rest of the story is history. Thorndike rounded up some stray cats from the alleys of New York City. He built a box with a door that could be opened by pressing a lever. Inside the box he placed a cat, outside the box he placed something the cat liked (typically one or more of his famous three Fs—fish, friends, and freedom). The problem was to get out, and the solution was to press the lever. When first put in this **puzzle box,** the cat went through its repertoire of responses—clawing at bars, hissing at Thorndike, spitting and snarling, smiling coyly at Thorndike, meowing and purring, and so on and so on—more or less at random. By chance, it finally hit on the Thorndike-ordained correct response. The second time the cat was put in the puzzle box, it took less time to get out—not because it now knew how to get out, but because it tended to spend more time where it happened to be when the door opened. In subsequent trials, it took less and less time until, finally, it went immediately to the lever and pressed it. If Romanes had entered Thorndike's

ANYTHING THAT EXISTS, EXISTS IN QUANTITY AND THEREFORE CAN BE MEASURED.

E. L. THORNDIKE

laboratory at this point and observed the cat casually walking over to the lever and nonchalantly pressing it, he would have run off to write yet another anecdote showing how very intelligent animals are. Thorndike, who had observed the mechanical process by which this apparently intelligent product was established, knew otherwise. Romanes had written a book called *Animal Intelligence* showing how smart animals are; Thorndike now wrote a book with the same title showing how dumb animals are.[217]

In that book, Thorndike presented his description of **trial-and-error learning.** Thorndike's learning theory is somewhat analogous to Darwin's survival-of-the-fittest principle. In a population of organisms, some are fitter to survive in a particular environment; in a repertoire of responses, some are fitter to survive in a particular situation. The fittest response is the one leading to a reward. According to the **law of effect,** a response followed by a reward is more likely to occur again. In other words, the link between this particular situation and the response followed by a reward is strengthened, whereas the links between this situation and the other responses not followed by a reward are weakened. Thus the fittest response survives and the other responses die, as diagramed in Figure 3-3a. Since *all* the responses are, strictly speaking, followed by the reward, the law of effect must be supplemented by the **gradient of reinforcement.** The sooner the response is followed by the reward, the more the link between the situation and the response is strengthened. Two implications of this principle have been verified: Rats tend to learn the last turns in a

a. The link between the situation and the response followed by a reward is strengthened and the links between the situation and all the other responses are thereby weakened.

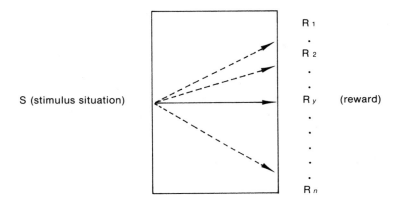

S (stimulus situation)

R 1

R 2

R y   (reward)

R n

b. The creation of a conditioned reflex by arranging that the CR permits access to the UCS.

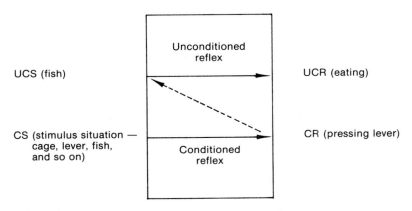

UCS (fish)

Unconditioned reflex

UCR (eating)

CS (stimulus situation — cage, lever, fish, and so on)

Conditioned reflex

CR (pressing lever)

Figure 3-3. The basic model of instrumental conditioning

maze first and the first turns last. Rats run faster and faster on a straight runway as they approach the goal at the end.

In Section 3.211 we asked the question "How does a stimulus, previously neutral, come to elicit a response?" Pavlov provided one answer; now Thorndike provides another: the response is instrumental in permitting access to a stimulus which already elicits a response that is intrinsically rewarding. This operation, called **instrumental conditioning,** is diagramed in Figure 3-3b.

3.222   The Work of Skinner

B. F. Skinner, the foremost living behaviorist, transformed Thorndike's puzzle box into what has come to be called, in his honor and to his dismay, the **Skinner box.** It contains a lever and a tray arranged so that pressing the lever permits a food pellet to fall into the tray. The index of learning is the number of times the lever is pressed rather than the time to get out of the box. Originally, the rewards were dispensed and the responses were recorded by Skinner himself. However, the Skinner box has now been automated, and the rat can run its own experiments without the aid of an experimenter. When the bar is pressed, two metal surfaces make contact, a circuit is completed, a disk turns, and a pellet drops into the tray. Thus the rewards are dispensed. When the bar is pressed, a pen touching a tape moves up one notch and leaves a **cumulative record** of the number of presses in each unit of time as the tape moves horizontally at a constant speed. Thus the responses are recorded. The only thing that prevents total automation is the fact that the rat must initially be taught to press the lever. This is done by a process called **shaping,** using the **method of successive approximations.** The rat glances toward the lever. Give it a pellet. The rat looks at the lever. Give it a pellet. The rat takes a step toward the lever. Give it a pellet. The rat sniffs at the lever. Give it a pellet. The rat raises its paw toward the lever. Give it a pellet. Each response that is a successively closer approximation to the desired response is rewarded, until the rat is pressing the lever and supplying its own pellets.

At first Skinner arranged for the rat to get a pellet every time it pressed the lever—**total reinforcement.** However, he got tired of making so many pellets and decided to give the rat a pellet only some of the times it pressed the lever—**partial reinforcement.** In this way he stumbled inadvertently onto a more true-to-life situation. The fisherman does not get a bite every time he casts his line, the saleswoman does not make a sale every time she delivers her pitch, and the wooer does not get a date every time he or she asks. We live in a world of partial reinforcement. Schedules of partial reinforcement may be **ratio schedules** or **interval schedules.** That is, reward may be a function of response or of time; for example, a pellet may drop after every 20 responses or after every 20 seconds. Schedules of partial reinforcement may be **fixed schedules** or **variable schedules.** That is, a pellet may drop after every 20 bar presses or 20 seconds or, on the average, every 20 bar presses or 20 seconds. Ratio schedules tend to produce a higher rate of responding than interval schedules, and variable schedules tend to produce a higher rate of responding than fixed schedules. That is, rats work better on piecework than on salary and when paid sporadically rather than regularly. The most powerful schedule of the four that result from combining those two dichotomies—the variable ratio schedule—is used in casinos to produce a high rate of feeding coins into one-armed bandits by gamblers and in homes to produce a high rate of crying in babies.

Skinner once found himself sitting next to the distinguished philosopher Alfred North Whitehead at a banquet and launched into an enthusiastic exposition of his project to explain all human behavior in terms of conditioning. The calm old philosopher listened benignly to the brash young scientist, conceded that he could perhaps explain nonverbal behavior with this model, but argued that it could not handle verbal behavior. There was no way, said Whitehead, that Skinner could predict why he chose, at that moment, to say "No black scorpion is falling on this table." Skinner began his book *Verbal Behavior* next morning and published it several decades later.[203] In this book he offered the following response to Whitehead's challenge. **Verbal behavior** is behavior reinforced through the mediation of other people. There are two ways in which Skinner could have gotten the salt at that famous dinner—by nonverbal behavior (reaching for it himself) or by verbal behavior (asking Whitehead to pass it to him). We use words, then, to gain reinforcement through the mediation of other people. How do we acquire them in the first place? Skinner proposes the three mechanisms diagramed in Figure 3-4. The child utters an imitation of a word in the presence of the word, and an adult gives approval (**echoic response**); the child utters the name of an object in the presence of the object, and an adult hands over the object (**tact**); the child utters the name of the satisfier of a need in the presence of the need, and an adult provides the satisfier of the need (**mand**). This response would seem to fall far short of meeting Whitehead's challenge. Skinner argues, however, that the scientist is not required to explain each specific event but only the general principles underlying the specific events. The physicist is not expected to predict the order in which leaves will fall from a tree and the pattern they will form on the ground but is expected only to state the general principles governing falling bodies. Thus, Skinner attempted to explain all behavior in terms of learning and all learning in terms of instrumental conditioning.

3.23 *Classical and Instrumental Conditioning*

3.231 *In Contrast*

In the previous two sections, we posed the question "How do we learn?" or, in the more prosaic but precise language of behaviorism, "How does a particular stimulus come to elicit a particular response?" In Section 3.21, we proposed one answer: the stimulus is presented together with another stimulus that already elicits that response. This is the process of classical conditioning. In Section 3.22, we proposed another answer: the response permits access to a stimulus that already elicits a satisfying response. This is the process of instrumental conditioning. The two processes are diagramed in Figure 3-5 so that their similarities and differences may be clarified. The processes are similar in that they both explain the basic fact of learning—that a particular stimulus can come to elicit a particular response. They both explain this fact with reference to a stimulus-response bond already wired into the organism. They differ with respect to the manner in which the newly acquired

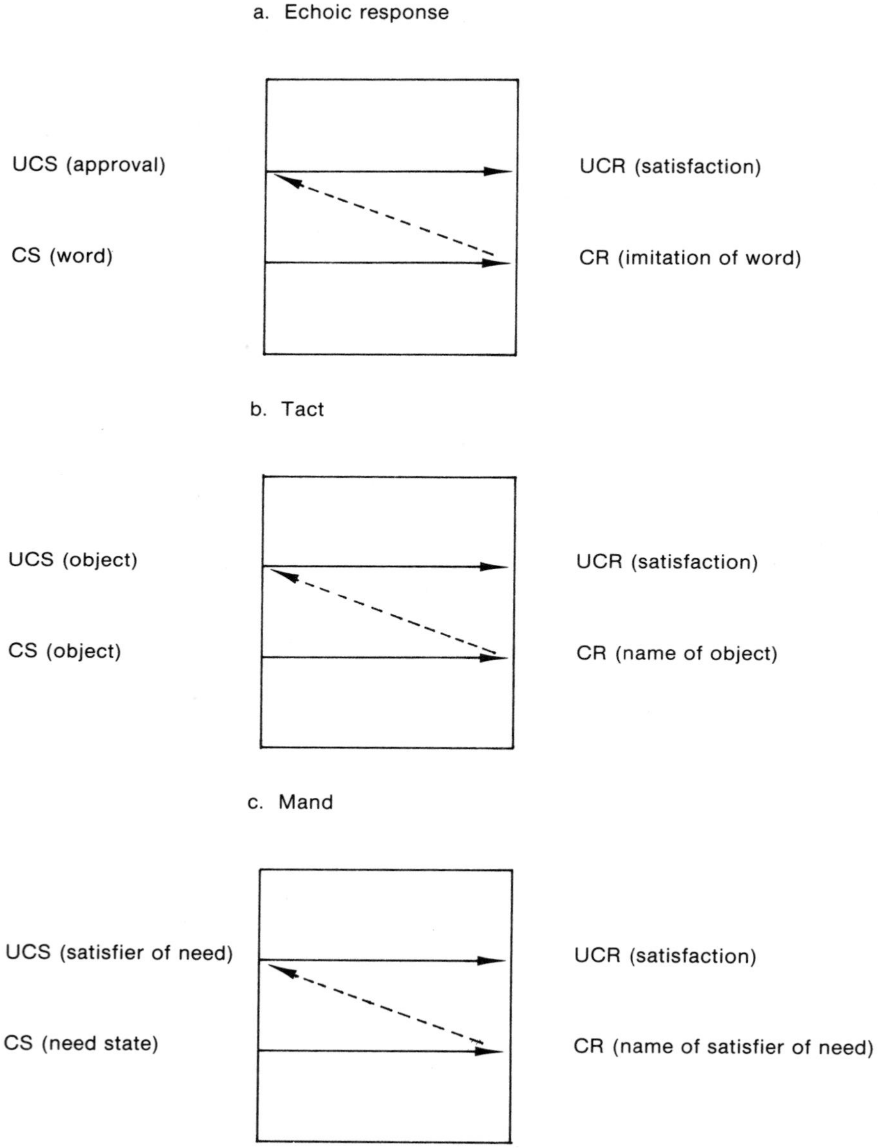

a. Echoic response

UCS (approval)   UCR (satisfaction)

CS (word)   CR (imitation of word)

b. Tact

UCS (object)   UCR (satisfaction)

CS (object)   CR (name of object)

c. Mand

UCS (satisfier of need)   UCR (satisfaction)

CS (need state)   CR (name of satisfier of need)

Figure 3-4. Skinner's three mechanisms for acquiring speech. Note that the CR is always a word, that it permits access to the UCS only through the mediation of another person, and that approval is assumed to be intrinsically satisfying.

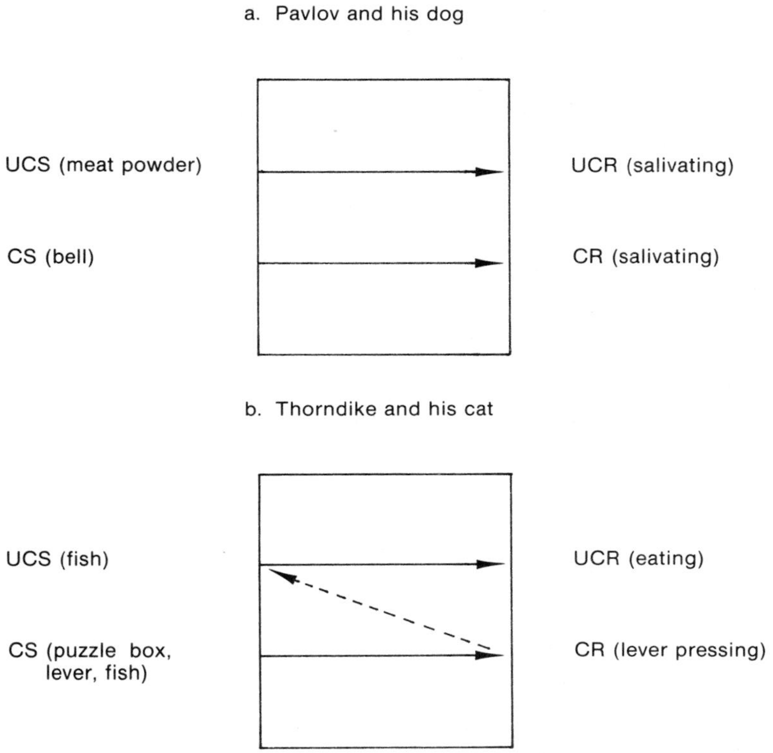

a. Pavlov and his dog

UCS (meat powder) ⟶ UCR (salivating)

CS (bell) ⟶ CR (salivating)

b. Thorndike and his cat

UCS (fish) ⟶ UCR (eating)

CS (puzzle box, lever, fish) ⟶ CR (lever pressing)

Figure 3-5. Classical and instrumental conditioning

bond (conditioned reflex) is related to the previously wired bond (uncon-ditioned reflex). Classical conditioning attributes learning to the fact that the CS and UCS are presented together; instrumental conditioning attributes learning to the fact that the CR permits access to the UCS. They could be considered, in a simple-minded way, as complementary processes. Classical conditioning involves the same response to different stimuli; instrumental conditioning involves different responses to the same stimulus. Classical con-ditioning is associated with the involuntary responses of the autonomic ner-vous system (that is, the part of the nervous system responsible for dealing with the internal environment); instrumental conditioning is associated with the voluntary responses of the central nervous system (that is, the part of the nervous system responsible for dealing with the external environment).

3.232   *In Combination*

Section 3.212 concluded with Watson's attempt to explain verbal behav-ior in terms of classical conditioning; Section 3.222 concluded with Skinner's attempt to explain verbal behavior in terms of instrumental conditioning.

Charles Osgood argues that verbal behavior can be explained, not by classical conditioning alone, nor by instrumental conditioning alone, but by a combination of classical and instrumental conditioning. Let us look at the work of Osgood and his coworkers as an illustration of how **neobehaviorists** attempt to explain behavior by combining and expanding the classical- and instrumental-conditioning models of the pure behaviorists.[162]

The central problem of verbal behavior (and, say some, of psychology) is the meaning of meaning. How can a word come to represent a thing? How can an arbitrary sequence of sounds or pattern of lines come to elicit responses related to the thing they represent? Osgood answers those questions in terms of conditioning. The word, being a previously neutral stimulus that comes to elicit a response, can be considered as the CS. The thing, being a stimulus that is already linked to a particular response, can be considered as the UCS. The inadequacy of either conditioning model alone can be illustrated by the case in which the UCS is Robert Redford and the CS is the words *Robert Redford*.* The classical-conditioning model will not do, since the UCR and the CR do not remotely resemble each other; that is, your response to the name *Robert Redford* would be very different from your response to Robert Redford himself. The instrumental-conditioning model will not do either, since the CR does not permit access to the UCS; that is, your response to the name *Robert Redford* will not, alas, gain you access to Robert Redford. Osgood suggests, however, that the two models in combination can explain how this arbitrary sequence of sounds can come to elicit a response related to the person they represent.

The presentation of a word and a thing together produces a response within the organism that is some part of the response to the thing (classical conditioning), and this response is instrumental in producing a stimulus within the organism that is linked to the CR (instrumental conditioning), as indicated in Figure 3-6. **Meaning** is this internal $(r_m - s_m)$ bond that acts as a

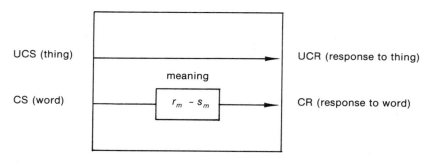

Figure 3-6.   Osgood's two-stage behaviorism to explain meaning

---

* Or Farrah Fawcett-Majors (if you prefer), or whatever sex symbol of whatever sex is current when you are reading this.

mediator between the CS and the CR. Osgood thus replaces one-stage behaviorism (which he labels the kiddie-car model of humans, Mark I—classical conditioning—and Mark II—instrumental conditioning) with two-stage behaviorism, in which input is provided by classical conditioning and output is produced by instrumental conditioning (which he labels the horse-and-buggy model of humans). Osgood found even this model too simple to explain the production and perception of sentences and replaced it with three-stage behaviorism—organization of stimuli, mediation, and organization of responses (which he called the Model-T Ford model of humans). If this model is, in turn, found inadequate to explain certain phenomena, must we continue to a four-stage behaviorism, or Ford Mustang model of humans? Will the ultimate model of humans be a further development along those lines, or are we on the wrong track? Will psychology progress through evolution or revolution?

3.24   *Teaching and Conditioning*

Every theory of learning is also, by implication, a theory of teaching. The stories of Pavlov and his dogs and of Thorndike and his cats are as much stories of how Pavlov and Thorndike teach as of how dogs and cats learn. "Theories of learning must be 'stood on their heads' so as to yield theories of teaching," said Gage.[64] Let us stand classical and instrumental conditioning on their heads.

3.241   *Classical Conditioning*

How did Pavlov teach? He presented a stimulus that was previously neutral together with a stimulus that already elicited a response. After a number of repetitions, the neutral stimulus came to elicit that response. I doubt that any teacher ever consciously uses such a teaching strategy in a classroom. This does not mean, however, that the classical-conditioning model is irrelevant. Teaching, as well as learning, may be unconscious. Awareness of the process may be useful not so much as a strategy to teach what you want to teach but as a way to avoid teaching what you do not want to teach.

Since the responses that can be classically conditioned are the involuntary responses of the autonomic nervous system, classical conditioning may be involved in the emotional responses of students to certain subjects. A teacher of mathematics who accompanies lessons with loud, threatening noises may classically condition some students to fear mathematics. You, of course, would never do such a thing, but you may have in your class victims of such previous "teaching." You may have to extinguish this conditioned response of fear by presenting mathematics without the loud, threatening noises, and without any pressure to perform. Students have to unlearn fear before they can begin to learn mathematics. Classical conditioning may also be involved in the emotional responses of students to certain teachers and of teachers to certain students. A student may be terrified of you because of some bad experience with a bearded man, or you may treat a student harshly because of some bad experience with a red-headed boy. Awareness of such a possibility may help you defuse some emotionally explosive situations. Conditioning is powerful because it is unconscious. By becoming conscious of the process, we can reduce its power.

The simple teaching Pavlov was doing can serve as a useful analogy to the complex teaching you will be doing. Principles of teaching can be seen more clearly in this simple model. Even this simple type of teaching results in generalization. In other words, by teaching a response to a conditioned stimulus, you simultaneously teach that response to stimuli similar to this conditioned stimulus. Generalization (or transfer, in the case of complex learning) is the very foundation of schooling. The process of schooling is based on the assumption that school learning transfers to out-of-school situations. We should teach so that the response generalizes to similar situations in which it is also appropriate. Even this simple type of teaching can be used to teach discrimination. Pavlov tried to teach a dog to discriminate between a light gray and a dark gray. The dog could not discriminate between them. He then taught the dog to discriminate between white and black, between a very light gray and a very dark gray, and so on until he came to the original pair. The dog could *now* discriminate between them. Teachers can help students make subtle discriminations by presenting the extremes of the dimensions along which the discriminations are to be made.

3.242 Instrumental Conditioning

How did Thorndike teach? He arranged the situation so that a particular response was followed by a reward. After a number of trials and errors, this response was always elicited by this situation. There is much more of Thorndike's kind of teaching than Pavlov's kind of teaching in the classroom. Teachers arrange the classroom situation so that certain responses are followed by reward and are thus reinforced, whereas certain other responses are followed by punishment and are thus extinguished. You may not like to think of yourself as conditioning your class. However, every time you smile or frown at a student you may be reinforcing or extinguishing previous behavior. It is not a question then of whether to use instrumental conditioning or not, but whether to use it well or poorly. Once again, awareness of the process will help you to use it well, or at least not to misuse it.

Every time you ask a question, Susie waves her arm violently in the air, bounces up and down in her seat, and hisses "Miiiisssss." You often invite her to give the answer just to shut her up. You are reinforcing bad behavior by oiling this squeaky wheel. Shy Johnny never raises his hand and you never invite him to answer. You want to keep at least one of them quiet. Johnny's passive behavior is encouraged because it saves him the embarrassment of having to talk in class.

DOING ANYTHING AT ALL THAT WOULD MAKE A TEACHER MAD AT HIM, SCREAM AT HIM, STRIKE AT HIM, WOULD ALSO HAVE BEEN A KIND OF RATIFICATION, EVEN IF IT WAS PAINFUL, THAT HE ACTUALLY WAS THERE. — MAYBE THE ONLY WAY HE COULD EVER IMPINGE UPON OTHER PEOPLE'S LIVES WAS BY INFURIATING THEM, BUT THAT AT LEAST WAS SOMETHING. IT WAS BETTER THAN NOT HAVING ANY USE AT ALL.

JONATHAN KOZOL
DEATH AT AN EARLY AGE

This example illustrates that reward and punishment vary from individual to individual. One person's meat is another person's poison. A sadist is a person who refuses to beat a masochist. Being invited to answer a question in class is a reward for Susie but a punishment for Johnny. Punishment may be a reward when it is the only attention you are getting. I once watched two women in a restaurant with a boy of about 3, who was apparently the son of one of them. They were chatting and completely ignoring the boy. He sat quietly for a while, playing with his cutlery, until he dropped a spoon. The two women immediately focused on him, the mother picked up the spoon and chided him gently, and then they returned to their conversation. The next time the boy dropped his spoon it was no accident. Once again, he got some attention before the conversation resumed. He escalated his disruptive behavior until the conversation was completely sabotaged and he was carried, kicking and screaming, from the restaurant. By contrast, what you assume to be a reward may often be a punishment. Sam may not want to clean your dirty blackboard—especially after recess when he split the seat of his pants climbing over a wall.

An awareness of what responses you reward and what responses you punish will help you discover and clarify your personal definitions of good behavior and bad behavior. Misbehavior is too often defined as that which inconveniences us. "The immature," said G. B. Shaw, "are a nuisance to the mature." There is an insidious (although understandable) process by which institutions designed for the benefit of the clients come to be run for the convenience of the managers. Schools are especially susceptible to this process because the clients are small, weak, and inarticulate. Your pattern of rewards and punishments betrays to your students your attitudes about teaching and learning. You, too, could discover those attitudes by observing those patterns. Some teachers punish a class by keeping it in late and reward it by letting it out early. They obviously believe that their classroom is not a good place to be, and their students pick up the message. School is apparently a prison where students are serving time but may get their sentences shortened for good behavior. Some teachers reward students by giving them certain kinds of extra work (handing out papers, cleaning the blackboard, and so on) and punish them by giving them certain other kinds of extra work (additional assignments, rewriting papers, and so on). Apparently, working for the teacher is a good thing but working for yourself is a bad thing.

An understanding of conditioning can, at the very least, help you avoid being conditioned by your students. The only joke in the behavioristic literature revolves around the question of who is conditioning whom. A cartoon depicting two rats in a Skinner box is captioned "I've sure got this guy conditioned. Every time I press this lever, he gives me a pellet." The following anecdote has been set in every major university in the world. A psychology professor taught his class about instrumental conditioning. At their next meeting, the class conspired to pay more attention every time the professor moved to the right. The class reputedly conditioned the professor right out the door. Such mass class conspiracies are rare, but individual students are conditioning teachers every day. Every time you look at Jimmy while you are speaking, you get a bright nod of approval. You assume that he understands everything you are saying. Comes the examination, you discover that your nodding acquaintance has been conning you.

3.243 *Teaching Machines*

In *The Technology of Teaching,* Skinner demonstrates how his principles of instrumental conditioning can be applied to the practice of teaching.[205] He argues that those who say "we learn by experience," those who say "we learn by doing," and those who say "we learn by trial and error" are like the three blind men holding, respectively, the tusks, trunk, and tail of the elephant. Each assumes that a little bit of the truth is the whole truth. Learning involves (1) the occasion upon which behavior occurs, (2) the behavior itself, and (3) the consequences of the behavior. This is the whole elephant. Learning by experi-

"TO ACQUIRE BEHAVIOR THE STUDENT MUST ENGAGE
IN BEHAVIOR."

B.F. SKINNER
"WHY WE NEED TEACHING MACHINES"

ence emphasizes the occasion; learning by doing, the behavior; and learning by trial and error, the consequences. Within this context, "teaching is simply the arrangement of contingencies of reinforcement"[205]—that is, the teacher creates occasions for desired behaviors and provides positive consequences to ensure that those behaviors will be repeated on similar occasions in the future. Whereas the teacher provides the first and third elements of learning—the occasion for and the consequences of behavior—the student must provide the second element—the behavior itself. In the traditional classroom with 30 or so students all behaving in their various ways and at their various rates, it is impossible for the teacher to monitor behavior with the precision necessary to provide the appropriate antecedent occasions and subsequent consequences. Skinner recommends that the process of teaching should, therefore, be automated. He designed a teaching machine, which is much more efficient as an occasion provider and reinforcement dispenser than a teacher. Since the **teaching machine** is simply a mechanical device for presenting a programmed text, let us focus on the latter. We are interested in the radio program rather than the radio or, as the engineers say, in the software rather than the hardware.

The **programmed text** consists of a series of statements and/or questions contained within a frame. The student responds to each frame and then turns to the next frame. This next frame contains the correct response to the previous frame (against which the student can check his or her response) and another statement and/or question. The teaching of the student by the programmed text is analogous to the teaching of the rat in the Skinner box. The teaching machine is a sort of Skinner box for students. The various principles applied in the design of programmed texts are derived from experiments with rats in the laboratory. The response is writing the answer rather than pressing the lever, and the reward is confirming that the response is correct rather than getting a food pellet. However, the principle that the reward increases the strength of the response is applied to both situations. The principle that the reward should follow the response as soon as possible is an application of the gradient of reinforcement. The principle that each frame should progress only a little beyond the previous frame is an application of the method of successive approximations. Programmed texts are designed so that most students get most answers correct, because behaviorists have discovered that reward is more effective than punishment.

There are basically two types of programs, linear and branching. In the **linear program,** all the students progress through all the frames in the same order; in the **branching program,** each student may take any one of a number of different routes through the program, depending on his or her answers to the questions. Thus, a student whose answer indicated understanding of the material would be directed to continue the program, whereas a student whose answer indicated a particular misunderstanding would be directed to a series of

PERHAPS THE TECHNICALLY MOST INTERESTING FEATURES OF SUCH AUTOMATIC DEVICES ARE THAT THEY CAN TAKE SOME OF THE LOAD OF TEACHING OFF THE TEACHER'S SHOULDERS, AND, PERHAPS MORE IMPORTANT, THAT THE MACHINE CAN PROVIDE IMMEDIATELY THE CORRECTION OR FEEDBACK TO THE STUDENT WHILE HE IS IN THE ACT OF LEARNING.

JEROME S. BRUNER
THE PROCESS OF EDUCATION

frames designed to remove this misunderstanding before continuing with the program.

Advocates of programmed instruction typically claim two major advantages over traditional instruction: programmed instruction is individualized instruction (students can proceed through linear programs at different rates and through branching programs by different routes), and programmed instruction is auto-instruction (students can teach themselves). Programmed instruction, however, may not simply augment traditional instruction but also improve it. The process of writing programs may be more important than the product. After writing a program, with its concern for the logical development of arguments and for feedback from the students, a teacher should be able to write better textbooks and deliver better lectures.

Some early advocates argued—before the bandwagon began to lose momentum—that the teaching machine would replace the teacher. Skinner did indeed plan his own obsolescence by automating the Skinner box to record responses and dispense rewards. No one argued that the Skinner box would replace Skinner. It simply replaced him as a response recorder and reward dispenser and set him free to do less mechanical things, like writing futuristic novels and defending his atheoretical theory. In the same way, his teaching machine takes over some of the mechanical aspects of teaching and frees the teacher for the more human aspects. Rather than being apprehensive about the teaching machine making the teacher the next victim of automation, we should be delighted with such a useful teaching aid (aide?) to take over boring chores like drilling and marking. The argument that the teacher can be replaced by the teaching machine betrays a very limited concept of the role of the teacher as a response recorder and reward dispenser. A mechanism, by definition, can only do mechanical things. Anyone who could be replaced by a machine *should* be replaced by a machine.

3.3   THE PERSON IS NOT RESPONSIBLE FOR BEHAVIOR

If the person is extrinsically motivated, then the person is not responsible for behavior. A person totally at the mercy of the environment is not free to act and thus is not responsible for his or her actions. This conclusion follows inevitably from the application of the determinism of science to the study of the nervous system. The two groups which have dominated psychology until recently—the Freudians and the behaviorists—both accept this implication. Your behavior today is determined, according to the behaviorist, by your conditioning in all your yesterdays; your behavior today is determined, according to the Freudian, by traumatic experiences in some long-forgotten yesterdays. This attitude may partly account for the popularity of behavior therapy and psychoanalysis. Behavior therapists and psychoanalysts are modern priests absolving their parishioner-patients of their sins as they lie on their confessional couches. They make soothing sounds. You are not to blame for whatever evil you have done. You are a victim of your past. You are depraved because you were deprived. The compulsive consumer who buys a new car every year is not responsible, then, for the ultimate impact of this consumption on the planet. Nor is the person who sells them, nor is the person who produces them, nor is the person who drives the bulldozer that gouges the required metals out of the earth. None of them is any more responsible than the bulldozer itself. They are all as extrinsically motivated as it is.

THE HYPOTHESIS THAT MAN IS NOT FREE IS ESSENTIAL TO THE APPLICATION OF SCIENTIFIC METHOD TO THE STUDY OF HUMAN BEHAVIOR. THE FREE INNER MAN WHO IS HELD RESPONSIBLE FOR HIS BEHAVIOR IS ONLY A PRESCIENTIFIC SUBSTITUTE FOR THE KINDS OF CAUSES WHICH ARE DISCOVERED IN THE COURSE OF SCIENTIFIC ANALYSIS. ALL THESE ALTERNATIVE CAUSES LIE OUTSIDE THE INDIVIDUAL.

B.F. SKINNER
SCIENCE AND HUMAN BEHAVIOR

3.4   THE PERSON HAS ONLY EXTRINSIC WORTH

If the person is not responsible for behavior, then the person has no intrinsic worth. He or she can't be blamed for bad behavior but, by the same token, can't take credit for good behavior. The person can't then gain any intrinsic worth. Since the person must gain worth somehow and can't gain intrinsic worth, then he or she must gain extrinsic worth—that is, acquire possessions. The fact that such extrinsic worth is not an adequate substitute for intrinsic worth does not make it any less potent as a motivator. Indeed, it makes it *more* potent. Intrinsic worth is real and can thus be attained; extrinsic worth is an appearance and thus cannot be attained. It is therefore pursued more and more ardently. The person accumulates more and more possessions in this futile search for satisfaction. Thus consumption becomes compulsive.

I will argue later that self-esteem is a real need of our species. This need will not go away simply because behaviorists do not recognize "self" and hence "self-esteem." The person can't gain self-esteem through possessions. You may be able to fool all of the people some of the time and some of the people all of

THE DENIAL OF FREEDOM, OF COURSE, IS A DENIAL OF RESPONSIBILITY: THERE ARE NO ACTS BUT ONLY EVENTS; EVERYTHING SIMPLY HAPPENS; NO ONE IS RESPONSIBLE.

E. F. SCHUMACHER
SMALL IS BEAUTIFUL

the time, but you can't really fool yourself at all. The person attempts then to gain prestige (worth in the eyes of other people) rather than self-esteem (worth in your own eyes). Prestige is not a satisfactory substitute for self-esteem. Other people are never really impressed by your possessions and, indeed, may be offended by them. They, too, may be seeking extrinsic worth by accumulating possessions. The bigger your pile, the less impressive their pile. Your greed clashes with their envy. Accumulation continues to escalate, however, because of—rather than in spite of—the fact that it is futile. Once you set out to impress, the less people are impressed, the more you try to impress them. The function of a thing is not its ostensible function, but to impress and thus to gain prestige. As many people as possible must know that you possess it. Thus consumption becomes not only compulsive but conspicuous.

3.5   THE PERSON IS AN INTERCHANGEABLE PART

If a person has no intrinsic worth, then she or he can be used as an interchangeable part in a social system. A person can, for instance, be fitted into a job. A job is defined by its functions, and the person who performs those functions can be replaced by any other person who performs those same functions.* Personnel officers fit the round pegs of people into the square holes of jobs. Exceptional people sometimes round the job to fit themselves, but most people are squared to fit the job. Just as Indian beggar boys are reportedly maimed to fit their "jobs," so most job holders are more subtly stunted to fit their jobs. The person becomes defined by the job. She or he answers "What do you do?" in terms of occupation, "Who are you with?" in terms of organization, and "What are you worth?" in terms of remuneration.† People who have trivial jobs (and most modern jobs are indeed trivial) see themselves as trivial people. This further contributes to the lack of intrinsic worth and compensating search for extrinsic worth. The fitting of the person to the Procrustean bed of the job also contributes to the irresponsibility mentioned earlier. If drivers of bulldozers ever have twinges of conscience about defacing the environment, then they can salve them by saying "It's my job." Milgram discovered that people who would not normally hurt another person would do so when commanded by an authority figure.[152] He called this the **Eichmann effect** because of Eichmann's defense, during his trial for exterminating Jews in a Nazi concentration camp, that he was merely doing his job as requested by his superiors. Le Bon, in a book entitled *The Crowd: A Study of the Popular Mind*, points out that the crowd has less responsibility than the individuals who compose it. A corporation is a crowd.

3.6 THE PERSON HAS CONTRACTUAL RELATIONSHIPS

If the person is an interchangeable part, then his or her relationships are contractual. The essence of a **contractual relationship** is that the people who make the contract are interchangeable. You have a contractual relationship with your grocer. There is an unwritten understanding that the grocer will give you food and you will give the grocer money. It does not really matter to you that this particular grocer gives you the food or to the grocer that this particular customer provides the money. You take the food home and your mate cooks it. It would seem reasonable to believe that your relationship to your mate is qualitatively different from your relationship to your grocer. However, the behavioristic concept of the person implies that it is only quantitatively differ-

* I once had the following conversation with an immigration officer: "How will you support yourself in the United States?" "My publisher will pay me." "They can't do that." "Why not?" "You will be depriving an American citizen of a job." "They can't pay anyone else to write my book." "A good point. Have a good trip." Few modern jobs offer such a satisfactory means of clinching an argument.

† Another conversation—this one at a party for advertising executives: "Who are you with?" "I came alone." "I mean, which advertising agency do you work for?" "Sorry. I'm not with any company." "What do you do?" "I do all sorts of things." "I mean, what's your job?" He didn't get around to asking me "How much are you worth?" but the look of disdain as he excused himself to find more congenial company implied that he had already decided I was not worth much.

ent. You simply present your mate with a longer and more complex shopping list. Your mate retaliates with an equivalent list. I'll scratch your back if you'll scratch mine. We know intuitively that it is important to Martha Jones that it is John Smith, the unique man she has chosen to live with, who is making her breakfast and that it is important to John Smith that it is Martha Jones, that unique woman he has chosen to live with, who is sharing his bed. That is, we know that some of our relationships are intimate rather than contractual. We realize that a marriage that can be described in contractual terms has degenerated into prostitution. (Indeed, prostitution could well be defined as a relationship that should be intimate but is contractual.) Intimate relationships are not possible, however, between people who are totally extrinsically motivated. If there is no self, what is there to be intimate with?

This cynical view of human relationships is not some 1984ish vision of a dehumanized world but a necessary deduction from the behavioristic concept of the person. As we saw earlier, Skinner makes this view explicit in his book *Verbal Behavior.*[203] There are two ways you can get something done: you can do it yourself or you can ask someone else to do it for you. The former involves nonverbal behavior and the latter involves verbal behavior. Verbal behavior is that behavior by which you get things done through the mediation of other people. Other people are means to your ends.

The relationship between the person and society is an extension of this relationship between any two members of society. The social contract is a set of explicit rules to ensure that all those implicit contracts between individuals are honored. Government is a protection racket. You pay your taxes and they pay police to protect you from exploitation by other people. Government is an insurance company. You pay your taxes and they support you when you are sick or old or unemployed. If relationships are contractual—that is, based on arbitrary and relative rules made by people to prescribe their conduct—then those relationships are very tenuous. You are constantly apprehensive that the rules will be broken. You assuage your anxiety by being excessively careful that you meet your commitments in your contracts. Maddi thus explains our obsession about doing our duty or, as it has come to be trivialized, doing our job.[127]

POST-EXERCISES

1. The Mystery of the Long-Shot Winners

In his novel *For Kicks* (London: Pan, 1965), Dick Francis, a jockey turned writer, confronts his hero with the following mystery.

A series of horses, which won races they were not expected to win, looked conspicuously stimulated, yet the dope tests after the race showed no evidence of dope. They came in frothing at the mouth, eyes popping, and bodies drenched in sweat. They had a high adrenalin count but no dope.

Shots of adrenalin had to be discounted, since adrenalin must be injected and acts instantly. There were no needle marks, and the horses were all calm and cool when they entered the starting gate. There were no batteries in whips or saddles to galvanize the horses into action.

The hero subsequently found out that the horses all won on courses with long straight runs to the finish line and that the horses had all, at some time, passed through a certain disreputable stable.

Can you solve the mystery?

(Subtle clue not offered to the hero of the novel: This is a post-exercise in a chapter on behaviorism.)

2. Self-Modification Project*

Do you eat or drink or smoke too much? Do you study or relax too little? Or do you, perhaps, study too much and drink too little?

Whatever behavior you might like to increase or decrease, you can do so using the behavioristic principles learned in this chapter. If you are perfect, go straight to the next chapter; if you are not perfect, try to modify your behavior using the following procedure.

a. Make a list of dissatisfactions in your life.
b. From this list, choose one or more items in which your problem can be stated in terms of your behavior in particular situations. Write a one-paragraph analysis of each, in which your problem behavior is linked to the particular situation in which it occurs (or does not occur).
c. Choose one of your problems-in-a-situation paragraphs and write an analysis of the problem, using as many behavioristic principles as you can; that is, translate it into the language of this chapter. Phrase the problem in terms as precise as possible, describing your behaviors or your feelings and the situations in which they occur.
d. Specify your problem as some behavior-in-a-situation that you wish to increase or decrease.
e. Collect baseline data on your target behavior—for example, the number of hours you study or the number of cigarettes you smoke in a day. Compute an average over two or three weeks to establish a stable baseline.
f. Find a reward that is appropriate for you—that is, something you like to do or to have or something you would not like to miss or lose. Ask yourself: Is it a reinforcer for me? Is it a strong reinforcer? Is it manipulable?
g. Draw up a contract—a written agreement with yourself that states what the target behavior is and what reinforcement you will gain for performing it.
h. Make a graph of your data, with time on the horizontal axis and number of occurrences of the target behavior on the vertical axis.

---

* Adapted from *Self-Directed Behavior: Self-Modification for Personal Adjustment*, by D. L. Watson and R. G. Tharp. Copyright © 1972 by Wadsworth Publishing Company, Inc. Used by permission of the publisher, Brooks/Cole Publishing Company, Monterey, California.

3. Living in a Behavioristic Society

B. F. Skinner admits to being a frustrated novelist. He spent some time as an aspiring writer in Greenwich Village, decided that he had nothing to write about, went back to school, and eventually became the foremost living authority on behaviorism. He now had something to write about. The novelist in him reemerged as the author of *Walden Two*, a futuristic novel describing a Utopian society based on his behavioristic principles.

If you want some idea of what it would be like to live in a society based on the behavioristic concept of the person, read the following source:

Skinner, B. F. *Walden Two*. New York: Macmillan, 1960.

Pay special attention to schooling in this society. Would you like to be a teacher in Walden Two? A student? Do the schooling practices follow from the behavioristic principles? Do you think such a school or such a society would work in practice?

Some people have tried to put *Walden Two* into practice. Their experiences are described in the following sources:

Kinkade, K. *A Walden Two experiment: The first five years of Twin Oaks Community*. New York: Morrow, 1973.
Kinkade, K. Commune: A Walden Two experiment. *Psychology Today*, 6(8), 35–42; 90–93 and 6(9), 71–82.

How did the factual Walden Two differ from the fictional Walden Two? Read Skinner's introduction to the above book for his explanation of those differences. How does Walden Two (fictional and factual) differ from the original Walden? What do you think Thoreau would think of those societies? What do you think of them?

Answer to Post-exercise 1

The villains at the disreputable stable had classically conditioned the horses to a high-pitched whistle (conditioned stimulus) by pairing it with a blowtorch applied to the hind legs (unconditioned stimulus). After a number of pairings of CS and UCS, the horse would bolt when it heard the whistle alone.

One of the villains would blow the whistle (which, being high-pitched, couldn't be heard by the other racegoers) when the horse started on the long straight run to the finish line. The horse bolted and won. The high adrenalin count, the frothing mouth, the popping eyes, and the sweating body were symptoms of fear, since horses are terrified by fire.

Humanism 4
and
Inside-Out Teaching

4 HUMANISM AND INSIDE-OUT TEACHING

PRE-EXERCISES

1. Critique of Behaviorism

The behavioristic concept of the person was presented in the previous chapter in the form of six propositions. Only the first two propositions are usually discussed in a presentation of behaviorism. "The person has only extrinsic needs" is discussed under "motivation," and "the person is conditioned from the outside in" is discussed under "learning." My exposition of behaviorism goes beyond the traditional presentation in textbooks in educational psychology, not because I am more impressed by it but, frankly, because I am *less* impressed by it. The full implications of the theory should be explored so that, if you do not accept those implications yet concede that they do indeed follow from the behavioristic theory of learning, which, in turn, follows from the behavioristic theory of motivation, then you may question those theories.

Do you accept those implications? Do you concede that they follow from the behavioristic theories of human motivation and learning? Do you, therefore, question those theories?

If you do, you are not alone. Here are some sources of critiques of behaviorism. Write your own critique and then read some of these sources to fill in some of the gaps in your presentation.

Chomsky, N. Review of *Verbal behavior* by B. F. Skinner. *Language,* 1959, *35,* 26–58.
Huxley, A. *Brave new world revisited.* New York: Harper, 1958.
Koestler, A. *The ghost in the machine.* London: Pan, 1967.
Matson, F. W. *The broken image: Man, science and society.* Garden City, N.Y.: Doubleday, 1966.
Matson, F. W. *Within/without: Behaviorism and humanism.* Monterey, Calif.: Brooks/Cole, 1973.
Wann, T. W. (Ed.). *Behaviorism and phenomenology: Contrasting bases for modern psychology.* Chicago: University of Chicago Press, 1964.

What theoretical framework would you recommend to replace behaviorism?

If the assumption that "the person has only extrinsic needs" leads to implications you find unpalatable, pursue the implications of the alternative assumption that "the person has intrinsic needs."

2. Critique of Traditional Education

What criticisms do you have of traditional education based on your own personal experience with it? What critiques by others have you read? To what extent do they conform to your personal critique?

Here are some critiques. You may like to read some of them to help articulate any sense you may have of shortcomings in traditional education. Do you see any relationship between the critiques of behaviorism, listed in Pre-exercise 1, and the critiques of traditional education listed below?

Dewey, J. *Experience and education.* New York: Collier, 1938.
Farber, J. *The student as nigger.* North Hollywood: Contact, 1969.
Freidenberg, E. Z. *Coming of age in America.* New York: Random House, 1965.
Goodman, P. *Growing up absurd.* New York: Vintage, 1956.
Illich, I. *De-schooling society.* New York: Harper & Row, 1971.
Marin, P., Stanley, V., & Marin, K. *The limits of schooling.* Englewood Cliffs, N.J.: Prentice-Hall, 1975.
Mayer, M. *The schools.* Garden City, N.Y.: Doubleday, 1963.
Pearl, A. *The atrocity of education.* New York: New Critics Press, 1972.
Postman, N., & Weingartner, C. *Teaching as a subversive activity.* Harmondsworth, Middlesex: Penguin, 1971.
Silberman, C. E. *Crisis in the classroom.* New York: Random House, 1970.

3. John Holt

The most prolific, and perhaps most persuasive, of the critics of traditional education is John Holt. What do you know about John Holt?

Here is a chronological list of books by John Holt. They are all available in paperback in your local bookstore. Perhaps you would like to read one or two or maybe a few. It is as hard to read one Holt as it is to eat one peanut.

His titles suggest that he has changed from a gentle to a harsh critic between 1964 *(How Children Fail)* and 1976 *(Instead of Education).* Do you think so?

Indeed, the last title suggests that he has moved into the school-is-dead school of critics—or, at least, the school-should-be-dead school. Do you think so?

Holt is very skilled at seeing beyond what children are supposed to be learning to what they are actually learning in the classroom. Make two columns headed "official curriculum" and "hidden curriculum" and list examples from Holt's books.

Holt, J. *How children fail.* New York: Dell, 1964.
       How children learn. New York: Pitman, 1967.
       The underachieving school. New York: Dell, 1969.
       What do I do Monday? New York: Dutton, 1970.
       Freedom and beyond. New York: Dutton, 1972.
       Escape from childhood. New York: Dutton, 1974.
       Instead of education. New York: Dutton, 1976.

Humanistic theory is presented here in the following six propositions about the person: the person has intrinsic needs, the person grows from the inside out, the person is responsible for behavior, the person has intrinsic worth, the person is not an interchangeable part, and the person has intimate relationships. Since each proposition implies the next, these six propositions constitute a system, and that system could be defined as the humanistic concept of the person. You will notice that the six propositions negate the corresponding six propositions in the behavioristic concept of the person.

4.1   THE PERSON HAS INTRINSIC NEEDS

Your nervous system is an element of you as a person, and you as a person are, in turn, an element of your society. The nervous system has a very special role within this hierarchy of systems within systems. It is the only system that can "know" your environment. It must know your environment in order to perform three broad functions—to mediate between your internal environment and your external environment (its biological function), to interact appropriately with other people (its sociological function), and to understand your environment and yourself (its psychological function). Underlying each of these functions are certain organic needs—biological, sociological, and psychological, respectively—which are designed to ensure that your nervous system performs each of these functions.

The biological needs and the mechanisms by which the nervous system satisfies them were described in the presentation of the behavioristic concept of the person in the last chapter. The humanistic concept does not replace the behavioristic concept of the person but subsumes it. **Humanism** does not replace behaviorism as Copernicus replaced Ptolemy but subsumes it as Einstein subsumed Newton. Humanism accepts behaviorism as far as it goes but points out that it does not go nearly far enough. Not only are there biological needs, but there are also sociological and psychological needs built into the nervous system.

4.11   Biological Needs

No evidence for **biological needs** was presented in the description of the behavioristic concept of the person in the last chapter. This was not in order to set the behavioristic concept up as a straw man to be knocked down by the humanistic concept. No evidence is necessary. The behavioristic and humanistic concepts agree with respect to biological needs. The best evidence for a need is that failure to satisfy it results in damage to the organism. If an organism is deprived of food and drink, it dies. Death is the dramatic documentation of the biological needs of hunger and thirst. Neither the behaviorist nor the humanist requires further evidence. Since deprivation of the sociological and psychological needs typically results in less dramatic damage, evidence for their existence is presented next.

4.12   Sociological Needs

Just as the biological needs are designed to ensure the survival of the individual, so the **sociological needs** are designed to ensure the survival of the species. Mother Nature loads Jack and Jill not only with hunger and thirst drives so that each of them will survive as an individual but with sex drives so that they will get together and our species will survive. Since an organism can survive without sex—a live organism but an unhappy organism—we tend to assume that the sex drive is less powerful than the hunger drive. However, Mother Nature is more concerned with the preservation of the species than with the preservation of the individual (like most parents, she aspires to be a grandparent) and would thus provide a powerful drive as a means to this end. The sex drive ensures not only that Jack and Jill will get together for that delightful experience designed to bribe us to procreate our species but that they will stay together to care for the resultant offspring during the long period of infant dependency. This caring mechanism is built into the child during the period of dependency so that the child will, in turn, take care of its child. Our cooperation with other people is based on this caring mechanism established within the family. Slater argues that it is cooperation rather than competition that has made our puny species the King of the Jungle.[206]

Total deprivation of sociological needs, like deprivation of biological needs, also results in death. The human infant is so dependent that it could not survive without the care of other people. A few dubious reports of feral children raised by animals indicate that, even if this is possible, the children become more like the animals that raised them than like the humans who bore them.[202] It is not ethically possible to study the effects of total sociological deprivation on human infants. However, Harlow has tested the effect on our close cousin, the Rhesus monkey.[90] Such deprived infants become neurotic, spending most of their time huddled in a corner of their cage. Spitz has studied the effect of partial deprivation of sociological needs on human infants.[212] He found that many orphans raised in foundling homes with minimum social contact die. Those who survive are physically, emotionally, and intellectually stunted. They die a little bit. They fall somewhat short of becoming fully human.

4.13   Psychological Needs

The **psychological needs,** unlike the biological and sociological needs, are not primarily concerned with survival. Our species is nature's first deluxe model with trimmings beyond those necessary for mere survival. We have more needs than we *really* need. The psychological needs reflect organic potentiality rather than organic requirements. They enrich rather than simply maintain life, they ensure that we thrive rather than merely survive, they make us competent in our environment rather than just adapted to it. As far as I can see, no one yet seems to understand why such luxury needs would evolve. Perhaps they evolved out of survival needs. We needed to know our environment in order to survive in it, but subsequently, as the threat to survival decreased, we needed to know our environment simply in order to know our environment. Psychological needs were means to an end but became ends in themselves. They became **functionally autonomous.**[4]

4.131   Need for Stimulation

Studies of **sensory deprivation** and of **dream deprivation** suggest that we have a need for stimulation. How would you like $40 a day for lying in a comfortable bed doing nothing, with visors over your eyes, pillows around your ears, and cuffs around your arms, so that your leisure will not be disturbed? It sounds like a good deal. (Actually, it was $20 a day, but those were 1956 dollars.) However, the McGill undergraduates who accepted the invitation into this paradise for students were soon clamoring to get out.[92] Such sensory deprivation turned out to be a very disturbing experience. Their thought processes deteriorated, their emotional responses became childish, and they had terrifying hallucinations. It seems that, just as the body needs food, the mind needs stimulation. This need for stimulation persists even when you are asleep. The discovery that rapid eye movements accompany dreaming has made it possible to conduct objective studies of this subjective state. Kleitman awakened some subjects every time they started to dream during several successive nights.[112] On subsequent nights, during which they were allowed to rest in peace, they dreamed significantly more than before. When you are deprived of eating, you subsequently eat more; when you are deprived of dreaming, you subsequently dream more. You have a need to eat; you have a need to dream.

The satisfier of the need to eat is food; the satisfier of the need for stimulation is novel stimuli. Just as you seek food when you are hungry, so you seek

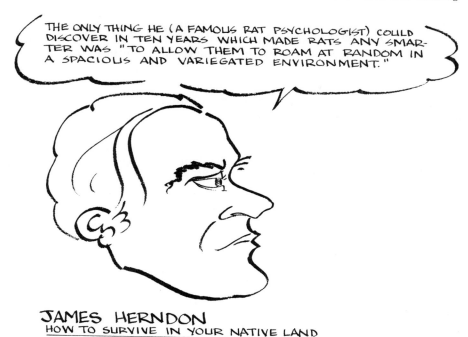

THE ONLY THING HE (A FAMOUS RAT PSYCHOLOGIST) COULD DISCOVER IN TEN YEARS WHICH MADE RATS ANY SMARTER WAS "TO ALLOW THEM TO ROAM AT RANDOM IN A SPACIOUS AND VARIEGATED ENVIRONMENT."

JAMES HERNDON
HOW TO SURVIVE IN YOUR NATIVE LAND

novel stimuli when you have a need for stimulation. A number of studies have demonstrated that organisms explore and manipulate their environment in search of novel stimuli. Rats will often choose the long, scenic route over the short, dull route between the start and goal boxes of a maze. They spend more time around unfamiliar objects put in their cages than around familiar objects. Monkeys will work hard to unfasten latches to open windows to see what is happening outside. Indeed, they will work to see nothing. They enjoy the manipulation of the latches as an end in itself. The activity is its own reward.

This need for stimulation may perhaps be explained in evolutionary terms. As long as your environment continues as is, you are in no danger. It is only novel stimuli that are potentially dangerous. Exploration and manipulation of your environment make the unfamiliar familiar. If the novel stimulus is indeed dangerous, you can remove it or remove yourself; if it is not dangerous, the threat is removed. Besides removing danger or threat of danger, exploration and manipulation incidentally enable you to get to know your environment. One peculiar property of novel stimuli may help explain why we have come to know more than we really need to know. Over time, a novel stimulus becomes less and less novel; that is, it ceases to become a satisfier of the need for stimulation. We must therefore continually search for new stimuli to satisfy this need. Perhaps, as our environment gets less and less threatening, the incidental function of getting to know our environment gets more and more important.

Alternatively, the need for stimulation may be explained in terms of a new conception of the structure of the nervous system. The traditional view is that the nervous system is composed of **projection** and **internuncial neurons.** The projection neurons are further classified into **sensory neurons,** responsible for the reception of stimuli, and **motor neurons,** responsible for the initiation of responses. The stimulus-response model of the behaviorist would theoretically require only the projection neurons. It is empirically obvious, however, that there are millions of neurons that are not directly linked to either stimuli or responses. This et-cetera category of all neurons that are not projection neurons was labeled *internuncial neurons.* They were presumed to mediate between sensory and motor neurons and account for that "waste of time" between the stimulus and the response.

The emerging view is that the nervous system is composed of **intrinsic** and **extrinsic neurons.**[186] The projection neurons are extrinsic, since they are directly associated with the environment; the internuncial neurons are intrinsic, since they are directly associated with the organism. The intrinsic part of the nervous system is not a mere mediator between the sensory and motor aspects of the extrinsic part. It is autonomous. It is central control. It actively seeks stimuli and initiates responses. The sensory and motor aspects of the extrinsic part are recruited to perform those functions. Thus, the extrinsic neurons are mediators between the intrinsic neurons and the environment. The intrinsic part of the nervous system adjusts responses on the basis of stimuli fed back to it from previous responses. The reflex arc of the behaviorist is replaced by the feedback loop of the humanist as the basic functional unit of the nervous system. The intrinsic part of the nervous system is not *entirely* autonomous. We saw in Section 3.13 how the reticular activating system keeps the organism awake and alert and, hence, alive by projecting diffusely onto the cortex. In order to do so, it requires stimulation from the environment. Thus the need for stimulation.

4.132   Need for Consistency

A group of psychologists arranged to have some observers infiltrate an organization whose members believed that the world would end at a particular time on a particular date.[55] They were curious to find out what would happen to the beliefs of the members when that time passed and the world remained. The psychologists found that those people who were only peripherally involved with the group ceased to believe, whereas those people who were strongly committed to the group (that is, those who had stated their beliefs in interviews with the press, who had sold their belongings and canceled their life-insurance policies, and so on) continued to believe. These true believers argued that the destruction of the world had been postponed, that there had been a mistake in the date, that the apocalypse had been canceled because of their vigilance, and so on and so on.

Those findings suggested to Festinger, the leader of the group of psy-

A FOOLISH CONSISTENCY IS THE HOBGOBLIN OF LITTLE MINDS, ADORED BY LITTLE STATESMEN AND PHILOSOPHERS AND DIVINES.

RALPH WALDO EMERSON
ESSAYS: FIRST SERIES

chologists, the concept of **cognitive dissonance.** When two items of information do not fit together, there is a tendency for one of them to be changed. For instance, the two items of information "I smoke" and "smoking causes cancer" are dissonant. Festinger found that significantly fewer smokers than nonsmokers believed the latter statement. People who had those two items of information within their subjective maps tended to stop smoking or to stop believing. Research on cognitive dissonance has led to a number of further findings that Grandmother would not have predicted. Not only do we own a car because we read ads for it, but we read ads for it because we own it; not only do we say what we believe, but we come to believe what we say; not only do we own things we like, but we come to like things we own; not only do we know what we like, but we come to like what we know. All these findings point to a need for consistency.

4.133 *Knowing and Understanding*

Whereas the need for stimulation provides the organic basis for knowing our environment, the need for consistency provides the organic basis for understanding our environment. Not only do we need to know, but we need to know what we need to know. What we know must be organized into a consistent body of knowledge; that is, we need not only to know but to understand. The need for stimulation and the need for consistency together provide an

"THE MORE A CHILD USES HIS SENSE OF CONSISTEN-
CY, OF THINGS FITTING TOGETHER AND MAKING
SENSE, TO FIND AND CORRECT HIS OWN MISTAKES,
THE MORE HE WILL FEEL THAT HIS WAY OF USING
HIS MIND WORKS, AND THE BETTER HE WILL GET AT
IT."

JOHN HOLT
HOW CHILDREN LEARN

organic basis for psychological growth. As we shall see in Chapter 5, Piaget describes the process of psychological growth as a series of alternating assimilations and accommodations. You assimilate information from your environment and adjust your subjective map to accommodate that information if it does not fit. The need for stimulation is the organic basis of assimilation, and the need for consistency is the organic basis for accommodation. The need for stimulation ensures a fresh supply of new information, and the need for consistency ensures that this information will be integrated into a consistent subjective map.

4.14   *Hierarchy of Needs*

Although the biological, sociological, and psychological needs must all be satisfied by the same nervous system, they are naturally in harmony. They are organized in a **hierarchy.**[135] Biological needs are most potent; when they are satisfied, sociological needs become most potent; and, when those needs are satisfied in turn, psychological needs become most potent.* That is, you shift gears up the hierarchy as lower needs are satisfied. The biological and sociological needs are so easily satiated that, in a healthy person in a healthy society, most time is available for the less satiable psychological needs. Eating ruins your appetite. The satisfiers of sociological needs—namely, other people—are in plentiful (indeed, too plentiful) supply. The satisfaction of the survival needs provides pleasant periodic interludes from the rigors of satisfying the psychological needs. Those priorities make sense. The necessity of surviving (biological and sociological needs) comes before the luxury of thriving (psychological needs). Perhaps psychological needs could be seen in terms of surplus energy, much as our economic luxuries can be seen in terms of surplus capital. Individual survival (biological needs) comes before species survival (sociological needs) since it is the individual who is arranging the

---

* My hierarchy is a simplification of Maslow's hierarchy, in which needs are clumped into three broad categories: biological, sociological, and psychological. His highest need—self-actualization—is considered here as the realization of the full human potential, which involves satisfaction of all those sets of needs.

THE HUNGRY MAN IS NOT CONCERNED WITH ARTISTIC SUCCESS, NOR IS THE FRIGHTENED CHILD INTERESTED IN LATIN.

G. W. ALBEE
"PSYCHOLOGY AND THE BODY OF KNOWLEDGE UNIQUE TO THE PROFESSION OF EDUCATION"

priorities. Mother Nature may be more concerned with the survival of the species, but I am more immediately concerned with my survival and you with yours.

4.15 *Intrinsic Motivation*

In Section 3.14, I argued that the traditional educational system is based on extrinsic motivation—that is, on the basic proposition of the behavioristic theory of the person that "the person has only extrinsic needs." Various critics of traditional education recommend an alternative educational system based on **intrinsic motivation**—that is, on the basic proposition of the humanistic theory of the person that "the person has intrinsic needs." Educational reform can be expressed most succinctly as shifting from extrinsic to intrinsic motivation.

The experimental evidence presented earlier leaves little doubt that intrinsic motivation exists. The need to know and to understand the world is built into the nervous system of our species, so there is no need for a system of rewards and punishments to bribe and threaten students into knowing and understanding the world. Indeed, it is surprising that the burden of proof is on those who claim the existence of intrinsic motivation. The essential feature of an organism, as compared to a mechanism, is that it is intrinsically motivated. No mother of a 2-year-old child requires any experimental evidence that our species, the most intrinsically motivated organism of all, will explore and manipulate the environment without rewards—and *despite* punishments.

If students have their own "motors" inside, there seems little point to pushing and pulling them around from the outside. It would appear, superficially, that this "outside" help could do no harm and might even save some wear and tear on the engine. However, there is strong evidence that extrinsic motivation does not add to the existing intrinsic motivation but destroys it. The student, unlike the car (being an organism rather than a mechanism), tends to switch off the motor.

"WE MAY LIKEN THE CHILD TO A CLOCK, AND MAY SAY THAT WITH THE OLD TIME WAY IT IS VERY MUCH AS IF WE WERE TO HOLD THE WHEELS OF THE CLOCK QUIET AND MOVE THE HANDS ABOUT THE CLOCK FACE WITH OUR FINGERS. THE HANDS WILL CONTINUE TO CIRCLE THE DIAL JUST SO LONG AS WE APPLY, THROUGH OUR FINGERS, THE NECESSARY MOTOR FORCE. —— THE NEW METHOD, INSTEAD, MAY BE COMPARED TO THE PROCESS OF WINDING, WHICH SETS THE ENTIRE MECHANISM IN MOTION."

MARIA MONTESSORI
THE MONTESSORI METHOD

Deci reviews a number of experiments demonstrating that extrinsic motivation destroys intrinsic motivation.[40] In one representative study, the experimenter asked nursery school children to draw pictures.[120] Half the children were told they would receive an award for drawing, and the other half were told nothing. Several days later, the children were allowed to play in a room containing the same drawing materials and a number of other things. The measure of intrinsic interest was the percentage of time spent working with the drawing materials. The children who had been rewarded spent significantly less time than the children who had not been rewarded. Their intrinsic motivation had been reduced by the extrinsic motivation. In a parallel experiment, it was demonstrated that the threat of punishment as well as the promise of reward can reduce intrinsic motivation.[41] Subjects were asked to solve puzzles. Half the subjects were told that an unpleasant buzzer would sound if they did not solve the puzzle within ten minutes and the other half were told nothing. When the subjects were later put in a free-choice situation in which solving similar puzzles was one of the options, the subjects who had previously worked to avoid the buzzer spent significantly less time doing the puzzles than those who had worked merely for the intrinsic satisfaction of solving the puzzles. Their intrinsic motivation had also been reduced by extrinsic motivation.

Why does extrinsic motivation destroy intrinsic motivation? White defines intrinsically motivated behaviors as those in which a person engages to feel competent and self-determining in relation to the environment.[232] Deci suggests that, when extrinsic motivation is introduced, the perceived locus of causality is shifted from internal to external.[40] People see themselves as behaving in order to win awards and avoid buzzers. They are "pawns" of rewards and punishments that push and pull them around. This shift in locus of control reduces their sense of competence and self-determination and thus reduces their intrinsic motivation.

Schools are designed so that students learn; innovations are introduced into schools so that students learn more. What innovations in traditional schools have worked?

Improving physical facilities in schools?   No.

Increasing the school day and the school year?   No.

Upgrading the quality of teachers by increasing qualifications and salaries?   No.

Changing teaching methods from lectures to seminars to tutorials?   No.

Integrating schools by busing?   No.

Preparing students by providing kindergartens and Project Head Start programs?   No.

Supplementing traditional teaching with television, programmed textbooks, computers, and other aids?   No.

This was the conclusion of a massive study sponsored by the U.S. Office of Education, based on data collected by a team of researchers over two years from 60,000 teachers and 570,000 students in 4000 schools, and published as the Coleman Report.[31] None of the school characteristics just listed (which one would assume to have some effect and into which billions of dollars have been poured) had any significant relationship to student achievement. The academic community reacted with understandable disbelief. Mosteller and Moynihan collected and analyzed critiques of the Coleman Report and came to essentially the same conclusions.[157] Jencks reanalyzed the data.[102] Same conclusions. Stephens conducted a similar analysis by reviewing reviews of research on factors affecting student achievement.[213] Same conclusions.

These depressing conclusions suggest that something is wrong with the basic assumptions about student achievement on which the various innovations to increase it are based. Traditional education is based on the limited behavioristic theory of the person, presented in Chapter 3. No amount of twiddling with the variables in such a system can produce any significant effect on student achievement. The behavioristic theory does not describe accurately why and how students learn, and an educational system based on this erroneous theory cannot, therefore, help them learn more. Students will learn more, however, in an educational system based on the more accurate humanistic theory of the person presented here in Chapter 4. The educational system must be not simply patched up but turned inside out.

The Coleman Report contains a clue that this is what is required. The one factor that *did* have an effect on student achievement was **destiny control:** the more students felt they could shape their own future, the more they achieved. Coleman's other significant finding, that social class is related to student achievement, supports the importance of destiny control. Lower-class students are less confident that they can shape their futures (partly because this is indeed true) and thus do not succeed as well in school as middle-class students. Destiny control is that "feeling of competence and self-determination," mentioned earlier, which is acquired through intrinsically motivated behavior and is destroyed by extrinsic motivation. An educational system based on intrinsic motivation will increase the destiny control—and, thus, the achievement—of the students.

Coleman suggests such a transformation of the schools.[32] He argues that the traditional school was designed to serve a society that was rich in action but poor in information. Children were actively involved in looking after themselves and siblings, helping at home and earning money from an early age. They went to school to augment the meager sources of information from their direct experience. Children now have little responsibility (indeed, childhood is extended considerably by putting young people into youth reservations to keep them off the streets and out of the job market until they are well into their 20s), but they are rich in information because of their access to the mass media. Schools have not accommodated to this new action-poor and information-rich society. Hence, there are bizarre discontinuities between school and society. First-grade children interrupt their playtime discussion of intercontinental ballistic missiles to go into class to read about Dick, Jane, and Spot from what one child described to me as a "broken-record book." This is why Marshall McLuhan insists that we interrupt our education by going to school. Coleman concludes that schools should provide the opportunities for responsible and productive action which are no longer available outside school. School should not protect children from society but prepare them to move out into it as responsible and productive adults.

4.2   THE PERSON GROWS FROM THE INSIDE OUT

4.21   Why Is Growth Stunted?

If the person has intrinsic needs, then the person grows from the inside out. Every normal child has the potential to be fully a person, just as every normal acorn has the potential to be fully an oak tree and every normal kitten has the potential to be fully a cat. Powered by the intrinsic system of needs described earlier, the child seeks satisfaction for them. In an appropriate environment, children are able to satisfy those needs and thus realize their human potential. The basic project of the child is to become an adult—not any old adult but a great and good adult. We therefore need to "explain" not the genius of an Albert Einstein or a Margaret Mead (or whoever *you* think has most fully realized the full human potential) but rather why we are not *all* Einsteins or Meads. Here are two alternative explanations.

4.211 Conflict between Needs: Freud

The process of realizing the human potential is so long and so complex that many things can go wrong. It is relatively easy for an acorn to become an oak tree and for a kitten to become a cat, but it is not easy for a child to become fully human. Freud's theory could be considered as a dramatic documentation of the many ways in which things can go wrong. His **id, superego,** and **ego** represent the forces striving for satisfaction of the biological, sociological, and psychological needs, respectively. Although these forces are naturally in harmony, as argued earlier, Freud shows how they come into conflict. Since the ego tries to maximize truth and the id tries to maximize pleasure, they come into conflict when truth and pleasure are incompatible. Berelson and Steiner, in summarizing scientific findings about human behavior, describe the human being as a "creature who adapts reality to his own ends, who transforms reality into a congenial form, who makes his own reality."[16] In the conflict between truth and pleasure, it seems that pleasure usually wins. Since the ego is concerned with laws and the superego is concerned with rules, they come into conflict when laws (propositions created by humans to describe their environment) and rules (propositions created by humans to prescribe conduct) are incompatible. Studies of conformity suggest that, in the conflict between laws and rules, rules usually win. According to Freud, the attempts by the ego to know and understand our world and ourselves is continually sabotaged by the id, which chants "I want," and the superego, which preaches "Thou shalt not." Any accuracy in our subjective maps of the objective world is a limited, hardearned, and precarious accomplishment. This will remain the case unless we can build a world in which truth is invariably pleasant and rules are invariably rational.

4.212 Lack of Satisfiers of Needs: Maslow

Maslow argues that so many of us fail to realize our full human potential, not because our needs are necessarily in conflict or because conflict is artificially introduced, but because we fail to shift gears up the hierarchy of needs. Most of the people on our planet must spend most of their time seeking satisfaction of their survival needs and have little "spare time" for the luxury of seeking satisfaction for their psychological needs.

In our affluent society, we have little direct experience of a subjective map in which biological needs are prepotent. We get an occasional glimpse of such a state when we are hungry and notice that we are highly sensitized to stimuli related to food. A psychologist once flashed nonsense syllables on a screen before lunch during a convention and got a significant number of food-related responses. Volunteers in an experiment on the effects of semistarvation reported that their consciousness became dominated by food. They talked about food, dreamed about food, replaced the pin-ups in their lockers with photographs of food, and exchanged recipes with the other volunteers. An anthropologist reports that food dominates not only the conscious but the unconscious lives of the members of an African tribe for whom food is scarce.[179] We are preoccupied not with sex, as Freud argues, but with whatever is scarce. The famished man does indeed live by bread alone.

We have more direct experience of a subjective map in which sociological needs are prepotent. Few people in our affluent society get stuck at the level of biological needs, but many get stuck at the level of sociological needs. Other people—the satisfiers of sociological needs—are, as I said, in plentiful supply. Perhaps so many of us get stuck in this second gear of sociological needs because we consider our relationships to other people as contractual rather than intimate. Maslow suggests that any benefit derived from visiting a psychiatrist may be due to the fact that she or he satisfies sociological needs and thus permits the client to move up the hierarchy of needs.[140] In our impersonal society, we need professional listeners to perform a function that should be performed by our intimates. Or perhaps our relationship to other people is marred by the futile attempt to replace self-esteem with prestige. The symptoms of the behavioristic personality, as described in the last chapter, may help to explain why so many people in our consumer society fail to realize their full human potential. We fail to satisfy our sociological needs and thus cannot move on to the satisfaction of our psychological needs.* Many students fail to gain from schooling because they are preoccupied with the satisfaction of their sociological needs. There is no computer time left for the luxury of knowing and understanding the world.

Maslow suggests further that the need to know may be overcome by the fear of knowing.[137] The person is torn between the safety of the survival needs (physiological and sociological) and the growth of the psychological needs. This conflict is most vivid in the image of the child clinging to the mother's apron strings in a strange environment, venturing out for longer and further explorations, and dashing back to home base after each foray when the environment gets too threatening. This conflict between the contentment of safety and the excitement of growth continues, in less blatant forms, throughout our

---

* A fine conversation I was having at a cocktail party was interrupted by a third person. The quality of the conversation shifted suddenly in some strange way that I did not understand at the time. I realize now that we had shifted down the hierarchy of needs from the psychological to the sociological level. We had been playing with ideas but had been shifted to working on interpersonal problems.

lives. Many of us fail to venture very far from our mothers' skirts (or whatever symbolic equivalent we have established). This emphasis on **deficiency motivation** at the expense of **growth motivation** (or, in Bruner's terms, on **defending behavior** at the expense of **coping behavior**)[26] often results from a threatening school environment. Dramatic changes in a child's competence when shifted to a nonthreatening environment may be interpreted as a switch from deficiency to growth motivation or, alternatively, from defending to coping behavior.

4.22 *Teaching as Facilitating Growth*

"The person is conditioned from the outside in," the second proposition of behaviorism (see Section 3.2), implies that the function of a teacher is to condition the student from the outside in. Teaching is an outside-in process. "The person grows from the inside out," the second proposition of humanism (see Section 4.2), implies that the function of the teacher is to facilitate the growth of the student from the inside out. Teaching is an inside-out process. The shift from an educational system based on behaviorism to an alternative system based on humanism requires, therefore, a corresponding shift from outside-in teaching to inside-out teaching. The role of the teacher shifts from dispenser of knowledge to facilitator of growth.

Facilitating growth requires a basic faith in growth. We tend to have this faith for the first nine months of growth (we accept the miracle of birth with surprising casualness) but then lose the faith. We assume that the child will not continue to grow right unless prodded and poked, pushed and pulled in what we think is the right direction. The new teacher must keep the faith. Children, powered by the intrinsic system of biological, sociological, and psychological needs described earlier, will seek and find satisfiers of those needs in a congenial environment. The major function of the teacher is to create such an environment. To provide an environment containing satisfiers of the needs of children requires an awareness of those needs. The teacher must, therefore, acquire the understanding skills (listening, reading, mnemonics) as well as the explaining skills (speaking, writing, heuristics), since the teacher is a receiver as well as a transmitter of information (see Section 9.2). Rogers suggests that the teacher should be like the therapist who listens rather than talks.[184]

4.3   THE PERSON IS RESPONSIBLE FOR BEHAVIOR

If the person grows from the inside out, then the person is responsible for behavior. Extrinsic motivation requires extrinsic control, whereas intrinsic motivation requires intrinsic control. The constraining force of society on a

person with extrinsic motivation may be replaced by the restraining force of a person with intrinsic motivation. This is reflected, within the discipline of psychology, by a shift in emphasis from other-control to self-control. The lay person has been appropriately apprehensive about the psychologist, because of the threat that, the better the psychologist understands you, the easier he or she can control you. This public image of the psychologist is somewhat justified, since the emphasis has indeed been on how to make organisms—whether rats or raccoons, pigeons or people—behave as the behaviorist wants them to behave. The recent burgeoning of research on self-control (a once taboo topic) is an encouraging sign that psychology is turning from yet another potential instrument of oppression to one of liberation.[81, 130] This does not mean that the psychologist must start again from scratch. Each technique for understanding and controlling others can be applied to self-understanding and self-control. Psychologists are beginning to present the powerful devices they have developed to the public so that people may use them for self-understanding and self-control. Behavioristic means can be used to humanistic ends. Power to the person.

This discussion of other-control versus self-control is a modern rephrasing of the determinism versus free will chestnut that philosophers have been roasting for centuries. Perhaps this controversy has been debated for so long because both positions are true. If you are determined to be determined, then

ALL THEORY IS AGAINST THE FREEDOM OF THE WILL; ALL EXPERIENCE FOR IT.

SAMUEL JOHNSON
1778

you are determined. If you think you have free will, then you have free will. The first act of free will is to believe in it. Two propositions that are incompatible with respect to the objective world may be perfectly compatible with respect to our different subjective maps of the objective world. People who have a behavioristic self-concept based on extrinsic motivation will tend to believe that their behavior is determined. The self-fulfilling prophecy (what you expect is what you get, to be elaborated in Chapter 12) ensures that their behavior is indeed determined. People who have a humanistic self-concept based on intrinsic motivation will tend to believe that they control their own behavior. The self-fulfilling prophecy, in this case, will ensure that they do indeed have free will. In this way, the determinist and the free-willist have both accumulated "evidence" for their respective theories throughout our history. Each theory is based on what feels good rather than on what seems true.* You do not believe it because it is true, but it becomes true because you believe it.

This shift from other-control to self-control in psychology corresponds to a shift from discipline administered by adults to self-discipline by children in education. The basic discipline problem is to shift from discipline by others to self-discipline. The Coleman Report considers "destiny control" (a child's feeling of capacity to shape his or her own future) to have a stronger relationship to achievement than all the other "school" factors together.[31] Anyone responsible for a child is mainly concerned with enabling that child to become responsible for himself or herself. It is in this sense that the statement "the function of parents and teachers is to plan their own obsolescence" is most apt. Sensitive teachers are aware how much self-control a child is capable of handling. They phase out other-control to allow this much self-control. Some of us permit too little too late, whereas others force too much too soon: throw off your chains or I'll beat you over the head. Freedom should not be forced on children unable or unwilling to handle it. The following plaintive plea was heard from a young child in a free school: "Do we have to do what we want to do today?" Structure is to freedom as the trellis is to the vine. Providing too much freedom with too little structure results in escape-from-freedom contortions as children squirm away from more freedom than they can handle.

---

* This was first pointed out to me by a wise old man I once met in Los Angeles. He had just emerged from a mental hospital, he was physically sick, his wife had left him, and his children did not respect or even like him. After a five-hour discussion during which we disagreed on every topic that arose, I suddenly saw an underlying pattern in our debate.

"I see now, old man, why we disagree. We consider each topic at such depth that we get right down to our basic philosophical assumptions, and I am a free-willist whereas you are a determinist."

"Of course, young man, you are a free-willist—your life is going well and you want to take the credit. And, of course, I am a determinist—my life is going badly and I don't want to take the blame."

4.4 THE PERSON HAS INTRINSIC WORTH

If people are responsible for their behavior, then they have intrinsic worth. They must accept blame for their bad behavior but can take credit for their good behavior. The words *bad* and *good* tend to scare scientists into scurrying off in search of philosophers. There seems no place for values in a world of facts. Western philosophers offer us a choice between pragmatic values (doing well) and ethical values (doing good). Some scientists are, however, beginning to evolve an alternative set of values based on natural laws rather than on cultural rules—that is, based on the propositions we have derived to describe our planet and ourselves rather than on the propositions we have derived to prescribe our conduct on that planet. Here is a summary of this system of values, as expounded by such diverse thinkers as Teilhard de Chardin, Kenneth Boulding, and Buckminster Fuller.

Our species on our planet is confronted not with an energy crisis but with an entropy crisis. Since energy can neither be created nor destroyed, we have as much energy today as we ever had or will ever have. It is **entropy**—the natural tendency of a system toward disorder—that is increasing. Any process that destroys structure or breaks complex systems down into simpler systems contributes toward this spontaneous tendency in the universe toward chaos. Biological systems, within their limited space and for a limited time, defy this law of entropy. During the period of growth, they become more rather than less structured. Our species, the most complex biological system, is the greatest antientropic force in the universe. Each of us is a defiant little package of antientropy fighting a brave battle against the forces of chaos. Consciousness emerges as a function of complexity and provides the ultimate weapon against entropy. It enables us to assimilate and accommodate information to create a microcosm of the universe within us. The more accurate this subjective map of the objective world, the better we fight the good fight. It is a futile battle, because eventually we must submit to the forces of chaos. However, although it is futile for each of us as individuals, it is not futile for all of us as a species. Each of us spawns other little packages of antientropy in our books or our movies or our children or the memories of our friends before we are recycled in the air our survivors breathe and the water they drink. The people who have this system of values recognize that they are a part of nature and not apart from it. Since they are an important element in the complex system of the universe, they have intrinsic worth. Their criterion of success is not wealth but health. They are healthy insofar as they realize their function in the universe—to satisfy their biological, sociological, and psychological needs—in other words, to be as fully human as possible.

When people recognize that they have intrinsic worth, they are said to have **self-esteem.** A certain level of self-esteem is already established in each child before school begins. Coopersmith concludes, on the basis of his extensive research, that parents of children with high self-esteem (1) accept the child in his or her own right, (2) lay down clear and enforceable rules of conduct, and (3) allow the child a wide latitude to explore within those boundaries.[34] A good teacher, like a good parent, can help maintain this high self-esteem by following those same principles. Firm and fair rules provide a secure world that makes sense, and freedom to explore it provides children with the confidence that they can make sense of it.

Covington and Beery argue that schools, on the contrary, often lower the self-esteem of students.[35] Self-esteem is linked by schools and other socializing agencies to intellectual ability which is, in turn, linked to scholastic performance. Since a competitive atmosphere is set up in the classroom, there can be only a few successes and many failures. Students become apprehensive about failing, since this reflects back on their intellectual ability which reflects, in turn, on their self-esteem. Many students become oriented toward avoiding failure rather than achieving success. Their various strategies for avoiding failure—passive indifference, underachievement, overstriving, and so on—are self-defeating for themselves (they fail because of the fear of failing) and frustrating for the teacher. The authors make a number of recommendations: (1) shift from a competitive to a cooperative classroom atmosphere, in which success is not scarce (see Section 4.63); (2) shift from a situation in which students compete with one another to one in which they compete with themselves (see Section 2.32); (3) set realistic standards for each student and allow them plenty of latitude to meet those standards in their own way at their own pace; (4) grant "freedom to fail" or, better, freedom to have temporary nonsuccesses on the way to success; and (5) shift from praise (which focuses on the standards of the teacher) to encouragement (which focuses on the standards of the student). Canfield and Wells provide further suggestions for enhancing self-esteem in your classroom.[29]

4.5   THE PERSON IS NOT AN INTERCHANGEABLE PART

A person who has intrinsic worth is not an interchangeable part. The shift from extrinsic to intrinsic motivation implies not only a shift from being controlled by others to self-control, but a shift from being employed by others to being self-employed. There are some encouraging signs that we can swell the ranks of the self-employed. The work of the world can be done without stretching and chopping us all to fit the Procrustean beds of jobs. We have developed mechanical slaves to do mechanical jobs. Instead of being apprehensive about being replaced by a machine, we should be delighted. So far, machines can do only monotonous, repetitive jobs. They free us for human activities. Technology has also freed us from the necessity of being in a particular place at a particular time to do a job. McLuhan once said "Executives drive to the office to answer the telephone." Two hours of gas-guzzling, air-polluting, nerve-destroying, ulcer-creating commuting—and there's a perfectly good telephone at home. I once overheard one of the editors in my publishing company say to another "I won't be in tomorrow, Terry, I've got some work to do." The most encouraging signs, however, are not technological innovations but changes in cultural attitudes. Serious recent consideration of schemes for a guaranteed annual income or negative income tax imply a shift from the view that there are those who work and those who are supported by charity to the view that everyone in an affluent society is entitled to the necessities of life and those who aspire to the luxuries may work to acquire them.

There is a growing counterculture of people who are content with the necessities and are not embarrassed about being "unemployed" and "getting something for nothing." They view themselves as "self-employed" and consider self-actualization as a legitimate form of self-employment. They do not consider the traditional distinction between work and play very useful. One person's work is another person's play. One person can work at taking children to a fun fair, and another person can play at solving quadratic equations. They prefer a distinction with respect to the subjective map rather than to the objective world. The distinction between doing what you must do and doing what you want to do is such a subjective substitute for the "objective" distinction between work and play. Their criterion of success is the average number of hours per day they are doing what they want to do. If you are healthy, what you want to do is to satisfy your organic biological, sociological, and psychological needs, to realize your full human potential, to self-actualize.

4.6 THE PERSON HAS INTIMATE RELATIONSHIPS

4.61 Intimate and Contractual Relationships

If a person is not an interchangeable part, then a person has **intimate relationships.** All relationships are potentially intimate. A stranger is just a friend you haven't met yet. The contract (or, rather, the understanding) with your grocer is that you tacitly agree not to realize your potential intimacy. You will limit yourselves to exchanging groceries and money. After all, you can handle only so much intimacy—if merely because of the simple fact that your time is limited. There is, however, a penumbra of intimacy around your contractual relationships. If your grocer falls off a stool while reaching for your cornflakes, you go to help. If you are out of work and thus out of money, the grocer may extend credit until you are on your financial feet again. Neither of you says "That's not in the contract." Whereas the contractual relationship is based on the rules of human beings, the intimate relationship is based on the laws of nature.[128] We recognize other people as members of the same species on the same planet in essentially the same predicament as ourselves. If God is dead, then there is no one here but us. Other people are the only personal element in an impersonal universe. They hold out the only hope of empathy, of understanding, of caring.*

4.62   Synergetic and Antagonistic Societies

Once again, the relationship between the person and society is a macrocosm of the relationship between one person and another. The relationship is **synergetic.** That is, what is good for the person is good for the society, and what is good for the society is good for the person. Ruth Benedict puzzled for years about the essential difference between the societies she liked and the societies she did not like. She finally concluded that, in the societies she liked, the ends of the person and the ends of the society were synergetic and, in the societies she did not like, the ends of the person and the ends of society were **antagonistic.** She gave her only copy of the notes on this synergetic-antagonistic distinction to Abraham Maslow, who used it in his consideration of our two basic problems—that of the good person and that of the good society.[138] Our prevailing philosophies of the relationship between the person and society (whether they be the bad-person, good-society view of Hobbes or the good-person, bad-society view of Rousseau) see them as antagonistic. There is no reason why the ends of the person and of society cannot be synergetic in our society. Society is a social invention, and we may as well invent a good society. The good society is one that provides the commodities to satisfy the true needs of the person, and the good person is one who has his or her true needs satisfied. The good person is created by the good society, and the good society is composed of good people.†

Social psychologists have tended to focus on antisocial behavior. It is more urgent and more dramatic. Some social psychologists have, however, begun to study **prosocial behavior.** Prosocial behaviors—caring, sharing, helping, and other positive acts—are the behaviors that would make a synergetic society possible. Mussen and Eisenberg-Berg have summarized the research so far on the development of such prosocial behavior in children. The authors

---

* These two basic attitudes toward other people are nicely represented by two gestures I encountered while traveling in Nepal. The traditional gesture is to hold your hands as in prayer, bow, and say "Namaste," which means "I honor the divinity in you." The modern gesture—alas, in urban areas where Western values have pervaded—is to hold out one hand palm up and say "Rupee." The shift from "Namaste" to "Rupee" is symptomatic of a shift from intimate to contractual relationships.

† I feel almost embarrassed to talk of the good person—it is so unfashionable. I once heard of a man who lived with a beautiful and talented actress and wondered why he was worthy of such a fine woman. He was pointed out to me in the street. He had a kind face but, no, he was not magnificently handsome. He was introduced to me. His conversation was lively but, no, he was not brilliant. He took me to his home. It was comfortable but, no, he did not appear to be fabulously rich. As I got to know him, I began to realize that he was simply good. It is an interesting comment on me and my times that it took so long to consider that possibility.

regret that there have been no studies as yet specifically of the role of teachers.[159] However, you can make reasonable inferences from each of the following findings. Prosocial behavior in children is increased by adults who (1) engage in prosocial behaviors (although not by adults who demand prosocial behaviors; do-as-I-say-not-as-I-do does not work); (2) reason with them as a means of discipline; (3) encourage them to reflect on the feelings and expectations of themselves and others; (4) assign them early responsibilities for others (like teaching younger children); (5) reward them for prosocial behavior; (6) provide them with role-playing and empathy-promoting exercises; and (7) make explicit demands that they act maturely.

4.63   Cooperative and Competitive Classrooms

The antagonistic society, based on contractual relationships, assumes competition among its members. The contract is merely a tenuous treaty to protect you in a human jungle in which each person is essentially in competition with every other person. It is assumed that the miniature society of the classroom should also be competitive to prepare its members for life in an antagonistic society. It may be, however, that such classrooms help create competitive people who, in turn, come to constitute the antagonistic society. Perhaps this vicious circle can be broken and replaced by a benign circle in which cooperative classrooms create cooperative people who, in turn, come to constitute a more synergetic society, based on intimate relationships. The **jigsaw method** was designed by Elliot Aronson, in cooperation with others, to create such a cooperative classroom.[7]

Suppose you are teaching the biography of Eleanor Roosevelt as part of a unit in social studies. You can teach it the usual way. You read the biography to the class and then ask them questions about it.

"Who was Eleanor Roosevelt?"

Those who think they know the answer (plus a few who fake it) raise their hands, and those who don't think they know the answer (plus a few who refuse to play the classroom game) don't raise their hands and, in some cases, lower their heads. You choose a hand.

"She was the first liberated First Lady."

"Wrong, Robin."

Wrong. Gong. One hand goes down and one ego goes down another notch. Jeers, sneers, cheers from classmates and mutters of "dummy" behind the steady hiss of "Misssssster" as they compete for the opportunity, open once again, to gain the approval of the teacher. You choose another hand.

"She was the wife of President Roosevelt."

"Wrong again, John."

Down go a dozen hands, and a dozen egos. Consternation in the class.

Only one hand left waving (the odds are too dangerous for those who were faking it). You choose it.

"Eleanor Roosevelt was the wife of President *Franklin* Roosevelt."

"Right, Mary."

You and Mary both beam in triumph at your superior knowledge that there were *two* President Roosevelts. Up go the egos of the 2 winners, and down go the egos of the 30 losers, all now "dummies" in the Smart-Alec and Dummy Game.*

After the oral quiz comes the written quiz—a multiple-choice examination at the end of the unit in which the students try, once again, to guess which is the teacher-ordained right answer. The examination is graded according to the normal curve; that is, there *must* be a few winners (the 5% who get "A"), a few losers (the 5% who get "F"), and many "second-rate," "third-class," "average" students (the 90% who are graded in between). Robin and her friend Sandy prepare for the examination together and make the same mistakes. Since they also sit together, you accuse them of cheating and flunk them both. So much for cooperation in the competitive classroom. In such a classroom, Eleanor Roosevelt herself could very well have flunked "Eleanor Roosevelt." She had difficulty remembering what she was supposed to think and do. That is why she thought and did so many original things. That is why an awkward, ugly girl never learned that she could not lead a successful life.

Or you can teach it another way. You divide the biography into six parts covering, let us say, early childhood, young adulthood, wife and mother, entrance into political life after husband's paralysis, First Lady, postwar years in world politics. You divide the class into groups of six and assign one part of the biography to one member of each group. Thus, for example, Robin is placed in group C and is assigned the second part of the biography on the "young adulthood" of Eleanor Roosevelt. Robin reads her part a number of times and then meets with Sandy, Tom, Dick, and Harriet, who have been assigned the second part of the biography for groups A, B, D, and E. It is now legitimate for her to cooperate with her friend Sandy, since the function of this meeting is for the "experts" on the second part of the biography to review it together and make sure they understand it. Robin now returns to her own group and teaches her part to them, and they, in turn, teach their parts to her.

Aronson and his colleagues found that cooperative classes, using this jigsaw method, learned as much (and sometimes more) about Eleanor Roosevelt (or whatever the content) as competitive classes.[8] They also learned more important things. The teacher is not the sole source of information and approval; the students can teach and appreciate one another. Each member of the group has a crucial and unique contribution to make and is dependent on

---

* Or, alternatively, *The Wrong Show*, by analogy with the television program *The Gong Show*, in which a contestant whose performance is not pleasing to the judges is eliminated by the sound of a gong.

every other member of the group. They are interdependent, since the whole jigsaw can't be completed without all the parts. They learned to like themselves (self-esteem scores increased), to like their classmates, and to like school. Everyone can be a winner.

POST-EXERCISES

1. An Alternative Educational System Based on Humanism

It could be argued that the behavioristic concept of the student, presented in the previous chapter, underlies the traditional educational system, and that the humanistic concept of the student, presented in this chapter, could serve as the basis for an alternative educational system.

Reread each of the propositions that constitute the behavioristic concept of the student. What are the implications of each proposition for schooling? Are those implications indeed embodied in traditional schools?

Reread each of the propositions that constitute the humanistic concept of the student. What are the implications of each proposition for schooling? Design an alternative educational system based on those implications.

Many people have, of course, tried to design alternative schools. Read the following sources and compare their designs with yours. Incorporate the features of their designs that you like into your design.

Bremer, J., & von Moschzisker, M. *The school without walls.* New York: Holt, Rinehart & Winston, 1971.

Cox, D. W. *The city as a schoolhouse.* Valley Forge, Pa.: Judson Press, 1972.

Glasser, W. *Schools without failure.* New York: Harper & Row, 1969.

Kohl, H. *The open classroom.* New York: Vintage, 1969.

Kozol, J. *Free schools.* Boston: Houghton Mifflin, 1972.

Montessori, M. *The Montessori method.* New York: Stokes, 1912.

Neill, A. S. *Summerhill.* New York: Hart, 1960.

Penha, J., & Azrak, J. *The learning community: The story of a successful mini-school.* New York: Paulist Press, 1975.

Troost, C. J. (Ed.). *Radical school reform: Critique and alternatives.* Boston: Little, Brown, 1973.

2. Summerhill and A. S. Neill

The most famous of the alternative schools is Summerhill, and the most famous of the alternative-school teachers is A. S. Neill. What do you know about Summerhill? What do you know about A. S. Neill?

Here is a list of books about Summerhill by its founder, A. S. Neill, and others. You may like to read some of them to augment what you already know about Summerhill and Neill.

Bernstein, E. What does a Summerhill old school tie look like? *Psychology Today,* 1968, 2(5), 37–41; 70.

Bull, R. E. *Summerhill USA.* Harmondsworth, Middlesex: Penguin, 1971.

Great Britain, Ministry of Education. *Report by H. M. Inspectors on the Summerhill School, Leicester, Suffolk East, inspected on 20 and 21 June 1949.*

Hart, H. H. (Ed.). *Summerhill: For and against.* New York: Hart, 1970.

Hemmings, R. *Children's freedom: A. S. Neill and the evolution of the Summerhill idea.* New York: Schocken, 1972.

Neill, A. S. *Summerhill.* New York: Hart, 1960.

Neill, A. S. *Freedom—not license!* New York: Hart, 1966.

Neill, A. S. *Neill! Neill! orange peel!* New York: Hart, 1972.

Popenoe, J. *Inside Summerhill.* New York: Hart, 1970.

Snitzer, H. *Summerhill, a loving world, in photographs.* New York: Macmillan, 1964.

Walmsley, J. *Neill and Summerhill: A man and his work: A pictorial study.* Baltimore: Penguin, 1969.

3. First-Person Accounts of Teaching Experiences

The recent spate of first-person accounts of teaching experiences could be viewed as attempts to design an alternative classroom based on the humanistic concept of the student. Read some of the following books and ask yourself the following questions. Is this an attempt to turn teaching inside out? What difficulties are involved in inside-out teaching within an outside-in educational system? How did each of these teachers deal with those difficulties? What practical principles do you derive from the experiences of these fellow teachers?

Ashton-Warner, S. *Teacher.* New York: Simon & Schuster, 1963.

Braithwaite, E. R. *To Sir with love.* Englewood Cliffs, N.J.: Prentice-Hall, 1959.

Conroy, P. *The water is wide.* Boston: Houghton Mifflin, 1972.

Craig, E. *P.S. your not listening.* New York: New American Library, 1972.

Daniels, S. *How 2 gerbils, 20 goldfish, 200 games, 2,000 books, and I taught them how to read.* Philadelphia: Westminster Press, 1971.

Decker, S. *An empty spoon.* New York: Harper & Row, 1969.

Dennison, G. *The lives of children.* New York: Vintage, 1969.

Grossman, H. *Nine rotten lousy kids.* New York: Holt, Rinehart & Winston, 1972.

Herndon, J. *How to survive in your native land.* New York: Simon & Schuster, 1968.

Herndon, J. *The way it spoze to be.* New York: Simon & Schuster, 1968.

Kaufman, B. *Up the down staircase.* New York: Avon, 1964.

Kohl, H. *36 children.* New York: New American Library, 1967.

Kozol, J. *Death at an early age.* Boston: Houghton Mifflin, 1967.

Rothman, E. *The angel inside went sour.* New York: McKay, 1971.

The Theory 5
of Jean Piaget

---

5 THE THEORY OF JEAN PIAGET

5.1 The Man
5.2 The Method
    5.21 Description of the Method
    5.22 Critique of the Method
    5.23 Value of the Method to Teachers
5.3 The Theory
    5.31 Function, Structure, and Content
    5.32 Stages of Development
        5.321 Sensorimotor Stage
        5.322 Concrete-Operations Stage
        5.323 Formal-Operations Stage
        5.324 Summary of Development

PRE-EXERCISES

1. An Essay on Jean Piaget

Write as many sentences as you can containing the name *Jean Piaget*. For example, "Jean Piaget is a child psychologist." "Jean Piaget was born in Switzerland."

Don't worry if you do not know much about Jean Piaget. This does not mean that you are stupid. It merely means that you have not yet been informed. This chapter is designed to inform you.

What would you like to know about Jean Piaget? Read on. Much of what you want to know may be contained in this chapter.

Organize your sentences into a coherent essay on Jean Piaget. It is not coherent? Why not? There are gaps in your knowledge? Read on. You may find missing parts of your essay in this chapter. You do not really understand his theory? Read on. This chapter may help you understand.

This exercise will appear again at the end of the chapter. The major function of this pre-exercise is to impress you with how much you have learned between the pre-exercise and the post-exercise.

2. Early Memories

What is your earliest memory? Are you sure you really remember this? Or are you remembering being told this?

Check the accuracy of your early memories by asking your parents about them. Ask your parents for anecdotes about things you said and did before your earliest memories. Do you remember those experiences now? If not, why not? Is it possible that the memory mechanism is not established until some years after birth?

You know how to grasp things but you do not remember learning how to grasp things. Is this type of motor memory somehow different from sensory memory?

Some people claim to remember experiences they had before they were 2 years old. Do you think this is possible?

Some people claim to remember how wonderful it was in the womb and how awful was the shock of being born. Do you think this is possible?

Some people claim memories of previous lives. What do you think of that, Cleopatra?

What do you remember of your first day of school? Conduct a conversation with that previous self who went off to school on that first day. What advice would your present self give to that previous self? What opinion would that previous self have of your present self?

Your previous self and your present self are the same person yet strangely different. In what ways are you the same and in what ways are you different? In the long interval between the first day of school and today, the you that woke up each morning recognized you as the same you that went to bed the night before. Does this ever surprise you? Or has it happened so often that you take it for granted, just as you expect the sun to rise each morning?

3. Propositional Logic

    a. Suppose you know that:

        If I have a marble in my right hand,
        then I have a marble in my left hand.
        I have a marble in my right hand.

        Then would this be true?

        I have a marble in my left hand.

        YES NO MAYBE

    b. Suppose you know that:

        If I have a marble in my right hand,
        then I have a marble in my left hand.
        I have a marble in my left hand.

        Then would this be true?

        I have a marble in my right hand.

        YES NO MAYBE

    c. Suppose you know that:

        If I have a marble in my right hand,
        then I have a marble in my left hand.
        I do not have a marble in my right hand.

        Then would this be true?

        I have a marble in my left hand.

        YES NO MAYBE

d. Suppose you know that:

If I have a marble in my right hand,
then I have a marble in my left hand.
I do not have a marble in my left hand.

Then would this be true?

I have a marble in my right hand.

YES   NO   MAYBE

5.1   THE MAN

Jean Piaget was a precocious child. He published his first scientific paper at 10, refused an important position as curator of a museum at 14, and completed his doctorate at 22. Unlike many such fast starters, he continued to outpace his peers and his times and is still precocious today in his 80s. (As I write this, I realize that today is his 80th birthday—Bonne anniversaire, Jean!) Precocious as he was, however, he still went through the same stages of intellectual development in the same order as you and I. This is his theory. Modest as he is, he may admit, if pressed, that he went through the same stages in the same order a bit faster than you and I.

Although Piaget was mainly interested in epistemology (the study of knowledge), he took his training in biology; and, although he was trained in biology, he has devoted his lifetime to developmental psychology. Such career choices would drive a guidance counselor crazy. Superficially, his decisions could be attributed to chance. A childhood in the country triggered an interest in the flora and fauna around him; hence the training in biology. A position in Binet's laboratory designing items for intelligence tests got him interested in the children's wrong answers; hence a career in developmental psychology. However, Piaget's career is more consistent than it seems. Developmental psychology (the subject to which he has devoted his life) is the link between biology (the subject in which he was trained) and epistemology (the subject in which he is primarily interested).

It is probably as important, but Piaget's theory is not so familiar as those of Freud and Darwin. This is so for a number of reasons. First, it is newer. A new theory tends to be greeted initially as preposterous and eventually as obvious. The theories of Darwin and Freud have been around long enough to become obvious, whereas the theory of Piaget, although no longer preposterous, is not yet obvious. Second, a new theory requires a new language. The usual difficulty of translating from French to English is compounded by the additional difficulty of translating from Piaget's idiosyncratic language into French. Third, his method is unpalatable and his theory is uncongenial to the

PIAGET, HOWEVER, IS OFTEN INTERPRETED IN THE WRONG WAY BY THOSE WHO THINK THAT HIS PRINCIPAL MISSION IS PSYCHOLOGICAL. IT IS NOT. IT IS EPISTEMOLOGICAL. HE IS DEEPLY CONCERNED WITH THE NATURE OF KNOWLEDGE PER SE, KNOWLEDGE AS IT EXISTS AT DIFFERENT POINTS IN THE DEVELOPMENT OF THE CHILD.

JEROME S. BRUNER
TOWARD A THEORY OF INSTRUCTION

prevailing behavioristic emphasis which has dominated psychology so far this century. Recently, his theory has finally become well known to psychologists and educators. Indeed, it has even become fashionable (perhaps to the detriment of the theory and to the embarrassment of the theorist). Since the methods and theories of Freud and Darwin are still more familiar, however, I will present those of Piaget by comparison with them. We will see that Piaget's method is similar to Freud's and that his theory is similar to Darwin's.

5.2   THE METHOD

5.21   Description of the Method

Piaget, like Freud, uses the **clinical method**; that is, he seeks to understand people by listening to them. Unlike Freud, however, he does not listen to adults talk about themselves as children. He has no faith in such retrospective accounts of childhood. Adults do not really know how it was to be a child, partly because their memory is too bad (it was so long ago and they have forgotten) and partly because their memory is too good (they "remember" things that never happened). Piaget himself describes his memories of being kidnaped even though his "kidnaping" was merely a story invented by his nursemaid to explain some scratches on his face. The main reason for his lack of faith is his own theory. As children develop into adults, they go through qualitative changes that make it impossible to think as they thought as children. Development is like climbing a flight of stairs rather than going up a ramp. Once you get on a stair, you can't see the previous stairs clearly by looking back. Unlike our physical growth, our mental growth involves qualitative rather than merely quantitative changes. We go through transformations. Our mental growth is like the physical growth of the tadpole into the frog or the caterpillar into the butterfly. Perhaps we are as unaware of our previous selves as the frog is of its career as a tadpole or the butterfly of its career as a caterpillar.

"IT IS AN UNCOMMON EXPERIENCE TO FIND OUT SOMETHING ABOUT CHILDREN'S BEHAVIOR WHICH REALLY SURPRISES, WHICH PRODUCES A SENSE OF SHOCK AND EVEN DISBELIEF: AFTER ALL, PEOPLE HAVE BEEN CHILD-WATCHING FOR A LONG TIME."

JOHN H. FLAVELL
THE DEVELOPMENTAL PSYCHOLOGY OF JEAN PIAGET

Piaget listens to *children* talk about themselves as children. Here, for example, is a child of 5 years, 9 months, talking—with some prompting from Piaget—about dreaming:[168]*

> Where does the dream come from?
> I think you sleep so well that you dream.
> Does it come from us or from outside?
> From outside.
> What do we dream with?
> I don't know.
> With the hands? . . . With nothing?
> Yes, with nothing.
> When you are in bed and you dream, where is the dream?
> In my bed, under the blanket. I don't really know. If it was in my stomach (!)
the bones would be in the way and I shouldn't see it.
> Is the dream there when you sleep?
> Yes, it is in the bed beside me.

---

*From *The Child's Conception of the World,* by J. Piaget. Copyright 1929 by J. Piaget. Reprinted by permission of Humanities Press, Inc., Routledge & Kegan Paul, Ltd., and Delachaux & Niestle.

(He tried suggestion.) Is the dream in your head?

It is I that am in the dream: it isn't in my head(!).

When you dream, you don't know you are in the bed. You know you are walking. You are in the dream. You are in bed but you don't know you are.

Can two people have the same dream?

There are never two dreams (alike).

Where do dreams come from?

I don't know. They happen.

Where?

In the room and then afterward they come up to the children. They come by themselves.

You see the dream when you are in the room, but if I were in the room, too, should I see it?

No, grownups (les Messieurs) don't ever dream.

Can two people ever have the same dream?

No, never.

When the dream is in the room, is it near you?

Yes, there! (pointing to 30 cms. in front of his eyes).

Sometimes Piaget will create some concrete situation as a basis for his conversation with a child. In the following example, he deflates a punctured rubber ball, directing the jet of air toward the child's cheek, and asks the child where the air came from and where it went. The child in this sample conversation is 8 years, 6 months old:[169]

What is happening?

There is air. Because there is a hole, then it comes out.

Where does the air come from?

They put it in.

Who?

The man. The man who took the ball and put air into it.

(The ball is deflated and allowed to fill itself again.)

It is coming back.

How?

By the hole.

But where from?

It is going in.

Is it the air of the room that is going in, or the air that I took away?

The air that you took away.

Piaget may invite the child to act as well as to talk. In the following example, he puts six counters on the table in a straight line with equal spaces between them and asks the child to pick out of a box the same number of counters. The child in this sample conversation is 4 years, 5 months old:[171]

Take the same number as there are there (6 counters).

(He put 7 counters close together, and then made the correct correspondence.)

Are they the same?
Yes.
(His row was then spread out.)
Are they the same?
No.
Has one of us got more?
Me.
Make it so you have the same number as I have.
(He closed his up.)
Are they the same?
Yes.
Why?
Because I pushed mine together.

In the case of young children who can't talk yet, Piaget can, of course, *only* invite them to act. Here is a description of one of Piaget's interactions with his daughter Jacqueline, when she was 1 year, 6 months old:[172]

Jacqueline is sitting on a green rug and playing with a potato which interests her very much (it is a new object for her). She says "po-terre" and amuses herself by putting it into an empty box and taking it out again. . . . I then take the potato and put it in the box while Jacqueline watches. Then I place the box under the rug and turn it upside down thus leaving the object hidden by the rug without letting the child see my maneuver, and I bring out the empty box. I say to Jacqueline, who has not stopped looking at the rug and who has realized that I was doing something under it: "Give Papa the potato." She searches for the object in the box, looks at me, again looks at the box minutely, looks at the rug, etc., but it does not occur to her to raise the rug in order to find the potato underneath.*

By really listening to what children are saying and by carefully watching what they are doing in many interactions such as these over half a century, Piaget has gained a glimpse into the mind of the child. Children tell him their secrets in words and show him their secrets in actions. As we shall see, Piaget is often surprised at what they show and tell him.

5.22 Critique of the Method

Piaget may have been surprised by the children, but psychologists were shocked by Piaget. The prevailing method in psychology is not his clinical method but the **experimental method.** Since he had never taken a course in psychology, Piaget did not know how he was supposed to do research. Even if he were to take a course in experimental psychology today, he would probably flunk. He breaks all the hallowed rules of the hallowed halls. He does not

---

*From *The Construction of Reality in the Child,* by J. Piaget. Copyright 1954 by Basic Books, Inc. Reprinted by permission.

review the relevant experiments of his colleagues or conduct experiments of his own. He does not set up precise hypotheses and the level of significance at which they will be knocked down. He does not select a careful sample of subjects. He does not manipulate an **independent variable,** control **extraneous variables,** and observe the effect on a **dependent variable.** In short, he does not use the experimental method.

If I may be so presumptuous as to put my Anglo-Saxon words into Piaget's Gallic mouth, he would argue as follows. The experimental method is indeed a powerful instrument that has greatly enhanced our understanding of the world and of ourselves. The logic of the experimental method is impeccable. If you vary the independent variable, control all the extraneous variables, and observe any change in the dependent variable, you can say that the variation in the independent variable is cause and the change in the dependent variable is effect. Such cause-effect relationships are the basis of science. What is questionable is not the logic of the method but its appropriateness for the study of all phenomena. It is not the logic used in thinking by children, nor is it the most appropriate logic for the study of the thinking of children. The experimental design is determined by the prejudices of the experimenter about how children think. This either forces the children to indeed think that way (another example of the self-fulfilling prophecy that will be discussed in Chapter 12) or to refuse perversely to think in the way the experimenter thinks they should think (thus causing the experimenter to stomp off muttering about confounding variables and confounded children). The experiment often reveals more about the thinking of the experimenter than about the thinking of the subject. It is necessary to use the clinical method, in which the behavior of the child determines the behavior of the adult, in order to preserve the spontaneous thinking of the child.

So much for the defense. Now to the attack. If you want to know how children think, you ask them—you don't tell them. This would seem obvious. You can't get to know by assuming that you already know. You ask them, but you don't ask them directly. "Hey, kid, are you adapting to your environment through alternating assimilations and accommodations?" They don't know how they think either. Indeed, I don't know how *I* think, and I bet you don't know how *you* think. But children think even though they don't know how they think, just as hens transform chicken feed into eggs and cows transform grass into milk without knowing how they do it. Children are, in a sense, the foremost authorities on thinking as children, and Piaget is the foremost authority on thinking about children thinking as children. So they work together. Children think and Piaget thinks about their thinking. Together they have developed a coherent and comprehensive description of mental development from child to adult. Like *children, description* is often qualified by *mere.* Such a put-down is no longer appropriate. Descriptive studies of development fell into disrepute because, in unimaginative heads, they tended to produce only variations on the statement "kids get better as they get older." Piaget and his army of children have made the description of development respectable again.

5.23 *Value of the Method to Teachers*

Piaget's method is simply a means to the end of his theory, which will be presented in the next section. However, even if you gain nothing from the theory, you can gain much from the method. His method embodies a respect—nay, reverence—for the spontaneous growth of the child. This is an appropriate attitude for the teacher to have toward the student (indeed, for anyone to have toward anyone else who has not proved unworthy of it). There is much talk of respect in education. However, it is usually about the student's respect for the teacher and seldom about the equally important teacher's respect for the student. The Black Power movement has sensitized us to our White chauvinism and the Feminist movement to our male chauvinism. Piaget helps sensitize us, White and Black, male and female, to our adult chauvinism. The Child Power movement is not very effective, since children are so small and powerless and tend to grow up and become the enemy. Children need the empathy of allies like Piaget who have never defected.

The method is useful not only as a general attitude but also as a specific tool. If you perform some of Piaget's experiments, you too can see the world once again through the eyes of a child. If you have a child around the house, you may want to try some of them right now. You will certainly want to try some of them when you have a class of your own. You will understand your students better and thus be better able to teach them. Just as an anthropologist must learn to see the world through the eyes of a preliterate tribal people in order to really communicate with them, so you must see the world through the eyes of a child.[167]

5.3 THE THEORY

5.31 *Function, Structure, and Content*

Developmental psychology was described earlier as the link between biology and epistemology. Developmental psychology is concerned with the *structure* of the nervous system, whereas biology is concerned with its function and epistemology with its content. Let's look in turn at function, structure, and content to see how structure links function to content.

Piaget, like Darwin, considers the function of the nervous system to be the adaptation of the organism to its environment. **Adaptation** involves the complementary processes of **assimilation** and **accommodation.** The nervous system assimilates information from the environment and, if necessary, accommodates to that information. The process of mental growth is like the progress of the worm, as it stretches its front forward and then pulls its back up. The alternating stretches and pulls of the worm correspond to the alternating assimilations and accommodations of the person. But what moves us to stretch and pull? The spate of evidence on the need for stimulation and the need for consistency (presented in Section 4.13) suggests the biological bases for assimilation and accommodation, respectively. We assimilate information from our environment because we have a need for stimulation, and we change to accommodate that information, if it is not consistent with the information already stored, because we have a need for consistency. A further analogy may help. The process of mental growth is, in another sense, like the progress of a person. Walking is a series of balancing and unbalancing acts. We throw ourselves off balance, recover our balance, throw ourselves off balance again, recover our balance again, and so on. Similarly, we throw ourselves off mental balance by assimilating input information that is inconsistent with stored information and recover our balance by changing to accommodate that information.

"——EVERY COGNITIVE INTERCHANGE WITH THE ENVIRONMENT INVOLVES BOTH ACCOMMODATION AND ASSIMILATION; EVERY INSTRUCTION FROM WITHOUT PRESUPPOSES A CONSTRUCTION FROM WITHIN."

JOHN H. FLAVELL
THE DEVELOPMENTAL PSYCHOLOGY
OF JEAN PIAGET

Because of the need for consistency, the stored information is organized into a structure. Inconsistent input information forces changes in this structure in order to accommodate it. When the structure changes qualitatively, the child is said to move into a new **stage.** There are three broad stages corresponding to three basic structures: **sensorimotor** (up to about 2 years), **concrete-operations** (2 to 11 years), and **formal-operations** (after 11 years). Of course, this is a very bold, bald statement. There are many substages within each stage, the transition from one stage to another is not abrupt, and the stages should not be tied too rigidly to ages. The content of your nervous system is the product of the alternating assimilations to and accommodations of those evolving structures. Your content is all the information you have assimilated from your environment. This information is not, however, simply poured in: it is assimilated to an organized structure of previous information, and that structure may have to change to accommodate it. Thus, structure mediates between function (alternating assimilations of and accommodations to information from the environment) and content (total information assimilated by the person from the environment).

This difficult relationship among the function, structure, and content of the nervous system may be clarified, perhaps, through analogy with human metabolism. The function of the metabolic system is also the adaptation of the organism to the environment. Adaptation involves the complementary processes of catabolism and anabolism. The metabolic system decomposes food into simple chemicals (catabolism) and then synthesizes those chemicals into the complex substances the organism requires in order to survive (anabolism). The processes of catabolism and anabolism in the metabolic system correspond roughly to the processes of assimilation and accommodation in the nervous system. Although any two normal metabolic systems are essentially the same in function and structure, they differ in content. The Eskimo eats whale blubber, the Englishman eats Yorkshire pudding, and the Carib reputedly ate other Caribs. Likewise, although any two normal nervous systems are essentially the same in function and structure, they differ in content. The Eskimo, the Englishman, and the Carib live in different environments and thus assimilate different sets of information from those environments. The analogy breaks down, however, because of qualitative differences between the two types of content—food and information. Whereas the metabolic system breaks down different foods into the same chemicals, the nervous system retains the different sets of information; that is, whereas whale blubber, Yorkshire pudding, and Carib are all reduced to the same chemicals, the perception and conception of whale blubber, Yorkshire pudding, and Carib are not. Your nervous system is your only contact with your environment, and it must "know" your particular environment so that you can survive in it. There is little biological point to the American stockbroker knowing the African jungle or the Pygmy knowing the Wall Street jungle. Piaget describes the catabolic-anabolic process of metabolism as follows: "When a rabbit eats cabbage, he is not changed into cabbage but, on the contrary, the cabbage is changed into rabbit."[174] However, the assimilation-accommodation process of the nervous system does, in a sense, change the rabbit into cabbage. As we assimilate information from our environment, our mind becomes a microcosm of that environment. As this map becomes more and more complete and more and more accurate, we become more and more adapted to our environment. We make ourselves at home in the world by making the world at home in us.

Piaget has done for **ontogenetic development** (from child to adult) what Darwin did for **phylogenetic development** (from animal to human). He has provided us with a three-dimensional description of development in all its length, breadth, and depth. Both Piaget and Darwin were confronted by essentially the same paradox, that development appears to be both continuous and discontinuous. They both resolve the paradox by describing development as a process of continuous discontinuity—continuous with respect to function, and discontinuous with respect to structure. Ontogenetic development, says Piaget, is continuous with respect to function (the person adapts to the environment through alternating assimilations and accommodations) but discontinuous with respect to structure (different structures emerge to accommodate to what is assimilated). Phylogenetic development, says Darwin, is continuous with respect to function (organisms evolve through adaptation to their environments) but discontinuous with respect to structure (different organisms evolve to fit different environments). Whereas Darwin had to convince us of the continuity, Piaget had to convince us of the discontinuity. Darwin had to overcome the prejudice that our species is unique; Piaget had to overcome the prejudice that the child is a miniature adult. Darwin and Piaget have humanized and matured us human adults by, paradoxically, showing us our kinship with animals and children.

5.32   Stages of Development

Now that Piaget has firmly anchored his developmental psychology to biology on the one side, through the structure-function relationship, and to epistemology on the other side, through the structure-content relationship, let us take a closer look. We already know that, as a different structure emerges, the child is said to move into a different stage, and that the three major stages are sensorimotor, concrete-operations, and formal-operations. Figure 5-1 may help you relate these unfamiliar stages to the more familiar dimensions of age and grade level. Here is a description of you during each of those stages.

5.321   Sensorimotor Stage.

You live in the here and now—not because your guru recommended it but because you have no option. Living in the there and then requires some internal representation of things that are not here and now. You have no such internal representation of your environment. You are interested in your environment only insofar as it is doing things to you (sensory) and you are doing things to it (motor). The behaviorists are right. You are indeed an S-R organism—up to the age of 2. Your work during your first two years is to coordinate stimuli and responses—stimulus with stimulus, stimulus with response, and response with response.

Coordinating stimulus with stimulus involves the acquisition of the object concept and object constancy. You now perceive the world as composed of objects, which continue to exist even when you are no longer looking at them **(object concept)** and which remain the same size despite variation in your distance from them, the same shape despite variation in your orientation to them, and the same brightness despite variation in the illumination on them **(object constancy).** That is, you believe the Statue of Liberty is still in New York harbor, where you last saw it, even though you are now back in Rattlesnake Gulch, Missouri, and that it would continue to be 150 feet high even if it were shipped back to France. It is difficult to imagine how the world could be seen otherwise. Yet children do, and you as a child did. When Piaget presented his daughter Jacqueline with a bottle, she made the appropriate reaching motions and gurgling noises as long as she could see it but lost interest in it completely when he put it behind his back. Out of sight, out of mind. This faith that an object exists independent of you (object concept) is a prerequisite

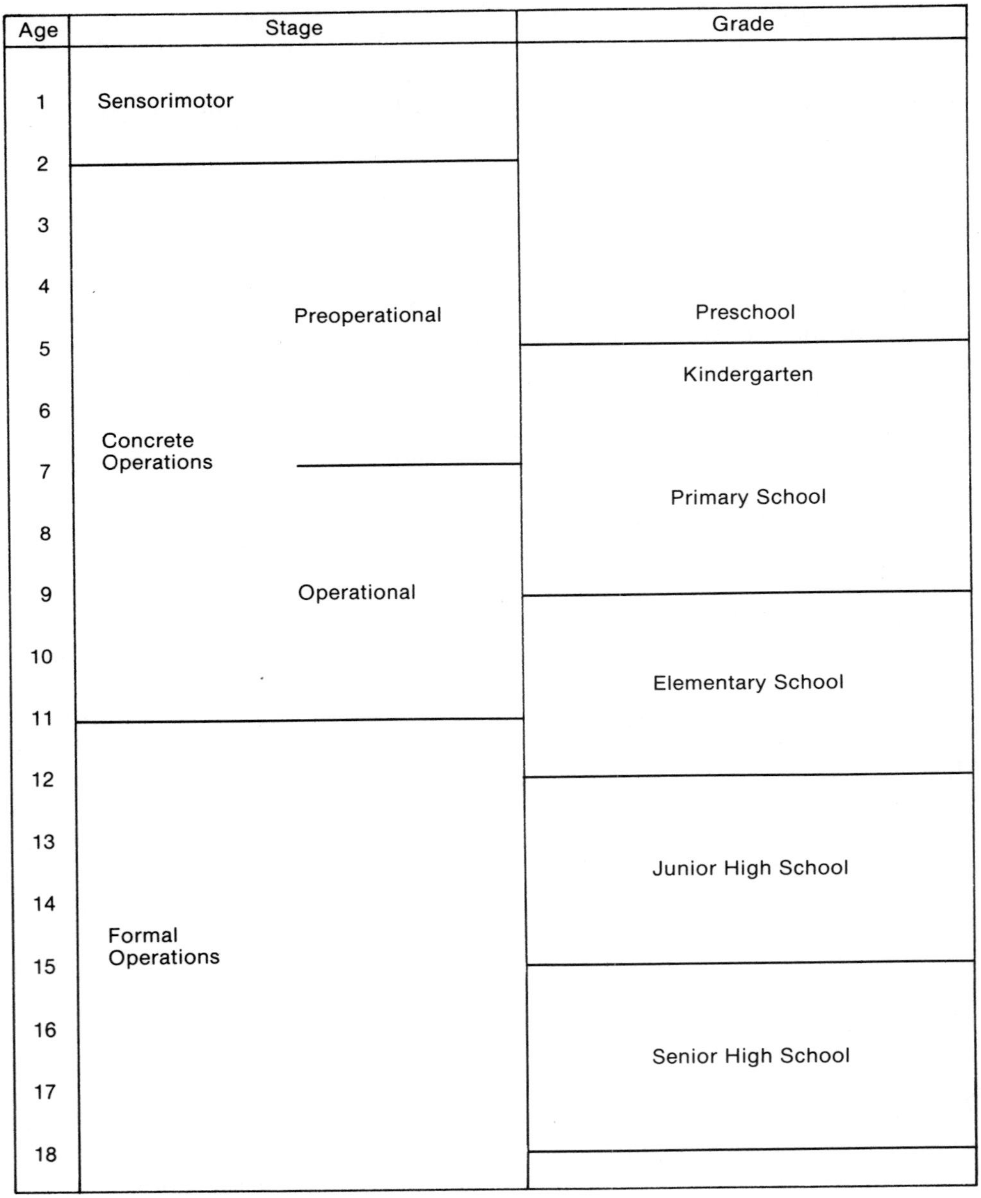

Age	Stage	Grade
1	Sensorimotor	
2		
3		
4	Preoperational	Preschool
5		Kindergarten
6	Concrete Operations	
7		Primary School
8		
9	Operational	
10		Elementary School
11		
12		Junior High School
13		
14		
15	Formal Operations	
16		Senior High School
17		
18		

Figure 5-1. Ages, stages, and grades

to the faith that it conserves its size, shape, and brightness despite variations in distance, orientation, and illumination (object constancy), and is one of your accomplishments during the sensorimotor stage.

Stimuli and responses get coordinated through a series of circular reactions. Between 1 and 4 months, you develop **primary circular reactions.** You happen to make the sound *ah* (response), you hear the sound (stimulus), you imitate the sound (response), you hear the sound again (stimulus) and so on as you imitate yourself again and again. Between 4 and 8 months, you develop **secondary circular reactions.** You happen to make a sound *dah* while your doting daddy is present (response), you see Daddy jumping up and down with excitement at being recognized (stimulus), you repeat the sound (response), Daddy jumps up and down some more (stimulus), and so on in that eternal process of two generations conditioning each other. This secondary reaction is centered on the environment, whereas the primary reaction was centered on the child. It is, in Piaget's words, "behavior designed to make interesting sights and sounds last." You have started to act on your environment. However, your behavior is not yet intentional. You have not yet disentangled your act as means from your desired end. You shake your rattle in order to produce those interesting sounds, but, if your rattle is taken away, you will continue to shake your arm. Between 12 and 18 months, you develop **tertiary circular reactions.** As before, you repeat a behavior that has an interesting effect, but you vary that behavior to see what change there will be on that effect. Thus, babbling is not just "ah, ah, ah, ah" as you imitate yourself in the primary circular reaction, nor just "dah, dah, dah, dah" as you perpetuate an interesting sight in the secondary circular reaction, but "ah, dah, mah, daah, damaa, maaaa" as you experiment to test the effect of your responses on your environment. You are conducting experiments. You are beginning your career as a scientist. You are not simply behaving in order to behave, you are behaving in order to check out your environment. Behavior was an end in itself, but it is now a means to other ends.

One president of the United States is reported to have said of another that he couldn't both walk and chew gum at the same time. This is true of all of us—up to the age of about 2. In your sensorimotor stage, you could not coordinate your responses. At birth, you have a small repertoire of reflexes: you can look at things, you can reach for things, you can grasp things, you can suck on things. During the first month, you exercise each of those reflexes individually. You look at, reach for, grasp, *or* suck on things. However, you cannot simultaneously look at and reach for a thing or successively look at, reach for, grasp, and suck on a thing. Your isolated responses are not organized into systems of responses until about 8 months. You then know objects purely in terms of those organized systems of responses to them. By 18 months, you begin to represent those objects as a system of internal responses. Such an internal representation of your environment heralds the beginning of mental life and the end of the sensorimotor stage.

5.322   *Concrete-Operations Stage*

As you move from the sensorimotor stage to the concrete-operations stage, you add indirect interactions with your environment to your repertoire of direct interactions. Such indirect interactions are made possible by internal representations of the environment, which are made possible, in turn, by the development of the **symbolic function**; that is, you learn to represent an object in your environment by something else. An object (such as a gun) may be represented by another object (a stick), a gesture (pointing a finger), a sound *(bang! bang!)*, a word *(gun)*, or an image (internal representation of a gun). Note that the word is only one of many possible representations of an object. The development of the symbolic function is a necessary condition for the development of language and not vice versa, as some theorists have argued.

IF YOU CALLED THESE SENSATIONS (SWEET AND SOUR) RESPECTIVELY BLACK AND WHITE, HE WOULD HAVE ADOPTED THEM AS READILY; BUT HE WOULD MEAN BY BLACK AND WHITE THE SAME THINGS THAT HE MEANS BY SWEET AND SOUR. —— IT IS NOT THE WORD, BUT THE CAPACITY TO EXPERIENCE THE SENSATION THAT COUNTS IN HIS EDUCATION.

HELEN KELLER
THE STORY OF MY LIFE
(QUOTING HER TEACHER, ANNE SULLIVAN)

The concrete-operations stage can be subdivided into **preoperational** and **operational substages.** In many classifications, preoperational is presented as a separate stage. However, I prefer to include it as part of the concrete-operations stage, since what is essentially a presensorimotor stage is included as part of the sensorimotor stage. Just as the sensorimotor child must practice isolated responses before organizing them into a system, so the concrete-operations child must practice isolated internal representations before organizing them into a system. The preoperational substage may perhaps best be considered as this preparatory phase of practice.

The preoperational substage can be described in terms of the "mistakes" you make as you explore your new, confusing world of symbols. Piaget illustrates two such mistakes in the following anecdotes about his children:[170]

When walking with his son, they passed a snail.
"There is a snail" said his son.
Later, they happened to pass another snail.
"There is the snail again" said his son.

Jacqueline, seeing her sister Lucienne in a new bathing suit with a cap, says to her mother:
"What's the baby's name?"
Her mother explained that it was a bathing costume.
However, Jacqueline pointed to Lucienne's face and asked:
"But what's the name of that?" repeating the question many times.
As soon as Lucienne had her dress on again, Jacqueline said very seriously: "It's Lucienne again" as if her sister had changed her identity by changing her clothes.

The first "mistake" (different members of a class—snail 1 and snail 2—in different contexts are the same member) and the second "mistake" (the same member of a class in different contexts—Lucienne-in-bathing-costume and Lucienne-in-dress—are different members) both illustrate that the child has concepts—the snails are fitted into the appropriate class of *snail* and Lucienne into the appropriate class of *baby*—but that the rules for dealing with the relationship between individual objects and classes of objects are not yet clear. When you reach the operational substage, those mistakes are corrected. You know that objects can be members of the same class yet be different objects and that an object may change contexts yet remain the same object. You can fit objects into classes and consider relationships between those classes. You are capable of **class reasoning.**

In the following experiment, Piaget illustrates another competence gained as you move from the preoperational to the operational phase of the concrete-operations stage.[171] Children are shown ten dolls of differing heights and ten miniature walking sticks also graded in height. They are told to arrange the dolls and sticks "so that each doll can easily find the stick that belongs to it." Preoperational children could not place the dolls or the sticks in order. They seemed to lack any organized procedure for doing this, such as finding the tallest doll, then the next tallest, and so on until the series is complete. They did not understand the principle that, if doll A is taller than doll B and doll B is taller than doll C, then doll A is taller than doll C. There was then a transitional stage during which the children could order the dolls and the sticks but could not assign the sticks to the dolls unless they were lined up evenly with them. Thus, if Piaget squeezed the row of sticks closer together or spread them further out, they could no longer tell which stick belonged to which doll. Finally, in the operational phase, the children could place both the dolls and the sticks in order and could assign the correct walking stick to each doll. Thus, at the end of the concrete-operations stage, you can place objects along dimensions and consider the relationships among them. You are capable of **ordinal reasoning.**

In summary, at the end of the concrete-operations stage, you are capable of both class and ordinal reasoning; that is, you can place things in your environment into classes and along dimensions. On this firm foundation of logic, you are now ready to build the superstructure of mathematics. Now that you know "doll A is taller than doll B" and "doll B is taller than doll C" implies "doll A is taller than doll C," you may be interested in making the more precise statement that "doll A is x units taller than doll B" and "doll B is y units taller than doll C" implies that "doll A is x plus y units taller than doll C." The natural numbers (1, 2, 3, . . .) make this possible. By placing those numbers evenly along your dimension, you can now see that doll A is, let us say, 9 units tall, doll B is 7 units tall and doll C is 4 units tall, that doll A is 2 units taller than doll B, that doll B is 3 units taller than doll C, and that, by implication, doll A is 5 units taller than doll C. Within this system of natural numbers, you can add and always get an answer. When you reverse this operation and subtract, you cannot always get an answer. Mathematicians invented zero to provide an answer when you subtract a number from itself and negative numbers to provide an answer when you subtract a number from a smaller number. When you multiply within this enlarged system of numbers, you can always get an answer, but when you reverse this operation and divide, you cannot always get an answer. Mathematicians invented fractions to provide an answer when you divided a number by another number that does not divide evenly. When you square within this system, you can always get an answer but, when you reverse this operation and take the square root, you cannot always get an answer. Mathematicians invented irrational numbers to provide an answer when you take the square root of a number that is not a perfect square. In the same way, more and more systems of numbers are invented to permit closure under more and more sophisticated operations, and thus the entire superstructure of mathematics is constructed. However, no matter how esoteric it becomes, it still rests on the foundation of class and ordinal reasoning, and you cannot assimilate it until you have mastered those basic logics.

5.323   *Formal-Operations Stage*

Having mastered concrete operations, you have the foundation for dealing with mathematical operations. You cannot yet deal, however, with some of the products of such operations. You cannot deal with negative numbers, irra-

"FINALLY, TO SAY THAT COGNITION IS RELATIVELY INDEPENDENT OF CONCRETE REALITY IS TO SAY THAT THE <u>CONTENT</u> OF A PROBLEM HAS AT LAST BEEN SUBORDINATED TO THE <u>FORM</u> OF RELATIONS WITHIN IT."

JOHN L. PHILLIPS
<u>THE ORIGINS OF INTELLECT: PIAGET'S THEORY</u>

tional numbers, or imaginary numbers (the square roots of negative numbers), because they have no concrete equivalents. You can deal with 5 oranges but not with –3 oranges or $\sqrt{7}$ oranges or $\sqrt{-2}$ oranges. You can see, smell, touch, and taste an orange but not a negative, irrational, or imaginary one. If I were to hand you three dolls—Mary, Sue, and Jane, Mary being taller than Sue and shorter than Jane—you would be able to line them up in order of height and tell me that Jane is the tallest of the three. However, if I merely *told* you that

YET MATHEMATICS CONSTITUTES A DIRECT EXTENSION OF LOGIC ITSELF, SO MUCH SO THAT IT IS ACTUALLY IMPOSSIBLE TO DRAW A FIRM LINE OF DEMARCATION BETWEEN THE TWO FIELDS — SO THAT IT IS DIFFICULT TO CONCEIVE HOW STUDENTS WHO ARE WELL ENDOWED WHEN IT COMES TO THE ELABORATION AND UTILIZATION OF THE SPONTANEOUS LOGICO-MATHEMATICAL STRUCTURES OF INTELLIGENCE CAN FIND THEMSELVES HANDICAPPED IN THE COMPREHENSION OF A BRANCH OF TEACHING THAT BEARS EXCLUSIVELY UPON WHAT IS TO BE DERIVED FROM SUCH STRUCTURES.

JEAN PIAGET
<u>SCIENCE OF EDUCATION AND THE PSYCHOLOGY OF THE CHILD</u>

"Mary is taller than Sue and Mary is shorter than Jane" and asked you "Who is the tallest of the three?" you would have great difficulty answering. You can do the problem in your hands but not in your head in much the same way as, at one point, you could count on your fingers but not in your head. In other words, you can perform operations on concrete objects but not on propositions about those objects. Your internal representation of your environment helps you deal more effectively with it, but you are not yet emancipated from it. You are capable of class and ordinal reasoning, but you are not yet capable of **propositional reasoning.** The following one-minute course in propositional logic may serve to demonstrate what you gained when you moved from the concrete-operations to the formal-operations stage.[69]

Let us imagine the box in Figure 5-2 as an empty universe and let us introduce into it the proposition. In the beginning, there was the proposition. At the risk of appearing unduly familiar at such early acquaintance, let us call it simply p. Propositions come in many guises—today is Thursday, now is the time for all good men to come to the aid of Jennifer, e equals m times c squared, Kafka is a kvetch—but they all have in common the fact that they may be said to be either true or false. Let us represent this fact, in shorthand, as p or $\bar{p}$, where p means proposition p is true and $\bar{p}$ means proposition p is false. Our proposition looks very lonely all alone in its empty universe. Let us then introduce another proposition, q, which, like all propositions, may be said to be either true or false. These two propositions together, all alone in an empty universe, will generate four possible states of affairs: p is true and q is true, p is true and q is false, p is false and q is true, p is false and q is false. These possibilities may be represented in shorthand as

$$p \cdot q \quad \text{or} \quad p \cdot \bar{q} \quad \text{or} \quad \bar{p} \cdot q \quad \text{or} \quad \bar{p} \cdot \bar{q}$$

There exists in the English language (and presumably in every language, although this is an open question worthy of empirical investigation) the means of eliminating every possible subset of alternatives from this set of four possible states of affairs. For instance, when we say "not both p and q," we are eliminating the first alternative; when we say "if p, then q," we are eliminating the second alternative; when we say "either p or q," we are eliminating the first and fourth alternatives; when we say "neither p nor q," we are eliminating the first, second, and third alternatives.

The following strategy may now be used to check your answers to the questions posed in Pre-exercise 3. The premises (the propositions after "Suppose you know that") eliminate certain of the four possible alternatives involving two propositions, and the status of the conclusion (the proposition after "Then would this be true?") is determined by the remaining alternatives. If the conclusion is contained in all the remaining alternatives, then it must be true (yes); if it is contained in some of the remaining alternatives, then it may be true (maybe); if it is contained in none of the remaining alternatives, then it can't be true (no). The answers, then, as indicated in Figure 5-2, are, respectively, yes, maybe, maybe, no.

	$p \cdot q$	$p \cdot \bar{q}$	$\bar{p} \cdot q$	$\bar{p} \cdot \bar{q}$
a. If p, then q		x		
$\quad p$			x	x
$\quad q$ YES				
b. If p, then q		x		
$\quad q$		x		x
$\quad p$ MAYBE				
c. If p, then q		x		
$\quad$ not p	x	x		
$\quad q$ MAYBE				
d. If p, then q		x		
$\quad$ not q	x		x	
$\quad p$ NO				

Column headings across the top of the figure:
$$p \quad (p \text{ or } \bar{p}) \qquad p \cdot q \text{ or } p \cdot \bar{q} \text{ or } \bar{p} \cdot q \text{ or } \bar{p} \cdot \bar{q} \qquad (q \text{ or } \bar{q})$$

Figure 5-2. Derivation of answers to questions posed in Pre-exercise 3.

A certain subset of propositions (for example, this is a typewriter, I am a Scotsman) states that a particular element is a member of a particular set. Because such propositions occur so often, the cumbersome "if x is a member of set A, then x is a member of set B" is compressed to "all As are Bs." The relations "some As are Bs" and "no As are Bs" can be generated in the same way. Class reasoning, involving the relations "all," "some," and "no," permits you to place the things in your environment into categories and to consider the relationships among those categories. In the same way, the subset of propositions stating the position of an element with respect to a point on a dimension generates the relations "is greater than," "is equal to," and "is less than"; and ordinal reasoning, involving those relations, permits you to place the things in your environment along dimensions and consider the relationships among their positions on those dimensions. In your concrete-operations stage, you can deal only with those two limited subareas of propositional reasoning—class reasoning and ordinal reasoning—because they refer directly to objects in your environment; in your formal-operations stage, you learn how to operate with propositions as well as objects and can thus deal with all propositional reasoning. The propositions need not be about objects in your environment. Indeed, the propositions can be counterfactual (If mice have ten legs, then they run faster than horses. Mice have ten legs. Therefore, mice run faster than horses.), nonsensical (If missions are stubils, then they are slevible. Missions are stubils. Therefore, missions are slevible.), or purely formal (If p, then q. p. Therefore, q.). The conclusion follows from the premises in each case because of the structure of the argument. The content does not matter. You are finally emancipated from your environment.

5.324   Summary of Development

In the most comprehensive book about Piaget available, Flavell lists 25 books and over 150 articles by Piaget and his coworkers (and this was in 1963, before Piaget really gained momentum).[58] It is presumptuous to compress this huge body of data, based on a lifetime of work, into a chapter, and it is very presumptuous to try to summarize it in a paragraph. Here is a very presumptuous paragraph.[*]

"INTELLECTUAL DEVELOPMENT MAY BE CONCEIVED AS A KIND OF TOYNBEEAN CHALLENGE-RESPONSE AFFAIR: AT SELECTED POINTS IN HIS DEVELOPMENT, THE SOCIUS THRUSTS THE CHILD INTO NEW ROLES WITH NEW AND DIFFERENT SETS OF COGNITIVE DEMANDS; THE CHILD RESPONDS TO THE CHALLENGE BY ACQUIRING THE NEW COGNITIVE STRUCTURES NEEDED TO COPE WITH THESE DEMANDS."

JOHN H. FLAVELL
THE DEVELOPMENTAL PSYCHOLOGY OF JEAN PIAGET

Your development was not the gradual accumulation of information and skills it appears when you look back on it. It was a series of revolutions in which you moved from one stage to another. "Each stage is qualitatively different from every other, but each results from the one that preceded it, and prepares the child for the one that follows."[119][†] First, you deal directly with your environment (sensorimotor stage), then with propositions about your environment (concrete-operations stage), and then with propositions about propositions (formal-operations stage). You free yourself from the tyranny of your environment by acting on it and thereby building up an internal representation of it. Your behavior is subsequently determined not only by your immediate environment but also by your map of it.

---

[*] Actually, my best rationalization is that I wrote it for a friend. I had been hibernating for the last few months reading books by and about Piaget. She asked what I had been doing. "Reading Piaget." "Who's that?" "Swiss psychologist who has a theory about child development." "What's the theory?" You too might find this paragraph useful for similar occasions.
[†] A little help from another friend.

POST-EXERCISES

1. An Essay on Jean Piaget

Write as many sentences as you can containing the name *Jean Piaget*. How does this post-exercise list differ from your pre-exercise list? Is it longer? Is it more accurate? What has happened in the interval? You gained some information from studying the intervening chapter? You got rid of some false information? "Jean Piaget is a Swiss lady who sells watches" was eliminated?

Organize your sentences into a coherent essay on Jean Piaget. How does this post-exercise essay differ from your pre-exercise essay? Is it more comprehensive? Is it more coherent? What has happened in the interval? You gained some understanding from studying the intervening chapter? You got rid of some misunderstandings?

Try to do this exercise without referring to this or any other book. If you are not yet satisfied with your essay, read the chapter again. You may find that some information that made no impression on you during your first reading will leap off the page at you during this second reading. This information is likely to be a missing part of your essay.

If you are still not satisfied with your essay, read other books and articles by and about Piaget until you *are* satisfied.

2. Piaget Experiments

Try some of Piaget's experiments. Note your results, your reactions to those results, and any understanding of children you gained through conducting the experiments. Try the same experiment with different children and different experiments with the same child. Note individual differences between children presented with the same task and differences among tasks presented to the same child.

The following books contain descriptions of experiments you may choose to conduct:

Almy, M., Chittenden, E., & Miller, P. *Young children's thinking.* New York: Teacher's College, Columbia University, 1966.

Forman, G., & Kuschner, D. *The child's construction of knowledge: Piaget for teaching children.* Monterey, Calif.: Brooks/Cole, 1977.

Ginsburg, H., & Opper, S. *Piaget's theory of intellectual development: An introduction.* Englewood Cliffs, N.J.: Prentice-Hall, 1969.

Lavatelli, C. S. *Piaget's theory applied to an early childhood curriculum.* Boston: American Science and Engineering, 1971.

The last book is accompanied by a teacher's guide and materials kit, *Early childhood education curriculum: A Piaget program.*

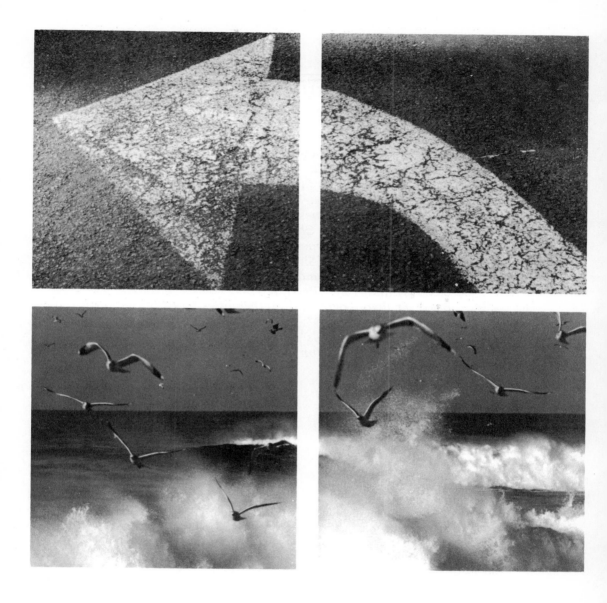

Readiness
and Critical Period

6

6 READINESS AND CRITICAL PERIOD

PRE-EXERCISES

1. A School System Based on Piaget's Theory

Think through some of the practical implications of a school system based on Piaget's theory. Could the arbitrary division of traditional schools (preschool, kindergarten, primary school, elementary school, junior high school, senior high school, college, university, graduate school) be replaced by a more rational division based on Piaget's stages (sensorimotor school, preoperational school, concrete-operations school, formal-operations school)? At what stage would it be appropriate to start formal schooling? To finish formal schooling? Are there stages when schooling would not help? If a child started school at a certain stage rather than a certain age, what would the entrance requirement be? How would a child "graduate" to the next school? What materials and procedures would be appropriate at each of these new schools?

"Sensorimotor school" is, of course, home. Is this first school better for some children than for others? What would be the effect of poor "schooling" at home on later schooling? How could a child with poor home schooling be better prepared for out-of-home schooling?

Schools based on Piaget's theory are not Utopian visions. They exist. Read the following books for descriptions of the new informal British elementary schools based on the theory of Piaget:

Featherstone, J. *Schools where children learn.* New York: Liveright, 1971.
Silberman, C. E. *Crisis in the classroom: The remaking of American education.* New York: Random House, 1970.

Weber, L. *The English infant school and informal education.* Englewood Cliffs, N.J.: Prentice-Hall, 1971.

Read the following book for a description of a school explicitly based on Piaget's theory but now—I regret—defunct:

Furth, H. G., & Wachs, H. *Thinking goes to school: Piaget's theory in practice.* New York: Oxford University Press, 1974.

Maria Montessori was, of course, "applying" Piaget's theory long before Piaget developed it. You may like to read Elkind's article summarizing the parallels and divergences between Montessori and Piaget:

Elkind, D. Piaget and Montessori. *Harvard Educational Review,* 1967, *37*(4), 535–545.

You might also like to read some books by Maria Montessori:

Montessori, M. *The Montessori method.* New York: Stokes, 1912.
    Spontaneous activity in education. New York: Schocken, 1966.
    The discovery of the child. Notre Dame, Ind.: Fides, 1967.

Here are some books *about* Maria Montessori:

Lillard, P. *Montessori: A modern approach.* New York: Schocken, 1972.
Rambusch, N. M. *Learning how to learn: An American approach to Montessori.* Baltimore: Helicon Press, 1962.
Standing, E. M. *The Montessori revolution.* New York: Schocken, 1966.

You might also visit a nearby Montessori school. Such Montessori schools will provide a foretaste of Piaget schools, since the Montessori methods are the Piaget principles in practice.

2. The Open Classroom

The most distinctive feature of the British elementary schools based on Piaget's theory, and more and more schools elsewhere, is the open classroom. The following sources may provide some useful suggestions for "opening" your classroom (or, at least, setting the door slightly ajar).

Barth, R. S. *Open education and the American school.* New York: Agathon, 1972.
Blitz, B. *The open classroom: Making it work.* Boston: Allyn & Bacon, 1973.
Brown, M., & Precious, N. *The integrated day in the primary schools.* New York: Ballantine, 1973.
Gingell, L. P. *The ABCs of the open classroom.* Homewood, Ill.: ETC, 1973.
Hertzberg, A., & Stone, E. *Schools are for children: An American approach to the open classroom.* New York: Schocken, 1971.
Kohl, H. R. *The open classroom: A practical guide to a new way of teaching.* New York: Random House, 1969.
Nyquist, E. B., & Hawes, G. R. *Open education: A sourcebook for parents and teachers.* New York: Bantam, 1972.

Perrone, V. *Open education: Promise and problems.* Bloomington, Ind.: Phi Delta Kappa, 1972.

Ramey, C. T., & Piper, V. Creativity in open and traditional classrooms. *Child Development,* 1974, *45,* 557–560.

Rathbone, C. H. Examining the open education classroom. *School Review,* 1972, *80*(4), 521–549.

Silberman, C. E. (Ed.). *The open classroom reader.* New York: Vintage, 1973.

Silberman, M. L., Allender, J. S., & Yanoff, J. M. (Eds.). *The psychology of open teaching and learning: An inquiry approach.* Boston: Little, Brown, 1972.

Sullivan, J. Open-traditional: What is the difference? *Elementary School Journal,* 1974, *74,* 493–500.

6.1 TIMING IN TEACHING

Many innovative educators—Dewey, Montessori, Rousseau, Neill, Rogers, Holt, and so on—have pointed out the need to respect the spontaneous growth of the child and to provide a congenial environment for that growth. However, their position was based on their intuition and personal experience. Piaget now provides a comprehensive and coherent theory, based on sound scientific evidence, for the practices they advocated. Furth and Wachs argue

WILLIAM WORDSWORTH
"MY HEART LEAPS UP WHEN I BEHOLD"

that an enlightened acceptance of Piaget's theory would bring about an educational revolution.[63] Let us see what an educational system based on Piaget's theory would perhaps be like by exploring some of its practical implications. One useful way to consider the practical implications of Piaget's theory is through the question of timing in teaching.

THE CHILDHOOD SHOWS THE MAN, AS MORNING SHOWS THE DAY.

JOHN MILTON
PARADISE REGAINED

An important skill in teaching (as in all arts) is timing. Outside-in teachers consider timing in terms of the optimal spacing of the appropriate sequence of instruction provided to the student. Inside-out teachers consider timing in terms of the optimal stage in the maturation schedule of the student for instruction. We learn about the outside-in process of instruction in courses on "Learning and Instruction," we learn about the inside-out process of development in courses on "Human Development," but we seldom learn how to coordinate those two sets of information to dovetail instruction to development.* This is the skill of timing. Conventional wisdom advises us to "strike while the iron is hot" and to "make hay while the sun shines." Since matura-

---

* Those were the titles of the two courses I was assigned at the University of Alberta. Such a division of content is necessary for administrative convenience. It was ironic, however, that the major point I made in each course was the intimate interaction between development and instruction. They can be separated only in college catalogs.

tion is a complex and hidden process, it is not easy to check whether the iron is hot or the sun is shining. Timing in teaching is, therefore, a subtler skill than it is in most other arts.

Timing involves being neither too early nor too late. We tend to assume that the issue of timing in teaching is much like that of catching a train: too late is a disaster, but too soon is merely an inconvenience. However, I will argue that too early can be as tragic as too late. Our progress through life could be summed up in terms of the instructions from the starter in a foot race—we "get ready," we "get set," and then we "go." A teacher can help students in their life race by providing appropriate instruction between the "get ready" and the "get set." "Get ready" corresponds to the concept of **readiness** and "get set" corresponds to the concept of **critical period.** Instruction must be neither too early, before the student is ready, nor too late, after the critical period is past. Let us look at each concept in turn.

6.2   READINESS

6.21   Thesis: Outside-In View

6.211   Guided Growth

Outside-inners consider timing in terms of **guided growth.** Growth is too important to be left entirely to the grower; it should be guided from the outside in. We have always known that motor development involves a series of stages, each of which is a prerequisite for the next. We must sit before we stand, stand before we walk, walk before we run, and run before we play soccer. We have recently learned that mental growth also involves such a series of prerequisite stages. We must determine the sequence of such stages and guide children through them. Extreme outside-inners argue that, not only is the mind a *tabula rasa,* or blank slate, at birth, but that the *tabula* will remain *rasa* unless they write on it. Completely denying the fact that the child is growing from the inside out, they attempt to "grow" the child entirely from the outside in. In the interests of efficiency, they "grow" the child as fast as possible.

"WHEN A PERSON IS READY, HE WILL MAKE HIS NEXT MOVE. FORCING HIM TO MOVE BEFORE HE IS READY IS LIABLE TO MAKE HIM OVERCAUTIOUS OR RELUC- TANT LATER, WHEN HE IS FACED WITH THAT NEXT MOVE. ON THE OTHER SIDE, AND PERHAPS EVEN WORSE, MAKING THE MOVE FOR HIM, AMONG OTHER CONSEQUENCES, DEPRIVES HIM OF THE EXPERI- ENCE OF KNOWING THAT HE IS CAPABLE OF DOING IT HIMSELF."

GEORGE BROWN
HUMAN TEACHING FOR HUMAN LEARNING

6.212   William James Sidis, a Force-Fed Child

Such an extreme outside-inner was Boris Sidis, a professor of abnormal psychology at Harvard University.[187] He believed that geniuses were not born but created by scientific teaching techniques and he proceeded to demonstrate his theory with his son, called William James in anticipation of emulating that other genius. William James Sidis had alphabet blocks suspended over his crib before he was 6 months old, was banging away on a typewriter at 2, learning Latin and Greek at 6, and banging on Harvard's door at 9. He was admitted at 11, lectured to the science faculty on four-dimensional bodies during his first year, and was graduated magna cum laude. So far so good. But then something broke. He abruptly withdrew from academic work and took the lowliest jobs he could find. Although he feigned stupidity with genius, he sometimes let his genius show through and had to refuse promotions. Most of his "genius" during his adult life was devoted to amassing a huge collection of streetcar transfers, to which he became fanatically attached as a symbol of his freedom during the streetcar rides between his home and Harvard University. This **force-fed child** grew into a tragic, lonely, obese man wandering around Boston with a spiked stick to rescue discarded streetcar transfers from the gutters.

6.22   Antithesis: Inside-Out View

6.221   Natural Readiness

Identical twins, T and C, were trained in stair-climbing just before the stair-climbing stage in motor development.[73] T was given six weeks' training and then C was given two weeks' training. After the eight weeks, both were tested and both did equally well. Thus, two weeks' training at the correct time is as valuable as six weeks' training at the wrong time. What is the correct time? The time at which the child is "ready" to climb stairs. It is futile to provide training for a task before the maturation necessary for performing that task has taken place. Maturation is not only a necessary condition for motor development but almost a sufficient condition. Instruction plays a very minor role. Hopi Indian children are strapped onto cradleboards as soon as they are born and remain there for the first three months (except, of course, for short periods when they are taken off to be washed) and for less and less time as they get older. Two Hopi Indian villages succumbed to the strange ways of the White man and left their children lying around loose. A study comparing the motor development of cradleboarded and noncradleboarded Hopi Indian children found no difference.[42] The children who spent most of their early months hanging around from their mothers' backs and the branches of trees unable to move anything but their heads developed just as well as those with complete freedom of movement. Thus, motor development is a matter of inside-out maturation relatively unaffected by outside-in learning. Surveys of such studies conclude that instruction is more effective when given to older children than when given to younger children.[11,87]

On the basis of those studies, inside-outers developed the concept of **natural readiness:** do not provide instruction until the children are ready for it. The best judge of readiness is the child. Let children learn in their own way at their own time and at their own pace. Extreme inside-outers (including one of my more naive former selves) argue that adults should not "interfere" at all in the maturation process. We should merely sit back and gaze, with awe, on the wondrous unfolding of the human potential. No one is sufficiently committed to this extreme view to let a child grow totally untrammeled by interference. The experiment has, however, been conducted by accident. A number of children, abandoned at an early age, have survived—usually with the help of animals. Let us consider, by way of example, one such **feral child.**

6.222   Victor, a Feral Child

Victor was 11 or 12 when he was spotted, completely naked, in the Caune Woods in France and captured as he climbed a tree trying to escape.[98] When news of his capture reached Paris, fashionable society speculated about Rousseau's "noble savage." Victor was more "savage" than "noble." He grunted like an animal, grubbed for roots and acorns to eat, and bit and scratched those who opposed him. Other romantics, who expected a fine physical specimen like, say, Tarzan, were equally disappointed. Victor was filthy, scarred, stunted, and trotted on all fours rather than swinging from tree to tree. All such feral children are more like the animals that reared them than the humans that bore them. Itard, who undertook the belated socialization of Victor, was never able to teach Victor to speak and could teach him to read only a few simple words and phrases, despite intensive efforts over five years.

6.23   Synthesis: Interactionism

6.231   Set Menu and Smorgasbord

We do not want our children to become like either Victor, the feral child, or William James Sidis, the force-fed child. No serious theorist would argue for either of the extreme positions that produced them. Every theorist advocates some position along a dimension ranging from total emphasis on inside-out maturation to total emphasis on outside-in instruction. Exponents of natural readiness tend toward the inside-out end of the dimension, and exponents of guided growth tend toward the outside-in end of the dimension.

Every theorist agrees that mental growth requires nourishment and that children should not be required to forage for their own food (extreme inside-out view) or be force-fed (extreme outside-in view). The debate is whether to present the intellectual fare as a smorgasbord or as a set menu. Advocates of natural readiness prefer the smorgasbord. Lay out a rich variety of resources and allow children to choose however much of whatever dishes in whatever order they desire. All you can eat for $4.50. If you have a big appetite, then you get your money's worth. Advocates of guided growth prefer the set menu. Find a healthy and balanced meal for the typical child at a given grade level and provide this set menu as the curriculum for that grade. Each "dish" is a prerequisite for the next. If you don't eat your potatoes, you don't get dessert.

"— ANY SUBJECT CAN BE TAUGHT EFFECTIVELY IN SOME INTELLECTUALLY HONEST FORM TO ANY CHILD AT ANY STAGE OF DEVELOPMENT. "

JEROME S. BRUNER
THE PROCESS OF EDUCATION

Bruner prefers the set menu. He dismisses natural readiness as a "mischievous half-truth" and then proceeds to present the alternative mischievous half-truth of guided growth.[25] Impressed by the ease with which children spontaneously learn to walk and to talk, devotees of natural readiness wait for them to develop mental skills spontaneously.* It will be a long wait. Bruner recommends that we not wait for them to get ready but get them ready. Readiness can be taught. It is the mastery of simple skills which are prerequisites for complex skills. If you wish to teach calculus in grade 8, then begin your teaching in grade 1 by teaching the prerequisite simple skills. Bruner's famous dictum—"any subject can be taught to anybody at any age in some form that is honest"[24]—provides a refreshing shift of onus from the student to the teacher. When we fail to teach, we should not shrug off our failure by saying "they are not ready yet" but should learn how to present our material in a form for which they *are* ready. However, two mischievous half-truths do not make one well-behaved whole truth. There is indeed an inside-out maturational schedule that cannot be ignored no matter how competent the outside-in instruction. There can be "too much too soon" as well as "too little too late." We will later consider the possibility of a child being "intellectually burned" by being introduced to numbers before the logical foundation for them is laid down (Section 6.232) and the unfortunately premature shift from the intrinsic motivation of thinking to the extrinsic motivation of reading (Section 6.233).

Piaget prefers the smorgasbord. Although he leans more toward the natural-readiness position than Bruner, he too argues against its extreme version. Development involves a complex interaction between inside-out matura-

---

* Natural readiness may apply to simple motor skills like walking and talking but not to *complex* motor skills. In a radio commentary on a soccer match the other day, I heard "the goalkeeper instinctively dived to the left to stop the point-blank shot." It took that goalkeeper years of tough, disciplined training to develop that "instinct." My instinct would have been to dive to the right, *away* from the ball.

tional processes and outside-in learning processes right from birth (or possibly even before). Readiness can never be "natural," then, in the extreme sense of totally spontaneous maturation. The child does not mature in a vacuum. Outside-in assimilation is necessary to trigger inside-out accommodation. There can be no accommodation without assimilation. Either accommodating in a vacuum or assimilating to a vacuum would be most "unnatural." Natural readiness refers to the stage of growth a child has reached through alternating assimilations and accommodations.

The distinction between activities that can be left to "doing what comes naturally" and activities that can't may be illustrated by a comparison between babbling and scribbling. Babbling is the basic act on which speaking is based, and scribbling is the basic act on which writing is based. Babbling and scribbling are both initiated spontaneously and are both maintained through feedback. However, feedback in the case of babbling is internal, whereas feedback in the case of scribbling is external. The child makes a sound, hears the sound, repeats the sound, hears the sound again, and so on in that "primary circular reaction" described in Section 5.321. An equivalent primary circular reaction maintains scribbling. The child makes a mark, sees the mark, repeats the mark, sees the mark again, and so on. When children were given paper and two tools, one of which made a mark and the other of which didn't, they continued to scribble with the marking tool but not with the nonmarking tool.[76] Feedback from the act itself is not enough to maintain it—the act must make some impression on the environment. Teachers can contribute to the continuation of such activities by arranging circumstances so that the child's environment is "impressed" by those activities.

This modified version of natural readiness is the basis of much modern practice. If readiness is a function of maturation *and* experience, then teachers can contribute to readiness by designing appropriate experience. Just as physical growth requires food and drink, so mental growth "feeds" on input and feedback information. Parents and teachers can provide stimulation and responsiveness for the minds of children just as they supply food and drink for their bodies. Just as a child can be physically stunted by inadequate or inappropriate food, so a child can be mentally stunted by inadequate or inappropriate information. The relative unreadiness of underprivileged children for schooling is due to limitations in the experiential rather than the maturational component of readiness. The Coleman Report concluded that social class showed a consistent relationship with academic performance.[31] It recommended that educational opportunity be shifted from equality of resources (input) to equality of achievement (output). Project Head Start was an attempt to compensate for the impoverished environment of lower-class children by providing them with the enriching experience that middle-class children get automatically at home. Television programs like *Sesame Street* and *The Electric Company* are alternative attempts to provide the enriching experience that primes readiness for schooling.

6.232 Development and Learning

I suggested earlier that the major dichotomy dividing educators is between those who advocate inside-out education and those who advocate outside-in education, and that education is, of course, some complex interaction between inside-out and outside-in processes. Piaget's view of the relationship between development and learning (roughly equivalent to inside-out and outside-in processes) helps clarify this complex interaction. Because of his emphasis on the intimate interaction between outside-in and inside-out processes, Piaget is often described as an **interactionist.**

Development is based on general experience, whereas **learning** is based on specific experience. General experience is that experience we all share as members of the same species on the same planet. Consider an Eskimo child living in an igloo, a Hottentot child living in a grass hut, and a New England child living in a bungalow. They share the experience that their dwelling—whether igloo, grass hut, or bungalow—maintains a constant size, color, and shape despite variation in distance from it, light shining on it, or orientation to it. This law of object constancy is learned by all children because it is a universal law of nature and they are all members of a species designed to know that law. The children differ, however, in specific experience. The Eskimo child learns that houses are made of ice, the Hottentot child learns that houses are made of grass, and the New England child learns that houses are made of shingles.

Laws, which become known through the inside-out process of development, are more substantial than facts, which are learned through the outside-in process of learning. They do not require extrinsic motivation. One of the functions of the nervous system of our species is to know those laws, and this function must be exercised. They cannot be forgotten. An adult Eskimo who has gone to live in a Los Angeles suburb may forget how to build an igloo but will never "forget" that igloos, like all objects, conform to the law of object constancy. Such laws are not subject to error. The outside-in information changes from place to place and from time to time, but the inside-out information does not change.

Development is the primary process, and learning is the secondary process. Development provides the structure for knowledge (laws), and learning provides the content (facts). Development is to learning as the basket is to the eggs. Learning theorists have failed to have a significant impact on education because they erroneously see learning as the primary process; they do not see it within the context of development. Indeed, they view development as the accumulation of successive learnings. Learning to learn is a step in the direction of developmentlike processes, but the first learning tends to be seen as similar to the second learning. Any mother could tell them that the developmental process they ignore is much more basic than the learning process. The child is growing from the inside out—not being "growed" from the outside in.

This does not mean that learning is unimportant. Development is a necessary condition for growth, but not a sufficient condition. There is little point in getting your basket if you are not going to gather any eggs. Indeed, as children grow older, learning becomes more important. Adolescents in the formal-operations stage have their baskets and now need lots of eggs. The full potential to be human is present at conception, but this potential can only be realized stage by stage. It is realized through learning. It is necessary to assimilate specific information from the environment (that is, to learn) in order to trigger the accommodation process that forces the child into the next stage (that is, to develop). The law that certain properties of objects remain constant despite variations in conditions under which they are viewed is a function of development, but this generalization can be reached only after assimilating experience with myriads of objects, which is a function of learning. Children are architects of their own growth, but they need materials with which to build themselves.

Now that Piaget has painted the broad picture of inside-out development, we can dovetail our outside-in teaching to it. The inside-outers are correct in emphasizing development, since development is the primary process and the secondary process of learning must be geared to it. However, the outside-inners are correct in emphasizing learning, since the teacher can do nothing about development directly. There are critical periods for the assimilation of particular information: the same information presented sooner or later cannot be accommodated. Rather than the traditional strategy of trying to maximize outside-in learning by cramming in as much information as possible as soon as possible, we are now able to optimize outside-in learning by presenting information appropriate to each level of development. What is appropriate? Hunt, who calls this "the problem of the match," suggests that the best criteria of appropriateness are spontaneous interest and surprise.[96] We tend to be interested in what is moderately novel—neither too familiar nor too unfamiliar. The appropriate level of difficulty of a task is, of course, neither too easy (students get bored) nor too difficult (students get frustrated). It should be within the students' capacity but should challenge them. Walker provides a theoretical basis for appropriate difficulty level and surprise value in terms of the optimal complexity of the material presented to the student.[226] A skillful teacher monitors the behavior of the student to maintain the complexity of the material within the range between the level at which the student quits working out of boredom and the level at which the student quits trying out of frustration.

It is obvious that an infant will not be interested in solving quadratic equations or an adolescent in piling blocks. It is in the less obvious cases that Piaget's timetable of development is useful. It has not been obvious, for example, that class and ordinal reasoning is a necessary condition for dealing with numbers. Students can gain nothing from instruction about numbers before this logical foundation is laid. The ruler in their heads is made of rubber. A premature introduction to numbers may be worse than useless. The children may get intellectually burned and decide that they are "not good at figures."* The teacher may also present information that is not only challenging but surprising. Dissonant information at the appropriate time unbalances students and facilitates the accommodation process required to regain balance. Children grow, paradoxically, by *not* having their expectations confirmed.

When Piaget describes a developmental process to a North American audience, he is invariably asked "How do you accelerate it?" We seem preoccupied with getting there fast even though we don't know where "there" is, why we want to "get there," or what to do when "there" is reached. Piaget's answer to what he calls "The American Question" is that development should be facilitated but not forced. We must respect the spontaneous growth of children. Let them grow in their own way and at their own rate. This rate is indeed faster for children from enriched environments than for children in impoverished environments. By all means, enrich impoverished environments, provide the input necessary to trigger mental growth. However, there seems little value in teaching laws of nature directly. The consensus of experimental evidence seems to be that any apparent gain is due to false accommodation to verbal formulas.[107,208] A great deal of such pseudolearning takes place in our schools, where teaching is not geared to the development of the child. Piaget himself points out:

> This is the big danger of school—false accommodation which satisfies the child because it agrees with a verbal formula he has been given. This is a false equilibrium which satisfies a child by accommodating to words—to authority and not to objects as they present themselves to him. A teacher would do better not to correct a child's schemas, but to provide situations so he will correct them himself.[181]

Collections of children's errors (for example, "The equator is a menagerie lion running around the earth and through Africa," "Our Father, who art in heaven, Harold be thy name," and so on)—often presented condescendingly as cute—are evidence of this empty verbalization. William James provides further evidence in this anecdote from his *Talks to Teachers:*

---

* Every time I introduced an equation or graph or anything that smacked of mathematics in my university class, many students shuddered with apprehension. The reaction was so intense that I assumed there was some biological basis for it. Their mothers had been scared by a square-root sign when they were in the womb, or they had had a traumatic experience with a surd when very young. Now I realize that it was not so much biological as a failure of culture to recognize biology. They are the people who were once burned and are now shy. This "math anxiety" is further illustrated by negative reactions of reviewers and students to the decimal system used in this book. This Section 6.232 is, obviously, the second sub-subsection of the third subsection of the second section of the sixth chapter. Yet some people would prefer a messy mélange of notations like Section 6 II c ii, since it looks less like mathematics. There is a course on "Math Anxiety" offered at the University of California at Santa Cruz. I just overheard a student saying "I'm not taking that course—I already *have* math anxiety."

A friend of mine, visiting a school, was asked to examine a young class in geography. Glancing at the book, she said: "Suppose you should dig a hole in the ground, hundreds of feet deep, how should you find it at the bottom—warmer or colder than on top?" None of the class replying, the teacher said: "I'm sure they know, but I think you don't ask the question quite rightly. Let me try." So, taking the book, she asked: "In what condition is the interior of the globe?" and received the immediate answer from half the class at once: "The interior of the globe is in a condition of igneous fusion."[101]

6.233 *Thinking and Reading*

Furth has argued that such empty verbalizations are due to an inappropriate emphasis on language at the expense of thought in early schooling.[62] This heavy emphasis is partly due to our **adultocentrism.** We look down on children from our lofty perspective and wonder how they may best be transformed into adults. This is a worthy end, since that seems to be the children's basic project, too. However, our means may be inappropriate. The most obvious difference between children and adults is that children are smaller. We recognize that we can do little about this from the outside in. We can only provide food and drink and leave physical growth to inside-out development. The next most obvious difference is that children are less articulate than adults. This we feel we *can* do something about from the outside in. We proceed to make them more articulate by teaching them language—as much as possible as soon as possible. Furth argues, on the basis of Piaget's theory, that our faith in physical growth from the inside out is equally justified with respect to mental growth. Provide food for the mind—stimulation and responsiveness—and leave mental growth to inside-out development. In this inside-out process, language plays a smaller role than is traditionally assumed. Language is a symptom of thought and not its source. As mentioned earlier, words are just one of many possible elements in the symbolization process. Adult articulateness is a function of superior logic rather than of a larger vocabulary.

If specific outside-in information were crucial to development, people with sensory limitations, like the blind and the deaf, would be at a great disadvantage. If language were crucial, deaf-mutes would suffer a double disadvantage. However, Furth has found that the mental development of deaf-mutes is only slightly retarded.[61] The example of Helen Keller, who developed a powerful intelligence although blind, deaf, and mute, is strong evidence for the relative importance of inside-out development over outside-in learning.[111]

A major advantage of an emphasis on thinking rather than reading is that the motivation for the inside-out development of thinking is intrinsic, whereas the motivation for the outside-in learning of reading is extrinsic. Thinking is an end in itself, whereas reading is too often a means to some other end—to please parents or compete with siblings, to imitate peers or impress teachers. Shifting from an emphasis on thinking to an emphasis on reading is like switching off the engine in your car and pushing and pulling it around. A child

BEFORE THE CHILD CAME TO SCHOOL, HE HAD TAUGHT HIMSELF TO DO A HOST OF THINGS THAT WERE MORE DIFFICULT THAN ANYTHING HE WILL EVER ACHIEVE AGAIN — HE TAUGHT HIMSELF TO TALK, HE TAUGHT HIMSELF TO USE EVERY MUSCLE OF HIS BODY, HE TAUGHT HIMSELF TO THINK, TO MAKE SOME KIND OF ORDER OUT OF THE CONFUSION OF THE WORLD.

W.R. WEES
NOBODY CAN TEACH ANY ONE ANYTHING

who has learned to think will come to realize the value of reading and will "learn to read in the easy, self-taught fashion of many preschool youngsters from homes where reading is an everyday activity."[62] Look at the world through a mirror. You will notice that certain aspects of your world look "funny"—street signs, billboards, storefronts—that is, those aspects containing writing. This exercise gives you a glimpse into the world of the illiterate. If you concede, as argued earlier, that a child is strongly motivated to make sense of the world, then you must agree that there is a strong intrinsic motivation to become literate.

6.234   *English, Logic, and Mathematics*

We learn English in English class and mathematics in mathematics class. Typically we close the English compartment of our minds with our English books and open the mathematics compartment with our mathematics books. Although good teachers of mathematics often point out that mathematics is simply English (or Eskimo or Egyptian or Ethiopian) made more precise, few students become fully aware that they are just two different aspects of language.

This fact becomes clear when we see the relationship between logic and English, on the one hand, and between logic and mathematics, on the other. The relationship between logic and English is presented in Chapter 9. **Language** is a hierarchy of units (phonemes, morphemes, sentences, and discourses) plus rules for combining units at one level to yield meaningful units at the next level. In English classes, you learn the rules for combining phonemes to yield morphemes (vocabulary) and for combining morphemes to yield sentences (grammar) but not for combining sentences to yield discourses (logic). The relationship between logic and mathematics was presented in Section 5.323. Class and ordinal logic enables us to deal with propositions (roughly speaking, that subset of sentences followed by a period rather than a question mark or an exclamation point) that place the things in our environment into categories and along dimensions. The natural numbers permit us to place them more precisely along dimensions, and the other number systems are introduced to permit closure under various operations. Mathematics thus evolves out of logic which, in turn, evolves out of English.

You may have answered yes to question 2 and no to question 3 in pre-exercise 3 to Chapter 5. Don't be upset. The majority of university students commit what logicians call the "fallacy of asserting the antecedent" and the "fallacy of denying the consequent." Be concerned, however. Since those rules are obviously not learned, they should be taught. Logic should be part of the

T'IS EDUCATION FORMS THE COMMON MIND:
JUST AS THE TWIG IS BENT, THE TREE'S INCLINED.

ALEXANDER POPE
MORAL ESSAYS

elementary and secondary school curriculum and not simply an optional, esoteric branch of philosophy in the university. Since logic is the link between English and mathematics, the failure to teach it drives a wedge between artists, who speak English, and scientists, who speak mathematics. It creates what Snow calls "the two cultures"—the innumerate artists and the illiterate scientists, who cannot communicate with one another and who cannot realize their full human potential by using all aspects of the most powerful human tool, language.[209]

Logic is just one of 12 aspects or, alternatively, one of 3 dimensions of what Ennis calls critical thinking. In an article and, subsequently, in a book, he provides a careful analysis of this neglected aspect of thinking—"the correct assessing of statements"—and argues convincingly for instruction in critical thinking in the schools.[51,52]

6.3 CRITICAL PERIOD

6.31 Imprinting in Animals

We tend to think that animal behavior is mainly determined by genetic factors whereas human behavior is mainly determined by environmental factors. As evidence for this, we point to the fact that there is little variation in the behavior of individual animals within a species and *much* variation in the behavior of individual humans within our species. This inference is essentially accurate but requires some qualification. We have already considered Maslow's argument that human behavior is more determined by genetic factors than is traditionally assumed. We are all moved by the same hierarchy of "instinctoid" needs, and the great diversity from individual to individual is due to the variety of means of satisfying those needs and degrees to which they are satisfied. Let us now consider Lorenz's argument that animal behavior is more determined by environmental factors than is traditionally assumed.[123] The little diversity from individual to individual within a species is due to the fact that, under normal circumstances, all members of the species are exposed to the same environment. Lorenz created abnormal circumstances and produced unnatural behavior.

Baby geese follow mother goose. Since all baby geese follow mother goose, it was assumed that this behavior was genetically determined. However, Lorenz arranged that the first large moving object goslings saw on emerging from the egg was not mother goose but Lorenz himself and observed that those baby geese followed him. It seems that nature leaves a blank in the genetic blueprint to be filled in by the environment, through an early, rapid, and more or less permanent form of learning called **imprinting.** Under normal circumstances (when there is no wise guy like Lorenz around interfering with nature's plans), the first large moving object is mother goose, and the biologically useful behavior of following mother goose is established. When Spalding performed a similar experiment, the baby geese did not follow him but, indeed, ran away from him.[211] This was not because Spalding was less motherly looking than Lorenz or because he was not large enough or did not move fast enough. It was because the geese saw him when they were 4 days old. There appears to be a critical period during which imprinting must take place or it will never take place.

Imprinting provides an interesting slant on instruction. Continuing our "every theory of learning implies a corresponding theory of teaching" theme, the study of imprinting is as much a study of how Lorenz teaches as of how geese learn. How does Lorenz teach? He changes the environment of growing geese during a critical period in their growth and thus changes their behavior. The relative importance of genetic and environmental factors in the development of animal and human behavior, respectively, translates, in our context, into the relative importance of inside-out maturation and outside-in instruction. Instruction plays a relatively small role in the development of animal behavior. The few examples of adult animals instructing their young are remarkable because they are so exceptional. Animals ain't got much culture to pass on from generation to generation. By changing the behavior of geese through manipulating their environment, Lorenz demonstrates that certain universal behaviors of animals are amenable to instruction. The effect of his teaching is severely limited. Nature leaves only a small gap to be filled in by the environment in the genetic program for developing a goose egg into a goose. You could usefully consider your teaching as changing the environment of growing children during a critical period in their growth and thus changing their behavior. The effect of your teaching is not so limited as that of Lorenz. Nature leaves a huge gap to be filled in by the environment in the genetic program for developing human infants into adults. As a teacher, you contribute to this filling-in process. The tremendous variation from individual to individual within our species is due to the fact that, during our long and complex development, the huge gap in the genetic program can be filled in by our different environments in such a wide variety of ways.

6.32   *Critical Periods in Humans?*

Are there equivalent critical periods in human development? The research on social deprivation by Harlow and Spitz (see Section 4.12) suggests that there is a critical period for emotional development. The limited consideration of the taboo topic of love has tended to focus on food. The infant who suckles at the mother's breast comes to love the breast, then the owner of the breast, then the owners of other breasts. Intrigued by the close attachment of infant monkeys to pieces of cloth provided for bedding (they carried them around as Linus carries his blanket and sulked when they were taken away to be washed), Harlow conducted a series of studies of **contact comfort.**[90] He provided infant monkeys with two mothers—one a wire mother from which they received food and the other a cloth mother from which they received contact comfort. The monkeys spent considerably more time on the cloth mother than on the wire mother. It appears that contact comfort is more important in the development of love than food. The infant monkeys treated the cloth mother much as they would treat a real mother. They ran to it when frightened, they used it as a base from which to explore a strange place, they worked hard to get a glimpse of it when separated. Monkeys raised with only wire mothers grew up to be neurotic, spending most of their time huddled in a corner of their cage. Monkeys raised with both wire *and* cloth mothers appeared normal but turned out to be poor lovers when they matured. The males were impotent and the females were frigid. The few females who conceived were poor mothers. Real mothers can't yet be replaced. Spitz discovered that human infants also need contact comfort.[212] Investigating the high mortality rate in foundling homes, he concluded that the infants were dying from a lack of tender loving care. Those who survived were physically weaker, less emotionally secure, and intellectually duller than children raised in normal homes. If we don't get the fondling we need during the early months of our lives, we will be permanently stunted.

Studies such as those of Harlow and Spitz suggest a critical period for "mothering." Is there a critical period for "teaching"? Whereas emotional development appears to be characterized by a **critical period,** during which certain input from the environment is crucial, intellectual development appears to be characterized by a **sensitive period,** during which a certain input from the environment is optimal.[207] The dramatic contrast between the ease with which we learn a first language at 2 and the difficulty with which we learn a second language at 20 suggests a critical period for learning language. However, the earlier period is not critical, since we can indeed learn that second language. The greater difficulty may be partly due to motivation. We need to learn that first language in order to communicate, but usually we do not *really* need to learn that second language. It is nice, but not necessary. The closer the simulation of the environmental conditions of learning a first language—total immersion, banning use of first language, and so on—the easier the learning of a second language becomes. Simulation can never be perfect, however, since it is impossible to force students to "forget" that they already know another language.

6.33   *Preschooling*

We have known for some time that "as the twig is bent, the tree will grow." This chapter simply adds the recent corollaries that "the twig won't bend until it is ready to bend" (readiness) and "if you don't bend the twig when it is ready to bend, then you will not be able to bend it later " (critical period) or, at least, "it will be more difficult to bend later " (sensitive period). More tentative corollaries have been suggested. "The twig bends easiest when it is growing fastest" and, since growth is most rapid at first, "the smaller the twig, the easier the bending." An understanding of the preschool child would appear superficially not to be relevant to an aspiring teacher who will be dealing with schoolchildren. However, paradoxically, the most sensitive period is before children go to school. A foundation is laid for schooling during those crucial first five years, and the quality of that foundation will determine whether they will have a solid or ramshackle intellectual structure.

To lapse into the vernacular, you can't know where children are at unless you know where they are coming from. Extreme environmentalists view the mind at birth as a *tabula rasa* (blank slate) on which environment writes. They are probably wrong about the first day of life, and they are certainly wrong about the first day of school. Many educational theorists seem to assume that the child comes to school with blank slate in head as well as in hand. When children toddle into that first class, their *tabulas* are far from *rasa*. Much has been learned at their mother's knee (and other low joints). They are not unschooled. They have been attending the big, round schoolhouse of our planet for four or five years.

Few learning jobs come advertised "no previous experience necessary." One of your functions as a teacher is to know what previous experience is a necessary prerequisite to the experience you are providing, to assess whether

IF A CHILD'S EDUCATIONAL ACHIEVEMENTS DEPEND SO HEAVILY ON WHAT HE LEARNED BEFORE THE AGE OF SIX, THE HOME – NOT THE SCHOOL – EMERGES AS THE MAJOR EDUCATIONAL INSTITUTION IN THE LAND.

MAYA PINES
REVOLUTION IN LEARNING

CHILDREN ARE DISMAYED BY THE SUDDEN AND TO THEM INCOMPREHENSIBLE DIFFERENCE BETWEEN THE FIRST FIVE YEARS OF THEIR LIVES, WHEN THEY USED THEIR BRAINS FOR FUN AND FOR SOLVING THEIR OWN PROBLEMS, NECESSARILY RELEVANT TO THEIR LIVES, AND THEIR LIFE LATER IN SCHOOL WHEN, WITH INCREASING FREQUENCY FROM GRADE ONE THROUGH THE END OF GRADUATE SCHOOL, MUCH OF WHAT IS REQUIRED IS EITHER TOTALLY OR PARTIALLY IRRELEVANT TO THE WORLD AROUND THEM AS THEY SEE IT.

WILLIAM GLASSER
SCHOOLS WITHOUT FAILURE

your students have that experience, and to provide that experience if they lack it. To do so, you need to know not only the school history of your students but their prehistory.

Understanding preschool children gives you that long perspective of a parent who sees a child grow from helplessness to competence, from needing a babysitter to being a babysitter. Such a perspective may help you contribute some continuity from preschooling to schooling to postschooling. Lack of this perspective creates those bizarre discontinuities which generate criticism of schooling as irrelevant. Those who do not understand preschool children often underestimate some of their capacities and overestimate others. A child who has to interrupt a conversation about intercontinental ballistic missiles during recess to read about Dick and Jane and Spot is receiving an early education about the irrelevance of school and the out-of-touchness of teachers. Another example is the discontinuity between play and work. We recognize that play is a preschool child's work, make a perfunctory gesture of incorporating this insight into the kindergarten curriculum, and then say suddenly, "Enough of this play—you have to get down to work." "All work and no play" does indeed make Jack a dull boy—especially when work involves sitting and listening to a teacher for most of five hours a day from Monday to Friday, although the less active parents have difficulty struggling through a half-hour sermon on Sunday.

POST-EXERCISES

1. A Manual for a Preschool Teacher

Write a manual for a preschool teacher. The preschool is, of course, the home, and the teacher is the parent. You may, however, want to test your manual with any preschool children lying around your house or around someone else's house if you are babysitting. Babysitting can be much more constructive for both "baby" and "sitter" than simply sitting.

Benjamin Spock has, in a sense, written such a manual in his *Baby and Child Care*. However, he is more concerned with emotional development and mothering than with intellectual development and teaching. His book is reputed to be second only to the Holy Bible on the worldwide, all-time best-seller list. Write a preschool manual to out-Spock Spock.

The following sources may help provide some theoretical background for the practical suggestions your manual will contain.

Beadle, M. *A child's mind: How children learn during the critical years from birth to age five.* New York: Doubleday, 1970.
Fraiberg, S. H. *The magic years: Understanding and handling the problems of early childhood.* New York: Scribner, 1959.
Frank, L. K. *On the importance of infancy.* New York: Random House, 1966.
Pines, M. *Revolution in learning: The years from birth to six.* New York: Harper & Row, 1966.

2. Feral and Force-Fed Children

Here are some sources for your further exploration of cases of children exposed to extremes in outside-in and inside-out education. I suggested in Section 3.241 that one function of a teacher is to present the extremes along a dimension so that a student may make more subtle distinctions along that dimension. This exercise may help serve that function.

Curtiss, S. *Genie: A psycholinguistic study of a modern-day "wild child."* New York: Academic Press, 1977.
Hale, H. *The wild boy of Aveyron.* Cambridge: Harvard University Press, 1976. (A later version of the "Victor" story—see Itard below—taking into account subsequent research.)
Hersey, J. *The child buyer.* New York: Knopf, 1960. (A fictional account of the forced growth of a child.)
Itard, J. M. G. [The wild boy of Aveyron] (G. & M. Humphrey, trans.). New York: Appleton-Century-Crofts, 1962. (Originally published, 1932.) (Itard's own account of his belated attempt to socialize "Victor.")

Mill, J. S. Unwasted years. In H. Peterson (Ed.), *Great teachers: Portrayed by those who studied under them*. New York: Vintage, 1946. (A more successful case of force-feeding. You may want to speculate why James Mill was able to make another great philosopher out of his son by intensive early training, whereas Boris Sidis was not.)

Rosenberg, S. The streetcar named Paradise Lost. In *The come as you are masquerade party*. Englewood Cliffs, N.J.: Prentice-Hall, 1970. (Biography of William James Sidis, the force-fed child described in the text.)

Singh, J. A., & Zingg, R. N. *Wolf-children and feral man*. New York: Harper, 1942. (Report on children apparently raised by wolves.)

Intelligence 7

7 INTELLIGENCE

PRE-EXERCISES

1. The Experience of Taking Intelligence Tests

Do you remember taking an intelligence test? Did you feel intelligent as you took it? Or did you feel stupid?

How well did you think you did? Did you ever find out how well you did? If not, why not? What do you think the effect would have been on you to find out that you did well? Poorly? Average?

Did the test seem fair? If not, why not? Did it seem reliable? That is, if you had taken it the previous Tuesday or the next Friday, would you have scored about the same? Did it seem valid? That is, did it seem to measure what it was designed to measure? What is this peculiar commodity—intelligence—that it was designed to measure, anyway?

How do you think your scores were used? Do you think your scores had any effect on your subsequent schooling?

Think of one of your friends who would have done very well. Think of one of your friends who would have done very poorly. Why did you think of those particular friends?

What did taking the test teach you about yourself?

How did the test differ from regular school achievement tests? How did it differ from any other test you have taken—aptitude test, interest test, driving test, pregnancy test, allergy test?

If you have had no previous experience with intelligence tests (and even if you have), you may want to gain some experience now. A counselor in the placement office of your university may administer one to you, or a graduate student in a course on testing may require volunteers as subjects. Or you can test yourself using the following book:

Eysenck, H. J. *Know your own IQ.* Harmondsworth, Middlesex: Penguin, 1962.

If you remember the name of any intelligence test you have taken, you can find out more about it by consulting the following book:

Buros, O. K. (Ed.). *Mental measurements yearbook.* Highland Park, N.J.: Gryphon, published annually.

This is a sort of consumer's guide to standardized tests. It provides information about the purpose of the test, evidence of reliability and validity, and instructions for administering the test and calculating the scores.

2. Tests of "Primary Mental Abilities"*

(1) VERBAL ABILITY

This is a test of your ability to understand what you read.
    Read proverb A.

A. Sail when the wind blows.

Two and only two of the following sentences have nearly the same meaning as proverb A. Find these two sentences.

    ✓   Strike when the iron is hot.
    ____   One must howl with the wolves.
    ✓   Make hay while the sun shines.
    ____   Make not your sail too large for the ship.

The first and third statements have been checked, because they have nearly the same meaning as proverb A.
    Now check the two sentences in the group below that have nearly the same meaning as proverb B.

B. Tall oaks from little acorns grow.

    ____   No grass grows on a beaten road.
    ____   Big streams from little fountains flow.
    ____   The exception proves the rule.
    ____   Great ends from little beginnings.

(2) VERBAL FLUENCY

In the blanks below, write as many different words as you can that begin with S and end with L. The words may be long or short. You may use the names of persons or places or foreign words. Errors in spelling will not be counted against you.
    As examples, the first three lines have already been filled in for you. Write as many other words as you can.

    1. *sell*
    2. *Saul*
    3. *spell*
    4. _____
    5. _____

*From *Primary Mental Abilities,* by L. L. Thurstone. Copyright 1938, 1966 by the University of Chicago Press. Reprinted by permission.

(3) NUMERICAL ABILITY

In this test you are shown some arithmetical problems that have already been worked out. Four answers are given for each problem. One of these is always the right answer. You are asked merely to check the right answer. You may use the space on the page for figuring, but do not waste time working out the exact answer.

In the first problem below you can readily see that the first number is nearly 4 and the second number is nearly 7. Since 4 × 7 equals 28, look for the answer that is nearest 28. This is the third answer, and it is checked.

$$4.12395 \times 6.82187 =$$

7.563327	_____
14.012468	_____
28.133051	✓
56.103378	_____

In the problems below use any tricks or shortcuts to find out which answer is correct, and check that answer. Do not waste time checking exact answers, because one of the given answers is the correct one.

$$\frac{53.29736}{5.01258} =$$

6.5654	_____
10.6327	_____
91.7136	_____
134.6973	_____

$$(197)^2 =$$

11,569	_____
23,417	_____
38,809	_____
62,187	_____

(4) SPATIAL ABILITIES

In this test you will be shown a series of pictures of hands. Some of these pictures represent right hands, and others represent left hands. Below each picture you will find two small squares.

If the picture represents a right hand, put a check mark in the right square; if it represents a left hand, put a check mark in the left square, as shown in the following samples, which are correctly marked.

Now mark the following samples in the same way.

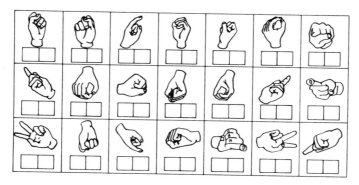

(5) PERCEPTUAL ABILITY

Here is a row of faces. One face is different from the others. The face that is different is marked.

Look closely to be sure that you see why the middle face is marked. The mouth is the part that is different.

Here is another row of faces. Look at them and mark the one that is different.

You should have marked the last face.

Here are more pictures for you to practice on. In each row mark the face that is different from the others.

(6) INDUCTIVE REASONING

Read the row of letters below.

ababab—

The next letter in this series would be *a*. Write the letter *a* in the blank at the right.

Now read the next row of letters, and decide what the next letter should be. Write that letter in the blank.

cadaeafa—

You should have written the letter *g.*
Now read the series of letters below, and fill in each blank with a letter.

cdcdcd—
aabbccdd—
abxcdxefxghx—

You should have written *c, e,* and *i,* respectively.
Now work the following problems for practice. Write the correct letter in each blank.

aaabbbcccdd—
axbyaxbyaxb—
abmcdmefmghm—
rsrtrurvrwrxr—
abcdabceabcfabc—

(7) MEMORY

In each row below is written a name. You are to learn the names so well that, when the last name is given, you can write the first name. Following this list, the last names are given in a different order. You will be asked to write the first names. If writing helps you to remember, you may copy the first and last names in the blanks below. Study silently until you are told to stop. Begin studying now. Do not wait for any signal.

First Name	Last Name	First Name	Last Name
Mary	Brown	_____	_____
John	Davis	_____	_____
Ruth	Preston	_____	_____
Fred	Smith	_____	_____

In the first row, the correct first name has been written. Without looking at the names above, write the correct first names in the other blanks.

First Name	Last Name
Ruth	Preston
_____	Brown
_____	Smith
_____	Davis

3. Some Tests of Divergent Thinking

a. List as many words as you can starting with *s* and ending with *tion.* You have five minutes.
b. List as many objects as you can that are round and edible. You have five minutes.
c. List all the uses you can think of for a wire coathanger. You have eight minutes.

d. Write as many sentences as you can with the following initial letters to the words:

W —— C —— E —— N ——

You have five minutes.

e. Here is a synopsis of a short story:

A missionary has been captured by cannibals. He is in the pot and about to be boiled when a princess of the tribe offers to have him released if he promises to marry her. He refuses and is boiled.

List as many titles as you can think of for this story. You have five minutes.

7.1   DEVELOPMENT OF INTELLIGENCE TESTS

7.11   One Intelligence: Binet

The minister of public instruction had a problem. Many children in the Paris school system for which he was responsible were not benefiting from instruction. This, he reasoned, could be due to two factors: either the child lacked the potential to benefit from instruction, or the potential was there but, for some reason, was not being realized. The solution to his problem would be different in each case. It was necessary, then, for him to find some means of distinguishing between those who lacked potential and those whose potential was not being developed, between those who could not learn and those who would not learn. In other words, he needed an instrument to measure the capacity to benefit from instruction. He presented the problem to a versatile young man named Alfred Binet. Although Binet was already a physiologist, a hypnotist, a lawyer, and a playwright, the minister of public instruction asked him to become, in addition, a psychometrician. Indeed, he invited him to become the world's first psychometrician.

Binet tackled the problem in a manner that was both obviously brilliant and brilliantly obvious. He constructed a large number of problems that seemed intuitively to him to test this capacity to benefit from instruction (items testing memory, vocabulary, discrimination, and so on) and presented the problems to a large number of children. On the basis of their responses, he selected the good items. What is a good item? Assuming that this capacity to benefit from instruction increases with age, a good item is one that is solved more easily as children get older. Figure 7-1a presents some representative good and poor items. He then placed the good items in groups, according to the age at which 50% of the children solved the problem. Thus, good item 1 in Figure 7-1a would be placed in the 8-year-old group, and good item 2 would be placed in the 14-year-old group. His test consisted of six such good items for each age from 2 to 16. A few illustrative items are provided in Figure 7-1b. This original test, constructed by Alfred Binet in 1904 and periodically revised by Terman and others at Stanford University **(Stanford-Binet test)**, is still one of the most popular intelligence tests.

a. Selection of items for Binet's test.

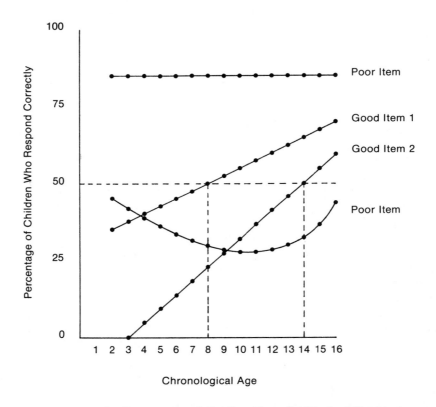

Chronological Age

b. Some representative items from the Stanford-Binet test.

50% of children of:

Age 5:   Define two of the following three words: *ball, hat, stove.*
          Fold a paper square twice to make a triangle after a
          demonstration by the examiner.

Age 8:   Distinguish between such words as *airplane* and *kite, ocean*
          and *river.* Know what makes a sailboat move. Know what
          to do if they find a lost 3-year-old child.

Age 12:   See the absurdity in such statements as "Bill Jones's feet
          are so big that he has to pull his trousers on over
          his head."
          Repeat five digits reversed.

Figure 7-1. Items for a Binet-style intelligence test

How is this instrument used to derive an index of the capacity to benefit from instruction (or **intelligence,** as this capacity has come to be called)? Let us say that 10-year-old Marie solves all the problems up to and including those in the 8-year-old group, four in the 9-year-old group, three in the 10-year-old group, two in the 11-year-old group, and none in the 12-year-old group. We are concerned with the range between the age for which she gets all the items correct **(basal age)** and the age for which she gets none of the items correct **(ceiling age).** Within this range, she gets two months' credit for each correct answer. Marie's total score then is 9.5 years, as calculated in Table 7-1a. This is called her **mental age (MA)** and is defined as the average chronological age of the children who have the same number of correct answers as she does. Since Marie is 10 years old, she is about average for her age. However, if 7-year-old Joe gets the same score, he is above average for his age, and, if 14-year-old Scott gets the same score, he is below average for his age. An index that takes chronological age into consideration would be useful. An obvious index is mental age divided by chronological age, and an obvious refinement is to multiply this index by 100 to get rid of the awkward decimal point. This index is called the **intelligence quotient (IQ).** The IQs of Marie, Joe, and Scott are calculated in Table 7-1b.

Table 7-1. Calculation of mental age and intelligence quotient

a. Calculation of mental age of Marie

		Credit	
Age Level	*Items Correct*	*Years*	*Months*
8	all	8	0
9	4	0	8
10	3	0	6
11	2	0	4
12	none	0	0
		9	6

b. Calculation of intelligence quotients of Marie, Joe, and Scott

	Mental Age	*Chronological Age*	*$\frac{MA}{CA}$*	*Intelligence Quotient*
Marie	9.5	10	0.95	95
Joe	9.5	7	1.36	136
Scott	9.5	14	0.68	68

When Alfred Binet presented the minister of public instruction with this first intelligence test, you could imagine (if you can ignore the anachronisms) the following hypothetical conversation:

Minister: Thank you, Mr. Binet, for providing me with an instrument for measuring the capacity to benefit from instruction (or intelligence, as it is now called). You have solved my practical problem. However, I am curious about what this mysterious commodity is. What precisely is intelligence?

Binet: Intelligence is what my intelligence test measures.

Minister: Don't put me on! You may have invented a measure of intelligence, but you didn't invent intelligence itself. Your definition implies that there was no intelligence until you measured it and that, as other tests are developed, there will be as many intelligences as there are measures of it.

Binet: I am simply giving you an **operational definition.** Rather than defining a concept vaguely in terms of other concepts, I am providing a precise set of instructions for arriving at the concept—just as a Zen master, asked to define Nirvana, may provide you with the steps to attain it, or a Scottish housewife, asked to define haggis, may provide you with a recipe to cook it.

Minister: Okay. So I administer your test according to your instructions, calculate the intelligence quotient, and thus obtain the intelligence of this child. By setting some arbitrary cutoff point, I can decide whether this child does or does not have enough capacity to benefit from instruction. How else could I use your measure of intelligence?

Binet: You could calculate the correlation between scores on my intelligence test and some scores representing success in your schools. If students who do well on my test also tend to do well in school and students who do poorly on my test also tend to do poorly in school, the correlation will be high. The higher this correlation, the greater the **validity** of the test—that is, the better you will be able to predict performance in school from performance on the test.

Minister: That is very useful. However, what if little Pierre happens to be having a bad day when he takes your test? Some little thing—a stomach ache, a rainy day, a quarrel with his mother—could result in a low score, brand him as unable to benefit from instruction, and thus bar him unfairly from that instruction.

Binet: The extent to which such day-by-day fluctuations affect performance on my test can be determined by giving the test to a large group of children and then giving it to them again some time later. The correlation between the scores on the first and second administrations is an index of the **reliability** of the test. The higher this correlation, the more reliable the test, and the more confidence you are justified in having in the accuracy of the scores on a single administration.

Minister: You've mentioned two correlations, one an index of validity and the other an index of reliability. Since you are the world's only psychometrician, would you calculate those indexes for me?

Binet: I'm very busy just now being a physiologist, a hypnotist, a lawyer, a playwright, and the world's first and only psychometrician, so let me just calculate one of them. I'll calculate validity, since a valid test must also be a reliable test; that is, if it measures what it claims to measure, then it must measure it consistently. However, a reliable test need not necessarily be a valid test. Your Social Security number divided by the distance between your ear lobes would be a reliable index of your intelligence, but it would not be a valid index.

Minister: Thank you. I look forward to receiving an index of the validity of your test. However, it still will not tell me what intelligence is.

Binet: Certainly it will. Intelligence is that which determines performance in school. This is a **practical definition.**

Minister: I like your practical definition as little as I like your operational definition. It just shifts from performance on the test to performance in school. Surely intelligence does not refer simply to certain responses made by the child, but refers to a certain something within. Surely it is some capacity of the person that underlies performance on the test and in school. The scores on the test and the indexes of school success correlate simply because of this capacity they have in common.

Thurstone (interrupting): Yes, indeed. Intelligence is something within the individual. However, it is not a single capacity but a set of capacities. This is an **analytical definition.** Binet's intelligence is a blanket term representing some rough average of a number of different capacities. I have stumbled on a means of discovering what those capacities are.

7.12   Seven Intelligences: Thurstone

The technique Thurstone used to discover the various intelligences underlying Binet's global intelligence is called **factor analysis.** His procedure was as follows. Like Binet, he administered a large number of items to a large number of children. However, rather than using the responses to determine the difficulty of the items, he used them to find the skills underlying the responses. He found the correlation between performance on each test item and every other test item. If this correlation is high (that is, those who did well on one item tended to do well on the other and those who did poorly on one item tended to do poorly on the other), then it is reasonable to assume that the same skill underlies performance on those two items. The simple correlation matrix in Figure 7-2 indicates that two distinct skills (one involving items 1 and 2 and the other involving items 3 and 4) underlie performance on the four items. A close look at the content of the items testing each skill suggests the nature of the skill. Thus, if items 1 and 2 both involved numbers, skill 1 is some sort of numerical ability, and, if items 3 and 4 both involved words, skill 2 is some sort of verbal ability. In this way, the statistical technique of factor analysis ferrets out the small number of latent skills underlying the large number of manifest responses. Thurstone isolated seven skills, which he called **primary mental abilities.**[218] Whereas Binet selected items that became easier as children got older, Thurstone selected items that best tested each of those seven skills. His test consists, then, of seven sets of items, with each set composed of those items most representative of each skill.

Thurstone's test differs from Binet's also in the method of administration. Whereas Binet's is an **individual test,** Thurstone's is a **group test.** The Stanford-Binet test is administered by one person to one student at a time; the

Test Item

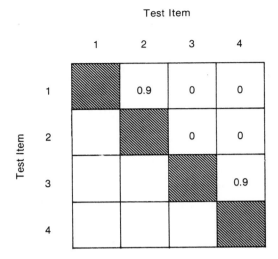

Figure 7-2. A matrix of intercorrelations between test items

Test of Primary Mental Abilities may be administered to a group of students simultaneously. The person who administers the Stanford-Binet test must be carefully trained in the procedure, whereas any person who can follow a simple set of instructions (for example, a teacher) can administer the Test of Primary Mental Abilities. Thurstone's test is obviously more convenient. However, it sacrifices accuracy at the altar of efficiency, so scores from a group test should not carry as much weight as scores from an individual test.

Pre-exercise 2 consists of one illustrative item testing each of the seven skills in Thurstone's Test of Primary Mental Abilities. Since they are just trial items, they are easier than the actual items. However, they may give you some intuitive feel for each skill and for your own competence with respect to each skill.

7.13   120 Intelligences: Guilford

This tool of factor analysis, like the computer, is often regarded with excessive awe by those who do not understand it. Such tools can be no better than the people who use them. What comes out of them is a function of what their user puts into them. Computer programmers use the expression GIGO (garbage in, garbage out), and factor analysts need an analogous expression—LILO (little in, little out). The skills that come out of a factor analysis are dependent on the items that are put in. Guilford put in a huge number of items of great variety (not just items that tested "school" intelligence, as did Thurstone) and, indeed, a large number of skills came out. There is not just one way to be intelligent, as Binet suggested, or seven ways to be intelligent, as

Thurstone suggested, but 120 ways to be intelligent, according to Guilford. Those 120 skills do not all emerge directly from the factor analysis. In examining the skills that did emerge, Guilford discovered that they could all be considered as involving a particular operation on a particular content to yield a particular product. By identifying five operations, four contents, and six products, he derived the 5 × 4 × 6, or 120, skills depicted in Figure 7-3.[82] Each skill involves one of the operations performed on one of the types of content to yield one of the products and is represented by the cube where the three intersect. Guilford is currently constructing test items for each of those skills.

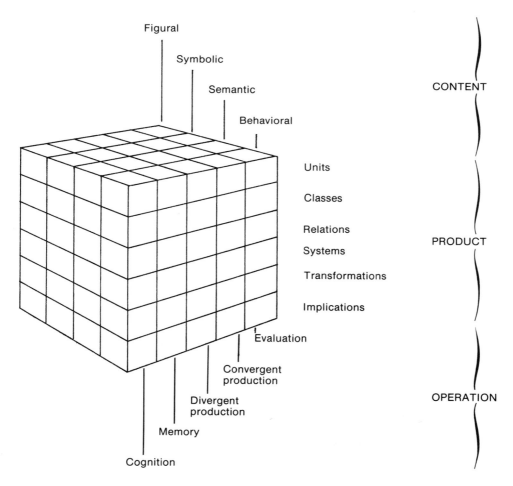

Figure 7-3. Guilford's three faces of intellect. (From "Three Faces of Intellect," by J. P. Guilford, *American Psychologist*, 1959, *14*, 469–479. Copyright 1959 by the American Psychological Association. Reprinted by permission.)

Guilford's structure of intellect reveals a limitation in both traditional intelligence tests and traditional schools. By defining intelligence narrowly in terms of the limited set of skills required by traditional schools, they fail to measure and develop many aspects of human potential. If there are, indeed, 120 different ways to benefit from instruction, then there should be 120 different types of instruction. The set of skills involving behavioral content, which constitutes social intelligence, is grossly neglected. Much more attention is devoted to our physical environment than to our social environment—hence that sad stereotype of our culture—the academic genius who is a social moron. Our interaction with other people is the important aspect of the play of life, with our physical environment serving merely as scenery, yet schools not only fail to teach social skills but actively inhibit social interaction. The slice of skills involving the operation of divergent production is also sadly neglected.

"EXAMINE THE TYPES OF QUESTIONS TEACHERS ASK IN CLASSROOMS, AND YOU WILL FIND THAT MOST OF THEM ARE WHAT MIGHT TECHNICALLY BE CALLED 'CONVERGENT QUESTIONS', BUT WHICH MIGHT MORE SIMPLY BE CALLED 'GUESS WHAT I'M THINKING' QUESTIONS.— SO WHAT STUDENTS MOSTLY DO IN CLASS IS GUESS WHAT THE TEACHER WANTS THEM TO SAY. CONSEQUENTLY, THEY MUST TRY TO SUPPLY THE RIGHT ANSWER."

NEIL POSTMAN AND **CHARLES WEINGARTNER**
TEACHING AS A SUBVERSIVE ACTIVITY

Most teaching involves convergent production; that is, we are taught to converge from a number of alternative answers to the one teacher-ordained "correct" answer. We are seldom taught to diverge from one question to a number of student-initiated alternative answers. Pre-exercise 3 consists of some of Guilford's divergent-production items, offered as a small counterbalance to your convergent-production education. If we wish to develop the full human potential, and if this full human potential can be usefully represented in terms of those 120 skills, then we should strive to realize all of those skills.

7.2 CRITIQUE OF INTELLIGENCE TESTS

7.21 A Challenge: Jensen

In 1869, Sir Francis Galton published *Hereditary Genius*, in which he argued, on the basis of evidence of the persistence of talent in eminent families, that genius was inherited.[68] His book triggered a controversy about the relative importance of genetic and environmental factors in determining intelligence. This debate flares up, from time to time, whenever someone has an axiom to grind for one or the other extreme position. In 1969, exactly 100 years after the controversy started, Jensen caused it to raise its hoary head again. He published an article "How Much Can We Boost IQ and Scholastic Achievement?" in the *Harvard Educational Review*, in which he argued, on the basis of the failure of compensatory programs like Head Start to live up to expectations, that lack of genius (to put his position as politely as possible) is inherited.[103] There is no point in continuing to pour money into such projects since, Jensen claims, intelligence is genetically determined, and non-White races are less endowed than White races and can't be brought up to the same level by manipulation of the environment.

> SENATOR DAUDIER ALWAYS STOOD IN OPPOSITION TO EVERY POLITICAL OPINION WITH WHICH HE WAS CONFRONTED AND INVARIABLY DEFENDED THE PERSON CRITICIZED BY WHOMEVER HE HAPPENED TO BE TALKING WITH, AND IN THE LAST PART OF THE SPEECH HE SYSTEMATICALLY AND INTENTIONALLY TORE DOWN WHAT HE HAD BUILT UP IN THE FIRST, SO THAT WHILE GIVING THE IMPRESSION THAT HE HAD VERY PRECISE OPINIONS ON EVERY SUBJECT, THE INVARYING RESULT OF WHAT HE SAID WAS A DRAW.

SALVADOR DALI
HIDDEN FACES

After Jensen threw down his gauntlet, the same tired ritual began again. Sides lined up. In the **hereditarian** camp, we find Jensen with his lieutenants, Shockley,[198] Herrnstein,[93] and Eysenck.[54] In the **environmentalist** camp is assembled a ragtag army of humanists, anthropologists, and assorted liberals.[19,104,154,180] The same old experiments are trotted out again. The basic strategy in such experiments is to keep one factor constant and attribute any variation in IQ to the other factor. Thus, the genetic camp presents studies in which environment is kept constant (for example, studies of unrelated children raised in the same home) and gleefully pounces on differences in IQ as evidence for the influence of genetic factors. The environmental camp counterattacks with studies in which genetics is kept constant (for example, studies of identical twins raised apart) and points to differences in IQ as evidence for the influence of environmental factors. Those who refuse to take to either trench point out, from no man's land, that it is empirically impossible to disentangle genetic and environmental factors completely. Unrelated children raised in the same home do *not* have a constant environment. Parents may assume that their natural children are more intelligent than their adopted children and thus may, consciously or unconsciously, transmit this attitude to the children. Identical twins raised apart do *not* have such very different environments, since they look alike and thus tend to be treated alike. The conclusions of the partisans in this debate tend to be exciting but inaccurate, whereas the conclusions of the nonpartisans tend to be accurate but dull. Since this is a textbook, we must settle for the accurate but dull conclusions. Here they are: There is much (indeed, very much) to be said on both sides. Intelligence is determined by some complex interaction between genetic and environmental influences. Further research is necessary.*

7.22   A Response

One new position (or, rather, one better-articulated version of an old position) has emerged from this most recent round in the nature-nurture fight. It has been known for some time that the average IQ for lower-class children is lower than that for middle-class children, that the average IQ for foreign-born children is lower than that for North-American-born children, and that the average IQ for minority-group children is lower than that for Anglo-Saxon Protestant children. Many critics have argued that those differences are partly due to the fact that the tests are designed by middle-class, North American, White, Anglo-Saxon Protestant psychologists. That bias is unconsciously built

---

* Since this is a footnote, I feel free to suggest a less accurate but more interesting conclusion. It was suggested to me by Leslie Fiedler (*Freaks.* New York: Simon & Schuster, 1978), who points out that the famous Siamese twins, Chang and Eng, had very different personalities. Chang was a drunk and womanizer, whereas Eng was a teetotaler and almost a celibate. Since genetic factors were identical and environmental factors were as similar as they could possibly be for any two people, their profoundly different personalities must be attributable to some third factor. Could it be that we are not determined entirely by genetic factors or environmental factors or some complex interaction between them, but that we "decide" how we are going to lead our lives? Chang decided on the short, happy life, whereas Eng aspired to the long, modest one. Most of us, unlike poor Eng, are able to make and act on such independent decisions.

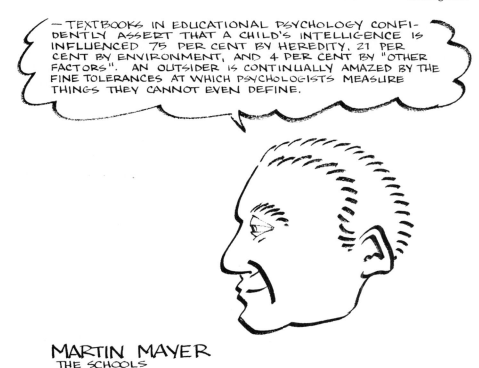

—TEXTBOOKS IN EDUCATIONAL PSYCHOLOGY CONFIDENTLY ASSERT THAT A CHILD'S INTELLIGENCE IS INFLUENCED 75 PER CENT BY HEREDITY, 21 PER CENT BY ENVIRONMENT, AND 4 PER CENT BY "OTHER FACTORS". AN OUTSIDER IS CONTINUALLY AMAZED BY THE FINE TOLERANCES AT WHICH PSYCHOLOGISTS MEASURE THINGS THEY CANNOT EVEN DEFINE.

MARTIN MAYER
THE SCHOOLS

into them is illustrated by the few cases in which items inadvertently favor usually less-favored groups. For example, lower-class children did better than middle-class children on an item involving the principle of the siphon.* In the turbulent wake of Jensen's article, this position has been considerably expanded.[102,108,109]

This later critique is qualitatively different from the earlier one. Whereas the earlier critique assumed the value of the intelligence test and merely tried to improve it by correcting for cultural bias, this later critique questions the value of the intelligence test and, indeed, points out that it has been used toward bad ends. Here is the gist of the argument, collected and collated from the sources just mentioned.

Every society seems inevitably to consist of the haves and the have-nots. The haves have not only more privileges but more power to protect those privileges. They can thus coerce or convince the have-nots to stay in their place. The haves in societies that *convince* the have-nots to maintain the status quo usually have some rationalization for the status quo: the have-nots

---

*Footnote for deprived middle-class kids: the principle of the siphon is applied in lower-class neighborhoods to steal gas from the tanks of parked cars.

have not because they are sinful in this life or were sinful in their last life, because they are criminal or crazy, and so on. In our meritocracy, the "explanation" is that the have-nots are stupid. Intelligence tests have been used, consciously and unconsciously, to convince the have-nots to buy this explanation. Since a huge industry, involving millions of dollars and thousands of jobs, has evolved around intelligence-testing, there are vested interests in perpetuating the myth that an intelligence test can differentiate between those who are bright and those who are dull or, by extension, between those who deserve privileges and those who do not.

"MERIT IS A SMOKESCREEN FOR THE PERPETUA-
TION OF PRIVILEGE. THE ABILITY OF IQ TESTS TO
PREDICT SCHOOL PERFORMANCE DOES NOT REBUT
THIS STATEMENT. AS ARTHUR JENSEN, THE
MOST RECENT DEFENDER OF IQ, POINTS OUT,
THE INTELLIGENCE MEASURED BY TESTS IS OPERA-
TIONALLY DEFINED AS THE ABILITY TO SUCCEED
IN SCHOOL."

EVERETT REIMER
SCHOOL IS DEAD

Consider the following two capsule careers.

Josef Smithski was born in a mining village in Poland. He spent much of his childhood playing in vacant lots with the children of other miners. He attended the local school for a few years. He did poorly, since he had little experience with, and hence interest in, books and ideas and such school stuff. He took an intelligence test and did poorly for the same reason. His parents did not encourage him to continue in school, since they wanted him to go to work early to augment the family income. He followed his father into the mine. During one two-week annual vacation, he went to the nearest town to seek a better job. However, he lacked the education necessary for a better job and could qualify for only the most menial tasks with little hope of advancement. Discouraged by this and by his loneliness among town dwellers who frowned on his unsophisticated village habits and attitudes, he returned home to the mine. Hearing that there were more opportunities in the United States of America, he tried to emigrate. However, because of the very low quota for Eastern European countries (established, by the way, partly on the basis of intelligence tests), his application was rejected. He married one of the local girls, had several children, and settled down more or less to repeat his father's life.

H. Joseph Smythe III was born in London, England. His father was a professor of economics at the London School of Economics and his mother the author of a number of novels and books of poetry. There were always good books and lively conversation around his home during his childhood. He attended Eton and Cambridge, where he did well because of his experience with and interest in words and ideas. For the same reasons, he did well on an intelligence test. His good grades secured him a fellowship to attend graduate school in the United States. His application for U.S. citizenship was accepted because of his British nationality and the recommendations of influential friends he had made in graduate school. On graduation, a friend of his father's offered him a job in his firm. He got along well with the other executives because of their common background and was soon earning $30,000 a year as vice-president of the Sales Division. He married a judge's daughter, a recent graduate of Vassar, whom he had met while skiing in Switzerland. They settled in a wealthy suburb of Boston and had two children.

Josef Smithski and H. Joseph Smythe III would both contribute to high correlations among IQ scores, number of years of school, income, socio-economic status, job level, status of spouse, or any other index of "success." Josef is low on all those scores, and Joseph is high on all of them. This does not mean, however, that Josef was born with an inferior nervous system that doomed him to his more limited life, as members of the genetic camp have argued. The intelligence quotient is only one of a complex of correlated variables. It is correlated with various indexes of "success" but is not the cause of such success. H. Joseph Smythe's success is due to a high status quotient at birth rather than a high intelligence quotient. His most intelligent move was to arrange to be born with a first-class ticket for the trip through life, and his various "successes" flowed from this initial "decision." He became smart be-cause he was rich, rather than rich because he was smart.

Jensen's centennial project has, therefore, backfired. His opponents have demolished his original arguments. One of his heroes, Sir Cyril Burt, on whose twin-study data he partially based his argument, has been exhumed from his beknighted grave and exposed as probably a bigot and possibly a fraud.[108] Jensen has a certain crazy courage, expounding these views in our egalitarian world (especially at Berkeley, of all places), and he has softened his hard posi-tion in later publications. The important issue, however, is not Jensen but **Jensenism.** Many of his liberal critics have forgotten this and have demon-strated that liberals can be as prone as conservatives to shift their attack from the theory to the theorist. The more substantial and extreme argument against intelligence-testing, which has developed in response to Jensen's argument, will be a powerful weapon when Jensenism (as it now seems fated to be called) raises its hoary head once again.

7.23   And a Reconciliation

As we saw in Chapter 5, Jean Piaget describes the complex interaction between genetic and environmental influences in terms of alternating assimi-lations and accommodations. He is in the genetic camp in the sense that he regards inside-out development (genetic influence) as primary and outside-in learning (environmental influence) as secondary. The relative importance of

genetic factors does *not* necessarily imply, as Jensen and others seem to assume, that there is a wide range of potential. It means only that we all share a
huge potential by being born as members of the most "intelligent" species on
the planet. We are all potentially very intelligent in the sense that our species
has a great capacity to benefit from experience—instruction being a limited
aspect of experience. There is no evidence of any intrinsic differences in the
quality of normal nervous systems. A nervous system is a nervous system is a
nervous system. Piaget thus demonstrates that it is possible to be in the genetic camp yet be a liberal and an optimist. This potential to benefit from experience can be realized only through interaction with the environment. It is
realized, as we saw, by assimilating information from the environment and
accommodating, if necessary, to that information. A person who lives in an
enriched environment will have much information to assimilate and will
realize this potential more fully than a person who lives in an impoverished
environment. Thus, Piaget is in the environmental camp in the sense that he
believes variation from individual to individual within our species is mostly
determined by environmental influences.

7.3   IMPLICATIONS FOR TEACHERS

If you were an administrator dealing with large groups, some general
index of capacity to benefit from instruction might be useful. Put yourself in
the shoes of the registrar of your university, who is required to select, let us say,
1000 freshmen from 5000 applicants. He could select those with the fairest
skins or those from the richest neighborhoods. This is obviously unfair. He
could list the candidates alphabetically and choose every fifth name. Such a
random process *seems* fair. However, it would result in the acceptance of many
who would not benefit from university instruction and the rejection of many
who would. Would it not be better to derive some index of capacity to benefit
from instruction and select those high on this index? Such an index is the IQ.
This procedure is far from perfect. It rejects many whose low potential is
compensated by hard work and accepts many whose high potential is destroyed by emotional instability. However, it must be evaluated against the
available alternatives rather than against some hypothetical ideal procedure.
Selection by test is certainly better than selection by whim, by prejudice, by
chance, by crystal ball, or by astrological sign.

Such a general index of potential to benefit from instruction is, however,
of little value to a teacher dealing with individual students. In the outside-in
tradition of education, IQ tests have too often been misused as rationalizations
for poor teaching. I can't teach you, not because I can't teach, but because you
can't learn. You are unteachable—you are low in the capacity to benefit from
instruction. Some critics have derisively compared schools with supermarkets
with students as customers, teachers as clerks, and administrators as execu-

tives. In a sense, they are worse. In the school supermarket, the customer is always wrong. Failures in communication are almost invariably attributed to the fact that students can't learn rather than to the fact that teachers can't teach.

— SOME GENUINE CAPACITY IS BEING TESTED. BUT WHETHER THIS IS THE CAPACITY TO PASS TESTS OR THE CAPACITY TO DEAL WITH LIFE, WHICH WE CALL INTELLIGENCE, WE DO NOT KNOW. — IF A CHILD FAILS IN SCHOOL AND THEN FAILS IN LIFE, THE SCHOOL CANNOT SIT BACK AND SAY: YOU SEE HOW ACCURATELY I PREDICTED THIS. UNLESS WE ARE TO ADMIT THAT EDUCATION IS ESSENTIALLY IMPOTENT, WE HAVE TO THROW THE CHILD'S FAILURE AT THE SCHOOL, AND DESCRIBE IT AS A FAILURE NOT BY THE CHILD BUT BY THE SCHOOL.

WALTER LIPPMAN
"THE RELIABILITY OF INTELLIGENCE TESTS"

In the inside-out tradition of education, there is a shift from using intelligence tests as a rationalization for poor teaching to using them as a rationale for good teaching. An intelligence test is one of the many instruments that can aid you as a teacher to understand students in order to be better able to teach them, and also to aid students to understand themselves in order to be better able to teach themselves. A set of tests for each of Guilford's "intelligences" would provide you with profiles of various students' competencies. Low scores would not be used to disqualify students from instruction in those areas but, on the contrary, to indicate where instruction might be useful to develop an unrealized aspect of their potential. High scores would indicate areas they might wish to pursue as a basis for choosing a vocation. The huge range of types of "intelligences" would serve to remind you that many types of instruction are required to help develop their full potential.

It would perhaps be better to speak of a profile of "interests" rather than of "intelligences." The term *intelligence* has become overlaid with value judgments. The fact that I am interested in taking photographs and you are interested in collecting stamps does not mean that either of us is superior to the other. We are simply different. We are *all* different, thank God. Vivent les différences! Our different profiles of skills are probably due mainly to our different interests which, in turn, are due to our different environments. Bruner points out that we get interested in what we get good at. If I may add that we get good at what we are interested in, then, between us, we have created an upward spiral of interest and competence. Interest increases competence, which further increases interest, which further increases competence, and so on and so on.

> AT PRESENT THE CURRICULUM TENDS TO BE A MORE OR LESS RIGID FRAME ON WHICH THE UNFORMED MIND IS FORCIBLY STRETCHED: IT DEMANDS CONFORMITY TO A SINGLE PATTERN OF BEHAVIOR, A PREDETERMINED STANDARD OF "INTELLIGENCE". WE SHOULD RATHER LOOK UPON THE CURRICULUM AS A MORE OR LESS FINITE SCALE OF <u>INTERESTS</u> UPON WHICH THE INDIVIDUAL MIND OF THE GROWING CHILD CAN PLAY ITS MELODY, ACCORDING TO ITS IMPULSE TO SELF-EXPRESSION, SELF-REALIZATION.

HERBERT READ
EDUCATION THROUGH ART

POST-EXERCISES

1. Dealing with Individual Differences in Intelligence

Various practical strategies have been devised in school systems to deal with individual differences in intelligence. These include streaming, individualized instruction, promotion and demotion, and skipping and repeating grades.

Which of those strategies were used in the various schools you have attended? What effects did those strategies have on you and your friends? What strategy do you prefer? Can you imagine a school system in which such strategies are not necessary? In the light of the discussion of intelligence in this chapter, consider the relative advantages and disadvantages of each strategy.

2. The Myth of Intelligence

Here is a title: *The Myth of Intelligence.* Now go off and write the book.
The title is not enough? Okay, here are some chapter headings:

"Intelligence was invented by Alfred Binet in 1904."
"Psychology is getting more intelligences, but it sure is not getting more intelligent."
"It's not that I'm not intelligent—I'm just not interested."
"Intelligence tests are paper tigers."
"The problem with the concept *average* is that half of us must be below it."
"Would any really intelligent person join an organization (Mensa) that excludes 95% of the population?"
"If Goethe had an IQ of 200 and Mozart an IQ of 180, does this mean that Goethe was a better writer than Mozart was a musician?"

Some people have already written similar books. Read the following to make sure that you have not been scooped. If not, write your book, publish it, and send me 1% of your royalties.

Blum, J. *Pseudoscience and mental ability: The origins and fallacies of the IQ controversy.* New York: Monthly Review Press, 1978.
Psychology Today, September 1972.
Harris, T. G. IQ abuse: An introduction, p. 39.
Garcia, J. IQ: The conspiracy, pp. 40–43; 92–94.
Mercer, J. R. IQ: The lethal label, pp. 44–47; 95–97.
Watson, P. IQ: The racial gap, pp. 48–50; 97–99.
Senna, C. (Ed.). *The fallacy of IQ.* New York: Third Press, 1973.
Sharp, E. *The IQ cult.* New York: Coward, McCann & Geoghegan, 1972.

Creativity 8

8 CREATIVITY

PRE-EXERCISES

1. Brainstorming

One tool for generating creative solutions to problems is the technique of brainstorming. It is based on the principle of deferred evaluation. A wind will extinguish a small flame but fan a large flame. The flame of creativity should be allowed to grow before the wind of criticism is applied to it.

The procedure is as follows. A chairperson presents a specific problem and invites an assembled group of people to suggest solutions. Criticism (of the ideas of others and your own ideas) is discouraged, and wild, way-out ideas are encouraged. The ideas are recorded as they are suggested, preferably on a blackboard so that they may serve not only as a record but as a trigger for more ideas. If the flame begins to flicker, the chairperson may try to revive it by tossing out some general strategies for solving problems. Those strategies are typically operations like add, subtract, multiply, divide, magnify, minify, separate, combine, adapt, modify, rearrange, substitute, and so on. The ideas are evaluated to determine which of them are useful or feasible.

Brainstorming was originally designed for group problem-solving. A group does indeed produce more new ideas than the sum of its members. Apparently, each person acts as a catalyst to the others, triggering ideas they would not have generated on their own. There is, however, no reason why you should not conduct an individual brainstorming session.

Here are a few exercises to practice brainstorming.

1. List as many functions as you can think of for (a) a wire coathanger, (b) a brick, (c) a bottle, (d) Scotch tape.
2. Suggest solutions to (a) downtown parking problems, (b) undone homework assignments, (c) tantrums in children and adults.
3. Suggest alternative titles to (a) movies you have seen recently, (b) articles in today's newspaper, (c) cartoons.
4. Suggest improvements in (a) screwdrivers, (b) hotels, (c) textbooks.

5. Write classified ads offering for sale (a) a vest-pocket exercising kit, (b) an untraceable poison, (c) a bed-making machine.
6. "A tenor is not a voice, it's a disease," said G. B. Shaw. Write a similar epigram on (a) a sophomore, (b) a politician, (c) television.

Although brainstorming was originally developed to generate new ideas in industry, you can adapt it to education. In the process of creating products, it also produces more creative people. Brainstorming can thus not only generate creative solutions to classroom problems but help your students become more creative. Organizing class projects, planning courses, solving discipline problems (with the disciplinee contributing, of course) are some possible applications.

The idea of brainstorming and the above problems were suggested in the following book.

Osborn, A. F. *Applied imagination.* New York: Scribners, 1953.

2. Collective Bulletin Board

Haefele devised the Collective Notebook method for generating creative solutions to problems. The procedure is as follows. A problem and some possible solutions are written in a notebook. The notebook is distributed to a number of people and collected at a specified time. In the interval, each person writes or diagrams his or her solutions in a copy of the notebook. The solutions are evaluated and useful solutions are rewarded.

This method has typically been used in factories. Lefrancois's Collective Bulletin Board is an adaptation to the classroom of Haefele's Collective Notebook method. The problem and possible solutions are written on the blackboard, and students are invited to add their solutions. This adaptation incorporates one of the advantages of brainstorming—ideas are triggered in each person by the ideas of the other participants—and avoids one of the disadvantages—the more vocal and uninhibited participants do not dominate the process. Lefrancois found that students who used this Collective Bulletin Board method for ten weeks did significantly better than a control group on tests of creative thinking. His own immense creativity was possibly enhanced simply by conducting the study.

You may like to try these methods in your classroom, both to solve problems and to increase the creativity of your students. Consult the following sources for further information about the Collective Notebook and the Collective Bulletin Board methods, respectively.

Haefele, J. W. *Creativity and innovation.* New York: Reinhold, 1962.
Lefrancois, G. R. *Developing creativity in high school students.* Unpublished M. Ed. thesis, University of Saskatchewan, 1965.

3. The Analogy Game

Any new idea is a combination of two or more old ideas. New ideas can thus be generated through analogies. *A* is to *B* as *C* is to ———? Whatever is placed in the blank may be a new idea. You can generate new ideas (new, at least, to you) by playing the analogy game.

The procedure is as follows. Draw a line down the middle of a sheet of paper and head each of the columns thus formed with the name of a system. List as many elements, states, relationships, events, and processes within the first system as you can think of. Try to fill in the space alongside the corresponding concept with respect to the second system. Repeat this process, starting with the second system.

I used this procedure in drawing the analogy between the metabolic system and the nervous system in Section 5.31. The section of my chart that I found useful is presented here.

Metabolic system	Nervous system
Adaptation	Adaptation
catabolism	assimilation
anabolism	accommodation
Food	Information

This exercise increased my understanding of both systems. The fact that the analogy was imperfect makes it no less illuminating. The manner in which the nervous system differs from the metabolic system forced me to consider its special status among the subsystems of which we are composed.

Use this procedure to think through, once again, at more depth, the various models of the teacher-student relationship listed in Post-exercise 1 of Chapter 1. Here is a start on the therapist-client model.

Teacher-student	Therapist-client
Homework	?
?	Transference

Use this procedure to think through the analogy between your classroom and your country.

Classroom	Country
Teacher	?
Discipline problem	?
Classroom climate	?
?	Domestic relations
?	Foreign relations
?	Form of government

Play the analogy game in your classroom by drawing the chart on the blackboard and eliciting concepts and their counterparts from the class.

4. Messing Around in the Matrix

Messing around in the matrix is an extension of the analogy game, in which there are more than two columns and in which you start by naming the rows.

Draw a matrix. Head the columns with any categories of interest to you and the rows with the same (or other relevant) categories. Consider each cell in terms of the relationship between the column and row categories it represents. The cell may contain a new idea.

Here are some examples.

a. Mixed drinks

Head the columns with the various liquors and the rows with the various mixers. Some of the mixed drinks that have already been invented are named in their appropriate cells. Invent drinks simply by focusing on an empty cell. Invent names for them. You may find that your names are more creative if you do this exercise empirically rather than theoretically.

	Whisky	Gin	Rum	Vodka
Soda water	scotch & soda			
Tonic water		gin & tonic		
Coca-Cola			rum & Coke	
Orange juice				screwdriver
Tomato juice				bloody Mary

Advanced course (for those still on their feet): head rows with liqueurs (Drambuie, Benedictine, creme de menthe, and so on) and enter the exotic world of "rusty nails," "ward eights," and "grasshoppers."

b. Sensory systems

	Vision	Audition	Touch	Smell	Taste
Receptor					
Entertainment	movies	talkies	feelies	smellies	tasties
Privacy					
Tools					

Running along the "entertainment" row suggests that the traditional movies, which involve only sight and hearing, could be augmented to incorporate other sensory modalities. Feelies have been suggested by Aldous Huxley and smellies have been tried, which leaves only tasties for you to invent.

Running along the "privacy" row triggers a consideration of our different concepts of privacy—not being seen, not being heard, not being touched, and so on. We find that this varies from culture to culture and from individual to individual within a culture.

Running along the "tools" row provokes some consideration of the various instruments we have devised for extending our sensory systems—telescopes, telephones, and so on. You may want to be more precise by considering more specific functions—such as tools to see without being seen (one-way mirror), to hear without being heard, and so on, or tools to make the small large enough to be seen (microscope), quiet loud enough to be heard, and so on.

c. Dual functions in classrooms

Head the columns with various classroom tools (blackboard, chalk, bulletin board, desk, and so on) and head the rows with the same tools. Examine each cell and consider how you could adapt each tool to perform a function of the other or how you could design a tool that would serve both functions. For example, how you could use the blackboard to serve the function of a book (students write a story with each student adding a sentence in turn) or a tool that could serve as both a blackboard and a book (story in large letters on a scroll suspended in front of class?). This exercise was suggested by a chute from classroom to playground, which doubled as a pleasant way to leave at recess and as a fire-escape.

d. Problems and theorists

Head the columns with the various theorists presented in this book (Skinner, Maslow, Piaget, and so on) and head the columns with various problems you anticipate as a teacher. Explore each cell and consider how each theorist could help in solving each problem. Even if this does not help you solve those problems, it does help you understand the theorists.

8.1   CREATIVITY AND INTELLIGENCE

Whereas outside-in education, based on the behavioristic model of the student, emphasizes intelligence as the dimension along which students may be placed, inside-out education, based on the humanistic model of the student, emphasizes creativity. Intelligence is the capacity to benefit from outside-in instruction, and **creativity** is the extent to which the potential of inside-out development is realized.

In the previous chapter, we discovered that intelligence is a blanket term covering a variety of human skills. Guilford identified 120 skills involving each of 5 operations on 4 types of content to yield 6 types of products.[82] Intelligence is a rough index of a subset of those skills. Creativity is a rough index of another subset of those skills. It would be useful to replace those vague terms *intelligence* and *creativity* with Guilford's more precise concepts of **convergent-** and **divergent-production skills.** "Intelligent" students are good at converging from a number of alternative answers to the one "correct" answer; "creative" students are good at diverging from one question to a number of alternative answers.

"IN A WORD, THEN, INTELLIGENCE IS INDICATIVE OF ACADEMIC GRADES BUT IT IS IRRELEVANT TO THE DISPLAY OF ANY FORMS OF EXTRACURRICULAR ACCOMPLISHMENTS WE INVESTIGATED. IDEATIONAL RESOURCEFULNESS — SOMETHING VERY DIFFERENT FROM INTELLIGENCE — IS WHAT PROVES TO BE IMPORTANT ONCE WE STEP OUTSIDE OF THE CLASSROOM."

M.A. WALLACH AND C.W. WING, JR.
THE TALENTED STUDENT

Getzels and Jackson used tests of divergent- and convergent-production skills to select two groups of students—the "highly creative" and the "highly intelligent."[74] The highly creative students were in the top 20% in divergent production but not in the top 20% in convergent production (that is, in conventional IQ tests), and the highly intelligent students were in the top 20% in convergent production but not in the top 20% in divergent production.

The flavor of the different styles of the "highly intelligent" and "highly creative" students is nicely captured in their responses to a **Thematic Apperception Test.** In this case, they have been shown a picture of a man writing in an office and invited to tell a story about what is happening. A typical story from a highly intelligent student:

> There's ambitious Bob, down at the office at 6:30 in the morning. Every morning it's the same. He's trying to show his boss how energetic he is. Now, thinks Bob, maybe the boss will give me a raise for all my extra work. The trouble is that Bob has been doing this for the last three years, and the boss still hasn't given him a raise. He'll come in at 9:00, not even noticing that Bob has been there so long, and poor Bob won't get his raise. *

A typical story from a highly creative student:

> This man has just broken into the office of a new cereal company. He is a private eye employed by a competitor firm to find out the formula that makes the cereal bend, sag and sway. After a thorough search of the office he comes upon what he thinks is the current formula. He is now copying it. It turns out that it is the wrong formula and the competitor's factory blows up. Poetic justice!

A comparison of the highly creative and highly intelligent groups of students yielded the following findings:

1. The two groups were not significantly different in scores of academic achievement (despite a 23-point difference in average IQ).
2. The highly intelligent students believe that the personality traits they prefer for themselves are the ones that lead to adult success and are favored by teachers; whereas the highly creative students believe that there is no relationship between the traits they prefer for themselves and the ones favorable to adult success, and a negative relationship between traits they prefer for themselves and traits regarded favorably by teachers.
3. In the use of imagination for the creation of fantasy, the highly creative students show significantly more stimulus-free themes, unexpected endings, humor, incongruities, and playfulness, and a marked tendency toward more violence.
4. In terms of career aspirations, the highly creative students see more careers as open to them, as well as many more unconventional ones—adventurer, inventor, or writer, for example, as opposed to lawyer, doctor, or professor.

---

* This and the following quotation are from *Creativity and Intelligence*, by J. W. Getzels and P. W. Jackson. Copyright 1962 by John Wiley & Sons, Inc. Reprinted by permission.

AN EXCELLENT PLUMBER IS INFINITELY MORE ADMIRABLE THAN AN INCOMPETENT PHILOSOPHER. THE SOCIETY WHICH SCORNS EXCELLENCE IN PLUMBING BECAUSE PLUMBING IS A HUMBLE ACTIVITY AND TOLERATES SHODDINESS IN PHILOSOPHY BECAUSE IT IS AN EXALTED ACTIVITY WILL HAVE NEITHER GOOD PLUMBING NOR GOOD PHILOSOPHY. NEITHER ITS PIPES NOR ITS THEORIES WILL HOLD WATER.

JOHN W. GARDNER
EXCELLENCE

8.2   *DEFINITION OF CREATIVITY*

As Lefrancois points out, much of the conceptual confusion about the vague term *creativity* can be cleared up by differentiating between the creative product, the creative process, and the creative person.[118] Let us consider each in turn.

8.21   *The Creative Product*

It is possibly most productive to consider the creative product in terms of the novel response—that is, a response the particular individual has never made before. This definition has a number of implications.

Creativity cannot be discussed in terms of the behavioristic model of the student. Learning involves a response from the repertoire of an organism which is followed by reinforcement which increases the probability of that response. Behaviorists can thus explain the persistence, but not the existence, of a novel response.

A FIRST-RATE SOUP IS MORE CREATIVE THAN A SECOND-RATE POEM.

ABRAHAM H. MASLOW
IN H.H. ANDERSON, CREATIVITY AND ITS CULTIVATION

Creativity is defined in psychological rather than sociological terms. A novel response is one that has never previously been made by a certain individual, rather than a response that has never previously been made by anyone. This individual is no less creative because other individuals have independently made the same response before.*

Creativity involves *any* novel response. It is not the exclusive domain of the few gifted artists ("gifted" implying that they were given it as a first-birthday present). There are uncreative poets and creative cooks. Creativity is not a characteristic of a few professions, nor is it a characteristic of a few people. It is a universal characteristic of our species.

8.22 The Creative Process

A number of artists and scientists have provided introspective accounts of the creative process.[84,164,177] The general consensus is that it involves the four stages of preparation, incubation, illumination, and verification, described by Wallas.[227]

---

* This may serve as some small consolation to you if, like me, you discover that most of your discoveries have been prediscovered (including this one). Each time I discover one of my discoveries, I reassure myself that I'm at least on the right track. "Yes," says my friend Guy, "but you're so far behind."

HE WISHED TO DISCOVER AMERICA. HIS GAY AND THOUGHT-LESS FRIENDS, WHO COULD NOT UNDERSTAND HIM, POINTED OUT THAT AMERICA HAD ALREADY BEEN DIS-COVERED, I THINK THEY SAID BY CHRISTOPHER COLUM-BUS, SOME TIME AGO, AND THAT THERE WERE BIG CITIES OF ANGLO-SAXON PEOPLES THERE ALREADY, NEW YORK AND BOSTON AND SO ON.   BUT THE AD-MIRAL EXPLAINED TO THEM, KINDLY ENOUGH, THAT THIS HAD NOTHING TO DO WITH IT.   THEY MIGHT HAVE DISCOVERED AMERICA, BUT HE HAD NOT.

G.K. CHESTERTON
"A FRAGMENT," IN THE COLOURED LANDS

The crucial stage in this process—**illumination**—is hardly a stage at all. It is that flash of insight when a solution suddenly appears. The **incubation** stage is inferred from the fact that this flash of insight often occurs, not while one is focusing directly on the problem, but when one is doing something else. Banting awoke in the middle of the night with the crucial experiment that led to the discovery of insulin. Darwin finally saw the elements of the theory of evolution click into place while he was relaxing, and Wallace developed essentially the same theory while ill with a fever. The unconscious process of incubation must be preceded by the conscious process of **preparation.** Banting had been preparing a lecture on diabetes the evening before the night he awoke with a cure for it, and both Darwin and Wallace had been struggling to understand the data that the theory of evolution explained. It is futile to hope for inspiration without shedding the preliminary perspiration. An appropriate solution will illuminate only a mind that is sensitized to the problem. Illumination must be followed by **verification.** At the moment of insight, you are absolutely convinced of the appropriateness of your solution. However, you have to convince your colleagues of its correctness by proving it to their satisfaction.

"TO ARRIVE AT THE SIMPLEST TRUTH, AS NEWTON KNEW AND PRACTICED, REQUIRES YEARS OF CONTEMPLATION. NOT ACTIVITY. NOT REASONING. NOT CALCULATING. NOT BUSY BEHAVIOR OF ANY KIND. NOT READING. NOT TALKING. NOT MAKING AN EFFORT. NOT THINKING. SIMPLY BEARING IN MIND WHAT IT IS ONE NEEDS TO KNOW. AND YET THOSE WITH THE COURAGE TO TREAD THIS PATH TO REAL DISCOVERY ARE NOT ONLY OFFERED PRACTICALLY NO GUIDANCE ON HOW TO DO SO, THEY ARE ACTIVELY DISCOURAGED AND HAVE TO SET ABOUT IT IN SECRET, PRETENDING MEANWHILE TO BE DILIGENTLY ENGAGED IN THE FRANTIC DIVERSIONS AND TO CONFORM WITH THE DEADENING PERSONAL OPINIONS WHICH ARE BEING CONTINUALLY THRUST UPON THEM."

GEORGE BROWN
LAWS OF FORM

Traditional education tends to emphasize the conscious and voluntary stages of preparation and verification. For example, a scientist is "prepared" by being presented with the accumulated information within the discipline and the tools used in that discipline to verify conclusions. This is understandable. Traditional educators talk about the conscious processes because it is possible to talk about them. Critics of traditional education tend to focus on the mysterious process of incubation and the dramatic process of illumination, while ignoring the more pedestrian stages of preparation and verification. This is like aspiring to give birth without being pregnant or raising the child. Both Darwin and Wallace discovered the theory of evolution, but Darwin gets the credit because he spent 17 years accumulating evidence for it before publishing *The Origin of Species*. Do you remember the sad story of Twitmyer (Section 3.211)? Both Pavlov and Twitmyer stumbled onto the phenomenon of classical conditioning, but Pavlov is remembered because he continued to study it for the next 40 years. The creative process involves both disciplined, conscious processes and spontaneous, unconscious processes.

8.23   The Creative Person

We all make novel responses. However, some of us make more and "better" novel responses than others. What are the characteristics of those of us who produce a great quantity and high quality of novel responses?

Maslow puzzled for years over a certain peculiarity of his self-actualizing subjects.[136] In his attempt to describe self-actualizing (creative) people, he could not decide whether they were selfish or unselfish, devoted to duty or bent on pleasure, ruled by the head or by the heart, childlike or mature. They seemed to fit into both categories. He finally realized that their basic characteristic was their capacity to transcend those simple-minded dichotomies. They were selfish in one sense but unselfish in another. Let us look at two important dichotomies that creative people transcend.

Creative people are open in one sense and closed in another. They have what Rogers calls "an openness to experience";[183] they are "relatively unfrightened by the unknown, the mysterious, the puzzling, and often are positively attracted by it."[136] They are closed, however, in the sense that, although aware of the judgments of others, they are relatively impervious to praise and blame. They have what Rogers calls "an internal locus of evaluation,"[183] they are "less enculturated; that is, they seemed to be less afraid of what other people would say or demand or laugh at."[136]

IT TAKES COURAGE TO BE CREATIVE. JUST AS SOON AS YOU HAVE A NEW IDEA, YOU'RE IN A MINORITY OF ONE.

E. PAUL TORRANCE

Have you ever participated in a conversation that goes something like this?

"Where'd you like to eat?"

"Let's go to Joe's."

"You always want to go to Joe's. We've been there a dozen times already."

"Well, why not? We know we can get a good steak there."

"Why don't we go to the Zanzibar (or whatever exotic restaurant)?"

"Is the food good?"

"I don't know. I've never eaten there. A friend recommended it to me."

"Why do you want to go somewhere you've never been?"

"Because I've never been."

"You can't go through your life dashing here and there doing new things all the time. You gradually find things that you like and do them again because you know you like them. It's called maturity."

If you are the person who wants to go to Joe's, you are a **teleophobe** (one who fears new things), and if you are the person who wants to go to the Zanzibar, then you are a **teleophile** (one who loves new things).* None of us, of course, are pure teleophobes or teleophiles. We tend to fall along a dimension ranging between those two extremes. Indeed, each of us shuttles back and forth along this dimension from situation to situation and from time to time. We all

WHENEVER I HIT UPON SOMETHING NEW THAT SUPPLIES ME WITH INTERESTING THINGS TO DO, I STICK TO IT UNTIL I GET THE FEELING THAT, WITH MY PARTICULAR BACKGROUND AND COMPETENCE, I AM UNLIKELY TO GET VERY MUCH FURTHER. THEN I DROP THE SUBJECT, AT LEAST FOR A WHILE. SINCE I HAVE BEEN IN A CONTINUOUS STATE OF MANIC EXCITEMENT ABOUT SCIENCE THROUGHOUT MY LIFE, I HAVE NEVER BEEN ABLE TO TAKE A REST AFTER EXHAUSTING A TOPIC. I HAVE MERELY CHANGED THE SUBJECT.

HANS SELYE
FROM DREAM TO DISCOVERY

* Don't bother looking these words up in the dictionary. I invented them (a trivial illustration of creativity in action).

fluctuate between the contentment of old, familiar things and the excitement of new, unfamiliar things or, phrased negatively, we all tread the tightrope between boredom and fear. The creative person, however, will tend toward the teleophile end. In that perennial battle between the need to know and the fear of knowing (see Section 4.212), the need to know usually triumphs. Because the need to know is strong, the creative person is open to experience. However, the creative person must be closed to the opinions of other people to weaken the fear of knowing. In the trivial case of venturing into a new restaurant, the fear of knowing is not a powerful force. However, the creative person must venture into unexplored territories and must not be daunted by the "here be dragons" signs that adorned the unexplored areas on ancient maps. The creative person needs what May calls "the courage to create."[142]

In Section 4.13, I discussed the need for stimulation and the need for consistency as the organic bases for knowing and understanding, respectively. The creative person is open to new experience because of a high need for stimulation. Openness is not enough. Your mind should be open, but not at both ends. You must be tolerant of ambiguity, but you must also aspire to resolve that ambiguity. In other words, creative people must also have a high need for consistency. They need not only to know but to understand.

Taylor and Barron conclude, on the basis of an extensive study involving clinical interviews and tests, that "young scientists are . . . marked by a strong

WE MUST BE ABLE TO USE DISCIPLINE TO GAIN GREATER FREEDOM, TAKE ON HABITS TO INCREASE OUR FLEXIBILITY, PERMIT DISORDER IN THE INTERESTS OF AN EMERGING HIGHER ORDER, TOLERATE DIFFUSION, AND EVEN OCCASIONALLY TO INVITE IT, IN ORDER TO ACHIEVE A MORE COMPLEX INTEGRATION.

FRANK BARRON
CREATIVE PERSON AND CREATIVE PROCESS

need for order and for perceptual closure, combined with a resistance to premature closure and an interest in what may appear as disorder, contradiction, imbalance, or very complex balance whose ordering principle is not immediately apparent."[214] This leads to a second dichotomy. The creative person must be both flexible (to accept new information) and persistent (to maintain a consistent structure of old information). Uncreative people find it difficult to maintain a balance between those two apparently incompatible characteristics. They tend to be too persistent as they lumber along dead-end streets leading nowhere or too flexible as they flit from street to street. They tend to be drudges or dilettantes. It is difficult to be persistent but not pig-headed and flexible but not flighty. The creative person transcends this dichotomy by being both persistent and flexible, when each is appropriate. Outside-in teachers tend to emphasize the persistence, which is necessary for the preparation and verification stages of the creative process, whereas inside-out teachers tend to emphasize the flexibility, which is necessary for the incubation and illumination stages.

8.3   CULTIVATION OF CREATIVITY

8.31   Importance of Creativity

Creativity is the source of all creations, but it can't itself be created. It can, however, be cultivated. The classroom should be modeled on the garden rather than on the factory. All normal children have the potential to grow into creative adults, just as all flower seeds have the potential to grow into flowers. However, this potential will not be realized unless the teacher-gardener provides the appropriate conditions for optimal growth, just as the seeds need sun, air, and water.* Creativity can't be created, but it can be destroyed. The question is not why creativity develops in a few, but why it is stifled in so many. The best evidence for this view is creativity in children. In our adultocentric view, child behavior tends to be seen as a poor imitation of our adult behavior. It is, rather, a creation in its own right. Piaget argues that each child is his or her own invention.[175] Creativity in children is most obvious with respect to language. A child invents the word *goed* by analogy with *walked* and *talked*. We smugly put this down as a mistake. The fact that it is "wrong" is a reflection on the eccentric exceptions in adult language rather than on the competence of the child. It is also an indication of creativity, since the child could not have acquired such a word by imitating adults.

The garden is worth cultivating. Creativity is what best distinguishes us from other animals. Despite their ingenious adaptation to the environment, bees create only more bees and honey and bears create only more bears (and

---

* Gardiner-as-teacher naturally likes the teacher-as-gardener metaphor.

havoc among the bees). They are adapted to their environment so that they may survive in it, but we can adapt our environment to ourselves so that we may thrive in it. The history of civilization is essentially the story of the discoveries and inventions of our species. On my desk in front of me right now there sit the creative products of many people. I owe my telephone to Alexander Graham Bell, my light to Thomas Edison, my typewriter to the three American inventors Sholes, Glidden, and Soule (and the many unsung inventors who made innovative improvements in its design), and a plethora of useful devices like ball-point pens, carbon paper, paper clips, thumbtacks, and rubber bands to obscure people who first invented them. I may have mixed feelings about the ends to which those tools are used. The telephone can be used to make obscene phone calls and the typewriter for writing threatening letters. However, there is no doubt that these tools can be used to enrich our lives.

Barron points to another factor that contributes to the importance of creativity.[14] He suggests that energy has two outlets—the constructive outlet of creativity and the destructive outlet of violence. In a letter to Albert Einstein, Sigmund Freud attributed the fact that both he and Einstein were pacifists to their ability to express their vitality positively in creativity, rather than negatively in violence.[46]

8.32   *Neglect of Creativity*

Although the importance of creativity is almost universally recognized, the cultivation of creativity is paradoxically neglected. Society places "creativity" with "democracy," "virginity," and "motherhood" as things to be worshiped in theory but demeaned in practice. Indeed, innovators often find that their novel ideas are discouraged rather than encouraged. The more novel the idea, the less adequate the standards for judging it. As argued in Section 5.1, creative ideas tend to be greeted initially as preposterous and eventually as obvious. When the idea is accepted only by its creator, people say "What?" and, when it diffuses throughout a culture so that it is accepted by "everyone," they say "So what?"

This resistance to new ideas may perhaps be explained by the same mechanism that explains their generation. The motivation underlying creativity is the need for stimulation and consistency. In the discussion of those psychological needs (Section 4.13), I suggested that we may be interested in novel stimuli because novel stimuli are potentially dangerous. You are in no danger as long as things remain as they are. That is why the hold-up man says "No sudden moves." Anything new in your environment must be explored and manipulated in order to remove the threat of danger. By exploring and manipulating their environment, creative people generate more novel things, which are threatening to other people. Conservatism is usually explained in terms of maintaining a comfortable status quo, but it is also used to avoid threatening change.

THERE IS ENTHUSIASM ABOUT THE IDEA OF NEW IDEAS BUT NOT ABOUT THE NEW IDEAS THEM-SELVES.

EDWARD DE BONO
THE USE OF LATERAL THINKING

This ambivalent attitude toward creativity is reflected in the school as well as in society. Schools tend to be instruments of stability rather than of change. They push in old ideas rather than pull out new ones. Getzels and Jackson found that their "highly creative" children were not so well liked by their teachers as their "highly intelligent" children.[74] Torrance suggests that creativity peaks at grade 2, after which children tend to adjust to the norm.[221] Three out of five of the eminent (and presumably creative) people studied by Goertzel and Goertzel had school problems.[80] It seems that, if the teacher is the gardener, then the creative student is the "pest" to be discouraged rather than the flower to be nurtured.

Perhaps you remember some creative child from your own experience in school. Indeed, perhaps you *were* such a creative child. You were not very concerned with the popularity contest among your peers (not only did you not win, you didn't even enter) or with grades to win teachers and influence parents. You were, let's face it, a kinda weird kid. Your future occupation took a back seat to your present preoccupation. The projects assigned by your teacher were neglected because you were preoccupied with projects of your own. Since your personal curriculum conflicted with the school curriculum, it was discouraged. You played with ideas rather than with spherical balls and social games. "Stop playing with your mind—it makes you crazy." You had dreams, since this was a first step to realizing them. "Stop dreaming." You would hazard a guess rather than psych out the correct answer when hit point-blank with a question. "Stop guessing." In an atmosphere that discouraged playing with ideas, dreaming, and guessing, you had little opportunity to develop your creativity. The only creativity in such a classroom was to think of creative excuses not to attend it or, if forced to attend, to devise creative strategies to let your wanderlustful mind be absent while your body was present.

8.33   *Creativity in Your Classroom*

In *your* classroom, creativity will, of course, be encouraged rather than discouraged. You will try to create an environment congenial to creativity. A study of the history of ideas suggests two important environmental determinants of creativity—the zeitgeist and serendipity. The **zeitgeist** (German for "spirit of the times") is the total intellectual climate. There was little innovation during the Dark Ages, since the zeitgeist was authoritarian; there was a massive explosion of discoveries and inventions during the Renaissance, since the zeitgeist was democratic. **Serendipity** is the art of discovering things by accident. Skinner stumbled onto partial reinforcement because he got tired of making enough pellets for total reinforcement; Olds found the pleasure center by missing the reticular formation. In the smaller environment of your classroom, zeitgeist corresponds to classroom climate, and serendipity can be facilitated by the use of creative tools. Let us look at each in turn.

In the cultivation of creativity, as in all cultivation, the climate is crucial. The classroom climate is determined largely by the teacher. Empirical evidence suggests that creativity thrives in classrooms, as in cultures, that are democratic rather than authoritarian. Students in informal schools were more creative than students in formal schools.[85] Students did better on tests of spontaneous flexibility under noncompetitive conditions.[1] Warm, spontaneous teachers encouraged creativity more than businesslike, organized teachers.[224] This empirical evidence is supported by the informed opinions of scientists who are experts in both the theory and practice of creativity. Carl Rogers considers psychological safety and freedom as necessary conditions for creativity.[183] Abraham Maslow characterized his self-actualized (that is, highly creative) subjects as being like happy, secure children.[136]

"CREATIVE MINDS DEVELOP BEST WHERE THERE IS A GENUINE RESPECT FOR CREATIVITY."

HANS SELYE
FROM DREAM TO DISCOVERY

Torrance makes the following suggestions for teachers in dealing with creative children in their classrooms: (1) provide a refuge; (2) use whatever power you have in your community to protect creative children from the pressure to conform; (3) help creative children understand their divergence and the good reason for it; (4) let them communicate their ideas by listening to them and helping them to get listened to by others; (5) try to get their creative talent recognized and rewarded; and (6) help parents, principals, and other authority figures to understand them.[222]

You don't have to be creative yourself to cultivate creativity in your students (a good coach is not necessarily a good player)—but it sure helps. You provide a model, not so much of what to do, but of how to do whatever you want to do. Uncreative books about creativity lack conviction, like advice from bald barbers and sick doctors. Children will be creative despite you, but, if you are creative yourself, they may also be creative *because* of you. Your teachers taught you how to teach. Not just your teacher-college teachers, for whom it was on the official curriculum, but all your other teachers, for whom it was on the implicit curriculum. One reason why our profession is so conservative is the tendency to teach as we were taught. Creativity is an antidote to such imitation.

Barron wonders whether the rarity of creativity in adults, as contrasted to the universality of creativity in children, is due to stultifying outside-in forces or is a natural aspect of inside-out growth.[14] He points out that, as we grow older, we seek and acquire order. This order prevents disorder but, unfortunately, also inhibits reorder. De Bono suggests how we can acquire the persistence of the adult yet not lose the flexibility of the child.[36,37] The adult brain is inflexible only when used normally in natural circumstances. De Bono recommends that we create abnormal circumstances and perform unnatural acts. He suggests, for example, that you open a dictionary at random and free-associate to the first word on the page, or that you wander around Woolworth's looking at objects with a particular design problem in mind. You will find such exercises in the spate of books he has written, which may help you remain as creative as your students.

The creative process provides us with tools to extend our nervous systems and, thus, to expand our lives. An important subset of such tools are the tools to create further tools. If those basic tools are not passed on to our children, our society will not be retooled for a fast-changing future. A number

"NOBODY CAN KNOW EVERYTHING, AND EVEN THE MOST PROFOUNDLY CURIOUS ADULT LIVES IN A UNIVERSE WHICH HAS BEEN CONVENTIONALLY STRUCTURED FOR HIM THROUGH 'LEARNINGS' WHICH ELIMINATE INCONVENIENT OR DISTURBING EXPERIENCES OR OBSERVATIONS. THE GROWTH OF MANY SUCH RIGIDITIES OF MIND IS NATURAL AND UNAVOIDABLE. TEACHERS ARE ALWAYS ASKING WHY CHILDREN LOSE THE WONDERFUL CREATIVITY OF THE KINDERGARTEN AGE, AND THE ANSWER IS PLAIN: 'BECAUSE THEY GROW UP.'"

MARTIN MAYER
THE SCHOOLS

of those tools were presented in the pre-exercises. There is some evidence that the use of such tools increases creativity.[86,118] It is ironic to note that those tools to create tools were developed in industry rather than in education. On reflection, it is not surprising that industry is interested in creativity. Capitalism is based—at least theoretically—on the idea that, if you invent a better mousetrap, customers will beat a path to your door. You may want to adapt those techniques to your classroom. We may or may not need better mousetraps, but we certainly need more creative people. Deschooling society may or may not be necessary, but retooling society certainly is essential.

POST-EXERCISES

1. Creative Teaching and Teaching Creativity

Use each of the tools provided in the pre-exercises (brainstorming, Collective Bulletin Board, analogy game, messing around in the matrix) to discover means for creative teaching. Consult the following sources to pick up further means you may have missed.

Hallman, R. J. Techniques of creative teaching. *Journal of Creative Behavior*, 1967, *1*, 325–330.

McLaughlin, F. (Ed.). *The mediate teacher: Seminal essays in creative teaching*. Philadelphia: North American, 1975.

Miel, A. (Ed.). *Creativity in teaching: Invitations and instances*. Belmont, Calif.: Wadsworth, 1961.

Zobes, L. *Spurs to creative teaching*. New York: Putman, 1959.

Use each of the tools to discover means for teaching creativity. Consult the following sources to pick up further means you may have missed.

Michael, W. B. (Ed.). *Teaching for creative endeavor: Bold new venture*. Bloomington: Indiana University Press, 1968.

Taylor, C. W., & Williams, F. E. (Eds.). *Instructional media and creativity*. New York: Wiley, 1966.

Torrance, E. P. *Guiding creative talent*. Englewood Cliffs, N.J.: Prentice-Hall, 1962.

Do you see any relationship between creative teaching and teaching creativity?

2. Testing and Teaching Creativity

A good testing device should double as a teaching device. Here are one or two sample items from each of a number of tests of creativity. Try them out on yourself, or on a class, if you have one handy. Consider how you could use them to teach creativity in your classroom. Glean the sources for further items.

a. ANAGRAMS

How many other words can you make out of the letters of the word *generation?*

Barron, F. Originality in relation to personality and intellect. *Journal of Personality*, 1957, *25*, 730–742.

b. INGENUITY TEST

As part of a manufacturing process, the inside lip of a deep cup-shaped casting is machine-threaded. The company found that metal chips produced by the threading operation were difficult to remove from the bottom of the casting without scratching the sides. A design engineer was able to solve the problem by having the operation performed

A.	i——p	h——h
B.	m——n	c——e
C.	f——r	w——l
D.	l——d	b——k
E.	u——e	d——n

Flanagan, J. Definition and measurement of ingenuity. In C. W. Taylor & F. Barron (Eds.), *Scientific creativity*. New York: Wiley, 1963.

c. REMOTE-ASSOCIATIONS TEST

In a paired-associates test, the subject is given a stimulus word and required to respond with the first word that comes into his or her head. Each of the following groups of three response words was made by subjects to a particular stimulus word. What was the stimulus word in each case?

pot	brick
butterflies	out
ulcer	boat

Mednick, S. The associative basis of the creative process. *Psychological Review*, 1962, *69*, 220–232.

d. CONSEQUENCES (OR JUST SUPPOSE) TEST

What would happen if animals and birds could speak a human language?

Just suppose that no one ever had to go to school anymore; what would happen?

Torrance, E. P. The Minnesota studies of creative behavior: National and international extensions. *The Journal of Creative Behavior*, 1967, *1*(2), 137–154.

e. INSIGHT PUZZLES TEST

Take away four matches from the following figure, leaving three squares and nothing more.

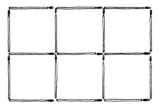

Make four equilateral triangles using six matchsticks.

Without lifting your pencil from the paper, connect all nine dots by drawing four straight lines.

· · ·

· · ·

· · ·

Crutchfield, R. S. Assessment of persons through a quasi-group interaction technique. *Journal of Abnormal and Social Psychology*, 1951, *4*, 577–588.

3. Exceptional Children

I have focused on individual differences in intelligence (Chapter 7) and creativity (Chapter 8) only, illustrating outside-in and inside-out approaches to individual differences, respectively. There are, however, many other dimensions and dichotomies that are relevant to teaching.

One blatant omission is a section on exceptional children, who may have to be treated in special ways. Since this book is for the general practitioner, I have not considered exceptional children in the text. However, if you aspire to be a specialist, or if you want to know enough to diagnose exceptional children in your class in order to refer them to appropriate specialists, or if you have to learn to adjust your teaching to them when no special facilities are available, then you may want to look at some of the following sources as an entrée into this vast literature. The titles indicate which exceptional children are being considered.

DeHaan, R. F., & Kough, J. *Helping children with special needs*. Chicago: Science Research Associates, 1956.
Dunn, L. M. *Exceptional children in the schools*. New York: Holt, Rinehart & Winston, 1963.
Erickson, M. *The mentally retarded child in the classroom*. New York: Macmillan, 1965.
Fliegler, L. A. (Ed.). *Curriculum planning for the gifted*. Englewood Cliffs, N.J.: Prentice-Hall, 1961.
Gallagher, J. J. *Teaching the gifted child*. Boston: Allyn & Bacon, 1964.
Kirk, S. A. *Educating exceptional children* (2nd ed.). Boston: Houghton Mifflin, 1972.
Kolstoe, O. P. *Teaching educable mentally retarded children*. New York: Holt, Rinehart & Winston, 1970.
Kough, J., & DeHaan, R. F. *Identifying children with special needs*. Chicago: Science Research Associates, 1955.
Robinson, H. B., & Robinson, N. M. *The mentally retarded child*. New York: McGraw-Hill, 1965.
Torrance, E. P. *Gifted children in the classroom*. New York: Macmillan, 1965.

Answers for Post-exercise 2

b. INGENUITY TEST

The coded answer is E, for "upside down." However, some ingenious students may have searched in vain for an answer involving the use of a magnet.

c. REMOTE-ASSOCIATIONS TEST

	pot		brick
stomach:	butterflies	*house:*	out
	ulcer		boat

e. INSIGHT PUZZLES TEST

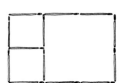 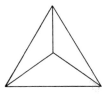

In each case, you have to overcome a set—an unstated assumption about the rules within which you must solve the problem. The sets in these cases are, respectively, "the three squares must all be the same size," "the four triangles must all be on the same two-dimensional surface," and "the lines must not go outside the square." The tendency toward such sets is one of the factors that limits our creativity.

Part Three

Teaching
the Subject
to the Student

Explaining and Understanding 9

9 EXPLAINING AND UNDERSTANDING

PRE-EXERCISES

1. Description and Explanation

Describing and explaining are important teaching skills. Here are a number of opportunities to practice them.

a. Describe the following.
   1. How to cook a favorite dish. This is, of course, simply a recipe. Look at various cookbooks for inspiration. How does the teaching style of James Beard differ from that of Graham Kerr? Can you derive principles for writing good cookbooks?
   2. How to play a favorite game. Look at instructions accompanying games and at books (for example, Hoyle's) describing the rules of games. How do the rules differ from principles of play?
   3. How something works. Look at operating manuals accompanying mechanisms (for example, cars, movie projectors) and at books (such as *How Things Work*) for inspiration.
b. Explain the following.
   1. Why something is as it is. During one of those rare times when the Canadian dollar was worth more than the U.S. dollar, a U.S. tourist made a 35¢ purchase in a Canadian store. She paid with a dollar bill, and the clerk took the 4% discount from the dollar. The tourist protested that she should pay the discount on 35¢ since she had made only a 35¢ purchase. The clerk said she had to pay on the full dollar because she had paid with the dollar. After a heated exchange, the tourist stomped off muttering something about Canadian crooks. Watching this, I thought that some skill in explaining could have done much for U.S.-Canadian relations. If you had been the clerk, how would you have explained it?

2. Why an apparent paradox is not really a paradox. For example, could someone out there explain to me why eggs get harder when I boil them, whereas potatoes get softer?
3. Why something goes wrong. A full description of how something works (as above) would include an explanation of how it sometimes does not work. Add to your description of the function of a system above an explanation of possible malfunctions.

2. Explaining and Giving Directions

Since I travel a lot and (for this and other reasons) get lost a lot, I have accumulated much experience in being given directions. The styles of giving directions reflect different teaching styles. This is not surprising, since the skills are similar. Teaching could be described as helping people get from where they are to where they want to go. Books from Bunyan's *Pilgrim's Progress* to Pirsig's *Zen and the Art of Motorcycle Maintenance* have used the journey as a metaphor for life. A teacher could be seen as a guide on this journey.

Stand at point A and ask passers-by directions to point B. Note the different "teaching" styles. Tease out different principles of teaching on the basis of the effectiveness of the directions.

Modify this procedure as a group exercise. One person specifies local points A and B, and the others describe how to get from A to B. Descriptions may be spoken or written. (It might be useful to record spoken directions for reference.) Compare teaching styles. Discuss principles of teaching that emerge.

9.1   OUTSIDE-IN AND INSIDE-OUT TEACHING

A distinction was made, in Chapter 1, between outside-in and inside-out teaching. The former is based on outside-in learning, and the latter is based on inside-out development. In Section 6.232 I argued that development is the primary process and learning is the secondary process. Because inside-out development is primary, I tend to favor inside-out teaching. My bias is no secret to anyone who has read this far. This does not mean, however, that I consider outside-in teaching unimportant. Indeed, there is a sense in which it is more important. We can do little about the inside-out process of development except respect its primacy, understand its stages, and dovetail our outside-in teaching to it. We can, however, have a profound impact on the outside-in process of learning. We help design the environment our students are assimilating; indeed, we are an important part of that environment ourselves.

Polemics against expository teaching are themselves examples of expository teaching. They share the same fate as Marshall McLuhan's books which inform us that books are useless. If they convince us, then they are wrong; if they fail to convince us, then they may be correct or they may simply have presented a poor exposition. It is fine to make romantic noises about the curiosity of children, but, if that curiosity is to be sustained, we must learn how best to satisfy it. Curiosity, unlike hunger, is whetted by being satisfied.

Indeed, the initiative must come from the child rather than the teacher. However, once the child says "Explain *X* to me," we should be able to explain *X* well. Explaining is at least one of the roads to understanding.

9.2   *THE COMMUNICATION UNIT*

One approach to the development of a psychology of teaching is through the psychology of learning. In Section 3.24 I argued that "every theory of learning is also, by implication, a theory of teaching." A second approach is through the psychology of communicating. Linking teaching with communicating may be more appropriate than linking teaching with learning. There is much teaching without learning and learning without teaching, but there is no teaching without communicating and, it could be argued, no communicating without teaching. Teaching, like communicating, is a process involving two or more people, whereas learning is a process within one person.

IT TAKES TWO OF US TO CREATE A TRUTH, ONE TO UTTER IT AND ONE TO UNDERSTAND IT.

KAHLIL GIBRAN

A useful model for considering the process of communicating is the communication unit of Shannon and Weaver.[197] A simplified version of the **communication unit,** consisting of a source and a destination linked by a channel, is diagrammed in Figure 9-1. As you are reading this, you are the **destination,** I am the **source,** and we are linked by the **visual channel.** If you were to

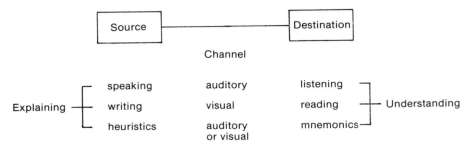

Figure 9-1. The communication unit and the explaining and understanding skills

stop reading and write me a letter of complaint or compliment about this book, then, as I read your letter, you would be the source and I would be the destination. If you chose to telephone rather than write me, we would not only reverse roles but switch channels. We would be communicating over the **auditory channel.** In our conversation over the telephone, we could rapidly alternate the roles of source and destination. This two-way communication is one of the advantages of the auditory over the visual channel. A counteradvantage of the visual channel, of course, is that cold print is more permanent than hot air. If you were to present your compliments or complaints face to face, we could add the nonverbal aspect of the visual channel (that rich language of gestures and expressions) to the verbal aspect and, if you were to become violent or affectionate, we might even add the tactile channel to our repertoire. The address, by the way, is R.R. 1, Alcove, Quebec, Canada J0X IA0 (if you are tired of being the destination and want to change roles), and the telephone number is (819) 459-2139 (if you want to switch channels). At least make our visual channel two-way by writing rude remarks in the margins.

Three major revolutions in the history of our species involve the acquisition of communication tools. We acquired the capacity to communicate over the auditory channel through the skills of speaking and listening; we acquired the capacity to communicate over the visual channel through the skills of writing and reading; we acquired certain techniques for organizing information at the source for effective transmission (**heuristics**) and certain techniques for organizing information at the destination for effective reception (**mnemonics**).* Let us refer to the set of skills at the source as **explaining skills** and to the set of skills at the destination as **understanding skills.** Those skills are presented in their appropriate places within the communication unit in

---

* This third revolution is not so familiar as the first two. This is due to the fact that the revolution is currently taking place (we are too close to see it clearly) and partly perhaps to the fact that I am just imagining it. I am tempted to invent new words to describe the source and destination skills involved in this revolution. However, rather than clutter up our language with yet more neologisms, I decided to use the closest available terms, *heuristics* and *mnemonics*, at the risk of violating some of the present meaning of those terms.

Figure 9-1. Teaching is traditionally associated with the explaining skills of speaking, writing, and heuristics, and learning with the understanding skills of listening, reading, and mnemonics. It is useful, however, to replace *teaching* with *explaining* and *learning* with *understanding*. The terms *teaching* and *learning* have become too intimately tied to the roles of teacher and student. The teacher teaches and the student learns; that is, the teacher is the source and the student is the destination. In fact, communication is a two-way process. Both teachers and students must acquire and use both explaining skills and understanding skills.

9.3   EXPLAINING AND UNDERSTANDING

9.31   Neglect of Processes

Explaining is the essence of teaching, and understanding is the essence of learning; yet both processes have been neglected by psychologists. The term *explaining* does not appear at all in the index of *Psychological Abstracts,* and the term *understanding* is followed by "see 'comprehension,' " thereby limiting it to the narrow sense of interpreting written and spoken material. The terms seldom appear in the indexes of textbooks on educational psychology. Only the textbook by Gage and Berliner contains a discussion of the process of explaining, and that is a description of their own work at Stanford University.[65] Only a few textbooks by behaviorists contain a discussion of the process of understanding, and those are merely criticisms of the concept *understanding* in contrast to their more precise behavioristic concepts. Psychologists are concerned, it seems, with understanding everything but understanding itself.*

9.32   Explaining

Philosophers of science, on the other hand, have devoted considerable effort to clarifying the concept of explanation. The best entrée to this literature for a teacher is possibly Jane Martin's *Explaining, Understanding and Teaching,* since, as her title suggests, she links explaining to understanding and embeds both within the context of teaching.[134] One point emerging from their discussion that is most relevant to the teacher is the subjective nature of explanation. What constitutes an explanation for one destination may not be an explanation for another destination. In our terms, explaining involves not

---

* Of almost 500 titles beginning *Understanding* listed in *Books in Print,* 1977–78—ranging from *Understanding Aging* to *Understanding Zen*—only two were entitled *Understanding Understanding.* One (Paul Ziff, Ithaca: Cornell University Press, 1972) was a philosophical analysis of the meaning of the word *understanding,* which I did not understand, and the other (Humphry Osmond, New York: Harper & Row, 1974) was not about "understanding understanding" at all but simply used it as a catchy title.

only knowing the subject but knowing the student. It is necessary to know a child in order to know what explanation would be satisfying to that child.

Consider, for example, the perennial question "Where do I come from?" The answer "Mummy's tummy" may be all that is initially required. The child goes off to assimilate that information and returns with "How did I get in

HOWEVER I BEGAN TO EXPLAIN TO HIM THEN AND AT INTERVALS ALL THAT WINTER I EXPLAINED IT TO HIM HOW EXPLANATIONS ARE CLEAR BUT NO ONE TO WHOM A THING IS EXPLAINED CAN CONNECT THE EXPLANATIONS WITH WHAT IS REALLY CLEAR, THEN CLEAR EXPLANATIONS ARE NOT CLEAR.

GERTRUDE STEIN
EVERYONE'S AUTOBIOGRAPHY

there?" "Daddy put you in" may be a satisfying (and, hence, satisfactory) answer. Having digested that, the child may come back with "How did he put me in?" and thus trigger further explanation. Subsequent questions would force more and more sophisticated explanations until, eventually, no further explanation is possible because we have reached the limit of our understanding within this domain. The parceling-out of information at higher and higher levels of explanation is recommended, not out of any sense of squeamishness about the topic, but out of a sense of the appropriateness of the explanation for children at different levels of sophistication. The best guide to what needs explaining is the questions children ask, and the best guide to the appropriate level of explanation is that the questions stop, indicating that the child is satisfied—for now—with the explanation. There is an optimal level of explanation. You can provide too much information as well as too little.* Sex-education books, like *How to Teach Your Child About Sex (Without Making a Complete Ass of Yourself)*, are designed to help parents gauge the appropriate level of explanation.

Students in schools stop asking questions—alas, not because they receive a satisfying answer, but, too often, because the answers they receive are so *un*satisfying that it is not worth asking further questions. They soon discover that schools are not set up to answer their questions and that, when they persist in asking them, teachers tend not to be equipped to answer them. The arguments against basing the curriculum on the questions of children are obvious. Each teacher must deal with 30 or so children, who are all asking different questions, and children are not sufficiently sophisticated about the world to know which questions to ask. However, the set of answers that constitutes a curriculum should surely, in some way, take into consideration the questions of the children to whom those answers are provided. Children, indeed, do not all ask the same questions. However, a little empirical research would reveal the typical questions asked by children of different ages. Children are, indeed, not so sophisticated about the world as adults. However, the best way to make them more sophisticated is to answer their questions so that they are forced to escalate to more and more sophisticated questions. They will acquire only a pseudosophistication if loaded with answers to questions they have never asked. Mayer describes a curriculum based on the questions of children at Orange Grove School in Whittier, California.[143]

Have you ever observed tourists who are inexperienced in talking to people who do not understand their language? When they are not understood, they tend to repeat their message over and over in a louder and louder voice. Talking to young children is much like talking to foreign-speaking people. Indeed, your own child is more "foreign" than an adult from Timbuktu. The foreign-speaking adult has only a different language structure, but, as Jean Piaget informs us (see Chapter 5), your child has a different thought structure. Inexperienced teachers tend to adopt the same ineffective strategy as the tourist. The lesson is repeated or shouted until at least the appearance of understanding is achieved. Teachers should learn not to play the same record over and over or to turn up the volume, but to adjust the tuning. Any message can be understood, as Bruner points out, if it is explained at the appropriate level, or in the appropriate form, for the children to whom it is addressed.[25] Having determined the typical questions at each age level, we should continue to determine the explanations that are typically satisfying. A spiral curriculum,

---

*Our tendency to overexplain is nicely captured in the anecdote about a father suddenly confronted by his daughter's question "What is sex?" He had been priming himself for such a question and launched into a long, detailed explanation of the facts of life. His daughter waited respectfully for him to finish and then pointed to the space marked "sex" on a questionnaire she was filling out.

"—WE CAN DISCOVER THE BOUNDARIES OF WHAT A CHILD KNOWS SIMPLY BY ASKING QUESTIONS, AND THE BOUNDARIES PROVIDE EVIDENCE OF READINESS FOR MOVING FROM THE FAMILIAR TO THE UNFAMILIAR. LEARNING OCCURS WHEN THE LEARNER PERCEIVES THAT A NEW EXPERIENCE RESEMBLES AN OLD ONE."

KARL H. PRIBRAM
"NEUROLOGICAL NOTES ON THE ART OF EDUCATING."

as advocated by Bruner, would be designed to meet the more and more sophisticated versions of the questions and answers to those questions that one would expect as children get older. An aspect of teacher education would be the presentation of questions and explanations that are appropriate to the grade the teacher will be teaching.

Another aspect of teacher-training would be respect for the explanations of children. What constitutes a good explanation is a function not only of the destination but also of the source. Since communication is a two-way process, students must sometimes explain and teachers must sometimes understand. A child's explanation should not necessarily be judged by an adult's standards. * Nor should a child's explanation be dismissed too readily because it is not immediately obvious. Jones, who is a therapist as well as a teacher, cites the following conversation in the sixth-grade arithmetic class of one of his clients, Billy: [106]

> *Teacher:* And now can anyone tell me what infinity means? (silence) What is infinity?
> *Billy:* (pause) Uh, I think it's like a box of Cream of Wheat.
> *Teacher:* Billy, don't be silly!

Later, Billy explained to his therapist what he was not allowed to explain to his teacher.

> *Therapist:* Billy, *how* is infinity like a box of Cream of Wheat?
> *Billy:* Well, think of a box of Cream of Wheat. It shows a man holding a box of Cream of Wheat. Right? And that box shows the same man holding the same box. Right? And that box. . . . You can't see them all, like you can't see infinity. You just know they're all there going on forever and ever.

Next time you look at a bottle of Dubonnet (the adult equivalent of a box of Cream of Wheat), see if *you* don't think of infinity.

---

* At one point in my elementary school career, I used to run to school pushing my gir (a metal hoop propelled by a hooked stick). One evening, I lost my gir; the next morning, I was late for school. "Why are you late?" "I lost my gir and had to walk to school." This still sounds like a perfectly good 8-year-old's explanation, but I was punished for "insolence."

9.33 *Defining Understanding*

9.331 *As Inverse of Explaining*

An **inverse operation** "undoes" a given operation. Thus, subtraction is the inverse operation to addition, and division is the inverse operation to multiplication. Speaking and listening are inverse operations: speaking is the process of encoding a message for transmission over the auditory channel, and listening is the inverse process of decoding the message for reception. Writing and reading are inverse operations: writing is the process of encoding a message for transmission over the visual channel, and reading is the inverse process of decoding the message for reception. Insofar as explaining is simply speaking and writing and understanding is simply listening and reading, then explaining

and understanding are inverse operations. However, since explaining is only one of the means toward understanding, understanding is not merely the inverse operation to explaining. Much can be understood that is not explained. When asked to explain his special magic in playing the trumpet, Louis Armstrong said, "If you don't know, I can't tell you; if you know, I don't need to tell you." You may remember Woody Allen's long search throughout the movie *Bananas* for that missing something which explained why a certain lady didn't love him. Such things are understood from the inside out—they can't be explained from the outside in. Indeed, such deep understanding can be damaged by explaining. Holt reports that a class of children who knew how to make paper fans no longer knew after it had been explained to them.[94]

9.332   *As Explaining to Self*

A foreign-speaking friend once gave me an insight into a more productive way of viewing understanding than as simply the inverse operation to explaining. She said "I can't explain that to myself" when she obviously meant "I can't understand that." As so often happens, "bad" grammar is good logic. Understanding can be considered as explaining to yourself. Someone explaining something to you may indeed help you explain it to yourself (that is, understand it), but this is only one of the ways. You can explain something to yourself in that intimate communication in which you are both source and destination. No one else need be present. You may discover, however, that another person helps you understand, not by explaining something to you but by permitting you to explain it to her. In the process of explaining it to her, you explain it to yourself. It is better to be the source than the destination, because you are actively involved in constructing the explanation. You are also more actively involved in the presentation of the explanation. You essentially attend your own class—a class you can't skip or sleep through. That is why you learn so much more by teaching than by "learning."

"I WENT THROUGH IT (QUANTUM THEORY) ONCE AND LOOKED UP ONLY TO FIND THE CLASS FULL OF BLANK FACES — THEY HAD OBVIOUSLY NOT UNDERSTOOD. I WENT THROUGH IT A SECOND TIME AND THEY STILL DID NOT UNDERSTAND IT. AND SO I WENT THROUGH IT A THIRD TIME, AND THAT TIME I UNDERSTOOD IT."

JEROME S. BRUNER
THE PROCESS OF EDUCATION

Even if understanding and explaining were inverse operations, the skills of explaining and understanding would not be perfectly correlated. Those who are good at multiplication are not necessarily good at division. However, the fact that understanding is more than the inverse operation to explaining makes the correlation even less perfect. Being able to explain something to yourself does not necessarily imply that you can explain it to someone else. As I said before, a good player is not necessarily a good coach. The skills that distinguish a good player who is also a good coach from a good player who is simply a good player are the special skills of the teacher. That is, teachers not only understand, but can explain what they understand to others.

9.333   *As Knowing How*

Understanding is, however, even broader than that which is explained—by self or others. Neither the farmer nor the cow can explain to the cow how to transform grass into milk. Yet the cow "understands" how to do it in a much more profound sense than the bovine biologist knows how. The cow can do it. In the same way, you and I "understand" how to breathe, how to maintain our balance, how to cure a cut (from the inside), and so on. We understand how to do those things but can't explain how to do them. Learned skills based on those organic processes tend to be difficult to explain.

EXPLANATIONS. WE TEACHERS — PERHAPS ALL HUMAN BEINGS — ARE IN THE GRIP OF AN ASTONISHING DELUSION. WE THINK THAT WE CAN TAKE A PICTURE, A STRUCTURE, A WORKING MODEL OF SOMETHING, CONSTRUCTED IN OUR MINDS OUT OF LONG EXPERIENCE AND FAMILIARITY, AND BY TURNING THAT MODEL INTO A STRING OF WORDS, TRANSPLANT IT WHOLE INTO THE MIND OF SOMEONE ELSE.

JOHN HOLT
HOW CHILDREN LEARN

Consider bicycling. No amount of explaining will bring you to that magic moment when suddenly you have the knack. You have to try again and again until the understanding is built into your body. There is no innate bicycle-riding instinct. Mother Nature could never have anticipated such a crazy invention when she designed you. There is, however, an innate ability to keep your center of gravity within your base to maintain your balance, and this ability can be adapted to situations in which your base is artificially transformed into a pair of skis, a couple of tires, a Pogo stick, or a rope stretched over Niagara Falls. The fact that such inside-out skills are understood but not explained does not mean that a teacher is unnecessary. It merely means that the role of the teacher changes. The teacher does not explain, but helps understand. One way to help understand is to serve as a model. Elkind suggests an alternative to the watch-me school of education.[49] The teacher watches the student rather than having the student watch the teacher. Elkind illustrates from his own experience of helping his son understand how to ride a bicycle. By watching his son closely, he discovered that he was, at any one time, either pedaling or steering. After this was brought to his attention, his son soon mastered the art of simultaneously pedaling and steering in order to maintain his balance.

During a personal energy crisis, I bought a bicycle. Although I had not ridden a bicycle for 15 years, I could ride it right away without any difficulty. Later, on returning from a month's vacation, I could no longer ride it. I had forgotten the number of the combination lock I bought for it. The inside-out learning to ride a bicycle was much more durable than the outside-in learning of my combination. This fact causes extreme inside-outers to argue that all important learning is inside-out learning. However, outside-in learning is important, too. My failure to remember my combination was as effective in preventing me from riding my bicycle as would have been my failure to remember how to ride a bicycle. Explaining from the outside in is necessary in those cases when it is impossible to understand from the inside out. There is no way nature could equip you with the means of "understanding" an arbitrary sequence of numbers. Indeed, if it could, my combination lock would be useless. You and the friendly neighborhood bicycle thief could learn my combination.

9.34 Measuring Understanding

As mentioned earlier, behaviorists deride the concept of understanding because of its vagueness. The fact that a concept is difficult to define and measure, however, does not mean that it is unimportant. Indeed, a case could be made that something which can be measured with our simple instruments must be so trivial that it is hardly worth studying. We should shift our focus from what is measurable, however clear, to what *is*, however vague. I have made an attempt to define understanding—as the inverse operation to explaining, as explaining to oneself, and as knowing how. Let me suggest some small steps toward measuring understanding.

In the army, an officer checks whether an order has been understood by requiring the soldier to repeat it back to him. When you send a telegram by telephone, the operator reads your telegram back to you to ensure that the correct message has been received. Schools have gone little beyond this primitive test of understanding. It is inadequate, since it can be passed by the simpler process of memorizing. Any success such a test has in measuring understanding is due to the fact that understanding does indeed help in the memorizing of long, complex messages. Such a test can, at best, measure understanding only in its simplest form, as the inverse operation to explaining.

Objective examinations are notorious for their emphasis on memorizing rather than understanding. They can, however, be designed to test for understanding. A multiple-choice item, for example, can be used to test understanding of the implications of a principle rather than simply recognition of the principle. If students understand the principle, they will be aware of its implications. An item can be designed so that a student who is aware of an implication of the principle will choose the appropriate alternative and a student who has certain misunderstandings of the principle will be fiendishly lured toward the other options. Another alternative is to devise a number of items all involving the same principle and define understanding of that principle as getting a certain number of those items correct. In my doctoral thesis, for example, I devised six items of varying content embodying each of a number of logical principles.[69] A student who got at least five of those items correct was said to understand this principle. This was a reasonable conclusion, since the probability of getting at least five out of six items correct by chance, when there are three alternatives for each, is very small—less than 1 in 50, to be more precise.

Essay questions in which the student is invited to explain some principle may be better tests of understanding. The assumption underlying such tests is that students who can explain the principle to others can explain it to themselves—that is, can understand it. However, just as understanding does not imply explaining, so the ability to explain does not imply the ability to understand. The explanation may simply be a parroting of the explanation provided by the teacher. The "in your own words" qualifier may be useful. The best test of an explanation is that it is understood by the destination. Essays should perhaps be evaluated, then, not by the teacher, who presumably understands the principle already and thus cannot tell whether this explanation contributed to his or her understanding, but by another student, who does not understand the principle. My grandfather was principal (and sole teacher) in a one-room schoolhouse for half a century. I once asked him how he could possibly teach all grade levels in one classroom. He said that he only taught the oldest child, who taught the next oldest, who taught the next, and so on down the line. Perhaps the reason so many of his students (including his own three sons and three daughters) did not suffer from the "disadvantage" of a one-room schoolhouse was that they learned to understand through explaining so that others understood. Is that clear? I'm trying to make this book so clear that even I understand it.

Understanding, in its most profound sense of knowing how, is, paradoxically, the easiest to test. The test for understanding how to ride a bicycle is riding a bicycle.

9.4   SPEAKING AND LISTENING

Communication over the auditory channel precedes communication over the visual channel in the history of our species. We were speaking and listening for many thousands of years before we learned, quite recently, the tricks of writing and reading. In our individual histories, each of us learns to use the auditory channel before learning to use the visual channel; that is, we speak and listen before we write and read. Within each channel, we learn to receive before we learn to transmit—we listen before we speak, we read before we write. Indeed, throughout our adult lives, we continue to be able to receive more than we can transmit. Our recognition vocabulary is always much larger than our use vocabulary. The capacity to transmit, in each channel, is based on the capacity to receive. You can't speak until you can listen; you can't write until you can read. Deaf-mutes usually are not born mute; they are born deaf. They can't learn to speak because they can't listen to themselves and others speaking. Listening is, therefore, the basic skill. Speaking is based on listening; writing and reading are, in turn, based on speaking and listening; other human skills are, in turn, based on these communication skills.

NATURE HAS GIVEN TO MEN ONE TONGUE, BUT TWO EARS, THAT WE MAY HEAR FROM OTHERS TWICE AS MUCH AS WE SPEAK.

EPICTETUS

The skill of listening is so basic, indeed, that it is taken for granted. Writing and reading always appear in the curriculum, speaking sometimes, but listening never. However, although it never appears officially in the curriculum, listening is, paradoxically, the most practiced skill. Students spend most of their time in school either listening or pretending to listen.* The skill of listening illustrates one of the most blatant discrepancies between the official curriculum (what is being taught) and the actual curriculum (what is being learned). In the traditional school, listening is never taught but always learned.

Most of the time, teachers speak and students listen. Teachers need practice in listening, and students need practice in speaking. Many apartment buildings have a device with a lever marked "speak" in one position and "listen" in another position for communicating with visitors at the front door. One of the occupational hazards of teaching is the tendency to get your lever jammed in the "speak" position. It is especially important for teachers to learn to listen. Children tend to be poor transmitters, and teachers must be good receivers, in compensation, so that communication will be effective. The most frequent complaint of teenagers who attempt suicide is that no one is listening. We must learn to listen, not just to the rational but to the emotional content, not just to the verbal but to the nonverbal aspects of the content, not just to what the children are saying but to what they are meaning. If children continue to ask for something after you give it to them, then perhaps what they are asking for is not what they want. One of the insights that may have emerged from pursuing the analogy between the teacher-student and therapist-client relationships, suggested in Pre-exercise 2 to Chapter 3, is that therapists are essentially professional listeners, and teachers may benefit from emulating their listening skills.

"THERE IS ONE BLANKET STATEMENT WHICH CAN SAFELY BE MADE ABOUT THE WORLD'S SCHOOLS: THE TEACHERS TALK TOO MUCH."

MARTIN MAYER
THE SCHOOLS

The acquisition of a first language provides a fine illustration of the interaction between inside-out developmental processes and outside-in learning processes. We have already looked at Skinner's attempt to explain the acquisition of language (Section 3.222) as an outside-in learning process. Perhaps he can explain why a child learns a *particular* language in terms of instrumental conditioning, but he can't explain why a child learns a language per se. Karena,

---

* Any appearance of intelligence in well-schooled people may be due to this prolonged practice in listening. One of my professors in graduate school told me that a distinguished visiting professor had been impressed by my intelligence. I recalled my only meeting with him, in the company of two other graduate students. My only contribution to the conversation had been a few nods and "mm-hmms." However, I was deeply interested in what he was saying and I had listened very intently. Since then, I've never worried about people I admire thinking I am stupid. There's no danger as long as I keep my mouth shut.

WHEN CHILDREN ARE NOT SATISFIED AFTER THEY GET WHAT THEY ASKED FOR, IT IS BECAUSE WHAT THEY ASK FOR IS ONLY A SUBSTITUTE FOR WHAT THEY REALLY WANT AND ARE NOT GETTING.

SYDNEY J. HARRIS
SAN FRANCISCO CHRONICLE

an Eskimo girl adopted by my neighbors here in Canada, speaks English. Skinner could explain why Karena speaks English rather than Eskimo. She is growing up in a community in which she can imitate English sounds and sentences and is reinforced for creating English sounds and sentences. Such a language community is a necessary condition for the acquisition of a language, but it is not a sufficient condition. The same neighbors also "adopted" a husky. Pattak spent his first few years in an Eskimo-language community and his later years in an English-language community, but Pattak (who would be bilingual now, were he a Skinnerian dog) has learned neither Eskimo nor English. Karena—but, alas, not poor Pattak—was born with the potential to speak a language, any language, and that potential could be realized by spending her early years in any language community.

Noam Chomsky explains the acquisition of language as an inside-out developmental process.[30] The child is prewired to acquire a language. Each child reinvents grammar. The outside-in contribution of the language community serves the necessary, but secondary, function of providing the "fuel" to keep the grammar-generating genetic machinery working. Sentences are not generated sequentially from left to right, as behaviorists imply, but hierarchically from **deep** to **surface structure.** You start with the intention of generating a sentence and then apply, in appropriate order, a number of rules. The sentence must contain a noun phrase and a verb phrase. The noun phrase must contain an article and a noun. The verb phrase must contain a verb and a noun phrase. By applying those vocabulary rules, the **kernel sentence** is churned out, as indicated in Figure 9-2. **Rules of transformation** may, then, be used to make this sentence ("The boy hit the ball") passive ("The ball was hit by the boy"), negative ("The boy did not hit the ball"), or interrogative ("Did the boy hit the ball?").

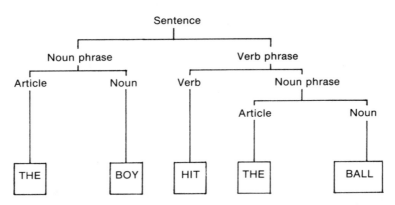

Figure 9-2. The hierarchical structure underlying the sequential generation of a sentence

9.5 WRITING AND READING

We do not teach children to speak and listen. Many critics of teaching argue that, if we taught them, they'd never learn. We do, however, teach children to write and read. This makes sense. Whereas speaking-listening is largely biologically determined, writing-reading is largely culturally determined. Writing, and the necessary inverse skill of reading, are cultural inventions. They must be passed on from generation to generation. In our terms, speaking-listening is based mainly on the inside-out process of development, whereas writing-reading is based mainly on the outside-in process of learning. Teachers can, therefore, contribute more to the writing-reading processes than to the speaking-listening processes.

The fact that we can teach it, however, does not mean that communication over the visual channel is more important than communication over the auditory channel. We should, of course, teach children to read and write. However, perhaps we should not base the entire elementary school curriculum on reading. Children (especially children who are not ready to read, as argued in Section 6.233) may not get the knack of it and be at a disadvantage throughout their school careers and, indeed, possibly throughout their entire lives. When reading is the key to the curriculum, many children are locked out. Our species has been communicating over the auditory channel for much longer than over the visual channel. We have been speaking and listening to one another for millions of years but have been writing and reading to one another for only a few thousand years. The overwhelming emphasis in schools is on those comparatively recent tricks of writing and reading.* We are like a child who gets a flashy new toy and abandons a faithful old teddy bear. Speaking is not only neglected—it is prevented. Little children should be seen and not heard. Silence is golden. This emphasis on the visual channel in school contributes to the failure to transfer between school and out-of-school activities. Writing-reading is emphasized in school, whereas speaking-listening is emphasized out of school. Students, therefore, tend to separate those things they write about (school things) and those things they speak about (out-of-school things). Enlightened parents find it difficult to persuade their children to speak about school things, and enlightened teachers find it difficult to persuade their children to write about out-of-school things. A salesperson gets several years of instruction in writing-reading, which he or she may squander on writing checks and reading timetables, but no instruction on speaking-listening, which he or she did after school and does after schooling most of the time.

No one is likely to do for writing what Chomsky did for speaking—that is, claim, with much supporting evidence, that our species has an innate potentiality to write, which will be realized if people grow up in a language community where they are exposed to writing. We can't expect children to start writing spontaneously as they start speaking spontaneously. This does not mean, however, that we can't capitalize on intrinsic motivation. I argued in Section 9.333 that, whereas we do not have an innate bicycle-riding skill, we can build that skill on an innate balance-keeping skill. In a similar way, there is an underlying organic basis to writing and reading. We have a built-in tendency to know and understand our environment (see Section 4.13). An important part of our modern environment consists of written material. As I suggested earlier, look at your present environment right now through a mirror. Some parts of it, you will notice, look funny (like this page, for instance, or the spines of the books in your library, or posters on your wall, or signs outside your window). To an illiterate, those parts always look funny. I once spent a week in a Japanese village in which no English was spoken or written. There was not even the comfort of familiar letters. This experience gave me a glimpse into the impoverished world of the illiterate and an insight into the intrinsic motivation of an illiterate in his or her own society—a child who has not yet learned

---

* Reasons for the emphasis on the visual over the auditory channel are obvious and understandable. Writing is quiet, whereas speaking is noisy. Writing produces a product, whereas speaking leaves no trace. Products produce an impression of productive activity. Those advantages are administrative rather than pedagogical. How do we prevent that tendency within institutions for procedures designed to perform a function to yield to procedures designed for ease of administration?

to read. The child is intrinsically motivated to write as well as to read. Gibson and Lewin conclude, on the basis of a large body of experimental evidence, that "children, given the tools and proper surroundings, will scribble, draw, and print spontaneously, improving their writing ability without formal instruction."[75] One major disadvantage of "disadvantaged" homes is that there is little written material lying around and, more important, there are few adults picking it up. There are seldom writing materials or models of adults using them. Therefore, as a teacher and as a parent, you can encourage writing and reading by providing writing and reading materials and models in the child's environment.

A number of teachers have shown how such outside-in influences can trigger inside-out motivation. O. K. Moore provides children with **talking typewriters,** which "say" each letter as the children depress each key.[156] No instructions are given—or, apparently, required. Children spontaneously play with those typewriters and, incidentally, learn to write and read. Sylvia Ashton-Warner bases her **organic method** of teaching writing and reading on intrinsic motivation.[9] She invites the children in her class to ask her for a word they would like to learn to write and read, and gives them each a "private" word printed on a large card. The child says the word and traces it. The cards are collected, shuffled, and dumped on the floor the next day. The children find their own cards, exchange words with partners, and go to the teacher for new words. When each child has accumulated a key vocabulary of 30 words, the children are encouraged to write their own key words and to write sentences, using their key words and some general vocabulary which is provided. The children are eventually able to write their own texts based on their own experience. Their chosen words are "captions of the mind pictures" rather than captions of some remote pictures in a McGuffey Reader.

The history of teaching children to read could be considered as a continuing debate between the advocates of the phonetic method and the whole-word method.[141]

The **phonetic method** piggybacks the new symbolic system for communication over the visual channel on the old symbolic system for communication over the auditory channel. The basic unit of the visual system is the **grapheme** (roughly corresponding to the letter), and the basic unit of the auditory system is the **phoneme** (roughly corresponding to the speech sound). Since children already know the phonemes, the basis of their established skills of speaking and listening, they can, by learning the equivalent graphemes, acquire the skills of writing and reading. The major difficulty with this argument is that English and other natural languages do not have a set of graphemes which correspond to one and only one phoneme. One phoneme may have many corresponding graphemes (for example, the sound o may be represented by the letters b*eau, oh,* d*oe,* wh*oa,* g*o,* m*ow,* s*ew,* th*ough*), and one grapheme may have many corresponding phonemes (for example, the letter *o* may represent the sounds b*o*ne, d*o*ne, *o*ne, g*o*ne). This problem can be solved by inventing an artificial written language in which there is perfect phoneme-grapheme correspondence. Such a language is the **Initial Teaching Alphabet (ITA),** consisting of 44 graphemes corresponding to the 44 phonemes which are the basis of the English language. Children quickly learn those correspondences and are soon reading and writing with this alphabet. The discrepancy between their "funny" books and "real" books becomes apparent, however, and the news must be broken to them that adults have many strange exceptions to the child's perfect system. They seem not at all surprised by such adult craziness and tolerantly proceed to learn those exceptions in order to be able to read "real" books. This procedure is very much like learning to drive a car by learning first with an automatic transmission and, once you have mastered the basics, taking on the additional complication of shifting gears.

Advocates of the **whole-word method** argue that, whereas the phoneme is, indeed, the smallest unit of spoken language, the **morpheme** (corresponding roughly to the word) is the smallest *meaningful* unit. The sounds *d, o, g* have no equivalents in the physical world, but the word *dog* has. Children should be taught to read, not by piggybacking the visual symbolic system on the auditory symbolic system, but by linking the visual symbolic system directly to their equivalents in the physical world. This method takes advantage of intrinsic motivation. Children are not interested in *d*'s, *o*'s, and *g*'s, but they are interested in *dogs*. The fact that children are interested in what dogs or other aspects of their own experience, physical or psychological, look like in writing is demonstrated by Ashton-Warner, whose little cards given to each child with their private words come back with the "dirt and disrepair of passionate usage."[9] Only one-look words are included in a child's key vocabulary, since words that are not recognized immediately as a whole presumably do not represent an important aspect of the child's experience.

Gibson and Lewin argue that this Great Debate about how best to teach reading has distracted researchers from the more productive question of how children learn to read.[75] The debate is fruitless, since the advocates of the two positions (like the blind men touching the tail, the trunk, and the tusks of the elephant) are merely looking at different parts of the whole. A language is a hierarchy of units (phonemes, morphemes, sentences, discourses) plus rules for combining units at each level to create meaningful units at the next level (phonemes to morphemes—vocabulary; morphemes to sentences—grammar; sentences to discourses—logic). Learning a language involves learning the rules at all levels. The phonetic versus whole-word debate reduces to the question of whether to begin at the level of the phoneme or the morpheme. Most modern methods of teaching reading use some combination of both methods. They take advantage of the motivational effect of recognizing whole words. It is, indeed, true that those who are taught by the whole-word method have an initial advantage because of this motivation. However, it is like learning to type by the two-finger, hunt-and-peck system. You are typing right away, but you soon reach a ceiling—your eyes and fingers can move only so fast. To get beyond this ceiling, you have to go back to learning the keyboard and typing at a slower initial rate. This is difficult, because you have to unlearn the hunt-and-peck habits and are unwilling to take a step backward in order to take two steps forward later. Most modern methods also take advantage of the economy of a phonetic system of language in which everything from the instructions on your cornflakes box to the plays of Shakespeare can be constructed out of 26 letters and 44 sounds.

9.6   HEURISTICS AND MNEMONICS

Heuristics were described earlier as the set of techniques for organizing information at the source for effective transmission, and mnemonics as the set of techniques for organizing information at the destination for effective reception. They are not inverse processes in the same sense as speaking-listening and writing-reading are inverse processes. Heuristics reduce the need for mnemonics; that is, if the information is organized at the source, it need not be organized at the destination. Since an active rather than a passive destination contributes to communication, a case could be made for a disorganized presentation by the source to force organization by the destination. Henry Luce, founder of *Time,* used to cut chunks out of the logical presentations of his writers to force readers to fill in those gaps in the argument themselves and, thus, get actively involved in the presentation. I once sat enthralled through a beautifully organized lecture but found that, when I later tried to tell a friend about it, I had not retained much of the content. The next time I listened to the same lecturer, I forced myself to take notes—although, as I took them, I was convinced that I would never need them. When I tried to recall it later, I had indeed forgotten most of it (although the act of taking notes had helped a bit) and could only resurrect the lecture by rereading the notes. Smooth lectures may be like all those smooth airplane trips you never remember. It may be useful to introduce some turbulence, as in that one flight you will never forget. This argument should not be used as a rationalization for not preparing lectures. It takes more preparation to create that orderly disorder which gets your audience actively involved than to create that order which encourages your audience to sit back passively and enjoy the show.

POST-EXERCISES

1. Note-Making

The first schools used the auditory channel. Teachers spoke and students listened. The printing press opened up the more efficient visual channel and made the traditional lecture obsolete. Teachers, bogged down by the inertia of tradition, continued to use the auditory channel but introduced a peculiar twist. Teachers read and students wrote. Teachers transformed from the visual to the auditory channel (they read their notes), and students transformed back from the auditory to the visual channel (they wrote *their* notes). This elaborate procedure employs 101 people for two hours to make 100 poor copies of the notes of the professor. A single secretary could duplicate 100 perfect copies during a coffee break. But, hush—the unemployment situation is bad enough.

If you find yourself participating in this peculiar academic ritual, then, instead of transferring to a secretarial school where you will also learn typing and shorthand, you may want to use this listening-and-writing skill of note-taking to practice your listening and writing skills. I recommend the following procedure, which I call note-*making* and which I used to learn to write.

a. During each lecture, get down as much of it as you can on the right side of your notebook. Use your own private shorthand, spelling, grammar—whatever is necessary to resurrect the lecture later.
b. As soon as possible after the lecture, while it is still fresh, rewrite your notes on the left side of your notebook opposite your original notes. As you rewrite, translate as much as possible into your own words, throw out redundant sentences and words, reorganize the material as logically as you can. Put a question mark in the margin opposite statements you don't understand, apparent inconsistencies, and logical leaps you can't make. Find the answers to your questions by consulting the textbook, the professor, or that bright classmate you wanted to talk to anyway. (This second step is a useful way to fill in those spare hours between classes.)
c. At the weekend, type up your notes for the previous week. Once again, as you type them, rephrase, organize, and condense the notes as much as possible. Eliminate redundancies from lecture to lecture. Tease out the hierarchical structure underlying the sequential presentation. Diagram this structure as a frame on which to hang the content. Add, in brackets, your personal reactions to the lectures.
d. Shortly before the examination, read through your notes for the course to reassure yourself that you know the material. You will be pleased to discover that you have learned it through the process of writing and rewriting it.
e. In the evening before the examination, go see a movie, sleep a guiltless sleep, get up fresh, and go collect your "A" (or, at worst, a "B," if you slip up badly).

I make it sound easy, you say? Of course. If I made it sound difficult, you wouldn't be tempted to try it. Besides, it *is* easy. All it takes is the simple discipline of writing and rewriting your notes day by day and week by week throughout the term. It is a sure way of surviving the university and getting into the graduate school or professional school of your choice, if that is a necessary step in realizing your goals. It is a very good way to learn to write. But it sounds like work, you protest? Sorry to disappoint you. It is. You wanted to learn to write without work? The best of luck. Oops, sorry—excuse me—here comes your fairy prince waving his magic wand.

2. Hierarchical Structure Underlying Sequential Presentation

Under normal circumstances, we are not allowed to speak for more than a few minutes without being interrupted. When we find ourselves in that unnatural situation of talking at length without interruption (giving a public speech or teaching), we tend to panic. It is not so much that we must talk to so many people at once; we would have no difficulty in talking to each of them individually, and it is really not much different to talk to them collectively. Simply as a matter of convenience, if you have the same thing to tell a number of people, you might as well get them together and tell them all simultaneously. The panic is mainly due to the fact that we must talk—not to many—but for so long. We have little opportunity to learn to organize a long presentation. Here is a technique for doing so. Try it the next time you must talk at length.

A lecture is a sequence of thousands of sounds, and it does, indeed, seem an impressive and difficult task to remember which order they come in. However, just as there is a hierarchical structure underlying the sequence of sounds that constitutes a well-formed sentence, so there is a hierarchical structure underlying the sequence of sounds that constitutes a well-organized discourse. If you diagram the hierarchical structure underlying your sequential presentation, then you do not have to remember thousands of sounds but only a few dichotomies. Two alternative ways of representing the hierarchical structure of a lecture on conditioning are provided in Figure 9-3 by way of example. You will recognize, of course, that

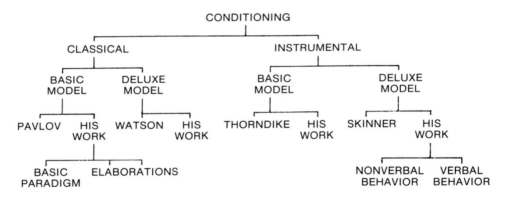

    1   *CONDITIONING*

        1.1 *CLASSICAL*
            1.11 BASIC MODEL
                1.111 *Pavlov*
                1.112 *His work*
                    1.1121 Basic paradigm
                    1.1122 Elaborations
            1.12 DELUXE MODEL
                1.121 *Watson*
                1.122 *His work*
        1.2 *INSTRUMENTAL*
            1.21 BASIC MODEL
                1.211 *Thorndike*
                1.212 *His work*
            1.22 DELUXE MODEL
                1.221 *Skinner*
                1.222 *His work*
                    1.2221 Nonverbal behavior
                    1.2222 Verbal behavior

Figure 9-3. Two ways to represent the hierarchical structure underlying a sequential presentation

the second alternative is the way I chose to represent the hierarchical structure of each chapter in this book.

Indeed, you don't even need to remember the few dichotomies. You can write the hierarchical structure on the blackboard to provide an outline for the audience. When you lose your place, you can refer to the outline under the pretext of reminding the audience where they are, where they have been, and where they are going. If you prefer, you can write the major headings on your fingertips and refer to them as you enumerate the points you are covering. Be careful, however, with prespeech cocktails. At a reception before giving a speech to the National Secretaries' Association, I drank a Scotch on the rocks. This had two detrimental effects. The Scotch thickened my accent, and the wet glass obliterated my notes. When I couldn't read my fingertip notes the first time I got lost in the lecture, I had to come clean—in more ways than one. Now that my dirty little secret is out, you may as well know it, too.

With a little practice using this technique, you will soon be able to give a two-hour lecture without reading, or even referring to, notes. Thus you will be able to maintain personal contact with the audience, which is, after all, the big advantage of the auditory over the visual channel.

3. Survey of Your Personal Mnemonics

Each of us has built up a set of personal mnemonics for dealing with everyday situations that recur again and again. (My personal mnemonic for spelling *mnemonic,* for example, is "just as it sounds but with an *m* for *my* in front.") The use of mnemonics is a shameful and secret activity. In certain circles, it is viewed as a disreputable trick. To encourage other closet mnemonists to come out, I confess my own experiences in conducting this exercise.

There are certain arbitrary conventions (the names of the notes in the musical scale, the number of days in each month, and so on) which are useful to remember. Mnemonics are simply tools to make the meaningless meaningful and facilitate memory.

a. What formal mnemonics do you use? Certain mnemonics have become part of the general culture and are shared by a large number of people, who pick them up somehow somewhere. My entire repertoire, as far as I can see, is "Thirty days hath September, ————" and "*i* before *e* except after *c*." Which do you use? Where did you pick them up?

b. What mnemonic do you use for distinguishing left and right? Distinguishing up and down is easy, under normal circumstances, since gravity ensures that means of distinguishing them are built in. However, the distinction between left and right is arbitrary, and each of us develops some idiosyncratic mnemonic for remembering which is which. Unlike the formal mnemonics above, these informal mnemonics tend to be unconscious. It was only when I performed this exercise that I became aware of an involuntary movement of my right hand (or in my image of my right hand?) into the writing position and realized that my mnemonic is "I write with my right."

Observe your experience carefully between the instructions "turn right" from your favorite backseat driver and your act of turning right. What is *your* mnemonic? Since I drive a lot in both North America (on the right side of the road) and in Great Britain (on the left side of the road), I have to replace the usual left-right mnemonic with one that applies in both cases—"I should be sitting on the side of the car away from the sidewalk" ("pavement" in Great Britain). Such a mnemonic should become unconscious to enable you to react quickly when confused on turning a corner or when confronted by a truck apparently in your lane on the brow of a hill. Once they become unconscious, however, they become dangerous when they no longer apply. I had to drill myself in new mnemonics when I took my right-hand car to left-hand Britain and when I drove from right-hand France through left-hand Sweden to right-hand Norway. What "disreputable tricks" do *you* use to stay alive?

c. What mnemonic do you use for judging large areas? For many years, I judged large areas in terms of an acre field which was part of a farm I lived in as a small child. On revisiting the farm as an adult, I discovered that this field, which seemed vast to me when I was relatively small and it constituted a large part of my world, was "actually" quite small. In all those intervening years, therefore, when someone mentioned their half-acre lot or 100-acre farm, my image of their properties was too large and, when I looked at a property, my estimate of its area was too small. Now that I have replaced my inaccurate mnemonic with a more accurate one—"an acre is about the size of a football field"—my judgments are more realistic. Do you have any old mnemonics that need revising?

d. What mnemonic do you use for calculating the ubiquitous 15% tip? I shift the decimal point in the bill total one space to the left to get 10%, halve this amount to get 5%, and add those two amounts to get 15%, and then round up or down depending on service (the last step is my defiant little gesture toward the original function of the service charge). I assumed that everyone did it this way.

However, my friend Guy Lefrancois showed me that he had a better way. He considers 15% as 15 cents in a dollar and simply rounds off the bill total to the nearest dollar and multiplies by 15. Guy patiently explained to me (Guy is good at explaining things—he wrote what used to be the best textbook in educational psychology) that his method is superior to mine since it requires only one arithmetic operation rather than three and that operation is not as difficult as it seems since, over many restaurant and bar bills, his 15-times table is as smooth as his 3-times table.

Compare your mnemonics with your friends'. Do you find surprising differences?

4. Bizarre Mental Images

Here is a mnemonic device you may want to add to your repertoire. Learn this rhyme:

One is for bun	1 Newspaper
Two is for shoe	2 Bananas
Three is for tree	3 Fish
Four is for door	4 Cigarettes
Five is for hive	5 Jam
Six is for sticks	6 Bread
Seven is for heaven	7 Whisky
Eight is for gate	8 Bacon
Nine is for line	9 Stamps
Ten is for hen	10 Toothpaste

Associate each of the items in a list you want to remember (as on the right) with each of the items in the rhyme, using a bizarre mental image. Spend about 15 seconds conjuring up your mental image. The bizarrer, the better, since bizarre images are unlikely to get confused with your regular images (which, presumably, are not bizarre).

Repeat the rhyme and write down your list of items in order. You will find that each line of the rhyme will trigger the appropriate image. For example, as you say "four is for door," an image of a smoking cigarette in the keyhole of a door will appear, and you will be able to write "4 cigarettes."

I have listed ten items so that you may be tempted to try this technique. These items suggest a shopping list, but the technique can be used for remembering any permutation or combination of up to ten items—series of topics in a lecture you are giving, series of points you want to make in an essay question you anticipate in an examination, a series of tests for diagnosing trouble in the internal-combustion engine, a number of ideas you have while driving that you want to record later, and so on.

I have used this same rhyme over and over again and, strangely, the images never get mixed up. The "bun" gets most use, since it is used every time, no matter how long my list. Like the driver's seat in a car, it should show most wear. However, although that "bun" has contained ashtrays, batteries, newspapers, elephants, Albert Einstein, the Taj Mahal, the Federal Bureau of Investigation, a teacher spreading curiosity as a contagious disease, the statue of the Thinker typing a book, plus a motley assortment of other objects, the correct image comes to mind when I need it.

In an experiment using this technique, untrained subjects were able to remember 500 pairs of objects with 99% accuracy. The experiment was terminated, not because the subjects ran out of skill, but because the experimenters ran out of patience. That experiment and this technique are discussed in the following source.

Miller, G. A., Galanter, E., & Pribram, K. H. *Plans and the structure of behavior.* New York: Holt, 1960, pp. 134–137.

The Discovery 10
Approach

10   THE DISCOVERY APPROACH

PRE-EXERCISES

1. Calculating Area

Find the area (in square units) of the shaded part of each of the figures on page 243. Note the process as well as the product of your thinking. You may find it useful to turn on a tape recorder and talk to yourself out loud.

2. Discovery and Invention

What is the difference between a discovery and an invention? Which of the following were discovered? Which were invented?

orange   cow
orange juice   Aberdeen Angus (a hardy
Tang (a synthetic   breed of cow)
   orange juice)   beef
Coca-Cola   corned beef
                                beef Wellington
ice
ice cube   truth
ice cream   sex
ice pick   communism

Lord of the Rings   Pythagoras
The Psychology of Teaching   the theorem of Pythagoras
   (the book in your hand)   hypotenuse (name for side of

a.

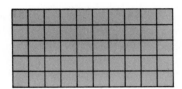

b.

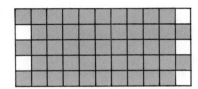

c.

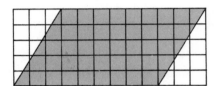

d.

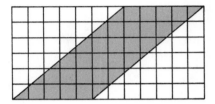

e.

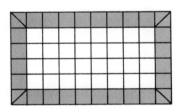

f.

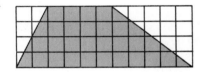

g.

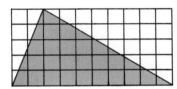

h.

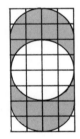

triangle opposite right angle)
π (ratio of circumference to
    diameter of a circle)

intelligence
Stanford-Binet intelligence test
IQ score

Loch Ness monster
mermaid

Marshall McLuhan
Evel Knievel

Lana Turner
you
me

childhood
adolescence

virus
serum
inoculation

In what sense can a person be discovered? Invented? I selected Marshall McLuhan, because a San Francisco advertising man once claimed that he had invented him; Evel Knievel, because it has been said that he invented himself, packaged himself, and sold himself to the media; Lana Turner, because she is reputed to have been discovered in a drugstore.

In what sense can a person be self-discovered? Self-invented?

It is difficult to think of childhood and adolescence as discoveries. However, Chapter 2 of the following book is titled "The Discovery of Childhood."

Ariès, P. *Centuries of childhood.* New York: Knopf, 1962.

You may like to read this chapter and consider whether adolescence and youth are possibly recent discoveries (or inventions?).

"I think I've discovered a new virus." "My boy, the last thing the world needs is another virus." In case you didn't notice, this is a joke. Why?

Albert Einstein was working in a patent office when he discovered (invented?) the theory of relativity. Could he take out a patent on it? Could the people who used this theory to discover (invent?) the atom bomb take out a patent on that?

Is it discoveries or inventions that endanger our species on our planet? What can you patent? What can you copyright?

Holt suggests that to invent is to discover for the first time (*How Children Learn,* p. 185). Do you agree?

All the above things have already been discovered or invented. What remains for *you* to discover or invent?

3. Inside-Out Teaching by the Socratic Method

Plato wrote a series of dialogues illustrating the teaching methods of his teacher, Socrates. Read the following excerpt from one of those dialogues, *Meno,** and then think through the questions that follow the dialogue.

Menon: Yes, Socrates. But what do you mean by saying that we do not learn, but what we call learning is remembering? Can you teach me how this is?

Socrates: You are a young rogue, as I said a moment ago, Menon, and now you ask me if I can teach you, when I tell you there is no such thing as teaching, only remembering. I see you want to show me up at once as contradicting myself.

Menon: I swear that isn't true, my dear Socrates; I never thought of that, it was just habit. But if you know any way to show me how this can be as you say, show away!

Socrates: That is not easy, but still I want to do my best for your sake. Here, just call up one of your own men from all this crowd of servants, any one you like, and I'll prove my case in him.

Menon: All right. *(To a boy)* Come here.

Socrates: Is he Greek, can he speak our language?

Menon: Rather! Born in my house.

Socrates: Now, kindly attend and see whether he seems to be learning from me, or remembering.

*Adapted from *Great Dialogues of Plato,* translated by W. H. D. Rouse. Copyright 1956 by New American Library, Inc. Used by permission.

Menon: All right, I will attend.

Socrates: Now my boy, tell me: Do you know that a four-cornered space is like this? [*Diagram 1*] [Note: There are no diagrams in the Greek text; they and the lettering have been added to assist the reader.]

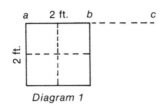

Diagram 1

Boy: I do.

Socrates: Is this a four-cornered space having all these lines [i.e., sides] equal, all four?

Boy: Surely.

Socrates: And these across the middle, are they not equal too?

Boy: Yes.

Socrates: Such a space might be larger or smaller?

Boy: Oh yes.

Socrates: Then if this side is two feet long and this two, how many feet would the whole be? Or look at it this way: if it were two feet this way, and only one the other, would not the space [i.e., area] be once two feet?

Boy: Yes.

Socrates: But as it is two feet this way also, isn't it twice two feet?

Boy: Yes, so it is.

Socrates: So the space is twice two feet?

Boy: Yes.

Socrates: Then how many are twice two feet? Count and tell me.

Boy: Four, Socrates.

Socrates: Well, could there be another such space, twice as big, but of the same shape, with all the lines equal like this one?

Boy: Yes.

Socrates: How many feet will there be in that, then?

Boy: Eight.

Socrates: Very well, now try to tell me how long will be each line of that one. The line of this one is two feet; how long would the line of the double one be?

Boy: The line would be double, Socrates, that is clear.

Socrates: (aside to Menon): You see, Menon, that I am not teaching this boy anything: I ask him everything; and now he thinks he knows what the line is from which the eight-[square] foot space is to be made. Don't you agree?

Menon: Yes, I agree.

Socrates: Does he know then?

Menon: Not at all.

Socrates: He *thinks* he knows, from the double size which is wanted?

Menon: Yes.

Socrates: Well, observe him while he remembers bit by bit, as he ought to remember.

Now, boy, answer me. You say the double space is made from the double line. You know what I mean; not long this way and short this way, it must be equal every way like this, but double this—eight [*square*] feet. Just look and see if you think it will be made from the double line.

Boy: Yes, I do.

Socrates: Then this line [ac in Diagram 1] is double this [ab], if we add as much [bc] to it on this side.

Boy: Of course!

Socrates: Then if we put four like this [ac], you say we shall get the eight-foot space.

Boy: Yes.

Socrates: Then let us draw these four equal lines [ac, cd, de, ea in Diagram 2]. Is that the space which you say will be eight feet?

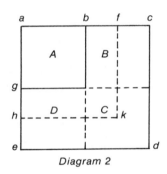

Diagram 2

Boy: Of course.

Socrates: Can't you see in it these four spaces here [A, B, C, D] each of them equal to the one we began with, the four-foot space?

Boy: Yes.

Socrates: Well, how big is the new one? Is it not four times the old one?

Boy: Surely it is!

Socrates: Is four times the old one, double?

Boy: Why no, upon my word!

Socrates: How big, then?

Boy: Four times as big!

Socrates: Then, my boy, from a double line we get a space four times as big, not double.

Boy: That's true.

Socrates: Four times four is sixteen, isn't it?

Boy: Yes.

Socrates: But what line will make an eight-foot space? This line makes one four times as big, sixteen, doesn't it?

Boy: That's what I say.

Socrates: And this four-foot space [A] comes from this line [ab], half the length of the long one?

Boy: Yes.

Socrates: Good. The eight-foot space will be double this [*double A*] and half this [*half A, B, C, D*].

Boy: Yes.

Socrates: Then its line must be longer than this [*ab*], and shorter than this [*ac*]. What do you think?

Boy: That's what I think.

Socrates: That's right, just answer what you think. Tell me also: Was not this line [*ab*] two feet, and this [*ac*] four?

Boy: Yes.

Socrates: Then the line of the eight-foot space must be longer than this line of two feet, and shorter than the line of four feet.

Boy: Yes, it must.

Socrates: Try to tell me, then, how long you say it must be.

Boy: Three feet.

Socrates: Three feet, very well: If we take half this bit [*half of bc*] and add it on, that makes three feet [*af*], doesn't it? For here we have two [*ab*], and here one [*bf*], the added bit; and, on the other side, in the same way, here are two [*ag*], here one [*gh*]; and that makes the space you say [*afkh*].

Boy: Yes.

Socrates: Then if the space is three feet this way and three feet that way, the whole space will be three times three feet?

Boy: It looks like it.

Socrates: How much is three times three feet?

Boy: Nine.

Socrates: How many feet was the double to be?

Boy: Eight.

Socrates: So we have not got the eight-foot space from the three-foot line after all.

Boy: No, we haven't.

Socrates: Then how long ought the line to be? Try to tell us exactly, or if you don't want to give it in numbers, show it if you can.

Boy: Indeed, Socrates, on my word I don't know.

Socrates: Now, Menon, do you notice how this boy is getting on in his remembering? At first he did not know what line made the eight-foot space, and he does not know yet; but he thought he knew then, and boldly answered as if he did know, and did not think there was any doubt; now he thinks there is a doubt, and as he does not know, so he does not think he does know.

Menon: Quite true.

Socrates: Then he is better off as regards the matter he did not know?

Menon: Yes, I think so too.

Socrates: So now we have put him into a difficulty, and like the stingray we have made him numb, have we done him any harm?

Menon: I don't think so.

Socrates: At least we have brought him a step onwards, as it seems, to find out how he stands. For now he would go on contentedly seeking, since he does not know; but then he could easily have thought he would be talking well about the double space, even before any number of people again and again, saying how it must have a line of double length.

Menon: It seems so.

Socrates: Then do you think he would have tried to find out or to learn what he thought he knew, not knowing, until he tumbled into a difficulty by thinking he did not know, and longed to know?

Menon: I do not think he would, Socrates.

Socrates: So he gained by being numbed?

Menon: I think so.

Socrates: Just notice now that after this difficulty he will find out by seeking along with me, while I do nothing but ask questions and give no instruction. Look out if you find me teaching and explaining to him, instead of asking for his opinions.

Now, boy, answer me. Is not this our four-foot space [*A in Diagram 3*]? Do you understand?

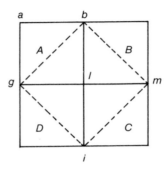

Diagram 3

Boy: I do.

Socrates: Shall we add another equal to it, thus [*B*]?

Boy: Yes.

Socrates: And a third equal to either of them, thus [*C*]?

Boy: Yes.

Socrates: Now shall we not also fill in this space in the corner [*D*]?

Boy: Certainly.

Socrates: Won't these be four equal spaces?

Boy: Yes.

Socrates: Very well. How many times the small one is this whole space?

Boy: Four times.

Socrates: But we wanted a double space; don't you remember?

Boy: Oh yes, I remember.

Socrates: Then here is a line running from corner to corner, cutting each of these spaces in two parts [*draws lines bm, mi, ig, gb*].

Boy: Yes.

Socrates: Are not these four lines equal, and don't they contain this space within them [*bmig*]?

Boy: Yes, that is right.

Socrates: Just consider: How big is the space?

Boy: I don't understand.

Socrates: Does not each of these lines cut each of the spaces, four spaces, in half? Is that right?

Boy: Yes.

Socrates: How many spaces as big as that [*blg*] are in this middle space?

Boy: Four.

Socrates: How many in this one [*A*]?

Boy: Two.

Socrates: How many times two is four?

Boy: Twice.

Socrates: Then how many [square] feet big is this middle space?

Boy: Eight [square] feet.

Socrates: Made from what line?

Boy: This one [*gb*].

Socrates: From the line drawn from corner to corner of the four-foot space?

Boy: Yes.

Socrates: The professors [Sophists, experts in some subject who gave lessons for a fee] call this a diameter [diagonal]: so if this is a diagonal, the double space would be made from the diagonal, as you say, Menon's boy!

Boy: Certainly, Socrates.

Socrates: Now then, Menon, what do you think? Was there one single opinion which the boy did not give as his own?

Menon: No, they were all his own opinions.

Socrates: Yet he did not know, as we agreed shortly before.

Menon: Quite true, indeed.

Socrates: Were these opinions in him, or not?

Menon: They were.

Socrates: Then in one who does not know, about things he does not know, there are true opinions about the things which he does not know?

Menon: So it appears.

Socrates: And now these opinions have been stirred up in him as in a dream; and if someone will keep asking him these same questions often and in various forms, you can be sure that in the end he will know about them as accurately as anybody.

Menon: It seems so.

Socrates: And no one having taught him, only asked questions, yet he will know, having got the knowledge out of himself?

Menon: Yes.

Socrates: But to get knowledge out of yourself is to remember, isn't it?

Menon: Certainly it is.

Is education a process of pulling out information that is, in some sense, already in a person, or is it a process of pushing in information? Are there perhaps certain kinds of information that are pulled out and certain other kinds of information that are pushed in? Is there some appropriate balance between pushing and pulling? As a teacher, do you think you will be a pusher or a puller?

The relationships elicited from the boy by Socrates were discovered by Pythagoras. He formed a secret society and shared his discoveries with the members. Any member who betrayed any of those "secrets" to a nonmember was thrown out of the society and, in some cases, into the sea.

Did Pythagoras share Socrates' opinion that everyone knew those relationships? Is there any way in which you (or the servant boy) could have learned those historical facts if no one had told you?

10.1   THE WORK OF KOHLER

10.11   The Island of the Apes

Wolfgang Kohler, one of the founders of **Gestalt psychology,** happened to be on an island when World War I started. Unable to return to his native Germany, he was marooned on the island for four years. On the island, there was a colony of apes. Kohler passed his time studying the apes.[115] He built a cage. Inside the cage, he put an ape; outside the cage, and outside the ape's reach, he put things that apes like. So far, substituting ape for cat and banana for fish, the situation is very much like that which Thorndike designed for his cats. The solution, however, is not to press a lever to get out of the cage to get the fish, but to pick up a stick which happens to be lying inside the cage, to pull in the banana. Like Thorndike's cat, Kohler's ape tried various responses: reaching through the bars, trying to pull the bars apart, beckoning to Kohler to pass him the banana, and so on and so on. Unlike Thorndike's cat, which continued such trial-and-error behavior until it happened to make the Thorndike-ordained response, Kohler's ape stopped trying after a number of trials and errors and sat down to consider the situation. Suddenly, it jumped up, grabbed the stick, and pulled in the banana. A high point in the intellectual history of the ape was reached when Sultan, an Albert Einstein among apes, joined two sticks together to reach a banana that was out of reach of either stick alone.

How does this learning of Kohler's ape differ from that of Thorndike's cat? The most obvious difference is the suddenness of the solution in this **insight learning** in contrast to the gradualness of the solution in trial-and-error learning. That is why insight learning is often called the **aha phenomenon** or the **Eureka effect.** The latter term comes from the story of Archimedes, who suddenly discovered the principle of specific gravity while lowering himself into his bathtub and ran naked through the streets shouting "Eureka."*

A second difference is the extent to which this insight learning can be transferred to other situations. The apes had grasped not only a stick and a banana, but a principle. The arm can be extended by using a stick. They were able to apply this principle in other situations. Kohler tested for transfer by suspending a banana out of reach overhead. Most apes transferred the principle of extending the arm horizontally to extending it vertically. One ape had a better idea. He surprised Kohler and defied gravity by planting the stick below the banana and scrambling up the stick to get the banana before the stick fell. This was a better solution than the one envisioned by Kohler, since he got an unbruised banana. The apes also transferred from extending the arm to extending the leg. They learned to pile boxes lying around the cage to get at the

---

* This is Greek for "I've found it" and not for "Good God, that water's hot," as some simple souls have suggested. Thus, on the same day, Archimedes discovered the principle of specific gravity and invented streaking.

banana. One ape had a better idea. He led Kohler by the hand to a position below the banana and used the great Herr Professor Doktor Kohler as he would a pile of boxes.

A third difference is the extent to which this insight learning involves understanding of the situation. Two apes would cooperate to pile boxes (although there was an obvious reluctance to place the last box, since the other ape would immediately clamber up and get the banana). The gestures and facial expressions of baby apes watching their elders working to get the bananas strongly suggest that they were empathizing. Such cooperation and empathy imply that the apes understood what was going on.

10.12   Insight Learning and Discovery Teaching

As mentioned earlier, each theory of learning implies a corresponding theory of teaching. How was Kohler teaching? He was using the discovery approach. He was arranging the environment (or, in Bruner's phrase, he was "engineering the situation") to increase the probability that the apes would make a discovery. The discovery approach is to insight learning as programmed instruction is to conditioning. Whereas Thorndike was controlling learning, Kohler was merely encouraging it. Thorndike's cat could *only* use blind trial and error, since the solution to the problem was arbitrary, ordained by teacher Thorndike. Kohler's apes could discover the solution, since it involved a principle intrinsic to the situation.

"WE HAVE GONE OUT OF OUR WAY TO PRESENT MATERIAL TO CHILDREN IN CONTRASTIVE FORM—FILM OF BABOON JUVENILES PLAYING, FOLLOWED BY HUMAN CHILDREN PLAYING IN AN IDENTICAL 'HABITAT'. THE CHILDREN DISCOVER QUITE READILY THAT LITTLE BABOONS PLAY MOSTLY WITH LITTLE BABOONS AND DO NOT PLAY WITH THINGS, THAT HUMAN CHILDREN PLAY WITH THINGS AND WITH EACH OTHER. THIS IS ENGINEERING A SITUATION."

JEROME S. BRUNER
THE RELEVANCE OF EDUCATION

Many discoveries in the history of science have been due to accidents. The most famous, although apocryphal, are the falling of the apple on Newton's head and the spilling of the water from Archimedes' bathtub. Experience may be the best teacher (and often an impish one, as in those cases), but it can use some teaching aids. Teachers who use the discovery approach are teaching aides to experience. They are metaphorically dropping apples and spilling water when they judge that such "arranged experiences" will trigger a discovery. They are creating accident-prone environments.

10.2   THE WORK OF WERTHEIMER

10.21   The Geometry Class

Max Wertheimer, another founder of Gestalt psychology, extended the study of insight learning from apes in a cage to children in a classroom (a considerable extension, I hasten to add).[231] He was visiting a classroom one day. The teacher had already taught the class that the area of a rectangle was length times width. He now taught them that the area of a parallelogram was base times altitude. When teacher and class were satisfied that they knew how to find the area of a parallelogram, Wertheimer asked if he might continue the lesson. He fiendishly drew a parallelogram such that the altitude missed the base; that is, he drew a parallelogram as in Figure 10-1b rather than as in Figure 10-1a. The class was shaken and stuck. One member voiced the complaint of the class—"We haven't had that one yet."

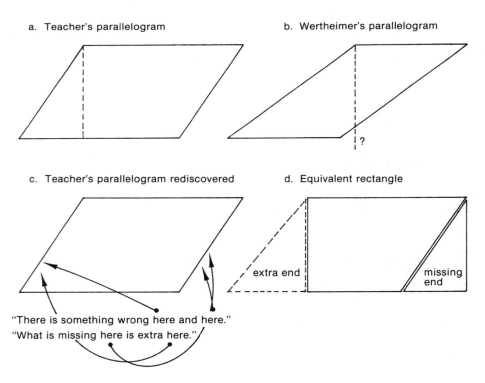

Figure 10-1.   Finding the area of a parallelogram by the discovery approach

Wertheimer proceeded to reteach the area of a parallelogram by the discovery approach. He cut a parallelogram out of cardboard and held it up. By casually allowing it to rotate, he triggered the discovery by one member of the class that his parallelogram was identical to the teacher's parallelogram. The fact that it was rotated through 90 degrees would not affect the area. Wertheimer's "funny" parallelogram, whose area the student thought he could not find, had the same area as the teacher's parallelogram, whose area he could find. In other words, he could transfer his understanding to another parallelogram rotated through 90 degrees. By casually leaving the scissors with which he had cut the parallelogram lying around, he triggered another insight in another student. She said "There is something wrong here and here" (pointing to the two ends). "What is missing here is extra here." Picking up the scissors, she cut off the "extra end" and placed it at the "missing end" (as in Figure 10-1d). The figure was now a rectangle, whose area they knew how to find. The students could now *understand* why the area of a parallelogram is base times altitude: the base is the length and the altitude is the width of the rectangle into which it can be transformed. Another student surprised Wertheimer by seeing a solution Wertheimer had not seen himself. She bent the parallelogram around to form a cylinder and then pointed out that the cylinder could be cut vertically at any point to yield the rectangle. Such surprises are one delightful aspect of this type of discovery teaching (that is, if you like surprises!). Although you set the problem, you do not set the solution. Since there is no teacher-ordained correct solution, you can be surprised by children, and even by apes.

10.22 Transfer

With the teacher's mechanical teaching, the students had memorized a procedure; with Wertheimer's discovery teaching, they had learned the principle underlying the procedure. One advantage of the latter technique is that the students could transfer this learning to other cases in which the principle applies. This was not possible when they had merely memorized a procedure (as demonstrated when a trivial change like the altitude missing the base could throw them into confusion). Since they knew the principle, they knew what was central and what was peripheral. Peripheral changes did not confuse them, and central changes alerted them to the fact that the principle did not apply. Wertheimer continued his lesson by demonstrating that they could transfer their principle to find the areas of figures b, e, and f in Pre-exercise 1. Here are the areas of the various figures in Pre-exercise 1, with the calculation suggesting one way to derive each area.

a. $10 \times 5 = 50$ b. $10 \times 5 = 50$ c. $9 \times 5 = 45$

d. $6 \times 5 = 30$ e. $\dfrac{10 \times 5}{2} = 25$

f. $\dfrac{4 \times 2}{2} + (4 \times 4) + \dfrac{4 \times 5}{2} = 30$ g. $(10 \times 6) - (8 \times 4) = 28$

h. $4 \times 4 = 16$ (Pushing the top and bottom semicircles into the central circle creates a 4×4 square.)

Transfer is an essential feature of schooling. If there is no transfer of those skills learned in school to out-of-school situations, then schooling is, indeed, as some critics have argued, merely a state-subsidized baby-child-adolescent-youth-sitting service. The wider the transfer, the better the schooling. Wertheimer was concerned not only with that superficial transfer from finding the area of a parallelogram to finding the area of a triangle, and not only with that deeper transfer involved when those principles are applied to finding how many pounds of seed or yards of cloth are needed for a given area, if the student subsequently becomes a farmer or a tailor. He was concerned with a way of thinking that can be applied to problems apparently remote from the problem to which this way of thinking was initially applied. The essential feature of good problem-solving is to look at the situation as a whole and try to discover how the situation and the problem are related. Wertheimer argued that Gauss, Galileo, and Einstein were good problem solvers, since they applied this way of thinking to their respective problems in mathematics and physics. By seeing the situation as a whole, they could see what was central and what was peripheral. Over long conversations with Albert Einstein, Wertheimer uncovered the thought processes behind the discovery of the theory of relativity. Within the paradigm of Newton, the speed of light was peripheral; within the paradigm of Einstein, the speed of light is central. The paradigmatic shift from Newton to Einstein is essentially this shift of the speed of light from peripheral to central. The thinking that produces such basic paradigmatic shifts, as described by Kuhn,[117] is so difficult because you have to see things whole in order to change them, and the strong structure of the whole system resists such changes in any of its elements.

10.23   Discovery and Expository Teaching

Teachers would appear superficially to play only a minor role in such insight learning. However, **discovery teaching** is much more challenging than **expository teaching.** Teachers themselves must understand the principles rather than simply memorize the procedures. Expository teaching is often the result of rote learning by teachers—they are simply parroting *their* teachers' procedures as their students, in turn, parrot their procedures. Discovery teachers must not only understand the principles they are teaching but the students to whom they are teaching them. They must know "where they are at" in order to arrange their situation to increase the probability that they will discover the principles. Few students will stumble spontaneously onto the problem of discovering the area of a rhombus. Teachers must create such problems for them, not simply by assigning them, but by inspiring them to make those problems their own. Teachers must present the problems in an appropriate order so that the principles are most easily discovered—the area of a square before the area of a rectangle before the area of a parallelogram before the area of a triangle before the area of a rhombus.

Discovery teachers are aided by the fact that there is a spontaneous tendency to make sense of things. Wertheimer found that young children confronted with a pattern of blocks with a few blocks out of place would spontaneously move those blocks to restore the pattern. Our nervous systems are designed to make sense of things. Expository teaching is difficult as well as ineffectual because it works against the natural tendency of the brain to work as it is supposed to work. We are not spontaneously stupid; mechanical teaching forces us to be stupid. Discovery teachers are also encouraged by the "eurekas" they hear from their students. This reinforcement can be quite dramatic (as when I flashed the old woman/young woman reversible figure on a huge screen in front of my class of 700 students and heard "ahas" and "Eurekas" resounding through the class as the figure reversed for each member), or it can be quite subtle (as when I glimpsed a sudden smile on the face of the woman in the fifth row, seventh from the left). Since the world is so new to infants, they are making discoveries all the time. Some developmental psychologists have argued that the smile is an infant's way of saying "Eureka." Look for those sudden smiles.

10.3 THE WORK OF BRUNER

10.31 A Theory of Instruction

In *Productive Thinking,* which he wrote during the last seven years of his life, Wertheimer summarized his lifetime of work.[231] It was published posthumously and was only the first of a series of books he had planned to write. His notes and papers are available in the Graduate Faculty of Political and Social Science, New School for Social Research, New York, so that others (perhaps you?) may continue his work where he left off. Jerome Bruner has continued his work in one direction by integrating insight learning into a theory of instruction.[26]

Information is transmitted from generation to generation both genetically and culturally. Since instruction can have no effect on genetic transmission, the theory of instruction must focus on cultural transmission. The important aspect of what is transmitted culturally is not so much the information, which our species has accumulated, but the tools for acquiring and organizing that information, which our species has discovered and developed. The product is less important than the process. Give a man a fish and he eats for a day; teach a man to fish and he eats for a lifetime. It is this capacity to discover and develop tools that best distinguishes us from other animals. We have acquired many

such tools throughout our human history, and, during our children's long period of infant dependency, we have an opportunity to pass these tools on to them. The best way for children to acquire these tools is to rediscover them on their own. The tools will be owned by them rather than simply borrowed. They will appreciate them more, just as they appreciate a bicycle they have bought with their hard-earned money more than a bicycle that was given to them. Bruner concedes that no one person in one lifetime can ever spontaneously rediscover a minute fraction of all the tools discovered by our whole species in its entire history.[27] However, they can rediscover many tools if discovery teachers guide insight learners as Kohler guided the apes and Wertheimer guided the geometry students. The function of schooling is to help the next generation rediscover the tools that previous generations have discovered. Only by discovering and using those tools can children realize their full human potential. The techniques by which discoveries are made are themselves discoveries. It is essential that each generation learn those techniques, since our further evolution will depend on further discoveries.

10.32 *Tools as Extensions of the Nervous System*

It is fruitful to consider those tools as extensions of the nervous system.[26] Since the nervous system consists of **motor neurons** (to make responses), **sensory neurons** (to receive stimuli), and **internuncial neurons** (to think), the tools may be classified as **motor tools, sensory tools,** and **reflective tools.** Motor, sensory, and reflective tools are extensions, respectively, of motor, sensory, and internuncial neurons. These tools are psychological rather than physical. However, the analogy between hardware and software tools is helpful. Bicycles and pliers are motor tools, since they extend the motor functions of the legs and arms; telescopes and telephones are sensory tools, since they extend the sensory functions of the eyes and ears; computers and slide rules are reflective tools, since they extend the reflective function of the brain. With psychological as with physical tools, you must know that they exist and that *you* can use them; you must know how and when to use them. Just as a person can never become a carpenter by watching a carpenter working or by being presented with a pile of furniture the carpenter has made, so a person can never become a thinker by watching a thinker thinking or by being presented with a pile of thoughts the thinker has thought. You must discover and use the tools yourself. The psychological tools are of more general use than the physical tools. The farmer must learn to use a pitchfork and a tractor, the tailor must learn to use a needle and a sewing machine, and the architect must learn to use a blueprint and a compass, but all must learn to use Euclidean geometry to find the areas of fields, fabrics, and floors.

As children grow, they develop motor tools, then sensory tools, and finally reflective tools. The periods during which they develop those tools corre-

"IT WAS NOT A LARGE-BRAINED HOMINID THAT DEVELOPED THE TECHNICAL-SOCIAL LIFE OF THE HUMAN; RATHER IT WAS THE TOOL-USING, COOPERATIVE PATTERN THAT GRADUALLY CHANGED MAN'S MORPHOLOGY BY FAVORING THE SURVIVAL OF THOSE WHO COULD LINK THEMSELVES WITH TOOL SYSTEMS AND DISFAVORING THOSE WHO TRIED TO GO IT ON BIG JAWS, HEAVY DENTITION OR SUPERIOR WEIGHT. WHAT EVOLVED AS A HUMAN NERVOUS SYSTEM WAS SOMETHING, THEN, THAT REQUIRED OUTSIDE DEVICES FOR EXPRESSING ITS POTENTIAL."

JEROME S. BRUNER
TOWARD A THEORY OF INSTRUCTION

spond roughly to Piaget's sensorimotor, concrete-operations, and formal-operations stages. However, Bruner does not view the person as passing through each stage into the next, but rather as retaining three parallel systems of tools for dealing with the environment. These three systems of tools provide **enactive, iconic,** and **symbolic representations,** respectively, of the environment. These alternative representations permit progressive levels of understanding. Bruner recommends a **spiral curriculum** designed to encourage understanding of a phenomenon at each of those levels. Children with an enactive representation of their environment can experience the phenomenon; those with an iconic representation can deal with a concrete embodiment of it; and those with a symbolic representation can deal with it abstractly. Thus, a child with an enactive representation can gain some understanding of the principles about area by playing with blocks or Cuisenaire rods (whose lengths are proportional to the numbers they represent), can subsequently gain a more sophisticated understanding on acquiring an iconic representation by working with cardboard cutouts of figures (such as Wertheimer used), and then an even more sophisticated understanding on acquiring a symbolic representation by dealing with algebraic formulas representing general principles about area— for example, $(a + b)^2 = a^2 + b^2 + 2ab$, meaning that the area of the square on the sum of two lines is equal to the sum of the areas of the squares on each line plus twice the rectangle created by the two lines.

Language is the most powerful tool within that most sophisticated set of tools which permit a symbolic representation of the environment. A thousand percepts of a thing in our environment can be grouped under a single concept—thus, the thousand cows we have seen can be grouped into a category and labeled with the concept *cow*. In a sense, a word is worth a thousand pictures. Rather than deal with millions of percepts, we need deal only with thousands of concepts. Those specific concepts can, in turn, be grouped under more general concepts. Thus, *cow* may be grouped with *horse* under *vertebrate*, *vertebrate* with *invertebrate* under *animal*, and *animal* with *plant* under *organism*. This hierarchical system of concepts enables us to represent and transform our environment. We can deal with our environment more effectively, just as we can deal with the mess after a party more effectively, by organizing things into categories—*rubbish* into the garbage, *returnable bottles* into their boxes, *records* into the cupboard, *dishes* into the kitchen, and so on. Discovery can be viewed as the invention of a new category system or a change in an old category system. Thus, the discovery of microbes added a new category under *organism,* and Darwin's theory of evolution took humans from an exclusive category and placed them firmly where they belong, with the other animals under *organism.*

10.4   CRITIQUE OF THE DISCOVERY APPROACH

10.41   Discovery Is Too Slow

Newton claimed modestly that he could see so far only because he stood on the shoulders of giants. A high school student can see even farther by standing, in turn, on the shoulders of Newton. Koestler describes, in *The Sleepwalkers,* the agonies and the ecstasies of the many brilliant thinkers who spent their lives trying to find the laws that govern planetary motion.[113] Newton's laws of motion, the culmination of all this effort, can be learned by a high school student in an afternoon. Why not simply hoist students up on Newton's shoulders by telling them those laws?

B. F. SKINNER
THE TECHNOLOGY OF TEACHING

We must indeed simply tell students much of what our species has discovered. However, if we pass on only the product of our discoveries and not the process of discovery, then the process will not continue. We may hoist our students up onto the shoulders of giants, but they will never become giants themselves. Besides, the shoulders of giants may be a rather precarious perch. If science progresses by a series of revolutions rather than by a gradual evolution, as Kuhn argues, then, come the revolution, the students may find themselves perched high and dry on some obsolete giant.[117] Indeed, they may get a leg up onto the shoulder of a giant and find that they can *not* see further. The view from the top is meaningless unless they have climbed there themselves. They must go through the process (or some simplified form of it under the guidance of a discovery teacher) to appreciate the product.

Discovery learning may be slower, but it is surer. Inductive generalizations from your personal experience are solidly backed by concrete evidence, whereas generalizations you have been told are not so firmly anchored. Rote learning only appears efficient because there is so much information transmitted. However, there is little information received. It does not "take," because it represents answers to questions students have not yet asked and solutions to problems they have not yet posed.

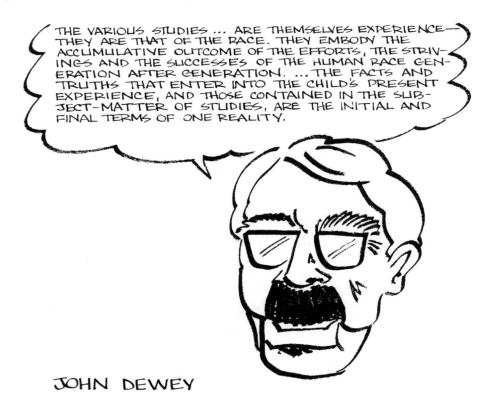

THE VARIOUS STUDIES ... ARE THEMSELVES EXPERIENCE—THEY ARE THAT OF THE RACE. THEY EMBODY THE ACCUMULATIVE OUTCOME OF THE EFFORTS, THE STRIVINGS AND THE SUCCESSES OF THE HUMAN RACE GENERATION AFTER GENERATION. ...THE FACTS AND TRUTHS THAT ENTER INTO THE CHILD'S PRESENT EXPERIENCE, AND THOSE CONTAINED IN THE SUBJECT-MATTER OF STUDIES, ARE THE INITIAL AND FINAL TERMS OF ONE REALITY.

JOHN DEWEY

10.42 *Perspiration Must Precede Inspiration*

There is little point in sitting around in bathtubs or under apple trees waiting for inspiration to strike. One must shed the preliminary perspiration. Archimedes had pondered his problem for some time before starting that aborted bath. A fallen apple, in the absence of Newton's prepared mind, would have remained simply a fallen apple. It took a Newton to transform this trivial, specific environmental event into the significant, universal law of gravitation. The spirit of the times may have been ready for the law of gravitation, but only Newton had drunk deeply enough of that spirit to discover it. Both Archimedes and Newton had assimilated much of the information currently available before their moments of insight.

Even the insights of Kohler's apes required some previous experience. Birch repeated Kohler's studies using apes that he had raised in cages and found that his apes did not have the insights Kohler reported.[18] He argued that the insight learning of Kohler's apes depended on previous learning—those apes had been raised in the jungle where they had had a great deal of experience with sticks. Harlow performed an experiment to test formally the role of such early experience on later problem-solving.[89] He taught a monkey to discriminate between two objects—say, a cup and a bottle. The objects were mounted on blocks, and the blocks were placed over two holes. A raisin was placed consistently in the hole below the cup. A barrier was raised. The monkey pushed aside one object and got a raisin if it chose correctly and nothing if it chose incorrectly. Harlow counted the number of trials until the monkey reached a certain criterion—say, six correct choices in a row. The monkey was then taught to discriminate between two other objects—say, a toy truck and an ashtray. Continuing with a number of unrelated discriminations, Harlow found that the monkey took progressively fewer and fewer trials to reach the criterion, until finally it learned in only one trial; that is, it would look under object A on trial 1 and, if it found a raisin, would continue to choose object A every time and, if it did not find a raisin, it would switch to object B on trial 2 and continue to choose object B every time. The monkey had changed from a trial-and-error learner for the first discrimination into an insight learner for the last discrimination. It had learned to learn. Thus Harlow suggests that trial-and-error and insight learning are not two different types of learning but two different phases of one continuous process.

10.43 *Discovery Is of Limited Application*

One aspect of teaching a skill is knowing which teaching method is most appropriate for certain subjects and certain students. For which subjects and which students is the discovery approach appropriate?

Certain subjects seem to lend themselves more readily to discovery teaching than others. The principles of mathematics and physics, for instance, are more easily discovered than the principles of history and geography. Since the principles in the former subjects are necessary, they can be discovered; since the principles in the latter subjects are somewhat arbitrary, they cannot be so easily discovered. Bruner has demonstrated that, insofar as principles of geography are necessary, they can be taught using the discovery approach.[26] He provided his students with the physical characteristics of a geographical area and had them deduce the location of the major cities, the industries, and so on. The more necessary the principles, the more appropriate the discovery method. It is entirely inappropriate only when the principles are entirely arbitrary. It is not possible to discover things when there is nothing to discover. Specific facts in the story of our species in time and space, which compose the bulk of history and geography, can only be discovered in the mundane sense of looking them up in reference sources. Since they are already available in those sources, it would be redundant to replicate those sources in your nervous system. It is important only that you know where to find those facts.

The discovery approach is not appropriate for certain students who do not believe that there are principles to discover or who, although they believe that there are principles to discover, do not believe that they personally can discover them. Scientists are so sure that the universe is orderly and that they can discover this order that they fail to realize this is a dogma not universally shared. Many children lack this faith, which seems basic to education as well as to science. Such children can learn only indirectly, from teachers, since the world has nothing to teach them. For them, the teacher is not a guide in understanding the world, since the world is not understandable, but an opponent in an intellectual badminton game in which they hit the shuttlecock back into the teacher's court. One argument against the discovery approach is that students will get upset at a teacher who withholds information from them. However, only those children who lack faith in their own capacity to discover their world would be annoyed at a teacher who refused to tell them all the teacher knew about it. Healthy children want to do things for themselves—from buttoning their coats to understanding their environment. Such a criticism points to a limitation in certain students rather than in the discovery approach.

POST-EXERCISES

1. Discovery versus Expository Learning

The relative merits of discovery and expository learning (or, in our terms, inside-out and outside-in teaching) have been debated throughout recorded history. Here are some sources that will help you participate in this debate. They are organized under tertiary, secondary, and primary sources, so that you can consider the debate at three levels of sophistication.

TERTIARY SOURCES

Ausubel, D. P., & Robinson, F. C. *School learning: An introduction to educational psychology.* New York: Holt, Rinehart & Winston, 1969. (The expository-learning position.)

Bruner, J. S. *The process of education.* New York: Knopf, 1963. (The discovery-learning position.)

Lefrancois, G. R. *Psychology for teaching.* Belmont, Calif.: Wadsworth, 1975. (Bruner's discovery learning, Ausubel's expository learning, and a reconciliation.)

SECONDARY SOURCES

Bruner, J. S. The act of discovery. *Harvard Educational Review,* 1961, *31,* 21–32.

Mosston, M. *Teaching: From command to discovery.* Belmont, Calif.: Wadsworth, 1972. (Dimension of teaching strategies ranging from extreme outside-in position—command—to extreme inside-out position—discovery.)

Skinner, B. F. *The technology of teaching.* New York: Appleton-Century-Crofts, 1968, pp. 109–111.

PRIMARY SOURCES

Craig, R. C. Directed versus independent discovery of established relations. *Journal of Educational Psychology,* 1956, *47,* 223–234.

Guthrie, J. T. Expository instruction versus a discovery method. *Journal of Educational Psychology,* 1967, *58,* 45–49.

Haslerud, G. N., & Meyers, S. The transfer value of given and individually derived principles. *Journal of Educational Psychology,* 1958, *49,* 293–298.

Hendrix, G. Learning by discovery. *Teacher,* 1961, *54,* 290–299.

Kittell, J. E. An experimental study of the effect of external direction during learning on transfer and learning of principles. *Journal of Educational Psychology,* 1957, *48,* 391–405.

Wittrock, M. C. Verbal stimuli in concept formation: Learning by discovery. *Journal of Educational Psychology,* 1963, *54,* 183–190.

2. The Case of the Missing Memory

As a teacher, you are intimately concerned with the process by which students assimilate information, store it, and then retrieve it. You tell your students something today, and they are able to repeat it tomorrow (or, at least, some of them can some of the time). They must have stored it somewhere somehow in the interval. How and where is it stored?

This case of the missing memory is, perhaps, the most tantalizing unsolved mystery in psychology. Here are some clues, and the sources of further clues, that you may like to follow. If you can solve this mystery, you may, as I will argue later, very well revolutionize the educational system.

Psychologists tend to assume that memory is stored in neural circuits. Nerve impulses break down the gaps between neurons and create permanent structures, which Hebb calls cell assemblies. A cell assembly is a hypothetical construct—that is, a structure that is assumed to exist but has not yet been found.

Hebb, D. O. *The organization of behavior: A neuropsychological theory.* New York: Wiley, 1949.

However, such structures have not been found. Lashley, who devoted his brilliant career to looking for them, was forced to conclude, whimsically, that learning was not possible.

Lashley, K. S. In search of the engram. *Society for Experimental Biology Symposium No. 4: Physiological Mechanisms in Animal Behavior,* 1950, pp. 454–482.

Such a conclusion suggests that our assumption was wrong.

Some experiments by McConnell pointed to an exciting alternative: memory is stored not neurologically but chemically, not in a neural circuit but within each neuron. In a typical experiment, McConnell taught some worms to turn right in a *t* maze. He then ground them up and fed them to other worms. The cannibal worms fed on trained worms took significantly less time to learn to turn right in the *t* maze than did cannibal worms fed on untrained worms. The information must have been stored chemically, since only chemistry survives being minced and eaten.

Thus, memory could not be found anywhere because it is everywhere. The ubiquitous is paradoxically elusive. Memory is not a part of the nervous system but a property of it—the capacity to retain information. We don't have memories—we *are* our memories. We are what we know.

McConnell, J. V. Memory transfer through cannibalism in planarians. *Journal of Neuropsychiatry,* 1962, *3*(Supplement 1), 42–48.

Alice Killackey, one of my students at the University of California at Santa Cruz, reviewed for me the literature about the chemical basis of memory that has accumulated since McConnell's experiments. A biology major who knows more about those matters than I, Alice reminded me that playing professor is a fine way to get an education. She concluded that the processes of depositing in and withdrawing from the memory bank are neurological but that storage is chemical. The mechanism by which neural impulses are transformed into chemical codes is not known, nor is the precise chemical that contains the code. It is probably one of the macromolecules—DNA, RNA, protein—or some combination of them.

Gurowitz, E. M. *The molecular basis of memory.* Englewood Cliffs, N.J.: Prentice-Hall, 1969.

Blakemore argues that, since DNA contains the code for "remembering" our phylogenetic experience (that is, all the experience we share as members of our species), it is reasonable that DNA or its close relatives, RNA and protein, may contain the code for "remembering" our ontogenetic experience (that is, the different amendments to the genetic code that each of us acquires through our different individual experiences). However, since all those macromolecules contain identical information in different forms, they must contain all the potentialities of which different aspects are actualized in each of us. This implies that learning is discovering something that, in some sense, the learner already knows (see the Socratic dialogue presented in Pre-exercise 3 of this chapter); that learning is essentially an inside-out process (as argued in this book) rather than an outside-in process (as traditionally assumed); that teaching is a process of facilitating discovery (as argued in this chapter).

Blakemore, C. *Mechanics of the mind.* Cambridge, England: Cambridge University Press, 1977.

An Operating Manual 11
for Species
Homo sapiens

11   AN OPERATING MANUAL FOR SPECIES HOMO SAPIENS

PRE-EXERCISES

1. Reactions to the Operating Manual

I have offered my manual to a number of people. "Hello! Are you a member of species *Homo sapiens*? Yes? I have just the thing you need—an operating manual for species *Homo sapiens*." Needless to say, there are a variety of interesting reactions. What would your reaction be?

Here are five typical arguments I've encountered and my counterarguments. Consider each in turn and reach your own conclusion.

Argument 1. I am not the operator.

If you think that you have free will, then you have free will; if you think that you are determined, then you are determined. This manual is of value only to those who believe that they control themselves from the inside rather than that they are controlled by outside forces. Organize a psychic coup d'état and seize control of your own life. You are the operator and here is your operating manual.

Argument 2. I should not be the operator.

Many problems are due, indeed, to operating our nervous systems badly, but the solutions involve learning how to operate them well.

UNINTELLIGENCE IS NOT WHAT MOST PSYCHOLO-
GISTS SEEM TO SUPPOSE, THE SAME THING AS
INTELLIGENCE ONLY LESS OF IT. IT IS AN ENTIRELY
DIFFERENT STYLE OF BEHAVIOR, ARISING OUT OF
AN ENTIRELY DIFFERENT SET OF ATTITUDES.

JOHN HOLT
HOW CHILDREN FAIL

Argument 3. I need my own personal manual.

We are all members of the same species in essentially the same predicament and with essentially the same equipment. A nervous system is a nervous system is a nervous system and, thus, what works for me will work for you. Albert Einstein and Margaret Mead simply learned better techniques for operating the same equipment.

Argument 4. The manual is dangerous.

The manual, like all tools, can, indeed, be used to bad ends. However, tools that are available to anyone should be available to everyone. People are not so much sinful or criminal or crazy as inept. They do not need so much to be exorcised or rehabilitated or cured as informed. This manual is an attempt to inform.

Argument 5. The manual contributes to mechanization.

The analogy between the nervous system and a machine, implied by "operating manual," is a simile rather than a metaphor; that is, it is useful to consider the nervous system as a machine in certain respects and for certain purposes. It allows us to stand back and get a clearer look at ourselves. We are dehumanized more by mystiques than by techniques. This manual attempts to destroy mystiques by revealing techniques.

2. The Information Crisis

Here are a number of personal anecdotes to illustrate what I call the information crisis. Read them and add equivalent experiences of your own.

What is the information crisis? How does it differ from the energy crisis? What is the solution to the information crisis?

a. When much younger, I made some attempts at education by enumeration—reading the Hundred Great Books, plowing alphabetically through an encyclopedia, learning all the words in a dictionary. Each of those grim tasks was a failure and would have been a failure even if I had completed it. I learned more than I ever needed (or even wanted) to know about aardvarks. Now that home computers can be purchased for under $600, I have decided to buy one rather than become one.

b. I met a man who had been described to me as "brilliant." He turned out to be merely well informed. He was so stuffed full of information that, every time he opened his mouth, it poured out. My encyclopedia would have been better company, since I could at least have looked up the topics *I* was interested in and learned what *I* wanted to know.

c. A student once asked me a general question about psychology. I found myself stuttering, to my embarrassment, "I'm sorry. I can't answer that question. I know too much about it." My answering mechanism got jammed by all the information rushing to meet the question at once.

d. While in my village in Scotland (where I feel relatively safe from the dangers of information overload), I was trying not to learn the outcome of the Ali-Liston fight before the BBC broadcast of it the next day. I had to stuff my ears against the threat of news from a neighbor's radio, run away from a transistorized kid in the street, avert my eyes from a newspaper being read by a man in front of me in the bus, avoid newspaper hawkers shouting the news in the street, silence two friends bursting to tell me, and turn off the television news when it shifted to sports. Despite all my efforts, the spoilsport announcer, so smugly sure that everyone would know, gave the result before the broadcast.

e. A student informed me that he had a lot of unlearning to do. Presumably, he thought that my class was the place to come and his mother asked him when he went home "What did you unlearn in school today, Marvin?"

f. Watching *The 64,000 Dollar Question* (a television quiz show in which "experts" sweated for money in soundproof booths over obscure and trivial questions), I wondered whether this bizarre concept of intelligence would be perpetuated in the lay public. It was later demonstrated that this show was an exhibit of another dubious concept of intelligence— commercial cunning. The show was fixed. The contestants had not cluttered their "home computers" with all that trivia but had simply memorized the answers and the agonized expressions the organizers had provided.

11.1   THE MISSING OPERATING MANUAL

One fruitful (and somewhat whimsical) way of extending the concept of education as the acquisition of tools is to consider education as the process by which one generation passes on the operating manual to the next generation. When I got my typewriter, I got an operating manual; when I got my car, I got an operating manual; but when I got my brain, the most complex and mysterious system in the universe—no operating manual. I kept checking my mail,

I'VE OFTEN THOUGHT THERE OUGHT TO BE A MANUAL TO HAND TO LITTLE KIDS, TELLING THEM WHAT KIND OF PLANET THEY'RE ON, WHY THEY DON'T FALL OFF IT, HOW MUCH TIME THEY'VE PROBABLY GOT HERE, HOW TO AVOID POISON IVY, AND SO ON. I TRIED TO WRITE ONE ONCE. IT WAS CALLED <u>WELCOME TO EARTH</u>. BUT I GOT STUCK ON EXPLAINING WHY WE DON'T FALL OFF THE PLANET.

KURT VONNEGUT, JR.
"AFTERWORD" TO
MARLO THOMAS, <u>FREE TO BE — YOU AND ME</u>

hoping that the manual would be delivered under separate cover. It has not yet arrived. Finally, after bumbling along as well as I could for 35 years, I decided to write my own manual. I was halfway through my life before I realized that it was a do-it-yourself project. If everything else fails, write the instructions.

The title—"An Operating Manual for Species *Homo sapiens*"—was too tempting to resist (even if only to impress potential publishers with the size of the market), but it is not quite accurate. Let me try to be more precise at the risk of being more prosaic. Species *Homo sapiens* consists of interacting subsystems—a circulatory system to process blood, a digestive system to process food, a reproductive system to process people, a nervous system to process information, and so on. The nervous system is the only one of those subsystems which is under voluntary control; that is, whereas it is reasonable to say "stop talking," because talking is a function of the nervous system, it is not so reasonable to say "stop bleeding," because bleeding is a function of the circulatory system. Therefore, the nervous system is the only system that can be "operated." This is, more precisely, then, an operating manual for the nervous system of species *Homo sapiens*.

Of course, other subsystems can be operated indirectly through the mediation of the nervous system. This will be illustrated with respect to the digestive system in Section 11.2. Equivalent sections could have been written on operating your circulatory system, your respiratory system, your reproductive system, and so on.

The brain (the "headquarters" of your nervous system) has been described as a "cerebral jungle" and as a "great, raveled knot." Day by day, however, the jungle is being cleared and the knot is being unraveled. It is becoming more and more possible to describe the function of the nervous system in terms of its structure. Each of the sections from 11.3 through 11.6 focuses on the subfunction of some substructure within your nervous system.

We tend to think of behavior as the output of the entire organism. It is, however, the output of a subsystem of the organism—the nervous system. Part of the environment of the nervous system is the rest of the organism, consisting of the other subsystems: the digestive system, circulatory system, endocrine system, and so on. The nervous system consists of an **autonomic nervous system** to deal with this internal environment and a **central nervous system** to deal with the external environment. Section 11.3 will focus on the operation of your autonomic nervous system.

Your central nervous system consists of an **old brain** (the more primitive structures in the brain stem which our species shares with other species) and a **new brain** (the cerebral cortex enveloping this brain stem, which evolved later in our species, and of which our species has a higher proportion than other species). You will remember that motivation was linked to the hypothalamus (Section 3.12) and that emotion was linked to the reticular activating system (Section 3.13). Both those structures are in the old brain. The old brain can, therefore, be roughly identified with your emotional responses to the external environment and the new brain with your rational responses. The old brain is the motor, and the new brain is the steering mechanism.

Your new brain may be further divided into a **right hemisphere** for the processing of percepts and a **left hemisphere** for the processing of concepts. This dichotomy could be roughly equated to the traditional distinction between the artist and the scientist. The artist operates mainly with the right hemisphere and the scientist operates mainly with the left hemisphere. An intuitive awareness of this distinction is contained in the traditional metaphor of the left hand (controlled by the right hemisphere) for the artist and the right hand (controlled by the left hemisphere) for the scientist. You are, of course, both an artist and a scientist. Shake your left hand with your right hand and say "hello" to your other half. Bridge the gap between the two cultures. Section 11.5 will focus on operating your right hemisphere, and Section 11.6 will focus on operating your left hemisphere.

This series of dichotomies, as summarized in Figure 11-1, enables us to talk more precisely (and, as seems inevitable, more prosaically) about the operating manual for species *Homo sapiens.* * It has the disadvantage, however,

---

* This series of dichotomies is presented here purely to serve this heuristic function. Such clear-cut distinctions between, say, the left and right hemispheres, as implied here, are very questionable. The discovery of this "neglected" part of the brain triggered a flood of speculation

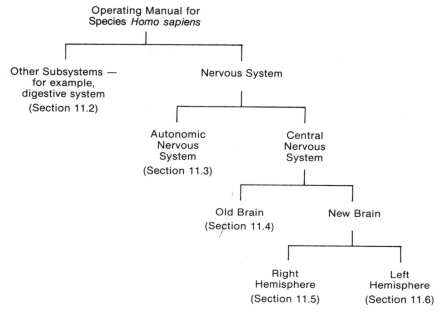

Figure 11-1.   Structure of operating manual for species *Homo sapiens*

of seeming to suggest that each subsystem within the nervous system can be operated independently of the others. Just as species *Homo sapiens* is an integrate (rather than an aggregate) of subsystems, so the nervous system is, in turn, an integrate of subsystems. Effective operation of your nervous system involves not only the effective operation of each subsystem, as discussed in the following sections, but effective orchestration among the subsystems. You must know which subsystem is appropriate to each subfunction and how to shift gears smoothly from one subsystem to another. You must get your right hemisphere together with your left hemisphere, your new brain together with your old brain, your central nervous system together with your autonomic nervous system, your nervous system together with your other subsystems, until, in the vague language of a previous generation, you "educate the whole person" or, in the equally vague language of the current generation, you "get it all together."

A further limitation of this manual is my tendency to emphasize the functioning of the left hemisphere of the new brain. This helps perpetuate the overemphasis in traditional schools on this limited part of the operating man-

identifying the right hemisphere with various "neglected" functions and groups—unconscious and nonverbal processes, thinking styles of women and minority-group members, and so on. Although those links are tenuous, they do serve, as here, as a useful way of talking about certain issues.

ual. However, as a product of traditional schools, this is what I know most about.* The recent surge of interest in the neglected parts of the operating manual is most encouraging and may result in a broader concept of education. Missing sections of the operating manual (such as Simeons' *Man's Presumptuous Brain*,[200] for operating your other subsystems through the nervous system; McKim's *Experiences in Visual Thinking*,[147] for operating your right hemisphere; and Trungpa's *Meditation in Action*,[223] for operating your autonomic nervous system) are appearing with increasing frequency. We must have a complete manual in order to maintain our balances on our planet.

LET US TEACH YOUNG PEOPLE THAT THEY DO IN SOME MEASURE HAVE A CONTROL OVER THEIR DESTINIES, NOT IN MATTERS OF NATIONAL WAR AND PEACE, PERHAPS, ALTHOUGH WE SHOULD LOVE IT IF IT REALLY WERE SO, BUT CERTAINLY IN MATTERS OF WHAT THEY SHALL STUDY TOMORROW, WHAT IT IS IMPORTANT FOR THEM TO LEARN TODAY. THE MOST IMPORTANT THING WE CAN TEACH IS THAT EACH STUDENT HAS CONTROL OVER HER OWN LIFE TO A LARGE DEGREE.

ESTHER ROTHMAN
THE ANGEL INSIDE WENT SOUR

* My bias was demonstrated to me by a friend who caught me saying "My poor feet—so neglected because they are so far away." "Far away from where?" she asked, revealing that I apparently think I live in my head. There followed a lecture of which I remember only snatches— "typical Western view of the body as an appendix dangling down from the brain to keep it from dragging on the ground," "looking down (literally and metaphorically) on my body from the conning tower of my head," "mind not only distinct from body but in conflict with it."

Here, then, is my operating manual, for what it is worth to whoever may find it useful. Sorry for the long delay between the delivery of your nervous system and the delivery of your operating manual. Your nervous system was issued by another department and I lost contact with it long, long ago. Sorry also that it is so sketchy and superficial. Perhaps I will be able to deliver a more complete manual in subsequent editions or, much better, perhaps you will be inspired to write your own. Perhaps you may pass on the operating manual, or at least the idea of the operating manual, to your students, so that they may, in turn, write their own manuals.

11.2   OPERATING YOUR DIGESTIVE SYSTEM

Only your nervous system can be operated directly, but your other sub-systems (your digestive system, your reproductive system, your respiratory system, and so on) can be operated indirectly through the mediation of your nervous system. We will consider the operation of your digestive system through your nervous system, by way of example. Similar chapters could be written about the operation of your other subsystems. The spate of books on the science and art of sex (*The Human Sexual Response, The Joy of Sex*, and so on) are parts of that potential chapter of the manual entitled "Operating Your Reproductive System." Breathing exercises recommended in some books on Yoga are part of the chapter entitled "Operating Your Respiratory System." Before considering the operation of the digestive system through the nervous system (Section 11.22), let us compare the two systems (Section 11.21). The nervous system may perhaps be clarified by analogy with the simpler digestive system.

11.21   *Comparison with the Nervous System*

The digestive system decomposes food into simple chemicals (catabolism), providing the body's cells with the raw materials needed to synthesize the complex substances the organism requires (anabolism). As mentioned earlier, Piaget likens the complementary processes of catabolism and anabolism to his complementary processes of assimilation and accommodation (see Section 5.31). The nervous system incorporates information into the subjective map of the world (assimilation) and then changes that subjective map to adjust to the information (accommodation). Although any two normal digestive systems are essentially the same in structure and function, they differ in content. The Eskimo eats whale blubber, the Englishman eats Yorkshire pudding, and the cannibal Carib ate other Caribs. Likewise, although any two normal nervous systems are essentially the same in structure and function, they too differ in content. The Eskimo, the Englishman, and the Carib live in different environments and thus assimilate different information from those environments. Within each of those cultures, each individual assimilates, within a narrower range, different food and different information.

The analogy breaks down, however, when we consider the nature of the content. Information is qualitatively different from food.* All your subsystems are energy systems, but your nervous system is also an information system. This is why it has a very special status. Let me illustrate. Whereas the digestive system breaks down those different foods into the same chemicals, which are then synthesized into the same substances, the nervous system retains those different bits of information and synthesizes them into different structures; that is, whereas whales, Yorkshire puddings, and Caribs are all reduced to the same things, the perceptions of whales, Yorkshire puddings, and Caribs are not. This is why we easily concede the fact that all digestive systems are the same (in structure and function) but not the fact that all nervous systems are the same. Your nervous system is your only contact with your environment, and it must "know" your particular environment so that you can survive in it. Your uniqueness is due to the fact that only you have experienced that exact sequence of environments you have survived so far. You are, in a sense, what you eat. You are, in a much more real sense, what you know.

Just as our digestive system needs an optimal amount of food, so our nervous system needs an optimal amount of information; that is, we can get too little or too much information, just as we can get too little or too much food. With our tendency to maximize rather than optimize, we find it difficult to imagine too much of anything. If some is good, then surely more is better and most is best. It is especially difficult for us to imagine too much information.† Yet, if the current energy crisis is that of too little energy, then the current information crisis is that of too *much* information. Since the digestive system is an energy system, it conforms to the principle of conservation of energy—energy can be neither created nor destroyed. There is no equivalent principle of conservation of information to apply to the nervous system. When I give you food, I no longer have it; when I give you information, I still retain it. That is why Scotsmen are so free with information. That is why you, as a teacher, can consider yourself a Robin Hood of information, taking from the rich and giving to the poor, without impoverishing the rich—and enriching yourself in the process. Energy conforms to the conservation principle, but information conforms to the proliferation principle. It can be created, but it cannot be destroyed.

---

* Educators are particularly prone to overdraw this analogy between the nervous system and the digestive system. Information is spoon-fed or force-fed throughout the school year and excreted at the final examination, with a review session just before as a laxative. Even Freud, in his oral and anal stages, placed education at the two ends of the digestive system.

† Unless, that is, we are members of the criminal underworld and know too well the disadvantages of knowing too much.

"WE ARE ALL OF US, NO MATTER HOW HARD WE WORK, NO MATTER HOW CURIOUS WE ARE, CONDEMNED TO GROW RELATIVELY MORE IGNORANT EVERY DAY WE LIVE, TO KNOW LESS AND LESS OF THE SUM OF WHAT IS KNOWN."

JOHN HOLT
THE UNDERACHIEVING SCHOOL

Although this information crisis affects us all, it is confronted in its most blatant form by professional scientists. The volume of research in each scientific discipline is increasing at such a rapid rate that no single scientist is able to read the stacks and stacks of research reports. Each scientist feels forced into narrower and narrower areas. Even within a specialty, scientists find themselves on a treadmill. As what they know increases, the ratio of what they know to what they know they "ought" to know decreases. The Sisyphus of ancient legend was compelled to roll a stone to the top of a slope, where it rolled to the bottom again. The Sisyphus of modern science is compelled to roll a stone to the top of a slope, where he discovers an even longer slope ahead.

Kuhn has demonstrated how we can avoid being trapped on the top of our ever-growing mountains of information.[117] He points out, in *The Structure of Scientific Revolutions*, that it is not the information itself which is important, but the structure of the information. Science does not progress, as conventionally assumed, by accumulating more and more information, but by organizing that information into more and more coherent structures. He shows how one **paradigm** (the structure around which information is organized) is replaced by another paradigm, which makes more sense out of more information. As a science meanders from paradigm to paradigm, those of us who are merely accumulating more and more information in some remote corner of that science may find ourselves stranded. As a science progresses, then, it does not get more and more difficult because there is more and more information; rather, it gets easier and easier because it is more and more coherent. As argued in Section 10.41, a high school sophomore can subsume Newton.

Some educators respond to current criticisms about the educational system by stepping up the volume of information. Audio aids, visual aids, Band-Aids, teaching aides are all enlisted to increase the volume. It is like throwing water to a drowning person. Students do not need information so much as the skills for organizing it. We should be providing students with better bullshit detectors* (or teaching them critical thinking—see Section 6.234—to be more polite) rather than equipping teachers with bigger shovels. It was such a bullshit detector (or bummer meter, or whatever the current term is for our personal censor) that Einstein was talking about when he attributed any success he had to his efficient "forgetory." It was probably (I realize now) what that

---

* A term borrowed, by the way, from Ernest Hemingway.

—GIVE EVERYONE AN EDUCATION THAT WILL MAKE HIM PROPAGANDA-PROOF.

ROBERT M. HUTCHINS
THE LEARNING SOCIETY
(QUOTING ARNOLD TOYNBEE)

student had in mind when he mystified me with the statement that he "had a lot of unlearning to do."

11.22   Operation through the Nervous System

When you were a newborn baby, people related to you mainly as a digestive system. They fed you at one end and cleaned you at the other. As you grew older, you took over those functions yourself. In other words, your digestive system came under the control of your nervous system. Since your nervous system is your only contact with your environment, it is the system which assures that you eat steaks and not sticks. It is also your nervous system that says no to that last piece of steak when you are no longer hungry. Through toilet training, elimination is also brought under conscious control—that is, under the control of the nervous system. Between ingestion and elimination, your digestive system pretty well gurgles along on its own.

One unique feature that distinguishes your nervous system from your other subsystems is that it can be observed from the inside as well as from the outside. If you could see me now as I write, you could observe the manifestation of the functioning of my nervous system from the outside—my behavior; I, in my exclusive inside seat, can observe the manifestation of the functioning of my nervous system from the inside—my experience. You can, therefore, control your digestive system through your nervous system either by changing your behavior or by changing your experience. Control through changing behavior has been well documented in the glut of diet books. Let us focus here on control through changing experience, which has not been so well documented.

Once, while I was revisiting Sir George Williams University, an attractive young woman approached and asked whether I remembered her. She was obviously, in that context, a former student, and I was tempted to feign recognition so that she would not feel unremembered but, finally, I had to confess that I didn't. She beamed with delight and gave me her name. She was the thin girl who had peered shyly out at me from a huge bulk within which she had been imprisoned. She explained that she had attended Weight Watchers and had lost 105 pounds.

"That's a whole person," I said.

"Yes, but there is another whole person I have to get rid of. Do you remember telling us in class about the phantom limb—that a person who has lost a limb still experiences sensations from it since he still has an image of the limb in his head? I have a phantom fat girl. I almost catapult myself out of bed every morning because I am applying enough force to raise my former self. I go to the mirror to remind myself of my new thin self and thus whittle away at that old fat self in my head. Even more important in this process is the mirror of other people. The phantom fat girl is being exorcised by the thin-girl feedback I am getting. I've gotten rid of the actual fat girl, but I still have to get rid of the image of the fat girl."

Maltz stumbled on the principles he expounds in his *Psychocybernetics* through a similar observation.[132] He was a plastic surgeon who observed that, although he could give his clients new faces, he could not ensure that they would also develop new images to match their new faces. The image is much more important. Ugly people with beautiful self-images are happier than beautiful people with ugly self-images. We can perform plastic surgery on our self-images by applying his principles of psychocybernetics.

An experiment I conducted on myself may help illustrate further how the digestive system can be operated through changing experience. I had gotten overweight from spending too much of my time sitting at this typewriter, and nature was charging me for excess baggage. I drew up a contract with myself that I would buy a bathroom scale, weigh myself every morning, and record that weight on a chart. The weights were averaged every week so that I would not be discouraged by day-to-day fluctuations. The chart was posted conspicuously on the bathroom wall so that kibbitzing friends could see it and provide that social facilitation which contributes to the success of Weight Watchers. This intimate little contact between I and me contained only this commitment to keep a daily record of my weight. There were no goals set, no exercise schedule, no diet regimes. My experience soon started to change. Lying in bed previewing the day, I'd remember my moment of truth on the scales. This would trigger a review of the previous day's eating and exercising. I would shudder as I remembered another day at the typewriter followed by a huge meal just before I went to bed. Sure enough, the scale would confirm that it had been another bad day at Fat Farm. Gradually, I began to think about those things *before* the next morning. I became more and more sensitive to my eating and exercising habits. Looking at my watch to see whether I am hungry. Continuing to eat even when no longer hungry merely in order to clean my plate (a residue of chidings about starving children in China during a wartime childhood?). Filling myself up in a restaurant, much like I fill my car up in a service station. Reading while incidentally eating. Eating so quickly that there is no time for tasting. As I became more and more aware of those bad habits, I ate less and less and enjoyed it more and more. The change in experience was reflected in the record on the wall. I lost an average of about a pound a week over 20 weeks. This does not sound like much, but, at this rate, in a year I would lose 50 pounds and in four years I'd be gone.

A fringe benefit is a greater understanding of the function of my digestive system. I became more aware not only of my eating habits but also of the comings and goings in my body. Once, when I could not wait to see the result of a very virtuous day, I weighed myself in the evening. The next morning, I found myself 2 pounds lighter. What had happened during the night? Was I just lying there evaporating? Of course, the body consumes energy just going about its basic business (about 90 calories an hour, I found out later) even while "I" am doing nothing. If I could lose 2 pounds just lying there not eating, then surely I could lose more by moving around and not eating. I found that I could indeed lose 3 or 4 pounds by fasting for a day. I found further that I could lose even more if I fined myself with a fast after a day in which I had gained. Apparently, it takes the body some time to assimilate the extra weight, and you can lose it again easily during that time. I knew all those things, of course, in my head. However, I had to have this personal experience of those principles in operation in order to really know them in my guts (so to speak!). It is exhilarating to find that you do indeed have so much control over those processes, and this exhilaration in turn provides the enthusiasm to maintain that control. Such little victories as discovering that you are a person who *can* eat one peanut may not seem like much, but they give you the confidence to go on to larger victories.

11.3 OPERATING YOUR AUTONOMIC NERVOUS SYSTEM

Your nervous system consists of an autonomic nervous system, for dealing with your internal environment, and a central nervous system, for dealing with your external environment. Until quite recently, we have assumed in Western cultures that the autonomic nervous system is, as its name implies, involuntary—that it could not be "operated"—and that there was, therefore, no point in learning how to operate it. The closest we come in our formal schooling is physical education, an optional extra in the curriculum. The only time we are normally required to be aware of the functioning of our autonomic nervous system is when a doctor asks us to describe our symptoms. We then find out how inept we are. We are better at describing the symptoms of disorders in our cars than in our own bodies.

Your autonomic nervous system is indeed basically involuntary, and fortunately so. If you had to control the beating of your heart, you would have no time for anything else. Your autonomic nervous system looks after the mundane maintenance matters of your internal housekeeping and thus sets your central nervous system free for "higher things." However, it has been discovered that the involuntary functions of the autonomic nervous system can be brought under voluntary control.[105] We are not normally aware of the function of our autonomic nervous system because it is overwhelmed by the function of our central nervous system, just as we are not aware of the light from the stars during the day because it is obliterated by the light from the sun. Western medical scientists have been looking for stars in the daytime and, finding none, have declared that they do not exist. Techniques have been developed for increasing the light from the stars (for example, **biofeedback,** which amplifies the signals from the autonomic nervous system) and for decreasing the light from the sun (for example, **meditation,** which cuts down the noise from the central nervous system). By those means, we have become aware of the functioning of the autonomic nervous system and have learned to control it.

Such techniques enable you to listen to your body. It is very wise, since it has learned how to operate over millions of years, and it can thus warn you when it is not operating well. Many diseases involve malfunctions in the control of the internal environment by the autonomic nervous system. Your autonomic nervous system could be viewed as a pharmacist dispensing the many complex chemicals required by your other subsystems. If you ingest unnatural substances, your body will write prescriptions for the appropriate, and possibly damaging, chemicals to deal with them. Your autonomic nervous system often dispenses prescriptions for chemicals that are not really required. For instance, anxious people may call unnecessarily for adrenalin to prepare them for fight or flight. The adrenalin generated by those false alarms is not used and causes damage to the body. We must be aware of the possible malfunction of the autonomic nervous system so that we can counter it. There is a need for an ecology of the internal environment as well as an ecology of the external environment.

11.4 OPERATING YOUR OLD BRAIN

11.41 "Human Teaching for Human Learning": Brown

George Brown and his colleagues on the Ford/Esalen Project in Affective Education are developing strategies for combining cognitive and affective education in what they call **confluent education.**[22,23] In our terms, they wish to educate both the old brain, for emotional responses to the environment, and the new brain, for rational responses to the environment. Or, in Bloom's terms, they wish to add to his *Taxonomy of Educational Objectives: Handbook I: Cognitive Domain*[21] (discussed in Section 2.12) the sequel, *Taxonomy of Educational Objectives: Handbook II: Affective Domain.*[116] They argue that traditional education has emphasized cognitive education at the expense of affective education, producing that caricature of our culture—the intellectual genius who is an emotional moron. When students do not thrive under our cognitive regime, we tend to give them more and more of the same. What is needed is not more cognitive education, but a qualitatively different kind of education—**affective education.**

Various experiential exercises developed at Esalen Institute and other growth centers are used to add the affective to the cognitive aspect of education. Thus, for example, a unit on William Golding's *Lord of the Flies* would not be, as is typical, a purely intellectual reading and discussion of a book about a group of boys plane-wrecked on a deserted island. It could contain an exercise in which the situation is simulated, with the classroom as the island and the students in the class as the group of boys. The simulation could be unstructured, so that the children could observe whether the same "types" emerge as in the book, or structured, with the children assigned the various roles, so that they could empathize with the various characters. The unit could contain the exercise called "finding a group." The students are invited to mill about the center of the room and, without talking, end up in groups of four. If there are five, one has to leave; if there are three, someone has to be found to join the group. The subsequent discussion of how the groups were formed may provide some understanding of the process by which the various subgroups formed among the boys in the novel and how Piggy felt on being excluded. The unit might contain an exercise called "animal fantasy." The children are invited to think of a person they can't stand, one they love, and themselves, and write all three names on a piece of paper. They are then to "turn all three into animals," visualizing animals that resemble those three people. They are then asked to place an adjective in front of the name of each of the three animals. In one use of this exercise, when the class shared their lists, they made some surprising discoveries about the character traits described. They were then invited to close their eyes and go in fantasy to a small clearing in a forest, where they imagined meetings between the animal that represented themselves and their "hated" and "loved" animals. The subsequent discussion and evaluation of the exercise illuminated the manner in which the boys in the novel visualized themselves and others as animals. Many other exercises—creating rituals, experiencing exclusion from a group, listening to the sound of surf in the dark, and so on—can make the novel much more "real" to the students. Such affective education makes cognitive education relevant by linking course content to the students' feelings and fantasies, emotions and motivations.

There is much talk about freedom and responsibility in orientation and graduation addresses at the beginning and end of schooling, but little *experi-*

I CARRY A WHOLE WASTE-PAPER BASKET OF IDEAS AT THE TOP OF MY HEAD, AND IN SOME OTHER PART OF MY ANATOMY, THE DARK CONTINENT OF MYSELF, I HAVE A WHOLE STORMY CHAOS OF "FEELINGS."

D.H. LAWRENCE
"LAWRENCE ON EDUCATION"

ence of freedom and responsibility in between. No amount of talk can substitute for the feeling of freedom and the feeling of responsibility. Citizens in a democracy must be both free and responsible, or the democracy will degenerate into anarchy, in which people are free but not responsible, or totalitarianism, in which people are responsible but not free. The only way in which people can become free and responsible is to experience freedom and responsibility, and one obvious place to gain such experience is the school.

11.42 *"Fantasy and Feeling in Education": Jones*

Richard Jones is concerned with extending traditional education from its focus on the left hemisphere of the new brain to include the right hemisphere (fantasy) and the old brain (feeling).[106] Fantasies and feelings are, unfortunately, viewed as disruptive of thoughts. Children are encouraged to be factual and objective. Fantasy is often discouraged as "daydreaming," "woolgathering," and even "lying." Emotion is viewed as the enemy of reason. Jones argues that fantasy and feeling enhance cognition, since we "learn best when we care most." The resistance to letting fantasy and feeling loose in the classroom is due to the fact that anything stimulating is also threatening. Few teachers are willing to face an exhilarating, but terrifying, roller-coaster ride every day.

11.5   OPERATING YOUR RIGHT HEMISPHERE

11.51   *Perceptual and Conceptual Maps*

Just as your digestive system processes energy to build your body, so your nervous system processes information to build your mind. This vague concept of *mind* can be clarified by considering it in terms of a **subjective map** of the objective world. The function of your new brain is to build a subjective map inside you of the objective world outside you. Your behavior is determined by this subjective map rather than by the objective world; that is, you deal with the world as you see it, rather than with the world as it is. An actual tree in the objective world can have no effect on your behavior unless you are aware of it, whereas imaginary enemies lurking behind that tree *can* have an effect on your behavior even though they are not there. The tree is in the objective world but not in your subjective map; the enemy is in your subjective map but not in the objective world. Much of education could be considered as the process of building an accurate subjective map of the objective world.

The new brain consists of two hemispheres side by side. We used to think of the left hemisphere of the brain as dominant and the right hemisphere as a sort of spare in case the left hemisphere was damaged. It is now clear that left and right hemispheres of the brain are not duplicates of each other, like left and right lungs or left and right ears, but have qualitatively different functions. We have assumed the left hemisphere to be "dominant" only because we have emphasized its function. The left hemisphere processes conceptual informa-tion, and the right hemisphere processes perceptual information. Alterna-tively, in the language used here, your subjective map has two aspects—a **perceptual map** and a **conceptual map.**

The basic unit of the perceptual map is the percept, and its counterpart in the objective world is the thing; the basic unit of the conceptual map is the concept, and its counterpart in the objective world is the word. The relation-ship between the percept and the thing is determined by the structure of the nervous system. This relationship is thus primary. The relationship between the concept and the word is determined by the arbitrary link between the percept and the concept in the subjective map and the arbitrary link between the thing and the word in the objective world. This relationship is thus sec-ondary. That is, the relationship between the percept and the thing is biologi-cally determined, and the relationship between the concept and the word is culturally determined. In Figure 11-2, the more stable link of the perceptual map to the objective world is indicated by a heavy line, and the less stable link of the conceptual map to the objective world is indicated by a light line.

The fact that the perceptual map is primary is supported by a study of the development of the nervous system. Both phylogenetic development (from animal to human) and ontogenetic development (from child to adult) are characterized by the progressive emancipation of the organism from the tyranny of its environment.

The amoeba is capable only of moving toward a particular source of energy or away from it. The response is entirely determined by the stimulus. The octopus is capable of the sophisticated behavior of *not* responding to a stimulus. Its spontaneous response to the stimulus "crab" is the response "grab." (Or, more accurately, "grab, grab, grab, grab, grab, grab, grab, grab.") Young has taught octopi to delay this response for a few seconds.[235] He has also taught them the even more impressive feat of detouring around a sheet of glass to get at a crab on the other side. This **detour behavior** is very significant. When the octopus turns away from the crab, its behavior must be directed by an internal percept of the crab rather than by the external stimulus of the crab. The octopus, then, has a perceptual map mediating between the stimulus and the response. It is this first flicker of mental life that enables it to say no to its

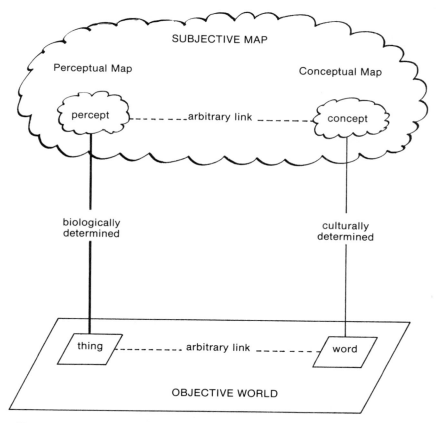

Figure 11-2. Perceptual and conceptual maps of the objective world

environment. With humans comes a further emancipation. We are capable of bundling a set of percepts of particular crabs into a general concept of a crab and of tagging that concept with the label *crab*; we have a conceptual as well as a perceptual map. Adler has argued that our conceptual map is what distinguishes us from all the other animals.[3]

Ontogeny recapitulates phylogeny. Somewhat. That is, our individual development is, roughly speaking, a high-speed rerun of the development of our species. We started off at the mercy of our environment. Our responses were determined by the stimuli impinging on us. We gradually built up a perceptual map that mediated between the stimulus and the response and then gradually abstracted a conceptual map from that perceptual map. As we learned to walk, we built up our perceptual maps; as we learned to talk, we built up our conceptual maps. As we grew older, we slowly shifted from an emphasis on the perceptual map to an emphasis on the conceptual map.

As with most innovations, this shift has both advantages and disadvantages. The conceptual map is a more efficient storage device. A thousand percepts of individual chairs can be stored under the one concept *chair*. One word is, in this sense, worth a thousand pictures. The conceptual map is also a more efficient retrieval device. You needn't rummage through the millions of snapshots your eyes have taken in your lifetime to find the one you want. Luria has described how an idiot savant performed impressive memory feats by retaining the perceptual map of childhood but could not handle conceptual problems because of "sensory overload."[125] Speaking enables us to trade labels so that we do not need to carry around a sack of objects in order to communicate about them. Writing enables us to record labels and thus "speak" to others remote in space and time. Mathematics helps us manipulate labels so that we can consider the relationships between them more clearly and concisely than we can in our heads. More recent innovations, like the telephone, the computer, the radio, and so on, have further improved the conceptual map as a more and more powerful means of making sense of the objective world. They all help us extend beyond the limited knowledge we can gain through our immediate experience in our short lifetimes.

Because of these advantages, we have tended to favor the conceptual map over the perceptual map. Educators have overemphasized those relatively recent innovations of reading, writing, and arithmetic. The conventional curriculum is based on the three Rs of the conceptual map and almost ignores the two Ls (looking and listening) of the perceptual map. Many millions of years of perceptual experience are neglected because of our fascination with a few thousand recent years of conceptual experience. Philosophers have also tended to favor the conceptual map over the perceptual map. Descartes said "I think, therefore I am," and generations of philosophers have echoed "He thinks, therefore I think too." They have Descartes before the horse. The conceptual map of thinking is based on the perceptual map. Since philosophers tend to study other philosophers rather than the phenomenon itself, much of the history of philosophy is the story of the elaboration of the error of Descartes—a pyramid of philosophers riding piggyback down a cul-de-sac.

One indication of the current bias in favor of the conceptual map over the perceptual map is the emphasis on **rationality** (the accuracy of your conceptual map of the objective world) over **veridicality** (the accuracy of your perceptual map of the objective world). You conceive a round earth, but you perceive a flat earth. You conceive the earth turning, but you perceive the sun setting. More truth is attributed to your conceptions than to your perceptions, but both are "true" at the appropriate level of analysis. Axioms based on your flat-earth perception would not get astronauts into orbit, but neither would axioms based on your round-earth conception get a hockey rink built. In our day-to-day life, we behave according to our perceptions rather than our conceptions. Try talking someone into walking with you part way round the earth to watch the earth turn, rather than down to the beach to watch the sun set.

"WORDS BECOME MORE REAL THAN THE THINGS THEY SIG-
NIFY. THE POWERFUL FACTORS IN OUR LIVES BECOME
LESS AND LESS THINGS THAT CAN BE TOUCHED AND
FELT, MORE AND MORE STATISTICAL INDICES AND VER-
BAL ABSTRACTIONS. IT IS WISDOM TO CUT THROUGH
SUCH ABSTRACTIONS AND ARTIFICIALITIES IN A
PERIODIC RETURN TO THE SOLID EARTH OF DIRECT
EXPERIENCE."

JOHN W. GARDNER
SELF-RENEWAL

Because of this bias toward the conceptual map, many of us suffer from the socialization disease. Check yourself out against the following symptoms: Peripheral blindness due to the donning of linguistic blinkers. Foveal blindness due to the inability to see things behind their labels (you can't see the wood for the "wood"). A tendency to lead a secondhand life as you deal more and more with the mediate world of words and less and less with the immediate world of things. A tendency to become a theory looking for facts rather than facts looking for a theory. An abstract attitude to match an abstract world (talking casually, for instance, about megadeaths). Loss of imagination. Alienation from former selves. Hardening of the categories.

The bias toward the conceptual map also prevents us from realizing the advantages of the perceptual map. For example, the perceptual map is often better for teaching and learning than the conceptual map. The immediate perceptual experience has more impact than the mediate conceptual knowledge. I "know" that the chair on which I am sitting is composed of myriads of atoms in rapid motion through a relatively vast space and that the planet on which the chair is sitting is itself only one of a myriad of planets in rapid motion through a vast space. However, I cannot experience those microscopic and cosmic views of the objective world without the microscope and the telescope to bring them within the range of my perceptual map. Failures of veridicality are more dramatic than failures of rationality. Demonstrating the Muller-Lyer illusion has much more impact than exposing the fallacy of denying the antecedent. Cuisenaire rods are useful teaching devices because they make the conceptual perceptual. A 5-year-old friend was demonstrating for me what added to 4 gave 6. She lined a 4 rod up alongside a 6 rod and then made the mistake of trying a 3 rod. As soon as she saw the protruding end, she tossed the rods away and started to cry. It is unlikely that she would have had such a spontaneous and dramatic emotional reaction if she had written $4 + 3 = 6$ and I had told her that she was wrong. It is certainly much more valuable for her to see that she was wrong than for me to tell her.

The bias toward the conceptual map continues, but rumblings of revolution are in the air. The voice of Merleau-Ponty is finally being heard as he nags us that the perceptual map is primary and the conceptual map is secondary.[150] McLuhan is offering to lead us out of the "linear literacy" wilderness of the conceptual map into the "all-at-once-ness" promised land of the perceptual map.[148] New-consciousness youth, raised with the television set as a third parent, is already there. Arnheim argues that creative thinking is the visual thinking of the perceptual map, with the verbal thinking of the conceptual map merely a device for organizing and communicating what has already been discovered.[6] Gibson takes us back to a time when the simple perceptual map of the world was not cluttered by the complex conceptual map superimposed on it.[77,78] He invites us to see the world again through the more innocent eyes of our remote ancestors, who knew the world through the perceptual map but did not know *about* the world through the conceptual map. Let us look at one example in which those rumblings have been heard and their implications for education evaluated.

Compensatory programs (like Head Start, Follow Up, and so on) and educational television programs (like *Sesame Street, The Electric Company,* and so on) are designed to provide artificially to minority-group children what other children receive naturally in their homes. The stimulation they provide is presumed to "compensate" for the stimulation children in minority groups lack. Ramírez and Castañeda argue that such programs, however well-meaning, condescend to minority groups by implying that their culture is "damaged" and must be "repaired."[178] This **damaged-culture theory** is rooted in the melting-pot social policy of the United States. Diverse peoples from around the world were to be boiled down to produce an amalgam called the American. This compound is presumed to be superior to each of the constituent elements in one of those rare cases in which a mongrel is valued over a pure race. The "pot" in which they were to be "melted" is, of course, the school, where aliens were to be transformed into Americans. It is, in many ways, a noble experiment and has provided a new identity for many peoples escaping oppressive conditions elsewhere. However, it has not worked so well for peoples already here (Native Americans, Eskimos, Mexicans) who were content with their old identity. The American compound turns out to be suspiciously like its most salient element, the Anglo, and Anglo culture is almost the antithesis of those native cultures.

Ramírez and Castañeda thus suggest an alternative explanation for the fact that Chicanos "fail" to benefit from schooling and, therefore, from the advantages of the upward mobility schooling offers. Chicano homes are not inferior to Anglo homes but simply different. When Chicano children go from a Mexican home to an Anglo school, they experience "culture shock." School culture involves not only a strange language and strange content but a strange style, in which assumptions about motivation, learning, human relationships, and communication differ from those of the home culture. They have the same disoriented feeling that you and I have when we visit a foreign country, and they exhibit the same symptoms—inappropriate behavior, dullness, lowered self-esteem. However, you and I know that being illiterate and inept is a temporary state caused by the environment, whereas the children have no such reassurance and may become convinced that they do indeed come from an inferior culture and are themselves inferior.

The solution is not to change the child to fit the school, but to change the school to fit the child. Chicano and Anglo cultures can be characterized roughly in terms of the relative emphasis on the development of the right and left hemispheres. Anglo schools are designed to teach and test the use of the left hemisphere (and are thus "half-witted" according to Ramírez and Castañeda). They should be redesigned to teach and test the use of both hemispheres. In such schools, children would become "cognitive switch-hitters," able to use each hemisphere when appropriate and to switch smoothly from one to the other. Peal and Lambert find that people raised as bilingual and bicultural in Montreal have more mental flexibility, superior concept formation, and a more diversified set of mental abilities than their monolingual and monocultural counterparts.[165] This is vividly illustrated by those brilliant politicians Pierre Trudeau, prime minister of Canada, and René Lévesque, premier of Quebec, both products of this bilingual and bicultural education. Such schools would permit Mexican-Americans to be both Mexicans and Americans—distinctive elements in a rich American stew, rather than boiled down into an anemic American consommé or drained off as an indigestible lump. Anglos, too, would be able to develop their human potential more fully. The limitations of the Anglo personality of which we have recently started becoming more aware—the inability to cooperate, the failure to establish intimate relationships and a sense of community, the tendency not to nurture others or to seek succor from them—are essentially the capacities that are developed in the Chicano culture.

11.52   *You as Movie Studio*

In my village in Scotland, there was one small cinema run by one man. He was barker. He would stand outside yelling "Roll up, roll up—only a few seats left." He was receptionist. When he persuaded someone to come in, he would rush around behind the ticket counter and sell the ticket. He was usher. He would rush around from behind the counter to show the customers to their seats before resuming his role as barker. He was projectionist. When he had finally collected a large enough audience to make it worthwhile, he would go upstairs and operate the movie projector. He was salesman. The film would stop (always, it seemed, at some exciting part, but I realize now at the end of a reel since he had only one projector), and he would walk around the cinema selling ice cream and chocolates until the audience had bought enough to bribe him to return to his role as projectionist.

This multiple-role feat is indeed impressive, yet each of us is performing a much more impressive feat. You are singlehandedly operating a movie theater of the mind. Not only that. Your mind is a movie studio as well as a movie theater. In that studio, you are making more magnificent movies than ever

TRUE, THE PICTURE OF THE OUTER, ADULT-CHOSEN PICTURES CAN BE MEANINGFUL AND DELIGHTFUL TO CHILDREN: BUT IT IS THE CAPTIONS OF THE MIND PICTURES THAT HAVE THE POWER AND THE LIGHT.

SYLVIA ASHTON-WARNER
TEACHER

came out of Hollywood studios. Your movies run continuously almost 24 hours a day throughout your lifetime.* Your movies do not just cater to vision and hearing but to all the sensory modalities—not only movies and talkies, but smellies and tasties and feelies, too. Isherwood wrote "I am a camera." He was much too modest. He is a magnificent mobile movie studio that doubles as a movie theater in which he can simultaneously watch his own show.† Your perceptual map of the objective world is built up as you move about in it making your automovie. You are producer, director, camera technician, script writer, narrator, and principal star—as well as the only member of the audience and the critic who reviews the movie the next morning.

11.53 You as Artist

The main limitation of your movie-studio-cum-movie-theater mind is that the movie theater has only one seat. There is no way you can invite me in to see your home movie as you see it. Stated more formally, the nervous system is a magnificent receiver but a poor transmitter. It is a good receiver because it has evolved as a receiver over billions of years. It is a poor transmitter because it has been used as a transmitter only relatively recently. In Chapter 9, we discussed the tricks of speaking/listening and writing/reading that our species has developed recently to improve the transmission facilities of our nervous systems. Since you cannot invite me in to see your home movie directly, you must learn how to show it to me indirectly. You can do so by speaking, writing, painting, taking photographs, making music, or simply by taking my hand and showing me things. The various arts are different ways of showing your home movies.

We tend to reserve the word *artist* for those who are especially good at showing their home movies. However, since we all share our automovies with someone somehow, we are all artists. The languages of the Eskimo and of the Balinese do not have a word for *artist* because, in those cultures, everyone does everything as well as she or he can. The best-selling book in history was written by fishermen inspired by a carpenter. Four lower-class lads from Liver-

---

* Once, during a two-day party, I ran out of color film and borrowed some black-and-white film. I took photographs with more abandon than before, since the film was cheaper. When I ran out of black-and-white film, I started snapping away with even more abandon using the empty camera. Then, it occurred to me that, since I was not going to get any permanent record of those shots, I did not need the camera. I began to compose scenes and "photograph" them by blinking. It finally dawned on me that I did not even have to blink. Why settle for stills when my life was a continuous movie?

† Once again, nature anticipates people. Each of our great innovations (movies, talkies) is simply an approximation to what already exists within each of us. We will one day design a vehicle equally at home on land, in water, and in air, only to realize that we have simply reinvented the humble duck.

pool have demonstrated that we are all potential musicians. By some insidious process, most of us are brainwashed into believing that we are not artists and relinquish this special status to those few who somehow survive this process. In my own case, I can pinpoint the day I ceased to think of myself as an artist. There was a competition for the limited seats in the art class in my first year at high school. I didn't get in and decided that I was not an artist. I have only recently rebelled against this arbitrary exclusion. On that day, the artist in me atrophied, although, fortunately, somehow the scientist in me survived. Most of us get excluded from *all* those special categories and settle into the miscellaneous category of "ordinary folk."

If you doubt that you are an artist, catch what you can of your own late show. Keep paper and pencil, or better, a tape recorder by your bedside and record as much as you can of your dreams. You may find in your nightlife much of the drama missing from your daylife. The dream is the poor person's drama. You entertain ideas by day, and they entertain you by night. It is in your dreams that you are most aware of that eerie but exhilarating sensation that "someone in here knows more than I do." You are (or, rather, some untapped part of you is) a fine dramatist in your dreams.

Two examples from my own nightlife. The word *postprandial* was used in one of my dreams. Since I didn't know what it meant and was an academic type, I staggered out of bed to look it up in the dictionary. I was among the *p*'s before I realized the strangeness of the situation. "What am I doing here? It's *my* dream." I continued anyway, discovering that it meant "after a meal" and had been used appropriately in the dream. I didn't know what the word meant, but someone in here knew. I used to lead my life in five-year installments for the convenience of biographers. At the time when I had completed my last five-year plan and was sweating over the decision about my next five-year plan, I had a series of dreams. The content varied from dream to dream, but the theme was always the same. Here is an illustrative dream from the series. Scene 1: I am in the playground of a rural school. The bell rings and I saunter into the classroom after the children. The teacher looks up as I enter and says "You're late but that's okay." Scene 2: Back out in the playground, I am laboriously climbing over a high fence at one end. A blond boy, who has just walked through a gate in the fence, is looking up at me with a quizzical expression. Scene 3: I am in a hut, which I recognize as the hut I lived in as an adolescent, at the time when I was planning my perfection. I am squeezing myself out of the window. The same blond boy is walking out the door. He turns (and, as he turns, I recognize myself as a child) and says "Cool it." Each of the dreams in the series involved my doing something with great effort and pain while someone else was doing the same thing in an easy and pleasant way and advising me to "cool it." I took the advice of this wiser part of me and, since then, my life has been easier, more pleasant, and, to my surprise, more productive.

11.6 *OPERATING YOUR LEFT HEMISPHERE*

11.61 *You as Laboratory*

All study is essentially the study of the human. Biology, psychology, and sociology study humans directly at different levels of analysis. English and mathematics are the study of languages created by humans to communicate with one another. History and geography are the study of the place of humans in time and space. Art and music as academic subjects are the study of the artistic products of humans. Political science and economics are the study of the institutions humans have created to handle power and resources. And so on and so on. In summary, all disciplines reduce to psychology.* Since all members of species *Homo sapiens* are essentially the same, you are representative of humans. You are therefore a handy, portable laboratory for all study. The Sinologist and the astronomer have, until recently, had an excuse for studying their subject matter secondhand. Psychologists have never had this excuse. We have always had ourselves.

You are the world's foremost expert on yourself. There is, however, a sense in which Freud knew more about you than you know about you, even though he may have died before you were born. You are like all people in some ways and like no other people in some ways. Insofar as you are like all people, Freud knew you better; insofar as you are like no other people, you know you better. There is no reason, though, why you cannot become as informed as Freud about those general laws we all share. We tend to become informed about those things in which we are interested. To you, you are the most interesting subject in the world.

One of the limitations of yourself as laboratory is that you can be only one person in one place at one time. You can never see the objective world as anyone else can see it, and you certainly can never see it as *everyone* else can see it. You must always view the world through that reducing (and distorting) lens of your particular nervous system. You cannot even be all your own possible selves. There is no way you can ever know those millions of other lives you could have led if you had made different choices at your many choice points. Life permits no controlled experiments. Your subjective map of the objective world, however, permits you to overcome this limitation somewhat. In your subjective map, if not in the objective world, you can be all people in all places at all times. On the stage of your mind, you can play the parts of Hamlet, Muhammad Ali, Indira Gandhi, or Mrs. Jones next door, and get some idea what it is like to be someone else. You can take a trip on a train of thought or a

---

* All professors will tell you, of course, that everything reduces to their discipline. This is the academic art of subsumemanship. Whenever you hear this, I recommend that you activate the aforementioned "bullshit detectors." However, in this case, the statement is true. All the other professors are wrong.

cruise on the stream of consciousness. You can sail, swim, scuba dive, snorkel, or ski on that stream or simply sit on the bank and watch yourself going past. Take a Scottish vacation—sit in your armchair and let your mind wander. Go around the world in 80 ways with your eyes closed. Your nervous system can serve not only as a spaceship but as a time machine. You can wander around the planets with HAL in the year 2001 and, next moment, be fighting alongside Robert the Bruce at the Battle of Bannockburn in 1314. In the subjective map, all time is now and all space is here.

11.62   *You as Scientist*

Very effective strategies for operating within the conceptual map have been developed by scientists. You can use those strategies in your everyday life, since *you* are a scientist. Indeed, as a child, you were a very good scientist. You performed magnificent scientific feats very early in your life. For example, you teased out the complex system of rules and exceptions that constitutes our language from the raw data of speech. These data are often confusing. Yet you figured out the meaning of *small* and *large,* for instance, even though the former had been used to describe cars and the latter to describe dogs. Admittedly, you made many mistakes. For instance, you said "I growed" for a time. But this is more a reflection of the ludicrous nature of our language. You had made a sound generalization which, for idiosyncratic reasons, happened not to be correct.

As you grew up, however, you learned that you were not a scientist. Scientists were a special sort of person. They were awesome figures with occult knowledge and supernatural skills. Or they were ivy-covered professors in ivory towers, puttering about in laboratories and muttering about in libraries. They were either aweful or awful. You learned that science was a private terrain, closed to the public and jealously guarded by the high priests of each discipline. Trespassers will be persecuted. Physics, chemistry, biology, and psychology became faraway places with science-sounding names. Science is the modern religion. Lay people used to be people who weren't clergy; now they are people who aren't scientists. We used to lend authority to our words by wearing a white collar backward; now we wear a white lab coat. If the white lab coat is not awe-inspiring enough, and if we are male, we grow a beard. I noticed that my classes were much more attentive when I wore a beard. The voice from the wilderness is more impressive than the cry from the clearing.

The sacred territory of science is guarded by a wall of mystique, which keeps "nonscientists" in their place outside. Scientists do not, of course, have a monopoly on this mystification process. Many counterculture gurus make a career out of the appearance of special knowledge and skills. Indeed, all people with special skills are prey to the temptation to present themselves as Very Special People. The mystique puts us at the mercy of specialists. We have all experienced that helpless feeling when mechanics warn us of dire consequences if we do not permit them to perform some expensive operation on our cars. We have all experienced the frustration of having a doctor shrug off our questions about our own bodies with a supercilious, you-wouldn't-understand attitude.

There are encouraging signs that more and more people are using their special skills to help people rather than to exploit them. Books like *The Tooth Trip*[144] and *The Well Body Book*[195] suggest preventive strategies that make us less dependent on dentists and doctors, respectively. Good professional healers, like good parents and good teachers, realize that their basic function is to plan their own obsolescence. Indeed, this may be the basic function of all good people, since the only thing we know for sure is that we are eventually going to have to be replaced. Such books destroy the mystique by revealing the technique. Clarity obliterates the appearance of profundity. Reputations for profundity *must* be based on obscurity. Any proposition which is clear is no longer judged as "profound." When you understand something, you see it as obvious, or even as a reminder of something you already knew.

Poor science education contributes to this process of convincing most of us that we are not scientists. The aim of science is to make the complex simple; the aim of science education is not, as it sometimes seems, to reverse this process. Science tends to be presented in terms of stinks and bangs rather than in terms of careful observation and clear reasoning. The product is emphasized over the process. Scientists are taking the universe apart to see how it works. Students of science should be invited to look over their shoulders to see what they are doing rather than be forced to rummage among the pieces at their feet. There is nothing in science that is intrinsically difficult. It is, however, often made artificially difficult by poor presentation. We blame the destination rather than the source and come to see science as something remote and special, rather than as simply common sense made systematic.

Lay people and off-duty scientists tend not to use careful observation and clear reasoning, which have proven so effective, in their everyday lives. They tend to upset that subtle balance between observation and reason that constitutes the scientific attitude. Some become extreme rationalists—"My mind's made up; don't confuse me with facts"—and some become extreme empiricists—"My mind is open, at both ends so that the facts may pour through." Extreme rationalists are a theory looking for facts. They seek out confirming facts and avoid contradicting facts. They thus reach foregone conclusions from unwarranted assumptions. Their brains instruct their sense organs to find only certain information, like a government that establishes a commission to find the facts and then specifies the facts it must find. They use information as a drunk uses a lamppost, for support rather than for illumination. Extreme empiricists are a disorderly pile of facts. They lack theory to organize those facts or even, at the very least, to help them discriminate between important and trivial facts. They are demented squirrels scampering from tree to tree, with swollen bellies and stuffed cheeks, gathering more nuts than they will ever need.

Often, we fail to apply the basic scientific principle "every effect has a cause" to ourselves, although we recognize that it applies to the *rest* of the natural world. Some recent changes in my relationship with inanimate objects suggest why we fail to apply this principle in our relationships with other people. I have at last stopped getting mad at inanimate objects. It has finally gotten through to me that doors that poke me in the eye, drawers that stick, socks that have holes, and screws that won't screw are not involved in a fiendish conspiracy against me. I have even stopped getting mad at my car, which has taken much abuse for its fickle habits. It dared to blow a tire on a thruway. I found that the tire was as bald as a billiard ball and that it was *I* who had almost killed myself. That was the last time I raged at my car. There is, however, one object that I still get mad at—the nozzle of my shower. I turn on the taps, lean over to test the water, and it treacherously clobbers me from behind with freezing or scalding water. When my temper and temperature have cooled, I am able to accept that, once again, I have conspired against myself. I have forgotten to put down the what-do-you-call-it that directs the water to the tap rather than to the showerhead. The reason I still get mad initially at the showerhead is that there is such a wide spatial and temporal gap between the cause (my turning on the water with the what-do-you-call-it up) and the effect (my getting clobbered from behind by the water). In the heat (or cold) of the moment, it appears to be doing this to me. The same mechanism may explain why we tend so often to blame external circumstances for things we are doing to ourselves in our interpersonal relationships. We are such complex systems that there is often a long delay between cause and effect. It took our species a long time, for instance, to recognize the cause-and-effect relationship between intercourse and birth. We can often see such complex cause-and-effect mechanisms working in other people—the man who gravitates, again and again, to bitchy women, or the woman who seems to get involved, again and again, with violent men. We see how they seek them out or bring out that aspect of their personality. It is not so easy to see the process in yourself. You are standing too close. Next time you find yourself blaming some external circumstance for your misfortunes, however, step back and try to see how you may be doing it to yourself. Perhaps you are reaping something you sowed, being hit by your own boomerang, or getting your karma back.

A more positive picture of the scientist can be pieced together from a number of books. Science educators seldom show those pieces, much less put the jigsaw puzzle together. Fuller's *Utopia or Oblivion* shows how science and technology can contribute more than politics and diplomacy to solving world problems.[60] Von Bertalanffy's *General Systems Theory* demonstrates how we can become Renaissance people in this second Renaissance.[225] Watson's *Double Helix*[230] uncovers the emotion and drama in the process of science. Koestler's *Act of Creation* reveals that creating hypotheses (aha experience) is no different from creating poems (ah experience) or puns (haha experience).[114] De

Chardin's *Letters from a Traveller* shows how the paleontologist's search under the earth is not incompatible with the theologian's search above the clouds.[38] Maslow's *Psychology of Science* presents science and humanism as comfortable bedmates.[139]

There emerges from books such as these the following composite picture of scientists.

1. They play a game with nature in which they ask questions and it gives answers. They know that they must ask precise questions to get precise answers, important questions to get important answers. They know that they need never appease nature since, although subtle, it is never whimsical. They respect nature and themselves as part of nature. They admire nature's art gallery and themselves as the only one of nature's creatures fully able to appreciate it.

2. They prefer the humble sound of tentative truth to the irritating noise of Absolute Truth. Those who know everything can't learn anything. An omniscient God is a boring know-it-all. They prefer the ugly truth to the beautiful falsehood. They look themselves straight in the eye and do not flinch from an unflattering reflection.

3. They are as unassuming as possible. Their theories are tentative and contain the seeds of their own destruction. They generate facts and may even generate contrary facts. They do not mind seeing beautiful big theories being destroyed by ugly little facts—although, admittedly, they mind more when they are their own beautiful theories than when they are their ugly facts.

4. They aspire to consistency in their lives as well as in their theories. They are not scientists in their laboratories and studies and lay people in their livingrooms and bedrooms. Scientists do not need to be split personalities. Their value systems can be consistent with their knowledge systems. They see themselves as defiant packages of negative entropy stalling the tendency of the universe toward chaos by assimilating and organizing as much information as they can. Fighting entropy is less romantic than fighting dragons, but it is more real.

5. They are serious yet not earnest, skeptical yet not cynical, solid yet not stolid, innocent yet not ignorant, childlike yet not childish.

11.63 *You as Participant Observer*

Your growth involves a complex interaction between the unfolding of your genetic program from the inside out and the assimilation of your culture from the outside in. You can affect your growth only through the latter. Education could be considered, in one broad sense, as the assimilation of your culture. An anthropologist studies a culture by being a **participant observer** in that culture. You can assimilate your culture by being a participant observer in your *own* culture. The culture of your "civilized" society seems much more complex than that of the "primitive" society. Lévi-Strauss assures us, however, that it is no more complex—it is simply more cluttered, since we have evolved cultural catch-alls (written language, cumulative science, videotapes, and so on) to hoard culture.[121]

As a participant observer, you operate on two levels of consciousness: you participate and you observe yourself participating. A number of psychologists have commented on this double consciousness. Hebb reports that, while lecturing to his classes, he often catches himself standing behind himself criticizing the lecture. Richard Alpert describes how he maintained his Baba Ram Dass Oriental cool when stopped by a traffic cop by observing himself as a character in a movie and the cop as an extra sent from Central Casting. Penfield's patients relive an experience from their pasts when he stimulates a part of their brains with an electrode, but are aware at the same time that they are sitting in an operating room.[166] Apparently, you *can* step into the same stream twice, but you must also sit on the bank and watch yourself going past. Those two states of being conscious and being conscious of your consciousness are qualitatively different. Reik recommends that couples not reminisce too much about the good old days. This tends to shift the quality of the memories from the former consciousness to the latter. They become like stories they have heard about others rather than those intimate, binding experiences they have shared.

This dual role of participant and observer is difficult to maintain. Like a drunk riding a horse, you tend to fall off one side or the other. You become a full-time observer, like academicians who observe at second eye and second ear as they lead secondhand lives, or television addicts who stop leading their own lives because the beautiful people on television live it so much better than they do. Or you become a full-time participant, like people who get so entangled in the minutiae of living that they cannot step back to observe the process of living. Or you switch artificially from one role to another—observing in school from 9 to 4 and participating out of school from 4 to 9, observing when very young and very old and participating in the years between. The vague noises about the lack of orchestration between learning and living or between thought and action could, perhaps, be more precisely translated into this failure to maintain that dual role of participant observer. The antiintellectualism fashionable among some students today could be an overemphasis on participation as a reaction against the overemphasis in the university on observation.* The public figure who refused yet one more interview with the statement "If I spend so much time talking about what I have done, am doing, and will do, I'll have no time to do it" was seeking to maintain that precarious balance between living and recording one's life. A friend once warned me that I was losing my balance by pasting the message "Life is an experience to be lived not a

---

*One of my students returned from a week at Goddard College to report that it was "a groovy place." Another student, disillusioned with the university, went off around the world and reported that his trip was "outasight." Neither of them, under intensive questioning, could be persuaded to be any more articulate.

problem to be solved" on my bathroom mirror to be read every morning before breakfast. He was right about me, but wrong about "life." It is, of course, an experience *and* a problem. To lead a full life, we must both live it as an experience through participation and solve it as a problem through observation.

Just as your two eyes permit you to see the world in three dimensions and your two ears permit you to hear the world in three dimensions, so those two states of consciousness provide you with a three-dimensional view of your culture. Participating provides the view from inside, and observing provides the view from outside. You gain knowledge *of* your culture through participation and knowledge *about* your culture through observation.

POST-EXERCISES

1. The Movie Studio of the Mind

You can learn to operate the right hemisphere of your new brain more effectively by considering yourself in your various roles in the movie-studio-cum-movie-theater of your mind.

Think of yourself as producer. How are you financing your movie? Are you still making grade-B exploitation films to finance your masterpiece? Or have you forgotten your original ideals and settled down to churning out third-rate movies?

Think of yourself as director. What is the message of your automovie? Who are you casting in the supporting roles? Are you still intent on that extravaganza with a cast of thousands? Or have you settled down to a low-budget domestic drama with a cast of two?

Think of yourself as camera technician. Is your eye-camera in good working order? Does the world still look as bright as when the camera was new? Have you tried your rose-colored filter lately, or has your gray filter gotten stuck on permanently? Is your zoom mechanism still working, or is it fixed at middle distance with far and near shots out of focus? After checking out your visual equipment, advise your sound technician to do the same with the audio equipment. And your smell technician and your taste technician and your feel technician.

Think of yourself as script writer. Are you writing your own script? Or was your script written by your parents with you merely mouthing the lines they assigned to you? Or do you believe that your script was written by the Great Ghostwriter in the Sky? Why not write a scenario for tomorrow's shooting as a step toward becoming your own script writer?

Think of yourself as narrator. Sit still for a moment with your eyes closed and listen to your narration. Do you hear the patter of tiny thoughts? How can you think with all this noise going on? Or *is* this thinking?

Think of yourself as principal star. What kind of character are you playing? Are you being typecast? Or are you a multifaceted diamond with a different character for each member of your supporting cast?

Think of yourself as the only member of the audience. Has your automovie degenerated into day after day of dittos in your diary? Why not try to do one little thing tomorrow you have never done before? You don't want to bore yourself, do you?

Think of yourself as critic. Do you usually give yourself a rave review in the morning for last night's performance, or do you look into the mirror and shudder as you wash your face? Do you evaluate each performance on its merits, or do you compare it with the performance of others? Do you pay little attention to your automovie since you are so obsessed with the autobiography you are going to abstract from it?

Why not leave that to those who will write your obituary and concentrate on making a beautiful automovie?

2. Keeping a Journal

One practical device to help you maintain that difficult role of participant observer in your own culture is the journal. Just as carrying a camera sensitizes you to the sights around you, so keeping a journal sensitizes you to the ideas around you. You may want to keep a journal of the day-by-day events in your classroom (which could evolve into one of those first-person accounts of teaching listed in Post-exercise 3 for Chapter 4) or a full-time journal, integrating your personal and professional lives.

Here are some suggestions based on keeping a full-time journal for the last seven years.

a. Carry your journal with you. So many potential journalists get discouraged because they don't have paper and pencil handy when they get ideas and have forgotten them when they get to their journal. I use a pocket day-timer so that I can carry my journal and my pen in my wallet, which is always with me.

b. Write your thoughts as soon as you think them. Experiences are so real as you are experiencing them that you assume you will never forget them. I'll never forget what's-his-name. Your friends may be nonplused at first, when you pull out your journal, but later they will be concerned when you don't. Didn't I say anything interesting today?

c. Write your own thoughts. Fish in your own stream of consciousness—don't poach in other people's streams. As your stream of consciousness rushes past (or trickles past on bad days) land only the fish you like.

d. Write to yourself. Since you are the reader as well as the writer of your journal, you can afford to be succinct. You as writer and you as reader have an even greater overlap of experience than an old couple together so long that they can communicate in grunts.

e. Reread your journals from time to time. The process of keeping a journal is more important than the product. However, rereading your journal may enhance its value. It can permit you to rerun your old movies—I remember reliving a sunny month in Ibiza one cold winter evening in Montreal. It keeps you in touch with your former selves—the authors of your previous journals. It helps you organize your thoughts. By reading your journal through over a long period, you get a bird's-eye view of your thoughts and may get insights not available from the worm's-eye view as you write day by day.

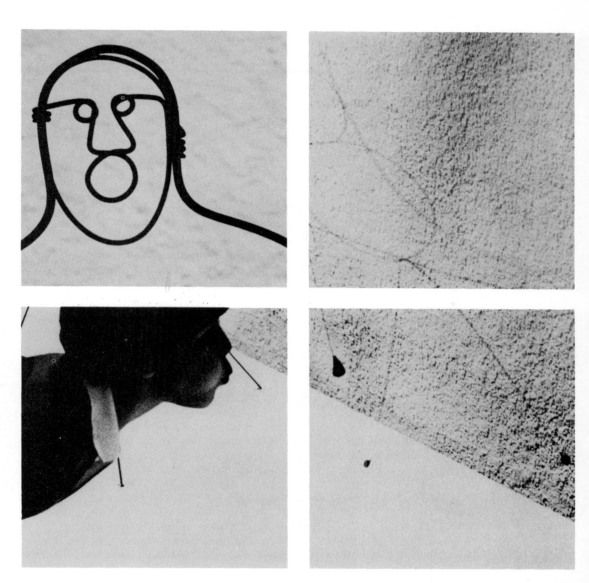

Observer Effects 12

12   OBSERVER EFFECTS

PRE-EXERCISES

1. Sixteen Facts in Search of a Theory

In *Six Characters in Search of an Author,* Pirandello, an Italian dramatist, introduces his six characters and invites the audience to write the play. This exercise parallels that of Pirandello. I have listed 16 facts and invite you to develop a theory to explain them. Clue: The title of another Pirandello play—*It Is So! (If You Think So).*

a.   Those (students, businesspeople, athletes, or whoever) who fear failure often do indeed fail.
b.   Girls tend to grow up girlish, and boys tend to grow up boyish.
c.   Patients are often cured when their doctors give them useless pills called placebos.
d.   Soon after the four-minute mile was finally broken by Roger Bannister, a number of other milers broke it too.
e.   The stock market crashed in 1929.
f.   Some people consistently have good trips on LSD, and some people consistently have bad trips.
g.   Zeigarnik never came up with any evidence against the Zeigarnik effect.
h.   Crystal-ball gazers, palm readers, and other "futurists" often do indeed predict events.
i.   The same people tend to be sent back to prison over and over again.
j.   Archie Bunker is prejudiced against Blacks and homosexuals and can indeed point to "evidence" justifying his prejudices.
k.   Dick always seems to get involved with bitchy women and Jane with violent men, and Sam never gets very involved romantically with anyone.
l.   The rich (whether economically or intellectually) tend to get richer and the poor tend to get poorer.

m. Many patients enter mental hospitals insane and come out sane, as would be expected, but many enter sane and stay in insane.

n. Clive Barnes, the influential drama critic for the *New York Times,* is reputed to be able, singlehandedly, to cause a million-dollar Broadway play to flop.

o. Nations that prepare for war tend to go to war.

p. Subjects who believe ESP is possible perform better at ESP tasks than subjects who do not believe ESP is possible.

2. Self-Fulfilling Prophecies

"It becomes so! (because you think so)." Are there any potential Pirandellos out there who would like to write a Pirandello-style play about the self-fulfilling prophecy—that is, about the very human tendency not to believe something because it is true, but to make it true by believing it?

Here is a list of personal experiences. Try to explain each of them in terms of the self-fulfilling prophecy.

a. I read an article about opinion polls. The author claimed that such polls not only predicted the outcome of the last U.S. presidential election but influenced that election by predicting its outcome.

b. I read Ken Kesey's book *One Flew over the Cuckoo's Nest.* Chief Broom in his only speech points out that he became a deaf-mute because he was not expected to hear or say anything.

c. A friend described to me the elaborate procedure by which the Dalai Lama, the spiritual leader of Tibet, is chosen as a young boy. I thought that possibly the most important factor was that a person treated as a leader from a young age will indeed become a leader.

d. I read in a newspaper the prediction by an important official of the International Monetary Fund that the pound would go down to $1.50 U.S. In the newspaper the next day, I read that the pound had dropped to $1.50 U.S.

e. I stumbled across the following statement while reading Colin Wilson's autobiography, *Journey to a Beginning:* "Certain army officers, sons of rich or titled men, seemed to give orders without effort, and were obeyed because they took it for granted that they *would* be obeyed."

f. I saw the movie *One Flew over the Cuckoo's Nest.* In the boat-outing scene, as each inmate was addressed as "Doctor," each dull face was momentarily transformed to bright.

g. I received a review of an early draft of this book. The reviewer argued that the level of discourse was too high for education majors.

h. A friend described a high school reunion 20 years after graduation. The class clown, who had become a distinguished executive, reverted to class clown at the reunion.

i. I read a review of the movie *Network,* in which the reviewer argued that the media not only report news but create it.

j. I had the following conversation:

"Mary is very unhappy."
"That's peculiar. She's always happy when she's with me."
"That's because she's with you. She's happy when she's with you, but she's often unhappy when she's not with you."
"I've never been with her when she's not with me."

Mary later pointed out that I expect her to be happy and thus force her always to present her positive side to me.

k. Most of these experiences occurred while I was working on this chapter on the self-fulfilling prophecy.

12.1 THEORY

12.11 The Hawthorne Effect

Children know about the **observer effect.** Jane tries to jump on the head of her shadow cast by the morning sun. She discovers that it is impossible. Dick stands in front of a mirror and opens his eyes very quickly to see how he looks when he is asleep. He discovers that it is impossible. Dick sets off to walk to the end of the rainbow and Jane to walk to the horizon. They discover that it is impossible. We all discovered the observer effect through such childhood experiments. Observation involves a relationship between the observer and the observed. There are certain things observers cannot do because, by trying to do them, they change this relationship.

Teacher-training supervisors know about the observer effect. The classes they observe can never be an unbiased sample of all the classes they could observe. They change what they observe by the act of observing it. The behavior of the teacher and of the students is affected by their presence in the classroom. Teachers may do worse than usual because they are nervous about being observed, or they may do better than usual because, warned of the observer's impending arrival, they prepared their lessons more diligently. Some classes behave worse and some behave better in the presence of a strange adult. The teacher may prepare for a supervisor's visit in more subtle ways than simply writing lesson plans. Some teachers tell their students they should behave well, since the inspector is coming to observe them rather than the teacher. One teacher found out that the inspector was in the school on a day when he had to teach a very difficult class. The teacher (who shall remain nameless) told this class that a gentleman was coming to observe how intelligent they were rather than how competent he was. In order to impress the supervisor, they should raise their right hand if they knew the answer to a question and their left hand if they did not know the answer. The supervisor came in. Everything was going fine until a very difficult question triggered a forest of left hands. The class cracked up as I (oops!) looked feverishly around for a right hand.

Scientists know about the observer effect. Physical scientists have recently discovered what schoolchildren and school supervisors have known for some time: what is observed may be changed by the act of observing it. Since observation is the basis of the scientific method, the observer effect poses a profound problem to scientists. Their method is limited. Every time you open the refrigerator door, you observe that the light is on. You can't conclude from this that the light is always on. This is obvious. What is observed is changed by the act of observing it. It is not so obvious that it is impossible to observe the absolute motion of a body through space. Since the observer is also in motion, only relative motion can be detected or even defined. This was not obvious to anyone until Einstein pointed it out in his theory of relativity, and it is still not obvious to most people. It is not so obvious that the position and momentum of a subatomic particle cannot be precisely determined at the same time. This was not known until Heisenberg pointed it out in his uncertainty principle, which upset Einstein's theory and was never accepted by Einstein. To observe the position of the particle, it is necessary to shine light on it, and this act changes its momentum. Once again, what is observed is changed by the act of observing it.

A group of social scientists encountered this limitation in the scientific method during a study they were conducting at the Hawthorne Works of the Western Electric Company in the 1920s.[182] They were investigating the effect of working conditions on the performance of workers. One variable was illumination. They increased the illumination. Production went up. They decreased the illumination. Production went up. They pretended to change the illumination but actually left it the same. Production went up. The same surprising finding resulted from varying other conditions in the workers' physical environment. Production could be increased by doing something—indeed, anything. It did not really matter precisely *what* was done. This **Hawthorne effect** has been attributed to the fact that any novelty decreases boredom and thus increases production, or to the fact that the researchers' interest in the workers improves morale and thus increases production.

12.12 *The Self-Fulfilling Prophecy*

The observer effect has so far been illustrated by examples from physical science (dealing with things) and from social science (dealing with people). There is an additional twist to the observer effect in the social sciences. The expectations of an observer can have no effect on things. Most of our species through most of our history "expected" this planet to be flat, but it refused to be flat and persisted in remaining round; most of us most of the time "expected" the sun to revolve around our planet, but the sun stubbornly insisted that the earth revolve around it. However, the expectations of an observer *can* have an effect on people. In the social sciences, the observed are also observers. Thus, the observed may change behavior not only because they are observed but because they observe that they are being observed. They may, consciously or unconsciously, pick up what they are expected to do and, consequently, do what they are expected to do.

This new twist introduces another observer effect into social science. Not only may behavior be changed by the act of observing it, but it may be changed in the direction expected by the observer. The prophecies of the observer may

IF YOU TREAT AN INDIVIDUAL AS HE IS, HE WILL STAY AS HE IS, BUT IF YOU TREAT HIM AS IF HE WERE WHAT HE OUGHT TO BE AND COULD BE, HE WILL BECOME WHAT HE OUGHT TO BE AND COULD BE.

GOETHE

fulfill themselves. Rosenthal and Jacobson have suggested that the Hawthorne effect may be due to such a **self-fulfilling prophecy.**[193] The researchers at the Hawthorne Works did not expect that production would increase no matter what way they manipulated the physical environment. Indeed, they were surprised by this discovery. However, they did expect that their intervention would improve production and could have communicated this expectation to the workers, who fulfilled their expectations.

12.13 The Experimenter-Bias Effect

Robert Rosenthal, a Harvard social psychologist, has studied this form of the observer effect in a series of experiments on experiments.[189] He argues as follows. An experimenter has certain expectations about the outcome of an experiment. Intentionally or unintentionally, the experimenter communicates these expectations to the subjects who, consciously or unconsciously, behave as they are expected to behave. Thus the hypothesis (that is, the proposition the experimenter expects to confirm) is confirmed, not because it is true, but because the experimenter expected it to be true.

This **experimenter-bias effect** may help to explain many controversies within science. Scientists on both sides of the controversy expect contrary

ANIMALS STUDIED BY AMERICANS RUSH ABOUT FRANTICALLY, WITH AN INCREDIBLE DISPLAY OF HUSTLE AND PEP, AND AT LAST ACHIEVE THE DESIRED RESULT BY CHANCE. ANIMALS OBSERVED BY GERMANS SIT STILL AND THINK, AND AT LAST EVOLVE THE SOLUTION OUT OF THEIR INNER CONSCIOUSNESS.

BERTRAND RUSSELL

results and thus get contrary results. Zeigarnik expects and finds evidence for the Zeigarnik effect, and critics expect and find evidence against the Zeigarnik effect. I know of no case in which a person who is so involved with a principle or theory that it is named after him or her has found evidence against it. Darwin made special note of any evidence against his theory of evolution, since he knew this was the evidence he tended to "forget."

Rosenthal's experiments on experiments have themselves generated a controversy. Barber and Silver reanalyzed and reinterpreted 32 experiments demonstrating the experimenter-bias effect and claimed that only a few of them did indeed demonstrate the effect.[12] Rosenthal reanalyzed and reinterpreted the experiments in another way and concluded that they still demonstrated the experimenter-bias effect.[190] Barber and Silver retaliated with a further reanalysis and reinterpretation.[13] Rosenthal was not permitted a last word in his defense. Since he is probably too polite to use this argument, let me present it on his behalf. A body of experiments can be analyzed and interpreted in a number of ways. The fact that Rosenthal's way results in evidence for his experimenter-bias effect and that Barber and Silver's ways result in evidence against his experimenter-bias effect is, in itself, evidence for the experimenter-bias effect. Although this line of reasoning is valid in this case,

THEY BELIEVE EVERYTHING THEY CAN PROVE, AND THEY CAN PROVE EVERYTHING THEY BELIEVE.

ARTHUR KOESTLER
"THE AGE OF LONGING"

Rosenthal need not resort to such a subtle ploy.* Barber and Silver concede that a number of the experiments they studied did indeed demonstrate the experimenter-bias effect. The fact that it exists at all is sufficient reason for studying it. The experimenter is an instrument in social-science research. Just as astronomers must be aware of sources of bias in their telescopes, so psychologists must be aware of sources of bias in themselves.

12.14   The Pygmalion Effect

The story of Pygmalion began, as so many stories begin, in ancient Greece, and the Roman poet Ovid used this figure as the hero in one of his legends. Pygmalion carved a statue of a beautiful woman out of ivory, fell in love with his creation, and persuaded the gods to bring Galatea to life. Pygmalion and Galatea got married and had a son, Paphos, who founded the city by that name in Cyprus. The myth also bore fruit. It inspired two plays— *Pygmalion and Galatea*, by W. S. Gilbert (of Gilbert and Sullivan fame), and

---

* Most closed theoretical systems contain some concept that enables the advocates of the system to argue that evidence against it is evidence for it. Thus, if you tell a Freudian that you do not remember wishing to kill your father and sleep with your mother, he will point out that this is evidence for repression. If you criticize a Marxist, she will dismiss your criticism as evidence of your bourgeois consciousness.

—YOU SEE, REALLY AND TRULY, APART FROM THE THINGS ANYONE CAN PICK UP (THE DRESSING AND THE PROPER WAY OF SPEAKING, AND SO ON) THE DIFFERENCE BETWEEN A LADY AND A FLOWER GIRL IS NOT HOW SHE BEHAVES, BUT HOW SHE'S TREATED. I SHALL ALWAYS BE A FLOWER GIRL TO PROFESSOR HIGGINS, BECAUSE HE ALWAYS TREATS ME AS A FLOWER GIRL, AND ALWAYS WILL; BUT I KNOW I CAN BE A LADY TO YOU, BECAUSE YOU ALWAYS TREAT ME AS A LADY, AND ALWAYS WILL.

GEORGE BERNARD SHAW
ELIZA DOOLITTLE IN
PYGMALION

Pygmalion, by G. B. Shaw. In Shaw's updated version of the myth, Pygmalion is replaced by Professor Higgins, a speech expert, and the raw material out of which he aspires to create *his* Galatea is not a block of ivory but an untutored Cockney flower girl called Eliza Doolittle. You are probably more familiar with the musical version, *My Fair Lady*, in which Rex Harrison transforms Audrey Hepburn from flower girl into lady by talking and singing at her. Rosenthal and Jacobson have carried the story a step further.[193] They argue that we are all Galateas, created by the **expectations** other people have of us, and that we are all Pygmalions, creating other people by the expectations we have of them. Each of us is supported by (or trapped in, depending on your point of view) a complex web of expectations other people have of us, and our behavior is determined, to some extent, by those expectations. Rosenthal and Jacobson focus, more specifically, on the effect of the expectations of teachers on the behavior of their students.

12.141 "Pygmalion in the Classroom"

During his investigation of the experimenter-bias effect, Rosenthal discovered that rats described as bright to the experimenters performed better than rats described as dull.[189] "If animals become 'brighter' when expected to by their experimenters, then it seemed reasonable to think that children might become brighter when expected to by their teachers."[193] He enlisted the aid of Lenore Jacobson, an elementary school principal, to conduct an experiment to check out this hunch. Here is a brief summary of that experiment based on their controversial book, *Pygmalion in the Classroom.*[193]

The experiment was conducted at "Oak School," an elementary school consisting of kindergarten and three streamed classes (fast, medium, and slow) at each grade level from 1 to 6. The "Harvard Test of Inflected Acquisition" was administered to all the children in Oak School who would be returning in the fall—that is, to kindergarten through grade 5. The test was presented to the teachers as a means of predicting which students would "bloom" academically during the following year, but it was actually **Flanagan's Tests of General Ability,** a standard but unfamiliar intelligence test. The test really served to provide an IQ score for each of the children, and the same test administered a year later provided an index of intellectual growth—score on posttest minus score on pretest. The following fall, the teachers were given a list of those students in their classes who were expected to bloom academically that year. This 20% of the students in the school were ostensibly selected on the basis of the test the teachers had administered the previous year but were actually selected randomly. Thus, the only difference between those "special" children and the other children was "in the mind of the teacher."[193]

The name of the school is false, the name of the test is false, and the list of potential bloomers is false, but the results are real. The "special" children showed significantly more intellectual growth than the other children. Not only did their IQs increase, but so did their performance on class tests. They were judged by their teachers as more intellectually curious, as happier, and, especially in the lower grades, as less in need of social approval.[193]

There were a number of interesting supplementary findings. This **Pygmalion effect** was more pronounced in the earlier grades. Perhaps younger children are more susceptible to the effect of expectations because the expectations others have for them and they have for themselves have not yet set. Their intellectual reputation is still not established. Although the "special" children did significantly better than the other children, the other children also showed intellectual growth. Perhaps the more positive attitude toward the "special" children created a more positive climate in the classroom and thus improved performance by the whole class, just as the better climate created in the Hawthorne factory improved performance by the workers. Children who showed much intellectual growth but were not expected to show such growth tended to be evaluated negatively by their teachers. Apparently, teachers are not exceptions to the rule that people tend to resent having their expectations shattered. We not only expect what we want, but we want what we expect.

12.142 *"Pygmalion Reconsidered"*

Since the Rosenthal and Jacobson experiment has been criticized on technical grounds, it is necessary, in order to understand those criticisms, to describe it in technical terms. An experiment involves (a) the manipulation of an independent variable, (b) the measurement of a dependent variable, and (c) the control of extraneous variables. If the independent variable is indeed manipulated, if there is a significant change in the dependent variable, and if all possible extraneous variables are controlled, then the manipulation of the independent variable can be considered as the cause of the change in the dependent variable, the effect. Such cause-and-effect relationships form the basis of science. The independent variable in the Rosenthal and Jacobson experiment is the teachers' expectations that certain "special" children in their classes will "bloom" during a certain academic year, and the dependent variable is the "intellectual growth" of those students during that year. Since those "special" children are a random sample from the children in the school, they differ from the other children only in terms of the expectations of their teachers; that is, all possible extraneous variables are controlled. Rosenthal and Jacobson feel justified in concluding, then, that the teachers' expectations were the cause of the significantly greater "intellectual growth" of the "special" children. The formal structure of the experiment is diagramed in Figure 12-1.

Criticism of an experiment typically consists of the negation of one or more of the three conditions for stating the cause-and-effect relationship: (a)

INTERVENING VARIABLES

```
                    ┌─────────────────────┐
                    │  climate            │
                    │                     │
                    │  feedback           │
                    │                     │
INDEPENDENT VARIABLE │  input              │   DEPENDENT VARIABLE
   expectation of  ──┼─→                   ├──→   "intellectual growth"
      teacher        │  output             │        of student
                    │                     │
                    │  experimenter-bias  │
                    │  effect?            │
                    └──────────▲──────────┘
                               │
                    EXTRANEOUS VARIABLES
                    experimenter-bias effect
```

Figure 12-1. Formal representation of the Rosenthal and Jacobson experiment

the independent variable was *not* manipulated, (b) the dependent variable did *not* show a significant change, or (c) all possible extraneous variables were *not* controlled. In their book *Pygmalion Reconsidered*, Elashoff and Snow have criticized the Rosenthal and Jacobson experiment on all three grounds.[47]

a. The independent variable was *not* manipulated. Rosenthal and Jacobson point out that teachers tended not to remember which of the children were "special." Indeed, in some cases, they may never have learned which children were "special": "While all teachers recalled glancing at their lists, most felt they paid little or no attention to them. Many teachers threw their lists away after glancing at them."[193] Elashoff and Snow conclude from this statement that "evidently the Pygmalion effect, if any, is an extremely subtle and elusive phenomenon that acts through teachers without conscious awareness on their part"[47] or, in less ironic and more formal terms, the independent variable was *not* manipulated. However, unless Elashoff and Snow can demonstrate that there was no significant effect on the dependent variable or that this significant effect was due to some extraneous variable, this evidence weighs in favor of the Rosenthal and Jacobson conclusion. Teachers' expectations caused intellectual growth *despite* the fact that some teachers did not remember, or even learn, that some children were "special." In his foreword to the Elashoff and Snow book, Gage points out that, since massive changes in the whole environment of a child have not produced consistent changes in IQ, it is implausible that the subtle change in the expectation of a teacher will do so.[47] Manipulations can be powerful, however, *because* they are subtle. A gentle twist of a key can open a door easier than massive blows with a sledgehammer. Rosenthal and Jacobson may have found the key and shown us the keyhole of one of the doors to academic achievement.

b. The dependent variable did *not* show a significant change. The dependent variable, "intellectual growth," was the difference between the child's pretest IQ score and posttest IQ score. Elashoff and Snow question whether such a difference represents anything so global as "intellectual growth." It is, indeed, a grand name for such a simple measure. However, Rosenthal and Jacobson are merely providing an operational definition of their concept. This is just as legitimate as giving the simple measure of an IQ score the grand name of "intelligence." If IQ is an operational definition of intelligence, then change in IQ is an operational definition of intellectual growth. Elashoff and Snow point out that significant increases in "intellectual growth" were found only in the first two grades. However, there was a significant difference between the "intellectual growth" of the whole experimental group and that of the control group. This confirmed the basic hypothesis of the experiment. The fact that this difference was mainly due to the first two grades is an additional finding worthy of note.

c. All possible extraneous variables were *not* controlled. The same teachers who had the expectations of the "special" children administered their IQ posttest; constructed, administered, and graded their achievement tests; and completed the questionnaire about their personalities. Perhaps the teachers' high expectations of those children caused them to grade them high on all those variables. Replications that demonstrate the Pygmalion effect to be more powerful when the dependent variable is class tests (over which the teacher has more control) than when it is intelligence tests lend support to this possibility. This means that the results are due, not to the Pygmalion effect, but to the experimenter-bias effect. This explanation depends on the teacher/ experimenter being aware, at some level, of which students are "special." Thus, this criticism merely reduces to the possibility that the Pygmalion effect is mediated by the experimenter-bias effect. This should be considered along with the other possible intervening variables suggested by Rosenthal.

12.143 *"The Pygmalion Effect Lives"*

This debate may be more a matter of style than of substance. I suggested earlier that rigor times relevance tends to be a constant in research on educational psychology. Rosenthal and Jacobson prefer to maximize relevance and thus sacrifice rigor, whereas Elashoff and Snow prefer to maximize rigor and thus sacrifice relevance. *Pygmalion Reconsidered* is an extended documentation of the accusation "you have sacrificed rigor." Rosenthal and Jacobson could plead that they have gained in relevance what they have lost in rigor. They have taken the experiment out of the laboratory into the classroom. The sacrifice of rigor is inevitable. The rigorous criteria of an experiment could only be met by taking the experiment back into the laboratory. However, this introduces an observer effect that has not been mentioned yet. Some phenomena are destroyed by being torn out of their natural environment and put into a laboratory. The flamboyant language, overenthusiastic conclusions, and premature popularization of *Pygmalion in the Classroom* are indeed inappropriate to rigorous research. However, it could be argued that they are appropriate to relevant research. Such devices contribute to the increase of positive expectations of teachers and, thus, to the improved performance of students.

In his review of 242 experiments on the Pygmalion effect, Rosenthal concludes that 84 studies demonstrated the effect.[191] An experiment on those experiments would demonstrate that this is a highly significant percentage. However, a phenomenon need not be replicated in all cases, or even in a significant number of cases, to be worthy of study. Science is the study of the exceptional as well as the universal. "Whatever is, is possible" (T. Love Peacock).[151] "Whatever is possible, is worth studying" (W. Lambert Gardiner). Roger Bannister ran a four-minute mile, Christiaan Barnard performed a heart transplant, Indira Gandhi became India's leader. No one would argue that we should wait for a significant number of replications before considering four-minute miles, heart transplants, and female world leaders. "A single success proves it can be done. Thereafter it is necessary only to learn what made it work."[151] Even the largely negative review of the literature included in *Pygmalion Reconsidered* concludes that "the question for future research is not whether there are expectancy effects, but how they operate in school situations."[47] Rosenthal cites 84 successes and suggests what made them work.[192] He considers four possible **intervening variables** that may mediate between the expectation of the teacher and the performance of the student:

> *Climate:* A teacher's high expectations for a whole class may create a warm atmosphere that improves performance. This Hawthorne effect may explain why the control group as well as the experimental group tend to do well in experiments on the Pygmalion effect.
>
> *Feedback:* Teachers with high expectations of "special" students praise them warmly for correct answers and, through such reinforcement, increase the probability of correct answers.
>
> *Input:* Teachers tend to spend more time with "special" students. Their high expectations are confirmed because they teach them more.
>
> *Output:* "Special" students are provided with more opportunities to respond. They are invited to answer more questions and are permitted more time to answer them.

Rosenthal suggests that all four factors may be operating, with the weights of the factors varying from teacher to teacher, child to child, and situation to situation.

The Pygmalion effect is not only surviving—it is thriving. Kash and Borich provide an elegant survey of subsequent research, which has expanded to include many aspects of teacher behavior besides those based on expectations and many effects of this behavior on aspects of students other than academic achievement.[110] They argue that affective education should not be, as traditionally assumed, simply a means to the end of cognitive education (the affective sugar to coat the cognitive pill) but an end in itself. Research on the effect of teacher behavior on five interrelated aspects of the self-concept is reviewed and supplemented by extensive quotations from the autobiographies of Eleanor Roosevelt, Muhammad Ali, Helen Keller, Bertrand Russell, and others, providing an experiential down-to-earthing effect rarely found in research reviews and an encouraging feeling that we are finally beginning to bridge the gap between the laboratory and life. They conclude that "pupils who are perceived as worthwhile, participating and contributing members in the classroom will eventually reflect that image of self not only in academic achievement but also in their role as members of society."

12.15   The Rosenthal Sensitization Effect

If a gentleman were to walk into your classroom some years from now and say "Hi, I'm Robert Rosenthal. I'd like to administer the 'Harvard Test of Inflected Acquisition' to your class, in order to predict who is likely to bloom intellectually during the next year," he would probably not get the same results as he did at Oak School. You would expect his study to be about expectations, and your expectations about expectations would contaminate the experiment.

Finn has referred to this as the **Rosenthal sensitization effect.**[57] Rosenthal may right now be conducting further research under an alias. In his work on the social psychology of the experiment described earlier, Rosenthal points to an experimenter-bias effect. This effect may operate in his own work. He expects expectations to have an effect, and those expectations about expectations may ensure that they do indeed have an effect. Rosenthal is an experimenter study- ing other experimenters. Perhaps we need experimenters studying experi- menters studying experimenters. It is an interesting theoretical problem to consider how to avoid an infinite regress of experiments on experiments on experiments.

12.2 PRACTICE

12.21 Using the Hawthorne Effect

The experimenter, in that perennial quest for objectivity in science, tries to eliminate any effect due to interaction between the experimenter and the subject. The Hawthorne effect is therefore usually considered a nuisance in research. It is an extraneous variable to be controlled, and elaborate devices (placebos, double-blind techniques, one-way mirrors, and so on) are created to control it. When such devices are not used, the results of experiments are dismissed by critics as simply due to the Hawthorne effect.

Some enlightened researchers in industrial psychology realized that the Hawthorne effect was not, as they first assumed, another extraneous variable to be controlled, but a powerful, new independent variable to be studied. The fact that, by studying workers, they could improve morale and thus increase production was an important finding in itself. This insight triggered a shift from the behavioristic time-and-motion studies, which focused on the physical work environment, to humanistic studies, which focused on the psychological climate of the work situation.

Perhaps the Pygmalion effect can do for educational psychology what the Hawthorne effect did for industrial psychology—that is, shift the emphasis from the physical plant to the psychological climate of the school, from deficiencies in the student to deficiencies in the teacher. The Hawthorne effect implies that it is the psychological climate of the factory that is important, that a bad climate, and hence poor morale and low production, are due to the managers rather than the workers; the Pygmalion effect implies that it is the psychological climate of the school and classroom which is important, that a bad climate, and hence low morale and poor "production," are due to the teachers rather than the students.

The Hawthorne effect may be a nuisance in the laboratory yet a conveni- ence in the classroom. The influence of the experimenter on the subject may indeed have to be controlled, but not the influence of the teacher on the student. The whole function of the teacher is to influence the student. Thus, what is a part of the problem in the theoretical world of the laboratory may be a part of the solution in the practical world of the classroom. A teacher who is very enthusiastic about a new teaching technique may indeed get better results using this new technique. The better results are due, however, not to the technique but to the enthusiasm, which improves morale and hence performance. Instead of derisively dismissing this as another flawed experiment, contaminated by the Hawthorne effect, we should welcome it as a way to improve performance. Consistent failure to find significant effects of different teaching techniques may be due to the fact that it does not really matter *which* new technique we try—what is important is the fact that we try new techniques. Variety is the spice of life in the classroom, too. Whereas the experimenter may want to eliminate the Hawthorne effect, the teacher may want to create it. Rosenthal and Jacobson list a number of studies in which subjects did better on IQ tests for warm examiners than for cool examiners.[193] A teacher can use the Hawthorne effect by being friendly, interested, and encouraging, creating a warm climate in the classroom, decreasing boredom, raising morale, and thus improving performance.

12.22   Using and Abusing the Pygmalion Effect

Your expectations as a teacher can affect the performance of your students. If you expect a particular student to be a good student, your expectation may help him or her indeed to be a good student. If you think your current class is the best class you have ever taught, then it may very well become the best class you have ever taught—until, that is, you think the same thing of your next class. You can create a benign spiral. High expectations lead to good performance, which leads to higher expectations, which lead to even better performance, which leads to. . . .

If you can't create benign upward spirals, you can, at least, avoid creating vicious downward spirals. For ethical reasons, Rosenthal has not conducted a companion experiment in which teachers are led to expect *poorer* performance from certain students. This "experiment" is conducted informally, however, every day, in thousands of classrooms around the world. Children are being made stupid by being told, in so many subtle and not so subtle ways, that they are stupid. Teachers, parents, and peers say "you are stupid" because they believe a child is stupid, but actually the child is stupid because so many people have said "you are stupid." Eventually, of course, they are often right. This dulling process due to low expectations by our various Pygmalions may be one of the major stunting factors that prevent us from realizing our full human potential.

You can break a vicious spiral which is already established by changing your initial poor expectations. Your expectations are based on your prejudg-

IT WASN'T ME THAT STARTED ACTING DEAF; IT WAS PEOPLE THAT FIRST STARTED ACTING LIKE I WAS TOO DUMB TO HEAR OR SEE OR SAY ANYTHING AT ALL.

KEN KESEY
CHIEF BROOM IN
ONE FLEW OVER THE CUCKOO'S NEST

ments (that is, prejudices) about students with different attributes. Awareness of the basis for your prejudgments may help correct any biases you may have. Some possible biasing factors are race, sex, name, social class, stream, intelligence quotient, and performance of older sibling. Some have argued for the abolition of intelligence-testing, since its function is precisely to provide the teacher with a reasonable expectation for each child.[57] Some have argued against streaming on the grounds that it prejudices teachers against whole classes.[133,176] Flowers assigned children randomly to streams and found that they tended to perform according to the stream to which they were assigned.[59] Perhaps, indeed, we should not add more potentially biasing factors to those which cannot be avoided, like race and sex. Teachers are going to notice that you are a Black girl, whatever the administrative procedures in the school, and perhaps further potential sources of bias should not be added by telling them that you have an IQ of 75 and have been assigned to the "slow" class on the basis of your previous performance. The important thing may be to make teachers aware of the various possible biasing effects, whether biological or cultural. Here is my contribution to this end—a notice to be copied, pasted on your mirror, and read each morning before going off to school.

> TEACHER, BE AWARE!
> I AM A TEACHER—NOT A JUDGE.
> I SHOULD NOT PREJUDGE PEOPLE ON THE BASIS OF THEIR RACE,
> SEX, OR INTELLIGENCE.
> THERE ARE NO STUPID PEOPLE—ONLY PEOPLE MADE STUPID BY
> BEING ASSUMED STUPID.

12.23 Self-Denying Prophecy

You may be suffering some detrimental effects of the self-fulfilling prophecy, day by day, right now as you attend a university. Although education is what the academic life is all about, education as a discipline is low on the academic totem pole. There is a tendency for textbook writers, administrators, professors, and other students to put down education majors as dull. Teachers of teachers may have low expectations of teachers which they, in turn, pass on to their students. A pessimistic Pygmalion stalks the university as well as the school. You can counter this pernicious effect by being aware of it. Such awareness may help some people to create their Galateas, but it will also give the Galateas a chance to fight back.[191] Insight can inoculate you against negative expectations. Hold still for your immunization shot!

Since Rosenthal could produce the Pygmalion effect by telling *teachers* that certain children were due to "bloom," one might assume that an even more powerful Pygmalion effect could be produced by telling the children themselves. This is not necessarily true. The fact that the teacher believes children are intelligent is important only insofar as it contributes to the fact that the children come to believe that they are intelligent. Vague statements about the enthusiasm of a good teacher being contagious can be made more precise by considering the "germ" as the expectation of the teacher which is "caught" as the **self-expectation** of the student. Children may not come to believe they are intelligent if told directly but may come to believe they are intelligent if told indirectly by a teacher who treats them, day after day, as if they were intelligent. The message "you are intelligent" can have no positive effects until translated into the message "I am intelligent"; and, alternatively, the message "you are stupid" can have no negative effects until translated into the message "I am stupid." In the latter case, the damage is done when a teacher's negative expectation is transformed into a student's negative self-expectation. By changing classes or schools, students can easily get away from the teacher, but, once having assimilated the negative expectations, they can't as easily get away from the *influence* of the teacher. Self-expectations are so much more powerful than expectations of others because we can never get away from ourselves. Students continue to fail, not because the teacher expected them to fail, but because they now expect themselves to fail.

I DO MY THING, AND YOU DO YOUR THING.
I AM NOT IN THIS WORLD TO LIVE UP TO YOUR
    EXPECTATIONS
AND YOU ARE NOT IN THIS WORLD TO LIVE UP TO
    MINE.
YOU ARE YOU AND I AM I,
AND IF BY CHANCE WE FIND EACH OTHER, IT'S
    BEAUTIFUL.
IF NOT, IT CAN'T BE HELPED.

F.S. PERLS
"THE GESTALT PRAYER"

Although negative expectations may make negative self-expectations more negative, they may also, paradoxically, make positive self-expectations more positive. If you have established positive self-expectations, then negative expectations may merely encourage you to greater efforts. Rosenthal might say that prophecies can be **self-denying** as well as self-fulfilling. I might say that a wind blows out a small flame but fans a big one. Grandmother would simply call it "cussedness." Could a small, ugly, one-eyed, Black Jew be a success in North America? "Yes, I can," said Sammy Davis, Jr. No one mentions, when listing his "disadvantages," that he never went to school. Perhaps, unconsciously, we realize that it was an advantage. He never learned that being small and ugly and Black were "disadvantages," and, by the time he became also one-eyed, Jewish, and married to a blonde actress, he had such positive self-expectations that he could overcome those "disadvantages" too. He is a success because he never learned that he "had" to be a failure.

POST-EXERCISES

1. Sixteen Facts Still in Search of a Theory

Fit each of the 16 facts listed in Pre-exercise 1 into the framework provided in Figure 12-1. In each case, write in the independent variable, the dependent variable, and some possible intervening variables. In each case, discuss at least one possible extraneous variable that could disqualify this fact as an illustration of the self-fulfilling prophecy.

The first fact is fitted into the framework below, by way of example.

a. Those (students, businesspeople, athletes, or whoever) who fear failure often do indeed fail.

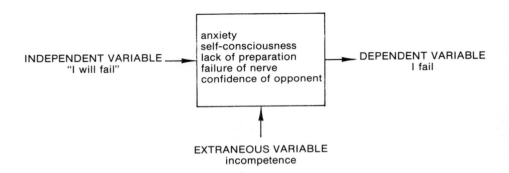

Note that the independent variable is a prophecy, and the dependent variable is the fulfillment of that prophecy. The prophecy cannot fulfill itself directly, but only through the mediation of some intervening variables. Some possible intervening variables in this case are suggested:

Fear of failure may increase anxiety or self-consciousness, which inhibits performance.
Expectation of failure results in lack of preparation (Why bother? I'm going to fail anyway) and thus poor performance.
Fear of failure causes a failure of nerve at crucial moments when risk is involved (the inspired guess in the case of the student, the informed gamble in the case of the businessperson, the just-right move in the case of the athlete). The capacity to take risks may separate winners from losers.
Lack of self-confidence is communicated to colleagues and opponents, decreasing the confidence of colleagues and increasing the confidence of opponents.

The prophecy may be fulfilled but not self-fulfilled because of the extraneous variable of incompetence. Failure may be due simply to incompetence; in this case, fear of failure is just a realistic awareness of the fact of incompetence. Failures may fail, not because they have an inferiority complex, but simply because they are indeed inferior.

2. Anecdotes Illustrating the Self-Fulfilling Prophecy

The following anecdotes illustrate the wide range of phenomena that may, perhaps, be partly explained in terms of the self-fulfilling prophecy. In each case, discuss how the self-fulfilling prophecy may be operating. Read the source from which each anecdote is taken to check whether the author adds anything to your discussion.

a. Cartwright Millingville, the president of the Last National Bank, noticed that the bank was unusually busy when he arrived at his office one Wednesday morning in 1932. His bank was a sound and solvent institution. It was, that is, until that Black Wednesday. A rumor had started that the bank was floundering. Depositors flocked to the bank to withdraw their savings before there were no savings to withdraw. More anxious depositors, hearing that other depositors were withdrawing their money, hurried to the bank to salvage *their* savings. The bank failed.

Merton, R. K. The self-fulfilling prophecy. In *Social theory and social structure*. Glencoe, Ill.: Free Press, 1949.

b. Clever Hans was a horse that could spell, read, solve problems of musical harmony, answer personal questions, and do arithmetic. His owner, a German mathematics teacher called Mr. von Osten, would ask a question, and Clever Hans would tap out the answer with his hoof. For example, Mr. von Osten would say "What is 2 plus 3?" and Clever Hans would tap his hoof five times. Mr. von Osten did not profit from the talents of Clever Hans, did not appear to be a fraud, and was willing to let others question Hans in his absence so that cues passed from owner to horse could be ruled out as an explanation. Pfungst conducted a series of experiments to explain this peculiar talent of Clever Hans. He discovered that Hans could only answer questions when he could see the questioner and when the questioner himself knew the answer. Finally, Pfungst discovered that the questioner unconsciously signaled to Hans to start tapping and to stop tapping. The signal to start tapping was a slight forward lean to see Hans's hoofs better, and the signal to stop tapping was a tiny head movement. By expecting Hans to stop at the right answer, the questioner unwittingly "told" him the right answer.

Pfungst, O. *Clever Hans: The horse of Mr. von Osten* (C. L. Rahn, Trans.). New York: Holt, Rinehart & Winston, 1965.

c. In 1794, Professor Ranieri Gerbi of Pisa discovered a cure for toothache. The sufferer crushed a small worm, *Curculio antiodontaligious*, between thumb and forefinger, and applied it to the tooth. An investigation was launched to check the validity of extravagant claims by Professor Gerbi for his cure. The committee of eminent scientists reported that 68.5% of hundreds of toothaches were indeed cured by the worm, but that those "cures" could not be attributed to the chemical composition of *Curculio antiodontaligious*.

Shapiro, A. K. A contribution to a history of the placebo effect. *Behavioral Science*, 1960, 5, 109–135.

d. A teacher found a list of the IQ scores of the students in his class on his desk near the beginning of the year. He kept it for reference and noticed during the year that those students with high IQs did better than those with low IQs. At the end of the year, he checked this out and discovered that there was indeed a high positive correlation (0.80) between IQ scores and achievement-test scores. When he took this information to his principal, he was informed that no intelligence test had been given to his class. The "IQ scores" were locker numbers.

Lefrancois, G. R. *Psychology for teaching* (2nd ed.). Belmont, Calif.: Wadsworth, 1975.

e. James Sweeney, a professor of industrial management and psychiatry at Tulane University, was responsible for the operation of the Biomedical Computer Center. George Johnson, a poorly educated Black, was a hospital porter. James Sweeney believed that George Johnson could become a computer operator. He appointed him janitor at the computer center. In the mornings, George Johnson cleaned the computer center; in the afternoons, he studied about computers. He was learning a lot about computers when it was discovered that he had to earn a certain score on an IQ test in order to become a computer operator. Johnson took the test, and his score indicated that he was not "supposed" to be able to operate a typewriter, much less a computer. Sweeney was not convinced by this "evidence" and threatened to resign if Johnson was not allowed to continue his studies. Johnson now runs the main computer room and is responsible for the training of new employees.

Look Editorial Board. "Sweeney's miracle." *Look,* November 16, 1965, pp. 117–118.

f. When he was 9, a boy stole a package of cigarettes, as a childish prank. His mother expected him to steal again and questioned him every time something was missing. When he was 15, the boy stole a car.

Knight, A. C. "Thief!" *Psychology Today,* March 1971, pp. 66–69.

g. Jane Elliott, a third-grade teacher in a small town in Iowa, was so deeply affected by the assassination of Martin Luther King that she decided to provide her students with direct experience of prejudice. She told them that brown-eyed people are better, cleaner, smarter, and more civilized than blue-eyed people. The "superior" brown-eyed students were given extra time at recess, allowed to go to lunch first and to sit in the front of the room, and were lavishly praised for correct answers; the "inferior" blue-eyed students were required to use paper cups rather than the drinking fountain, to wear paper collars as a sign of their lower status, were not allowed to use playground equipment, and were treated as stupid when they gave wrong answers. After a few hours of this regime, brown-eyed and blue-eyed children were convinced of their superiority and inferiority, respectively. Brown-eyed students would mistreat their blue-eyed classmates and demand an apology; blue-eyed students who had been confident before became tense, clumsy, and unsure of themselves. The same startling changes in behavior occurred when the roles were reversed.

Peters, W. *A class divided.* Garden City, N.Y.: Doubleday, 1971.

3. Following Up "Pygmalion in the Classroom"

It is interesting to follow up an article or book to find out what impact it had; it is especially interesting when that impact is impressive. Most studies produce a few ripples and eddies; *Pygmalion in the Classroom* left turbulent waves in its wake that have not yet subsided.

The first wave of reaction is the reviews in the relevant journals. You can find those reviews by consulting the *Book Review Digest* for the year the book was published and continuing through the following years until reviews peter out. Here are the sources of some reviews of *Pygmalion in the Classroom.*

JOURNAL	VOLUME	DATE	PAGES
Adult Leadership	18	Sept. 1969	95
American Educational Research Journal	5	1968	708–711
Reply by Rosenthal	6	1969	689–692
American Sociological Review	34	Apr. 1969	283
Childhood Education	45	Jan. 1969	284
Choice	5	Feb. 1969	1614
Contemporary Psychology	14	Apr. 1969	197–199
Educational and Psychological Measurement	29	Spring 1969	226–228
Educational Research Journal	5	1968	709–711
Encounter	32	May 1969	89
Instructor	78	Oct. 1968	56
Kirkus Reviews	36	July 1, 1968	746
Library Journal	93	Nov. 15, 1968	4291
New Yorker	45	Apr. 19, 1969	170
New York Review of Books	11	Sept. 12, 1968	30
New York Times Book Review		Sept. 14, 1969	55
Personnel and Guidance Journal	47	Feb. 1969	575
Saturday Review		July 20, 1968	56
		Oct. 19, 1968	62
Teachers College Record	70	May 1969	805
Time		Sept. 20, 1968	62
Urban Review		Sept. 1968	

The second wave of reaction is the series of empirical investigations designed to replicate or expand on the study. You can find those studies by consulting *Psychological Abstracts* or the Education Index under the topic "Expectations," or the Citation Index under the title of the article (this reference lists all the articles in which it is cited). Here are a few such studies.

Fleming, E. S., & Anttonen, R. G. Teacher expectancy or My Fair Lady. *American Educational Research Journal,* 1971, *8*(2), 241–252.

José, J., & Cody, J. J. Teacher-pupil interaction as it relates to attempted changes in teacher expectancy of academic ability and achievement. *American Educational Research Journal,* 1971, *8*(1), 39–49.

Meichenbaum, D. H., Bowers, K. S., & Ross, R. R. A behavioral analysis of teacher expectancy effects. *Journal of Personality and Social Psychology,* 1969, *13*(4), 306–316.

Rothbart, M., Dalfen, S., & Barrett, R. Effects of teacher's expectancy on student-teacher interaction. *Journal of Educational Psychology,* 1971, *62*(1), 49–54.

Sacks, E. L. Intelligence scores as a function of experimentally established social relationships between child and examiner. *Journal of Abnormal and Social Psychology,* 1952, *47,* 354–358.

Shore, A. L. Confirmation of expectancy and changes in teachers' evaluations of student behavior. *Dissertation Abstracts International,* 1969, *30*(A 5–6), 1878–1879.

The third wave of reaction is theoretical reviews, which attempt to integrate and evaluate the original study and the studies it inspired. Some such reviews evolve into books, often supplemented by material from the first and second waves. Research is typically judged by its fertility (the number of empirical studies and the amount of theoretical discussion it generates) rather than by its "truth." Only a few studies create this third wave of theoretical reviews, and only a very few studies inspire a book. Writers of those reviews and books seldom point out that their publication is evidence that the original publication was a valuable piece of research. Here are a theoretical review and a book.

Rubovits, P. C., & Maehr, M. L. Pygmalion analyzed: Toward an explanation of the Rosenthal-Jacobson findings. *Journal of Personality and Social Psychology,* 1971, *19*(2), 197–203.
Elashoff, J. D., & Snow, R. E. *Pygmalion reconsidered.* Worthington, Ohio: Charles A. Jones, 1971.

4. Racism and Sexism

A number of people have attempted to explain the perpetuation of racism and sexism in terms of the self-fulfilling prophecy. Read the following sources for this point of view.

RACISM

Davis, A., & Dollard, J. *Children of bondage.* Washington, D.C.: American Council on Education, 1940.
Merton, R. K. The self-fulfilling prophecy. In *Social theory and social structure.* Glencoe, Ill.: Free Press, 1949.
Rist, R. C. Student social class and teacher expectations: The self-fulfilling prophecy in ghetto education. *Harvard Educational Review,* 1970, *40,* 411–451.
Rist, R. C. *The urban school: A factory for failure.* Cambridge: MIT Press, 1973.
Rose, A. *The Negro in America.* Boston: Beacon, 1956.
Rosenthal, R., & Jacobson, L. Teacher expectations for the disadvantaged. *Scientific American,* April 1968, pp. 19–23.
Warner, W. L., Havighurst, R. J., & Loeb, M. B. *Who shall be educated?* New York: Harper & Row, 1944.
Williams, T. Teacher prophecies and the inheritance of inequality. *Sociology of Education,* 1976, *49,* 223–236.

SEXISM

Condry, J., & Condry, S. Sex differences: A study in the eye of the beholder. *Child Development,* 1976, *47,* 812–819.
Goebes, D. D., & Shore, M. F. Behavioral expectations of students as related to the sex of the teacher. *Psychology in the Schools,* 1975, *12*(2), 222–224.
Motta, R. W., & Vane, J. R. An investigation of teacher perceptions of sex-typed behaviors. *Journal of Educational Research,* 1976, *69,* 363–368.
Palardy, J. M. What teachers believe, what children achieve. *Elementary School Journal,* 1969, *69,* 370–374.

Various Views 13
of the Classroom

13 VARIOUS VIEWS OF THE CLASSROOM

PRE-EXERCISES

1. The Ideal Classroom

Consider the architecture of the various classrooms you have spent so much time in during your long career as a student. Do they differ much from one another? How did your elementary school classrooms differ from your high school classrooms? From your university classrooms? Are the differences a function of the personality of the teachers, or of different techniques of teaching? What "mistakes" in classroom design have you noticed? How do classrooms today differ from the classrooms your parents spent time in? Your grandparents?

Design the ideal classroom in which you would like to teach. You may find squared paper useful to sketch the layout. Don't worry about money. Go crazy. Why do you think the real classroom you will find yourself in differs so much from your ideal classroom?

If you feel ambitious, design a perfect school around your ideal classroom. If you feel really ambitious, design a perfect society around your perfect school. Would it be possible to maintain your ideal classroom within an imperfect school, or your perfect school within an imperfect society? Would it be possible to design a perfect classroom without also designing perfect students?

2. The Politics of the Classroom

A class could be considered as a miniature society. Each class, like each society, has a characteristic political style.

What political style best characterizes the various classes you have been in?

Here are some styles to choose from. There are more where these came from—*Roget's Thesaurus*—if you want to consider other styles.

anarchy	democracy	monarchy
aristocracy	dictatorship	oligarchy
autarchy	gerontocracy	socialism
autocracy	matriarchy	theocracy
communism	meritocracy	totalitarianism

Look up the less familiar styles of government and consider whether they are represented in any type of school you know of. What style of government would you like to "impose" on your class? Or is this a contradiction in terms? By appointing you teacher, are the people who hire you also setting you up as king or queen of the class? Do you have any real power, or are you simply a puppet leader? Can you abdicate? How would you go about abdicating? Should styles of government differ as a function of the personality of the teacher? the age of the students? the subject being taught? What would be the best style of government in a classroom as preparation for living in a democratic society?

In this chapter, let us shift our focus from **psychology** (the study of the individual) to **sociology** (the study of the group) and to that hybrid discipline, **social psychology** (the study of the relationship between the individual and the

EDUCATION CAN BE REGARDED AS SOCIALIZATION, TO MAKE THE YOUNG CONFORM HARMONIOUSLY TO SOCIETY — OR IT MAY BE REGARDED AS THE EFFORT TO PERFECT PEOPLE AS SUCH.

PAUL GOODMAN
THE COMMUNITY OF SCHOLARS

group). Let us turn, that is, from the psychology of teaching to the sociology of teaching and the social psychology of teaching. The sociology of teaching will focus on that group we call a class in a typical classroom, and the social psychology of teaching will focus on the relationship between the teacher and the class.

A classroom can be viewed in many ways. Just as we have many different models of the relationship between a teacher and a student (see list in Post-exercise 1 for Chapter 1), so we have many different models of the classroom. Some see it as an oasis to protect children from society, and some as a reservation to protect society from children; some see it as a garden in which growing plants are nourished, and some as a factory in which cogs are shaped. Let us look at some more formal models as seen through the eyes of various experts. Imagine four experts—a sociologist, a social psychologist, an ecologist, and a communication theorist—sitting at the back of a typical classroom (preferably behind a one-way screen to avoid those disturbing observer effects discussed in Chapter 12). Let us look at the classroom through their expert eyes.

13.1   THE VIEW OF THE SOCIOLOGIST

13.11   Schooling as an Aspect of Socializing

The sociologist views the classroom within the larger context of the school, the community, and the culture. Schooling is an aspect of socializing. In the history of our species on the planet, formal universal schooling, as we know it, is only a small, recent, local aspect of socializing. **Socialization** is the process by which a child is initiated as a member of a society. School shares responsibility for this process with home, church, peer group, mass media, and other socializing agencies. The child learns adult **roles** and what to expect of others in *their* adult roles. Those roles are learned incidentally and unwittingly in the course of social interaction.[48]

Parsons points out that the home teaches roles based on biology (sex, age), but, when the child goes to school, she or he learns roles based on nonbiological factors.[163] It is at school that one first acquires achieved as opposed to ascribed statuses. The teacher is usually the first significant adult in the life of

"—THE KINDERGARTEN CLASSROOM IS THEIR INTRO-DUCTION TO A SOCIALIZED WORLD, WHERE A COMMUNITY OF PEERS MUST ACT IN CONCERT. IT IS A BIG STEP TOWARD THE ONLY STATUS THAT MEANS MUCH TO A SMALL CHILD: THE STATUS OF GROWNUP."

MARTIN MAYER
THE SCHOOLS

a child who is not a relative—that is, the first interchangeable adult. One can talk of a former teacher but not of a former father. The child must, therefore, internalize a relationship to a role rather than a person. Basic attitudes to adult authority may be established in this relationship with teachers in the early grades.

Illich argues that school is the major socializing institution.[97] It socializes children into the role of consumer. Passive consumers of information in school will grow up to be passive consumers of goods in society. He advocates that we de-school society and thus destroy the consumer society by cutting off its supply of consumers.

I AM USING THE TERM "HIDDEN CURRICULUM" TO REFER TO THE STRUCTURE OF SCHOOLING AS OPPOSED TO WHAT HAPPENS IN SCHOOL, IN THE SAME WAY THAT LINGUISTS DISTINGUISH BETWEEN THE STRUCTURE OF A LANGUAGE AND THE USE THE SPEAKER MAKES OF IT.

IVAN ILLICH
AFTER DE-SCHOOLING, WHAT?

The teacher has been socialized not only into the general role of adult but into the specific role of teacher. Lortie describes the elaborate initiation ceremonies by which members are recruited for the teaching profession, which constitutes a highly developed subculture.[124]

One important role into which we are socialized is our **sex role.** Volumes have been written about the subtle and insidious ways in which boys are taught to be boyish and manly and women are taught to be girlish and womanly. Since those roles are learned "incidentally and unwittingly in the course of interaction,"⁴⁸ we have only recently become aware of this process. Most of the attention has been justly devoted to the manner in which women are victimized by this process. However, Sexton has argued that men are also stunted by being forced into stereotyped sex roles by institutions whose goals are incompatible with the goals of the child.¹⁹⁶ Just as corporations are uncongenial environments for women, so schools tend to be uncongenial environments for boys. Elementary school, in which most of the teachers are female, emphasizes female values. Boys either conform to those values in order to succeed and in the process become feminized, or rebel against them and become behavior problems and dropouts. Since the two major socializing agencies in early childhood, the home and the school, are dominated by women, the boy has no male models to emulate. Elkin tells the story of two kids playing house.⁴⁸ The boy put on his hat and coat, picked up his briefcase, kissed his "wife" good-bye, and went out the door. The girl was bustling about cleaning up the kitchen and doing the dishes when the boy came back "home" a few minutes later. He didn't know what daddies did after they kissed mommies good-bye.

13.12 Implications for Teachers

The teacher should be sensitive to the larger cultural context in which the classroom is embedded. No matter how insular you try to make your class, the broader cultural influences will percolate in under the door and over the transom. Teachers, like parents, may find themselves in conflict with powerful and pervasive socializing agencies, which threaten to swamp them. Television is such an influence. A Native American friend overheard her children playing Cowboys and Indians. Both of them wanted to be cowboys and kill the evil Indians. Vegetarian friends, who were trying to raise their children on healthful foods, discovered that the children were demanding and getting junk foods advertised on television from indulgent grandparents.

The descriptions of the television set as "a third parent" and as "the little square schoolhouse" suggest that it is taking over some of the socializing functions of the home and the school. You need spend only one day with a small child to understand the tremendous temptation to sit Joe down in front of the television set so that you can enjoy a few hours of peace and quiet while he sits hypnotized by the moving images. The bawling baby is replaced by a blaring television, but at least it does not tug at your sleeve. You rationalize that he is just looking at the movements and not understanding the content. However, when he begins to understand the content, he has withdrawal symptoms when you try to drag him away. Anyway, you say, we'll soon be able to send him to school. In this way, according to Newton Minow, Joe logs 15,000 hours of television, as opposed to 12,000 hours in the classroom, by the time he graduates from high school. Television is probably as powerful as it is perva-

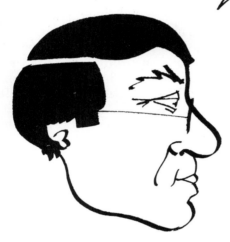

THE TEACHER IS NOW IN COMPETITION WITH A HOST OF RIVAL COMMUNICATORS, MOST OF WHOM ARE SMARTER, RICHER, AND CONSIDERABLY MORE EFFICIENT.

WILLIAM GLASSER
SCHOOLS WITHOUT FAILURE

sive. Television producers, who sell advertisements for thousands of dollars with the argument that they influence the behavior of viewers, argue that the programs they jam in between the advertisements do *not* influence them. Research suggests otherwise. One study finds a significant relationship between "an index of violence in favored programs as reported by parents" and "a rating of aggressive behavior by peers in grade 3" for a large group of boys.[53] Winn makes the more general criticism that television-viewing, per se, is bad for children, regardless of content.[233] The medium is the message, and the message is "Stay passive. Live in the never-never land of Peter Pan. Don't grow up."

"THE USE OF TELEVISION, AS IT WAS EMPLOYED IN THE UNITED STATES IN THE 1960'S, CAN BE PUT IN ITS PROPER LIGHT BY SUPPOSING THAT GUTENBERG'S GREAT INVENTION HAD BEEN DIRECTED ALMOST ENTIRELY TO THE PUBLICATION OF COMIC BOOKS."

ROBERT M. HUTCHINS
THE LEARNING SOCIETY

13.2   *THE VIEW OF THE SOCIAL PSYCHOLOGIST*

The classroom can be viewed as a political system. It is a microcosm of a country, in which the various styles of government are simulated. The traditional classroom tends to be autocratic—the dictatorship being benevolent or malevolent, depending on the personality of the teacher. Jackson brilliantly probes beneath the official curriculum to uncover the **hidden curriculum** in the classroom.[99] He shows the various strategies children learn to cope with this, their first institution. If it is an autocratic institution, then the strategies children learn will be useful later if they join the army, a corporation, or any other hierarchical organization. They will not be useful for coping with their responsibilities as citizens in a democratic society. Many have argued that a democratic classroom would provide better preparation for life in a democratic society.

IF WE PREACH DEMOCRACY IN OUR SCHOOLS BUT WE PRACTICE AUTOCRACY, WHAT ARE WE REALLY TEACHING?

MARY GREER AND BONNIE RUBENSTEIN
WILL THE REAL TEACHER PLEASE STAND UP?

In the classical study of political systems, autocracy, democracy, and anarchy were simulated by providing groups of boys, working on various tasks, with **authoritarian, democratic,** and **laissez-faire leadership,** respectively.[122] The "authoritarian" group was rebellious or submissive. They were productive when the leader was present, but aggressive and destructive when he was absent. The "democratic" group was task-oriented, cooperative, friendly, and more resistant to frustration. They showed even more independence and initiative when the leader was absent. The "laissez-faire" group was unproductive, hostile, and prone to scapegoating. They tended to be more productive when the leader was absent.

The various political systems were created by experimentally varying the leadership styles. The leader in the classroom is, of course, the teacher, and the classroom climate is determined by the teacher's personality. Although students may challenge the teacher's leadership, there is no doubt that the teacher has been set up as the monarch of the class. The teacher may abdicate. However, by doing so, he or she merely determines, by default, that the political system will be anarchy. Children are good meteorologists and weather forecasters. They learn, within a few weeks, that the prevailing weather in Ms. Jones's class is "sunny with light showers" and in Mr. Smith's class, "overcast with occasional thunderstorms." Within a few minutes of entering Mr. Smith's class on a stormy day, they can feel the electricity in the air and brace themselves for the thunder.

Critics of traditional education pounced on the superior attitudes and achievements under democratic leadership as evidence for their argument that teachers should shift from autocratic to democratic leadership. Subsequent studies of democratic leadership in classrooms have, however, been disappointingly inconclusive.[5] Dunkin and Biddle have argued that, in reacting simultaneously against the cold climate and authoritarian control of traditional classrooms, progressive educators failed to disentangle two important dimensions—warmth and directiveness.[43] They divided the world into two camps—us (the democratic "goodies" who are warm and nondirective) and them (the authoritarian "baddies" who are cold and directive). Such a dichotomy leaves out teachers who are warm and directive (the **benevolent dictators**) and teachers who are cold and nondirective (the **malevolent democrats**).* However, Dunkin and Biddle's analysis of the literature in terms of those two dimensions did not yield any conclusive support for the improvement of teaching by creating either a warm climate or a nondirective atmosphere.

A more promising approach is through the belief systems of teachers.[91] Those with **concrete belief systems** tend to have extreme, inflexible attitudes, to be ethnocentric and jingoistic, to utter platitudes and normative statements. Those with **abstract belief systems** tend to have moderate, flexible attitudes, to give individualistic and relativistic responses, and to see the complexities involved in issues. In one study, abstract teachers:

---

* This latter figure is less known but is becoming increasingly familiar. It is the teacher who forces more freedom on students than they can handle (see Section 4.3). "Throw off your chains, or I'll beat you over the head." It is malevolent when it is merely a rationalization for irresponsibility and laziness.

——TELLING THEM THIS IS A DEMOCRATIC SOCIETY BUT NOT SHOWING THEM HOW TO <u>MAKE IT</u> DEMOCRATIC FOR <u>THEM</u>. THERE WOULD BE NO WAY FOR THE CHILDREN TO <u>EXPERIENCE</u> THAT DEMOCRACY IN ACTION.

NAT HENTOFF
<u>OUR CHILDREN ARE DYING</u>

expressed greater warmth toward the children, showed greater perceptiveness of the children's wishes and needs, were more flexible in meeting the interests and needs of the children, maintained more relaxed relationships with the children, were more encouraging of individual responsibility, gave greater encouragement to free expression of feelings, were more encouraging of creativity, displayed greater ingenuity in improvising teaching and play materials, invoked unexplained rules less frequently, were less rule oriented, were less determining of classroom and playground procedure, manifested less need for structure, were less punitive, and were less anxious about Os' [observers'] presence [pp. 378–379].

A factor analysis grouped those behaviors into three main factors: resourcefulness, dictatorialness, and punitiveness. "Dictatorialness" corresponds roughly to "directiveness," and "punitiveness" to "warmth." Perhaps the missing factor in the studies reviewed by Dunkin and Biddle is this third factor of "resourcefulness." Love is not enough. You must also be competent.

13.3   THE VIEW OF THE ECOLOGIST

The view of the social psychologist is limited because it considers the relationship between the teacher and the class without considering the classroom setting within which they interact. This setting is a stage on which an adult and a group of children play the roles of "teacher" and "student." They are playing what has been called the Classroom Game according to a set of rules so rigid that classroom behavior is a predictable but atypical sample of behavior.[15] This is reflected by the fact that students are often surprised at how "human" a teacher is outside the classroom, and teachers are astonished at the profound personality changes in students in out-of-school settings. Studying children in a classroom is much like studying animals in a zoo (no slur intended). It is not their natural habitat, so they will not display their natural habits. A most competent survey of systematic studies of the process of teaching in the traditional classroom yielded little by way of practical advice for those responsible for hiring teachers or for the teachers themselves.[43] The role of the teacher on the traditional classroom stage is so rigidly prescribed that variations in personality from individual to individual have little effect. It matters little what teachers do in the classroom, because they can merely cope as well as they can with a most difficult situation, in which most of the problems are artifacts of the situation itself. Studies of the traditional classroom are like detailed descriptions of the dodo bird. They may, at best, suggest why it is becoming extinct and how it may be replaced by a better bird.

Ecology is the study of the relationship between an organism and its environment (which may, of course, include other organisms). The relationship between the student and that special environment of the traditional classroom has only recently received some limited attention from ecologists. Sommer found that, when students sat in a circle seminar-style, those directly facing the teacher participated more than those on the sides; when students sat in rows lecture-style, those in front participated more than those in back, and those in the middle participated more than those at the sides.[210] Eye contact seems to be the most important variable in both settings. The seminar arrangement would thus contribute to student-student communication, and the usual imbalance in contributions from members of the class could be somewhat corrected by seating the less aggressive students opposite you. Adams and Biddle corroborated this finding that students in the periphery of the classroom are spectators rather than actors in the classroom drama.[2] The majority of sources and destinations of communication, whether students or teachers, are located in the front and center of the classroom. A quiet student sitting at the side will be encouraged to participate more and a noisy student sitting in the middle to participate less merely by inviting them to switch seats.

The neglect of the study of classroom ecology is reflected in the lack of significant change in classroom architecture. Future archaeologists will be able to reconstruct our philosophy of education from the surviving symptoms of our edifice complex. There is more information in bricks than in books, in mortar than in mortarboards. The blackboard tells more than what is written on it about chalk and talk persisting well into the age of the computer and the television set. Excavating a traditional classroom, archaeologists will find desks bolted to the floor (learning is a passive rather than an active process), all facing the "front" (the teacher is the source of all knowledge), where the desk of the teacher is topped with a lectern (the word of the teacher is Gospel).* One trivial example will illustrate how little thought has gone into improving classroom design. The door in the traditional classroom is almost invariably at the "front" of the class (where the teacher is enthroned). How many thousands of hours have been lost due to classes being disturbed by late-comers or visitors entering by that front door? How much embarrassment has been caused by students forced to interrupt a class or miss it? How much more interruption and embarrassment before we learn to put the door at the back of the class? Ministers typically preach only a couple of hours a week, but they know enough to avoid interruptions during the service and embarrassment to their parishioners by arranging to have the entrance at the back of the church.

13.4 THE VIEW OF THE COMMUNICATION THEORIST

In Chapter 9, we focused on the communication unit, consisting of a source and a destination linked by a channel. The classroom can be considered as a communication system, consisting of a number of such communication units. **Communication systems** can be classified in terms of the number of sources and destinations. Four possible systems are listed below, with the names of those systems within the classroom setting.

one source	one destination	tutorial, individual instruction
one source	many destinations	lecture, demonstration
many sources	many destinations	seminar, class discussion
many sources	one destination	real-life situation

The first three communication systems represent the three major settings within the classroom—the **tutorial,** the **lecture,** and the **seminar.** Each of them requires a different set of teaching skills. We all know teachers who can talk to 100 students with ease but have difficulty talking to 1 student. The fourth communication system represents the real-life situation from the point of view of each student. He or she is one destination impinged on by many sources. Let us look at each communication system in turn.

13.41 One Source, One Destination

The tutorial has traditionally been viewed as the ideal communication setting for teaching and learning. This view is best expressed—or, at least, best remembered—in Arthur Gutterman's misquotation of James Garfield's state-

---

* Whenever I see a lectern in a classroom, I am tempted to grasp it with both hands and intone, in my best Presbyterian voice, "We shall commence reading from the Book of Gardiner, Chapter 4, Verse 7." I often succumb to this temptation. That's the best way to deal with it.

ment putting Mark Hopkins and James Garfield on opposite ends of a log. This traditional view is supported by modern research. Bernstein concluded, from reviewing 200 articles on remedial arithmetic, that tutoring improved performance and raised self-esteem.[17] Researchers tend to gravitate toward tutorials as a means of demonstrating the effectiveness of their methods. Bloom uses tutorials in his mastery approach.[20] Englemann uses tutorials to demonstrate that IQ can be raised by instruction.[50] Bruner uses tutorials to generate evidence for his anything-can-be-taught-to-anyone thesis.[26]

"FOR EDUCATION IS MAKING MEN;
SO IT IS NOW, SO IT WAS WHEN
MARK HOPKINS SAT ON ONE END OF A LOG
AND JAMES GARFIELD SAT ON THE OTHER."

ARTHUR GUTTERMAN
"EDUCATION"

The tutorial is ideal in theory but impossible in practice. There is no way in which such one-to-one teaching can be a major weapon in the arsenal of a teacher in the typical one-to-thirty class. However, although there are seldom "official" tutorials in the typical classroom, there are often unofficial tutorials. A teacher responds to a request for help with an arithmetic problem. Hey, presto—a tutorial! A student stays after class to ask a question. Hey, presto—another tutorial! Such spontaneous tutorials are often the highlight of a dull one-to-many day for a teacher or student.

Since it is difficult for the teacher to conduct tutorials, a number of surrogate teachers have been constructed to do so. We have already seen how tutorials can be conducted by teaching machines (Section 3.243). Computers have also been recruited as tutors. In **computer-assisted instruction,** the student may push buttons in response to multiple-choice questions, touch a cathode-ray tube with a special light pen, or answer a series of questions appearing on a TV-like screen.[10] Two books may help temper our North American tendency to seek simple technological solutions to complex human problems. In *Run, Computer, Run,* Oettinger and Marks remind us that computers as used in classrooms are too often complex devices misused to perform simple functions, that they can cause more rather than less mechanical work for the teacher, and that the juxtaposition of expensive equipment and clumsy children often leads to rigid rules that interfere with learning.[160] In *The Teacher and the Machine,* Jackson reminds us that we should not fear the machine itself, but people who are willing to treat *us* as machines.[100] The talking typewriter is an ingenious tutor designed by O. K. Moore and Alan Anderson.[156] The talking typewriter can be set so that a recorded voice pronounces each letter as the key is struck (free exploration); so that a letter appears on a screen and all the other keys are locked (search and match); so that a word appears on a screen and a recorded voice spells it out (word construction); and so that sentences or paragraphs with illustrations appear on a screen and a recorded voice reads them (reading and writing). Moore and Anderson have taught preschoolers to read by shifting them through those four phases involving larger and larger units.

It is ironic, perhaps, that this most intimate person-to-person setting of the tutorial is the one in which the person is most often replaced by a mechanism (and a further irony that the most elaborate of those mechanisms was invented by a man named Omar Khayyam). In the modern version of the tutorial, that "simple bench" of James Garfield would have to be very strong to hold James Garfield IV on one end and a teaching machine, a computer, and a talking typewriter on the other, and that "log hut" would have to be equipped with plenty of electrical outlets.

Another alternative is to replace the teacher as tutor with another student. "The best way to learn is to teach" has been repeated so often that it has degenerated into a cliché. However, the practical implication of this statement had not been explored formally until recently. A number of studies have demonstrated that students would learn better if they could be teachers rather than students.[72] Students were invited to tutor younger students who were having difficulty learning. The tutees gained, but the tutors gained more. They gained not only in the subject they were tutoring but in other subjects, too. Perhaps they were learning how to learn or were acquiring self-esteem through the role of teacher. In retrospect, it is not surprising that the children were good teachers. Children who have just learned something understand the difficulties in learning it and thus have more empathy than experts. These findings have encouraged people to recommend "multi-age grouping to facilitate cross-age tutoring." We used to call it a one-room schoolhouse. More ironies. It has taken years of research to stumble on what we have been saying (if not believing) for a long time—the best way to learn is to teach—and to recommend what we have had for a long time—the one-room schoolhouse.

Although it is difficult to conduct "official" tutorials in the typical classroom, you may consider some variations on the tutorial method. Reading over papers with each student (a few each day after school, perhaps) is a useful alternative to that dull ritual of taking home a pile of papers and "marking" them. It takes longer, but there are many compensations for the extra time. It is

"A CHILD OF THREE IS A BETTER MODEL FOR A CHILD OF ONE, BOTH BECAUSE THE THINGS IT DOES ARE MORE WHAT THE YOUNGER CHILD WOULD WISH TO DO, AND BECAUSE ITS POWERS DO NOT SEEM SO SUPERHUMAN."

BERTRAND RUSSELL
EDUCATION AND THE GOOD LIFE

a lively rather than a deadly process. By asking the student to think out loud, you can see thought in action and thus gain insight into not only *this* student's thought processes but the thought process in general. The tutorial offers a fine opportunity to turn education inside out. It is possible to let the student take the initiative and to focus on the ends of the student. Teachers tend to be so set in their one-way channel of communication that tutorials degenerate into lectures with an audience of one.* Tutorials should not only be individual (that is, involve only one student) but individualized (that is, involve this particular student).

13.42   One Source, Many Destinations

We seldom talk about lectures in elementary and high school teaching, but much class time is devoted to that one-source–many-destinations communication setting I am calling the lecture. The "lectures" tend to be presented as explanations, interrupted by questions, concluded by seatwork, and aided by props (thus shading into **demonstrations**). As the student gets older, the lectures get longer, questions, student activities, and props grow fewer, until, in the university, most of the contact time between teacher and student is devoted to "pure" lectures. What starts as "show and tell" ends simply as "tell."

Since the lecture is the core of traditional education, it is fiercely frowned on by those aspiring to alternative education.† Let's consider the major criticisms of the lecture to see whether we can throw out some bathwater without losing the baby.

13.421   What's Wrong with the Lecture?

a. The lecture was made obsolete by the printing press. The argument goes something like this. The first schools used the auditory channel. Teachers spoke and students listened. When the more efficient visual channel was opened up to a large public by the printing press, schools continued to use the auditory channel, because of the inertia of tradition. However, since the visual channel was more efficient, a peculiar twist was introduced. Teachers read from their written notes, and students wrote as they listened. The result of all this effort is a large number of poor copies of the teacher's notes.

---

* I remember a photograph in a Montreal newspaper of a class in which only one student had shown up during a snowstorm. The teacher was sitting at the teacher's desk and the student was sitting at his regular desk. Perhaps the picture was posed—but, then, perhaps not. Had it been a university class and this one student arrived late, he might have found that the professor had already started to lecture.

† At a conference I attended at Goddard College held to expand on the revolutionary views of Richard Jones (see Section 11.42), he was rash enough to expound those views by way of introduction. The assembled reformers got very hostile. How dare he lecture to them!

The lecture is indeed too often a means of transmitting information from the notebook of the professor to the notebook of the student without passing through the mind of either. Such a lecture should follow the chastity belt into the museum, and such a lecturer should follow the dinosaur into extinction. The students should send their tape recorders to "listen" to the tape recorder of the professor. If his or her notes have not yet been published, the professor should duplicate and distribute them. Lectures like this survive only because the large lecture course is profitable and because a pile of notes provides the student with a certain illusion of learning. Products seem to imply productivity. However, the inspiration provided by a good lecture can't be gained from a book. No one would suggest that Shakespeare should no longer be performed because his plays can now be read. In our electronic age, information is easy to obtain. Indeed (as I suggested in Pre-exercise 2 to Chapter 11), it is difficult to avoid. We need no longer attend lectures, or even go to a university, in order to gain information. Most of us, however, have to attend a university and attend lectures to gain inspiration. I understood very little of the content of the lectures of two of my most inspiring professors in graduate school. But I could tell that those two men were very excited about something and I wanted to share that excitement. Their curiosity spread by contagion. Fortunately, the state-sponsored immunization had not taken in my case, and I was infected. Such lecturers, who provide inspiration rather than transmit information, are not made obsolete by the printing press. Nor can they ever be replaced by *any* mechanism, because the inspiration is due to the identification of the student with the lecturer.

b. The content of lectures is irrelevant to the students. There is certainly a wide gap between what the lecturer usually wants to teach and what the students want to learn. Too often lecturers are talking to themselves, with the students eavesdropping on a soliloquy. Many lecturers realize that they are not getting across. Some do nothing about it. They feel that, to do so, they would have to pander. However, content does not have to be pap to be palatable. Some do something about it. They turn up the volume. Audio aids, visual aids, Band-Aids, or whatever technological aids are available are recruited to augment the lecture. This barrage of stimulation is still not getting across to some students. The lecturers decide that they should be adjusting the tuner rather than turning up the volume. They adjust the tuner—way down to the low end by stooping to pun and way up to the high end by swooping to oratory. Yet, even when they play the entire range of the dial, they still fail to make contact with some students.

Failure of communication may be due in some cases to flaws in the destination rather than in the source. Some students may be irrelevant to school. If they are not tuned in, they can't be turned on. You can lead a girl to Vassar, but you can't make her think. Some irrelevant students are victims of the adult conspiracy that the only vehicle to success or salvation is the Ivy League express. Only a few are truly interested in academic matters, but many are pushed through school. The teacher is like a deaf person answering questions that are not being asked. The student is like a squirrel hoarding answers for four years to questions he or she has not asked and may never ask. Here is a little dialogue from one of my too typical early classes. I am gazing over a sea of scalps as the students are busily scribbling my words as if I were Moses reading out the Ten Commandments. One precocious head rises and I find myself, God forbid, looking into a face:

"Those are good answers, but where are the questions?"

"They'll be in the final exam."

"But I'm not interested in the artificial exam questions. I'm interested in real questions."

"Oh, the real questions will arise after you leave the university. Then you will be able to match up my answers with your questions."

"But what if those questions don't come up?"

"Shut up and keep writing."

The function of education is to make sense of experience, but many students have little experience to make sense of. Many middle-class students raised in a sensory-deprivation chamber in darkest suburbia are culturally deprived. A student from an upper-middle-class residential district near Montreal was asked to write an essay about something preposterous that had happened to her. She wrote "Nothing preposterous ever happened to me. I come from the Town of Mount Royal." **Cultural deprivation** is usually applied to lower-class children to explain away their failure in middle-class schools. However, if you abandoned a 10-year-old lower-class kid and a 10-year-old middle-class kid in downtown Manhattan equidistant from their homes, who do you think would be home first? Which one of those kids is culturally deprived? I noticed this great discrepancy in sophistication once while having supper with two of my students. One—from a large, lower-class Black family in Mississippi—had somehow scraped together enough money to get to Montreal and rent and furnish his own apartment. He was doing well in his technician job during the day and in his university courses in the evening. The other—an only child from a middle-class family in suburban Montreal—considered coming downtown a great adventure but was nervous about crossing a busy street without holding someone's hand. Who was culturally deprived? Perhaps parents, instead of paying their children's first-year fees, should buy them one-way tickets to Australia. After working their way back, they might have some questions and come pounding on the doors of the university demanding answers. Life is good preparation for school. Perhaps free schools could serve as a sort of Project Head Start for adolescents. They would provide the experience, whereas the more structured schools would provide the education to make sense of the experience.

c. Lecture classes are too large. Too large for what? For two-way communication. But students listen to records for hours with even less hope of responding. It seems entirely reasonable that, if I have something to tell Joe and Harriet and Bob and Alice and so on and so on, I bring them all together in one place and tell them all at once. They can each make it a two-way and personalized process by creative note-making in which they record what interests them and their reactions to it. Perhaps what is offensive is that they must focus on what the lecturer says rather than on their reaction to it, since they will be examined on what the lecturer says. Too large for individual attention? But students return from the excitement of being together with 500,000 at Woodstock to complain about the anonymity of being together with 500 in Psychology 211.

Perhaps the complaint is not so much about the lecture per se but about the one-way communication of the lecture being the major, and sometimes only, means of communication in the university. Our consumer mentality extends even to the university. The student is viewed as a passive consumer of information. There is no hope of understanding as a consumer of information, just as there is no hope of happiness as a consumer of goods. Rather than step up the stimulation, as innovators typically try, we should provide students with opportunities to create their own stimulation. Students should be R-S organisms, acting to produce their own stimulation, rather than S-R organisms, reacting to stimuli impinging on them. All this input without output at the university is not only ineffectual but may even be damaging to the healthy nervous system. May I offer "No impression without expression" as a slogan for a *second* American Revolution?

d. Lectures are usually dull. Perhaps students are critical not so much of lectures as of bad lectures. The average lecture is just about as dull as the average sermon. Parents who can hardly stay awake during a half-hour sermon on Sunday condemn their children for being critical of lectures they have to sit through all week. A good lecture, like a good film, should provide an experience. The experience is too often that of sitting in a lecture hall listening to a lecture. The dullness of most lectures may be the central problem. If lectures were exciting, students would not consider them obsolete, irrelevant, and impersonal.

13.422   How May the Lecture Be Improved?

a. Realize that they can be improved. In everyday life, one is seldom permitted to talk for more than a few minutes without being interrupted. We get little practice, then, for that unnatural situation teachers find themselves in when they are permitted to talk on and on. We acquire the skill with practice and improve it with more practice. Like most acquired skills, it fades with disuse. On returning to teaching after a six-year absence, I found that I had to stumble through a 50-minute lecture whereas, six years before, I had no trouble with a 2-hour lecture.

Thyne suggests that explanations can be organized into four steps:

1. Be sure you understand the question being asked.

2. Identify the elements, variables, concepts, or events involved in the question.
3. Find the relationship between those elements.
4. Show how this relationship is an example of a more general relationship.[219]

Miltz taught this strategy of explaining to 30 teacher trainees and presented pretraining and posttraining explanations to judges who did not know which was which.[153] Judgments of organization, clarity, and overall quality of post-training explanations were significantly higher than those of pretraining explanations. Sheer dogged practice is not enough. You can move beyond that comfortable plateau where practice gets you to higher skills based on technique.

b. Don't be nervous. You can speak to each member of your audience individually, can't you? There is no reason, then, why you can't speak to them when they happen to be all together. It's the same thing—only more convenient. I used to be nervous for two days before speaking in public. When I started lecturing six times a week, I realized that I would therefore be nervous all the time. There was no point in that, so I decided not to be nervous. It's worth becoming a teacher even if just to force that decision.

c. Speak to one person, and let the rest of your audience eavesdrop. Switch, of course, from one person to another throughout the presentation. One of my graduate school friends at Cornell used to lecture only to a bountiful blonde who always sat cross-legged in the front row. He gave himself away by walking in one day, when she was absent, and saying "Where is everyone?" The major advantage of speaking and listening over writing and reading is that it permits personal contact. This advantage is best preserved in public speaking by creating the illusion that you are having a private conversation with one member of the audience. Studies have shown that students learn more when the lesson is directed to a specific member of the class than when it is vaguely presented to the class as a whole.

d. Don't read notes. Don't even refer to notes, if you can manage it. Remembering a one-hour lecture seems like a difficult task when you consider it as a sequence of thousands of sounds. Chomsky has demonstrated that the structure of language is hierarchical rather than sequential.[30] As I pointed out in Chapter 9, a sequential presentation on conditioning could have, underlying it, the hierarchial structure shown in Figure 9-3 (page 236). You do not need to remember a long sequence of words, but only a few dichotomies. Teasing out the hierarchical structure underlying your sequential presentation is a valuable aid in both organizing and remembering your lecture. With a little practice, you can easily deliver an organized two-hour lecture without glancing at a note.

e. Emulate entertainers. By observing professional entertainers, we could learn how to project our voices, establish conventions with the audience, and rehearse.* Talk of entertainers is repugnant to most educators. I once suggested

---

* Rehearsing is less exhausting if you write your lectures. The next year you have a nucleus on which to improve. After a few years, a book emerges, a second bird falls to the same stone, and you, now obsolete, can go off and do something useful.

somewhat whimsically at a meeting about problems in large classes that lectures be prepared by a writer in consultation with a teacher and delivered by an actor. Someone snapped indignantly "We are not entertainers—we are educators," a murmur of sympathy rippled through the assembled educators, and the discussion ended. However—let's face it—when you are handed a class of 700, you are in show biz. The art of the entertainer is to appear spontaneous although prepared; the art of the educator is, too often, to appear prepared although spontaneous. There is no reason why the arts cannot be reversed. One teacher approached me after the meeting at which I had suggested cooperation among a writer, a teacher, and an actor and agreed that it was an interesting idea but impractical, since it would take so much time. Perhaps here we come to the core of the problem with lectures. A writer would shudder at the prospect of writing eight hours of new material each week, and an actor would revolt at the prospect of presenting eight hours of new material each week. Yet the teacher, who has neither of their skills, is required to do both. It has been said that most people have one book in them, some people have two books in them, but no one has a weekly column. Certainly no one has a thrice-weekly lecture. The best of us have perhaps ten lectures in us, but all of us are required to deliver hundreds. In bravely attempting an impossible task, we settle for those dull collages of bits and pieces from the works of others. Few of us have the brilliance of Charles Hockett, who was able to present his own original work in his two-hour lectures every Wednesday afternoon at Cornell University. Yet even he could not sustain his creativity at that pace. He had the courage to open and close one seminar with the words "Today's lecture was to be about the language of history. I don't yet understand the language of history. Perhaps I will next week. Class dismissed."

Most teachers are miscast as lecturers. Very few of us have the flair of Richard Eakin, who delivers his lectures on the history of science at Berkeley in the words and dress of famous scientists.[44] Average teachers in normal circumstances are trying an impossible task. The Beatles, with all their charisma and electronic equipment, could entertain adolescents for at most a few hours. A high school teacher is required to "entertain" them for several hours every week. A minister can put a congregation of adults to sleep in an hour on Sunday, but a teacher is required to keep a class of restless children attentive for six hours a day from Monday through Friday. Many of the much discussed problems of traditional education are not due to inadequacies in teachers but to the impossible situation in which the teacher is placed.

13.43 *Many Sources, Many Destinations*

The class discussion or seminar (as it becomes formalized in the university)—a small group in face-to-face contact focusing on a topic of common interest—would appear superficially to be a good setting for learning. Yet they seldom catch fire. Class discussions and seminars tend to degenerate into bull sessions—a pooling of ignorance, a series of anecdotes about personal experience. Sometimes they degenerate into lectures by the teacher or, what is often worse, by a student. The chairman and the bored. The speaker and the silent majority. The tedium is the message. How can those twin tendencies be avoided? Seminars seem to degenerate into bull sessions because of too little structure and into lectures because of too much. How can an optimal amount of structure be achieved?

a. Provide some common experience. Some structure can be introduced by focusing on some experience shared by the members of the class. A film, a demonstration, a skit performed by members of the class, or a reading of an article in the morning newspaper may serve this function. I remember a lively discussion on the accuracy of the testimony of witnesses triggered by a scream-ing woman chased by a masked man in one door of the classroom and out the other.

b. Capitalize on spontaneous interest. The careful complex of seminar schedules created for an experimental program I was participating in disinte-grated. One day, I realized why. Montreal police went on strike, and violence erupted overnight. Spontaneous seminars ignited the next morning. I argued with the police, the strikers, and the students to no avail. "This is only No-vember," I pleaded, "and 'violence' is not scheduled till February." We are aware of the artificiality of the we-are-gathered-here-to-be-happy atmosphere of the New Year's Eve party, of the we-are-gathered-here-to-be-honest atmo-sphere of the encounter group, but not so much of the we-are-gathered-here-to-be-intelligent atmosphere of the seminar. There is, of course, no need to start riots on Wednesday evening to trigger interest for a scheduled class discussion of violence on Thursday morning. You can anticipate spontaneous interest. We were taken by surprise by the interest in violence and did not have materials ready to fan the flames of the subsequent spontaneous combustion. However, we did anticipate interest in President Nixon's scheduled visit to China and were prepared to capitalize on it by having materials handy to flesh out a discussion of the history of China.

c. Pose problems rather than provide solutions. Class discussions too often take the form of what John Holt calls "answer-pulling."[95] During my early seminars, I remember tossing out questions, waiting impatiently for the students to complete their bumbling attempts to answer them, and then pro-viding the Gardiner-ordained "correct" answer. This authoritarian attitude is encouraged by teacher's manuals which instruct the teacher to conduct a discussion to bring out the following points. This is analogous to a government department setting up a commission to get the facts on an issue but adding "here are the facts I want you to get." The findings of many a commission have been rejected because they were not the findings that were supposed to be gotten. The role of the student in such a "discussion" is like that of a witness being cross-examined by a judge or, worse, of a prisoner being grilled by a police officer. Rowe analyzed over 800 tape recordings of science lessons and found that the average teacher asks questions at the rate of two or three per minute and that a student must start a reply on the average within one second.[194] Many educators who question the value of speed-reading fail to recognize how much of our schooling is a course in speed-thinking. Such "discussions" are essentially disguised lectures in which the teacher tells the class while pretending to ask them.

Maier recommends **developmental discussion.** Such classes are neither nondirective (which tend to degenerate into bull sessions) nor autocratic (which tend to develop into bully sessions, as described earlier).[131] The role of the teacher is to formulate problems rather than to suggest solutions. The teacher divides the problem into parts that can be solved in steps, sets certain constraints on the discussion, and orients it toward a definite set of goals. Discussion may range freely within this framework as a function of the interests of the students.

d. Displace yourself from the center of the group. For many personal and practical reasons, teachers find it difficult to give up their central position of control in the group. There is indeed much justification for maintaining control because, unless the class has learned democratic procedures, the alternative to teacher control is no control. You are set up as king or queen of the class, and it is difficult to abdicate. Even if you want to, your subjects will often not let you. Most teachers not only do not encourage communication between two students in the class but actively discourage it. It is viewed as an interruption. Whenever a discussion evolves into a debate between two students, many teachers think it has gotten out of hand.

Centralized structures, like the wheel, chain, and Y patterns in Figure 13-1, in which the teacher is a powerful pivotal figure, cause students to feel peripheral and unimportant.[33] **Decentralized structures,** like the all-channel and circle patterns, help foster discussion.

e. Vary the format. Class discussions, even when not simply question-spraying and answer-pulling sessions, tend to have a bland sameness. Here are a number of possible variations within the many-sources–many-destinations theme.

Buzz groups. Divide the class into small groups, each of which conducts a discussion. Research suggests that five is the optimal number—large enough to provide varied input and small enough to permit everyone to participate. Perhaps the soporific effect of the traditional seminar and class discussion is due to the strain of such a large group to subdivide into smaller groups, as it does spontaneously at dinner parties. It is often useful to reconvene the group as a whole and invite volunteers from each small group to present the consensus of their group.

Brainstorming session. State a problem and invite the class to fire solutions at you. The problem can be theoretical (What can you use a wire coathanger for?) or practical (How can the class raise money for the end-of-the-year party?). The basic rule is "no criticism." Any idea, however bizarre, is accepta-

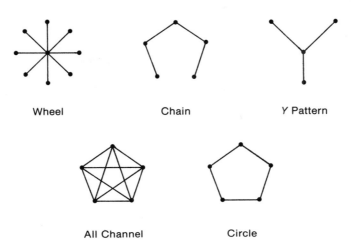

Wheel   Chain   Y Pattern

All Channel   Circle

Figure 13-1. Centralized (top) and decentralized (bottom) structures

ble. It is a good idea for you to write the ideas on the blackboard as they are thrown out by the class. Later, in the case of practical problems, the class can go through the various suggested solutions and winnow out the impractical ones.

Debate. Invite members of the class to conduct a formal debate on some predetermined issue of interest. You may want to act as moderator or invite a student to moderate and record the points pro and con in two columns on the blackboard as they are presented. A variation is to invite the participants to switch positions to demonstrate how debate can be an intellectual rather than an emotional matter, how lawyers can play "devil's advocate" by presenting one side of an issue, and how scientists can explore both sides of an issue.

13.44 *Many Sources, One Destination*

In looking at the points of view of the various experts, we should not lose sight of the point of view of the student. The three communication settings just described—tutorial, lecture, seminar—are the dominant communication settings in schools, but, from the point of view of the student, the most important is the remaining setting, since each student is one destination being bombarded from many sources. Unless we take the cynical view that the school system is a make-work project to provide jobs for teachers, the point of view of the student is the most important. We often forget this because of the tendency for institutions to shift emphasis from the service of clients to the convenience of managers.

"SUBJECT PEOPLES BOTH APPEASE THEIR RULERS AND
SATISFY SOME PART OF THEIR DESIRE FOR HUMAN DIG-
NITY BY PUTTING ON A MASK, BY ACTING MUCH MORE
STUPID AND INCOMPETENT THAN THEY REALLY ARE,
BY DENYING THEIR RULERS THE FULL USE OF THEIR
INTELLIGENCE AND ABILITY, BY DECLARING THEIR
MINDS AND SPIRITS FREE OF THEIR ENSLAVED
BODIES. DOES NOT SOMETHING VERY CLOSE TO THIS
HAPPEN OFTEN IN SCHOOL?"

JOHN HOLT
HOW CHILDREN FAIL

From the point of view of the sociologist, we saw the process through which a child is socialized by various agents—parents and peers, teachers and preachers, radios and televisions, books and films, and so on and so on. Turning things inside out and looking at this process from the point of view of the student, we see things very differently. Students are not trying to be socialized—indeed, they are resisting it—and the dynamic interaction between their goals and those of society is what is shaping their personalities. A child no more wants to be society-broken than a dog wants to be house-broken. As the world's foremost experts on themselves, children are sorting out the myriad, often conflicting, communications from those various socializing agencies and deciding what makes sense to them. You as teacher are only one of many sources impinging on each child in your class. In the orchestra to which they are listening, you play only one instrument. If William has a fara-way look when you are talking, he may be listening to a different drummer. If Mary has a pained look, then your instrument may be out of tune with another instrument she hears. A teacher should try to remain aware of those other influences so as not to strike too many discordant notes.

POST-EXERCISES

1. Debate among Experts

Choose one of the four expert positions; that is, imagine yourself as a sociologist, a social psychologist, an ecologist, or a communication theorist. What arguments would you present to the other experts as evidence that your point of view is a "better" point of view? What do you mean by "better"? What practical payoff from your theoretical point of view could you offer a teacher? A student? If you can find another member of the class willing to play one of the other experts, debate with him or her the relative fruitfulness of your approaches. Perhaps you could persuade your teacher to organize a debate in class between experts (or teams of experts) representing each position. Is there some other theoretical position that you consider more fruitful than any of the four presented in this chapter?

Imagine now that you are viewing an open classroom (Pre-exercise 2, Chapter 6) rather than a traditional classroom. Compare the open and the traditional classrooms, using the language of your chosen "expert." Still using your chosen language, state the advantages and disadvantages of open and traditional classrooms.

2. The Process of Socialization

Schooling has been described as an aspect of socializing. The process of socialization differs from time to time, from place to place, and from subculture to subculture. The following books describe socialization at times, in places, and in subcultures different from those with which you are probably familiar. You may find them useful as a means of removing, as far as that is possible, those cultural blinkers you inevitably acquire as a result of being socialized in a particular culture. Consider the role of schooling within each of these "different" cultures.

a. Differences from time to time.

Ariès, P. *Centuries of childhood: A social history of family life.* New York: Knopf, 1962.

b. Differences from place to place.

Bronfenbrenner, U. *Two worlds of childhood.* New York: Russell Sage Foundation, 1970.
Spiro, M.E. *Children of the kibbutz.* Cambridge: Harvard University Press, 1958.

c. Differences from subculture to subculture.

Cleaver, E. *Soul on ice.* New York: McGraw-Hill, 1968.
Coles, R. *Children of crisis: A study of courage and fear.* Boston: Little, Brown, 1967.
Coles, R. *Children of crisis: Migrants, mountaineers and sharecroppers.* Boston: Little, Brown, 1972.
Deloria, V., Jr. *Custer died for your sins.* New York: Macmillan, 1969.
Gonzales, R. *I am Joaquin.* New York: Bantam, 1973.
Rothchild, J., & Wolf, S. B. *The children of the counterculture.* Garden City, N. Y.: Doubleday, 1976.

Epilogue 14

14   EPILOGUE

14.1 *Behaviorism and Outside-In Education*
14.2 *Humanism and Inside-Out Education*
14.3 *Interactionism and Future Education*

PRE-EXERCISES

1. Defense of the Teaching Profession

In Pre-exercise 1 of the Prologue, I invited you to consider the question "What am I doing here?" Here, in Pre-exercise 1 of the Epilogue, I am inviting you to meet the challenge "What are you doing there?" The following critics are, in their various ways, asking this question. How would you defend your potential profession against each of these familiar criticisms?

a. *The school is dead.*

The schoolteacher is, therefore, out of work. Here are some sources to familiarize you with the argument.

Illich, I. *De-schooling society.* New York: Harper & Row, 1971.
Illich, I., Gartner, A., Greer, C., & Reissman, F. (Eds.). *After de-schooling, what?* New York: Harper & Row, 1973.
Levine, D. U., & Havighurst, R. J. (Eds.). *Farewell to schools???* Worthington, Ohio: Charles A. Jones, 1971.
Reimer, E. *School is dead.* Harmondsworth, Middlesex: Penguin, 1971.

b. *The school is deadening.*

A number of quotations by prominent thinkers imply that a better education can be acquired out of school.

"My grandmother wanted me to have an education, so she kept me out of school." (Margaret Mead)

"The information level outside of school is so much higher than inside the school, that one interrupts one's education by going to school." (Marshall McLuhan)

c. *Education is an initiation rite.*

Elementary school, high school, university, graduate, and professional schools are a series of higher and higher hurdles that children must jump to qualify for more and more lucrative and prestigious positions in our meritocracy. There is, therefore, no genuine interest in improving teaching. This would be like lowering the hurdles and, thus, permitting too many people to claim the top positions. There's no more room at the top.

Or, to change the metaphor, the schooling process is to an industrialized society as circumcision rites are to a primitive society. The educational innovator offering devices to make learning easier is like someone offering a local anesthetic to a witch doctor about to perform circumcision rites on pubescent boys. He is not interested in something to dull the pain. The pain is the point.

d. *The teacher is made obsolete by the teaching machine.*

Imagine yourself on a lifeboat with representatives of a number of other professions. Your only hope of survival is for some of you to sacrifice yourselves to the sharks (since there is not enough food for all of you) and for the rest to reach an uninhabited island, where they must set up a new society. You are debating the potential contribution of your various professions to that new society. The engineer has just claimed that, in addition to his engineering skills, he can contribute a teaching machine, which will replace you.

The sharks are circling the boat. It is your turn to speak.

The three subsections of this epilogue parallel Chapter 3 ("Behaviorism and Outside-In Teaching"), Chapter 4 ("Humanism and Inside-Out Teaching"), and Chapter 5 ("The Theory of Jean Piaget"). This is no coincidence. I wish to summarize my argument here, and the essence of that argument is contained in those three chapters. The other chapters could be considered as extensions of those three. Chapter 7 ("Intelligence") and Chapter 8 ("Creativity") are discussions of individual differences from the points of view, respectively, of the theories expounded in Chapters 3 and 4; Chapter 9 ("Explaining and Understanding") and Chapter 10 ("The Discovery Approach") are discussions of the teacher-student relationship from those two points of view. Chapter 6 ("Readiness and Critical Period") considers some practical implications of the theory expounded in Chapter 5, and Chapter 11 ("An Operating Manual for Species *Homo sapiens*") is my personal view of the educational process, based on this theory. Chapter 12 ("Observer Effects") and Chapter 13 ("Various Views of the Classroom") are close-up and long-range perspectives on the teacher-student relationship, as viewed by someone who considers that Piaget's theory, as expounded in Chapter 5, is currently the best basis for this relationship.

14.1 BEHAVIORISM AND OUTSIDE-IN EDUCATION

I argued, in Chapter 3, that the behavioristic concept of the student is the basis of outside-in teaching, which is, in turn, the basis of traditional education. I do not mean, of course, that behaviorism preceded traditional education chronologically but, rather, that it underlies it logically. In historical terms, education is not based on behaviorism or *any* explicit theory. Traditional education is based on—tradition. Our schools tomorrow will be modeled on our schools today, which are, in turn, modeled on our schools yesterday. How did this tradition start? When the noble experiment of universal education was introduced, it was financially feasible to have only 1 teacher for about 30 students. The history of education is the story of a series of pragmatic solutions to such basic practical problems.

    If you believe that teaching is an outside-in process, and if you find yourself in a classroom with your designated quota of 30 children, then you will do precisely, with your own personal variations, what I did, and what your teachers did, and what their teachers did. Teachers of teachers often complain that their students teach as they were taught rather than as they are taught to teach. But, under the circumstances, there is no option. If you view teaching as an outside-in process, then the entire structure of the traditional classroom makes perfectly good sense. The best way for you to pass on the accumulated information of our culture to your 30 assigned members of the next generation is for you to talk and for them to listen. They must pay attention to you (or face the "front" to create at least the illusion of attention). They must sit still to be filled with information. They must be quiet since, when one child is making noise, the other children can't hear what you are saying. The familiar catalog of rules against inattention, activity, and noise must be enforced so that your information can be transmitted.

WE KNOW ONLY TOO WELL THE SORRY SPECTACLE OF THE TEACHER WHO, IN THE ORDINARY SCHOOL-ROOM, MUST POUR CERTAIN CUT AND DRIED FACTS INTO THE HEADS OF THE SCHOLARS. IN ORDER TO SUCCEED IN THIS BARREN TASK, SHE FINDS IT NECESSARY TO DISCIPLINE HER PUPILS INTO IMMOBILITY AND TO FORCE THEIR ATTENTION.

MARIA MONTESSORI
THE MONTESSORI METHOD

As I discovered with respect to the Presbyterian principles with which I was raised, there is a need for a rule against something only when one would be tempted to do it, and one is tempted to do it only if it is enjoyable. (That is why such lists of rules are useful guides to the good life!) Rules against inattention (that is, daydreaming, fantasizing, or otherwise attending to your own thing), activity, and noise (the inevitable by-product of children's activity) are necessary, then, because they are enjoyable to children, and they are enjoyable because they involve the exercise of their natural functions. The traditional classroom violates much of what research and personal experience tell us about the nature of children. Most discipline problems are essentially artifacts of this unnatural situation. We are shocked and surprised when we hear of a student attacking a teacher. It is a tribute to the essential good nature of children and the competence of teachers that, in this bizarre situation, such an event is infrequent enough to be newsworthy.

Behaviorism provides an after-the-fact rationalization for traditional teaching rather than a before-the-fact rationale. It makes explicit the implicit theory. To that basic question—"What am I doing here?"—it provides a precise answer. You are, in Skinner's words, "arranging contingencies of reinforcement."[205] Skinner then proceeds to demonstrate that this can be done much

JEAN PIAGET
SCIENCE OF EDUCATION AND THE
PSYCHOLOGY OF THE CHILD

more efficiently and effectively by a teaching machine. By thus providing us with a valuable device for performing the traditional outside-in function of the teacher, he frees us to perform the more human function of inside-out teaching, which is suggested by the alternative humanistic theory of the student. Skinner is a courageous man. One of the dangers of clarity is that people know what you are saying and can thus attack it. His explicit statement of the nature of traditional teaching reveals that it is trivial. If teaching is *only* an outside-in process, as traditionally conceived, and this can be performed better by a machine, then it is a mechanical process.

14.2 HUMANISM AND INSIDE-OUT EDUCATION

Throughout recorded history, critics of outside-in education have been trying to turn it inside out. As I said, a history of education could be written in terms of the continuous debate between those who advocate the outside-in and the inside-out positions. The inside-outers have, however, always formed the loyal opposition. They have spawned isolated schools here and there— Dewey's Laboratory School in the United States, Neill's Summerhill in England, Tolstoi's Yasnaya Polyana in Russia, and so on—that shone brightly against the gray backdrop of traditional schooling and then faded out. Let us consider some of the reasons why inside-out schools have never seriously challenged outside-in schools as the prevailing system of education.

"— OUR SCHOOL SYSTEM, AS MUCH UNDER LEFT-WING AS UNDER RIGHT-WING REGIMES, HAS BEEN CONSTRUCTED BY CONSERVATIVES (FROM THE PEDAGOGICAL POINT OF VIEW) WHO WERE THINKING MUCH MORE IN TERMS OF FITTING OUR RISING GENERATIONS INTO THE MOLDS OF TRADITIONAL LEARNING THAN IN TERMS OF TRAINING INVENTIVE AND CRITICAL MINDS."

JEAN PIAGET
SCIENCE OF EDUCATION AND THE PSYCHOLOGY OF THE CHILD

An obvious first reason is the inertia of tradition. However, this conservative effect has never been as strong with respect to other professions. Changes in education are much more threatening to the status quo than changes in medicine or engineering. It is difficult to imagine a doctor or engineer being executed for practicing innovative techniques, yet Jesus Christ was crucified and Socrates was forced to drink hemlock. Such powerful resistance to educational innovation is a testimony to how very important our profession is.

A second reason is that inside-outers have tended to lack sound theory and strong empirical evidence for their position. They have simply reacted against the prevailing tradition. As we saw in Chapter 4, the humanistic theory of the student can best be described in terms of the negation of the behavioristic theory of the student. This thesis-antithesis style of debate tends to produce a pendulumlike swing between the positions of extremists. We see today the beginning of another boring swing back again to the conservative end. Articulate criticism of the inarticulateness of the "products" of the schools is reaching a crescendo.[126,201] All aboard for the bandwagon headed "back to the basics." You and I know, however, that reading, 'riting, and 'rithmetic (not to mention spelling) are far from basic. They are sophisticated aspects of our conceptual maps and, if not firmly anchored to our more basic perceptual maps, will condemn us to a life in a disembodied world of words. Someday, perhaps, those critics will do their history homework, so that they don't have to repeat it, and consider the possibility that the problem with the three Rs may be too much too soon, rather than too little too late. The principle that "if some is good, then more is better, and most is best" is being challenged at its source in economics; it certainly never has applied or ever will apply in psychology.

A third reason is that, whenever research is conducted to test the relative effectiveness of outside-in and inside-out teaching, the results are evaluated in terms of the prevailing outside-in standards. It is not just a case of the defending champion having an advantage; it is rather as if the defending champion is a boxer, the challenger is a karate expert, and the contest must be fought according to the rules of boxing. Experimenters who tried to replicate the results of Getzels and Jackson found that highly intelligent children did better than highly creative children in academic achievement. This is not surprising. Traditional schools train and test convergent-production skills. They cannot test divergent-production skills with their objective instruments, because those skills require students to produce their own answers rather than choose from among alternative answers provided for them. Intelligence tests and academic achievement tests are, therefore, two alternative measures of the same thing. They should indeed be correlated.* As we saw in the case of H. Joseph Smythe III and Josef Smithski (Section 7.22), correlations between intelligence tests and various indexes of "success" do not imply a causal relationship. They are not independent measures. They are simply indexes of a complex of interdependent variables.

Despite this advantage in favor of outside-in teaching, research is accumulating that is overwhelmingly in favor of inside-out teaching. It is as if

---

*A homespun example may help to make this point clearer. An equivalent error once caused me to miss an important appointment. I didn't trust the clock in the kitchen stove, since I didn't know whether it had been reset after an electricity cut a few days before. However, I was reassured by the fact that my roommate's watch gave the same time. Both measuring instruments turned out to be equally slow, since (as I found out too late) he had set his watch by the clock.

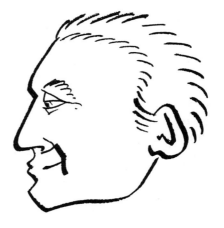

IT IS ALWAYS A PLEASURE TO HEAR EDUCATORS INSIST THAT THERE MUST BE A CLOSE RELATIONSHIP BETWEEN READING ABILITIES AND INTELLIGENCE, BECAUSE CHILDREN WHO SCORE WELL ON READING TESTS ALSO SCORE WELL ON INTELLIGENCE TESTS WHICH MUST BE READ.

MARTIN MAYER
THE SCHOOLS

the karate expert is so superior to the boxer that he can win even though they are fighting according to boxing rules. Massive studies of traditional education consistently fail to demonstrate any consistent effect of varying different aspects of the system (see Section 4.15). Educational innovators within the outside-in system are like engineers tinkering with an automobile. They adjust the carburetor to provide a higher proportion of gas by enriching the curriculum. No effect. They tune up the ignition system by changing the curriculum. No effect. They find better drivers by upgrading the quality of teachers. No effect. They improve the operating manual by designing better textbooks. No effect. Some of us are finally beginning to realize that the engine is missing. The "engine" is the intrinsic motivation of children to become adults. My argument in Chapter 4 is that an alternative educational system can be based on inside-out teaching, which is, in turn, based on the humanistic concept of the person, which is, in turn, based on the assumption of intrinsic motivation.

Research within the outside-in tradition contains some clues pointing to the missing engine. Coleman finds that the only variable significantly related to academic achievement is "destiny control" (and social class, which I suggest is related).[31] Numerous studies report the "Hawthorne effect"—the introduction of *any* novel teaching technique improves academic achievement. "Destiny control" tends to be dismissed, since it implies free will, which makes no sense within the outside-in tradition; and the "Hawthorne effect" is controlled as an undesirable extraneous variable. However, both those variables make sense within an alternative inside-out framework, and their positive relationship to academic achievement suggests that education can be improved by turning it inside out. Research supports this suggestion. De Charms demonstrates that learning can be improved by increasing the internal locus of control.[39] McKeachie summarizes the research on the outcome of instructor-centered (outside-in) and student-centered (inside-out) instruction.[145] He concludes that the student-centered approach produces greater gains in the ability to supply concepts in new situations, motivation to learn, attitude change, and group-membership skills. Thistlewaite reported on the characteristics of teachers named by a group of National Merit Scholars as those who contributed most to their desire to learn.[216] Those teachers allowed time for classroom discussion, modified the course content to meet students' needs and interests, treated students as colleagues, and took a personal interest in students. In other words, their teaching style was inside-out rather than outside-in. This research suggests that we should be putting the engine back in—or, rather, trying not to take the engine out.

14.3 INTERACTIONISM AND FUTURE EDUCATION

Rather, the solution is not so much to turn education inside out, as suggested by the humanistic theory presented in Chapter 4, as to discover the optimal orchestration between inside-out and outside-in processes—interactionism—which I have exemplified by the theory of Jean Piaget in Chapter 5. We do not thereby compromise between the two extreme positions but transcend them. Development is such an intimate interaction between inside-out growing and outside-in learning that it is impossible to disentangle them. Behaviorists and humanists show us different parts of the elephant; interactionists invite us to stand back and see the whole elephant.

One source of resistance to the introduction of psychological theory, such as Piaget's, into educational practice is the argument that children should not be used as guinea pigs. However, as Piaget points out himself, current practice is simply a bad experiment based on a bad theory.[173] The theory is confused, unconscious, unarticulated, adultomorphic—and basically wrong. Every practice is based on some theory. Good practice is based on good theory. Piaget's theory is, in my opinion, the best theory we've got right now.* You may not

---

* It does, of course, have a number of flaws. Some critics point to one or more of those flaws and think they have thereby disproved the theory. This is a little like abandoning your Cadillac because the ashtray is full and there is a scratch in the paint. If you are very rich, this is fine. However, developmental psychology is not very rich in theory. If we give up our Cadillac, then we are back to the humanistic Model-T Ford or the behavioristic bicycle. Perhaps we should keep our Cadillac and fix up the flaws.

"THERE CAN BE NO SIGNIFICANT INNOVATION IN EDUCATION THAT DOES NOT HAVE AT ITS CENTER THE ATTITUDES OF TEACHERS, AND IT IS AN ILLUSION TO THINK OTHERWISE. THE BELIEFS, FEELINGS, AND ASSUMPTIONS OF TEACHERS ARE THE AIR OF A LEARNING ENVIRONMENT; THEY DETERMINE THE QUALITY OF LIFE WITHIN IT."

NEIL POSTMAN AND CHARLES WEINGARTNER
TEACHING AS A SUBVERSIVE ACTIVITY

want to adopt it, but you certainly should adapt your emerging theory to "accommodate" this deep, broad, and long theory of the development that you, as a teacher, will be facilitating.

Although there are wide differences of opinion about solutions, there is almost universal agreement that traditional education has profound problems. The three major sets of solutions are deschooling (see Pre-exercise 1 to this chapter), free schooling (see Post-exercises 1 and 2 to Chapter 4), and reschooling. I am recommending here the last, and least radical, solution—that the schools change to conform to what we have come to know about children through accumulated experience, including that arranged experience called research. What we have learned about our bodies is reflected in the improved facilities in our hospitals; what we have learned about our minds has not yet percolated into our schools.

John Holt, looking strangely out of place with his short hair, jacket, and tie, was surrounded by wild-haired, idealistic youths complaining bitterly because he was not singlehandedly transforming the educational system right away. From the fringes of the group, I heard him say gently "Each of us does what we can with what we have got." So I'm doing what I can with what I've got. I'm writing a textbook. It would seem almost contradictory to write a textbook advocating an inside-out educational system, since the textbook is part of the apparatus of the outside-in tradition. I am trying, however, to get away from the traditional "text" book, with its authoritarian tone of gospel truth. Perhaps it should be called a teaching book. It is difficult to have an inside-out teaching book accepted in an outside-in system. This book is in your hands only because I have a very open-minded publisher and you have a very open-minded professor.

You will have equivalent difficulties if you try to be an inside-out teacher within our outside-in system. From time to time, an educational administrator will condescendingly concede that the most important element within the system is "the frontline soldier"—the teacher. The metaphor betrays the fact that such administrators view the organization as hierarchical, like the army, with administrators as generals, principals as sergeants, teachers as privates—and children, presumably, as "the enemy." This top-to-bottom organization perpetuates outside-in schooling. Turning teaching inside out will also require

I HAVE COME TO A FRIGHTENING CONCLUSION. I AM THE DECISIVE ELEMENT IN THE CLASSROOM. IT IS MY PERSONAL APPROACH THAT CREATES THE CLIMATE. IT IS MY DAILY MOOD THAT MAKES THE WEATHER. AS A TEACHER, I POSSESS TREMENDOUS POWER TO MAKE A CHILD'S LIFE MISERABLE OR JOYOUS. I CAN BE A TOOL OF TORTURE OR AN IN-STRUMENT OF INSPIRATION. I CAN HUMILIATE OR HUMOR, HURT OR HEAL. IN ALL SITUATIONS IT IS MY RESPONSE THAT DECIDES WHETHER A CRISIS WILL BE ESCALATED OR DE-ESCALATED, AND A CHILD HUMANIZED OR DE-HUMANIZED.

HAIM GINOTT
TEACHER AND CHILD

turning the educational system upside down. Schools are for students. The most important people working in the schools are the teachers. The principals and the administrators are useful teaching aides to look after the administrative matters.

John Holt is doing what he can with what he has got. I'm doing what I can with what I've got. Now, you do what you can with what you've got (and I hope you've "got" more as a result of working with my teaching book). Together we may make a bit of the world a bit better for some children.

POST-EXERCISES

1. Inspirational Literature

Teaching, like all professions, has its inspirational literature—that is, books designed to inspire more than to inform. When you are doubtful about your choice of profession or, once you have embarked on it, when you are discouraged, you may be reassured and encouraged by the following books. You don't need to wait until you are doubtful or discouraged.

No response is required of you in this exercise. Just read the books and feel good.

Barzun, J. *Teacher in America*. Boston: Little, Brown, 1945.

Colman, J. E. *The master teachers and the art of teaching*. New York: Pitman, 1967.

Eble, K. *The craft of teaching*. San Francisco: Jossey-Bass, 1976.

Highet, G. *The art of teaching*. New York: Vintage, 1957.

Highet, G. *The immortal profession: The joys of teaching and learning*. New York: Weybright & Talley, 1976.

Peterson, H. (Ed.). *Great teachers: Portrayed by those who studied under them*. New York: Random House, 1946.

Ulich, R. S. *Three thousand years of educational wisdom*. Cambridge: Harvard University Press, 1954.

References

1. Adams, J. C., Jr. The relative effects of various testing atmospheres on spontaneous flexibility, a factor of divergent thinking. *Journal of Creative Behavior,* 1968, 2, 187–194.
2. Adams, R. S., & Biddle, B. J. *Realities of teaching: Explorations with video tape.* New York: Holt, 1970.
3. Adler, M. J. *The difference in man and the difference it makes.* New York: World, 1967.
4. Allport, G. W. The functional autonomy of motives. *American Journal of Psychology,* 1937, 50, 141–156.
5. Anderson, R. C. Learning in discussions: A resume of the authoritarian-democratic studies. *Harvard Educational Review,* 1959, 29, 201–215.
6. Arnheim, R. *Visual thinking.* Berkeley: University of California Press, 1969.
7. Aronson, E., et al. The jigsaw route to learning and liking. *Psychology Today,* February 1975, pp. 43–50.
8. Aronson, E., Bridgeman, D. L., & Geffner, R. Interdependent interactions and pro-social behavior. *Journal of Research and Development in Education* (in press).
9. Ashton-Warner, S. *Teacher.* New York: Simon & Schuster, 1963.
10. Atkinson, R. C., & Wilson, H. A. (Eds.). *Computer assisted instruction: A book of readings.* New York: Academic Press, 1969.
11. Baer, C. J. The school progress of underage and overage students. *Journal of Educational Psychology,* 1958, 49, 17–19.
12. Barber, T. X., & Silver, M. J. Fact, fiction and the experimenter bias effect. *Psychological Bulletin Monographs Supplement,* 1968, 70, 1–29.
13. Barber, T. X., & Silver, M. J. Pitfalls in data analysis and interpretation: A reply to Rosenthal. *Psychological Bulletin Monographs Supplement,* 1968, 70, 48–62.
14. Barron, F. *Creative person and creative process.* New York: Holt, Rinehart & Winston, 1969.
15. Bellack, A. A. *The language of the classroom.* New York: Columbia University Press, 1966.
16. Berelson, B., & Steiner, G. A. *Human behavior: An inventory of scientific findings.* New York: Harcourt, Brace & World, 1964.
17. Bernstein, A. L. Library research: A study in remedial arithmetic. *School Science and Mathematics,* 1959, 59, 185–195.
18. Birch, H. G. The relation of previous experience to insightful problem solving. *Journal of Comparative Psychology,* 1945, 38, 367–383.
19. Block, N. J., & Dworkin, G. (Eds.). *The IQ controversy.* New York: Random House, 1976.
20. Bloom, B. S. Learning for mastery. Evaluation Comment 1, Number 2. Los Angeles: Center for the Study of Evaluation, University of California, 1968.
21. Bloom, B. S., Englehart, M. D., Furst, E. J., Hill, W. H., & Krathwohl, D. R. (Eds.). *Taxonomy of educational objectives: Handbook I: Cognitive domain.* New York: David McKay, 1956.
22. Brown, G. I. *Human teaching for human learning: An introduction to confluent education.* New York: Viking, 1971.

23. Brown, G. I. *The live classroom: Innovation through confluent education and Gestalt.* New York: Viking, 1975.

24. Bruner, J. S. *On knowing: Essays for the left hand.* Cambridge: Harvard University Press, 1962.

25. Bruner, J. S. *The process of education.* New York: Knopf, 1963.

26. Bruner, J. S. *Toward a theory of instruction.* Cambridge: Harvard University Press, 1966.

27. Bruner, J. S. *The relevance of education.* New York: Norton, 1973.

28. Buros, O. K. (Ed.). *Mental measurements yearbook.* Highland Park, N.J.: Gryphon, annual.

29. Canfield, J., & Wells, H. C. *100 ways to enhance self-concept in the classroom: A handbook for teachers and parents.* Englewood Cliffs, N.J.: Prentice-Hall, 1976.

30. Chomsky, N. *Aspects of the theory of syntax.* Cambridge: MIT Press, 1965.

31. Coleman, J. S. *Equality of educational opportunity.* Washington, D.C.: U.S. Department of Health, Education & Welfare, Office of Education, 1966.

32. Coleman, J. S. The children have outgrown the schools. *Psychology Today,* February 1972, pp. 72–75; 82.

33. Collins, B. E., & Raven, B. H. Group structure: Attraction, coalitions, communication and power. In G. Lindzey & E. Aronson (Eds.), *The handbook of social psychology* (2nd ed.) (Vol. 4). Reading, Mass.: Addison-Wesley, 1969.

34. Coopersmith, S. *The antecedents of self-esteem.* San Francisco: Freeman, 1967.

35. Covington, M. V., & Beery, R. G. *Self-worth and school learning.* New York: Holt, Rinehart & Winston, 1976.

36. De Bono, E. *Five-day course in thinking.* New York: Basic Books, 1967.

37. De Bono, E. *The use of lateral thinking.* Harmondsworth, Middlesex: Penguin, 1967.

38. De Chardin, P. T. *Letters from a traveller.* London: Collins, 1962.

39. De Charms, R. *Personal causation.* New York: Academic Press, 1968.

40. Deci, E. L. *Intrinsic motivation.* New York: Plenum Press, 1975.

41. Deci, E. L., & Cascio, W. F. Changes in intrinsic motivation as a function of negative feedback and threats. Paper presented at the meeting of the Eastern Psychological Association, Boston, 1972.

42. Dennis, W., & Dennis, M. G. The effect of cradling practices upon the onset of walking in Hopi children. *Journal of Genetic Psychology,* 1940, *56,* 77–86.

43. Dunkin, M. J., & Biddle, B. J. *The study of teaching.* New York: Holt, Rinehart & Winston, 1974.

44. Eakin, R. M. *Great scientists speak again.* Berkeley: University of California Press, 1975.

45. Educational Testing Service. Judges disagree on qualities that characterize good writing. *ETS Development,* 1961, 9(2).

46. Einstein, A., & Freud, S. *Why war?* International Institute of Intellectual Cooperation, League of Nations, 1933.

47. Elashoff, J. D., & Snow, R. E. *Pygmalion reconsidered.* Worthington, Ohio: Charles A. Jones, 1971.

48. Elkin, F. *The child and society: The process of socialization.* New York: Random House, 1960.

49. Elkind, D. *The child's reality: Three developmental themes.* Lectures delivered at University of Alberta, Edmonton, Canada, March 21, 22, 23, 1977.

50. Englemann, S. The effectiveness of direct instruction on IQ performance and achievement in reading and arithmetic. In J. Hellmuth (Ed.), *Disadvantaged child* (Vol. 3). New York: Brunner/Mazel, 1971.

51. Ennis, R. H. A concept of critical thinking. *Harvard Educational Review,* 1962, *32*(1), 81–111.

52. Ennis, R. H. *Logic in teaching.* Englewood Cliffs, N.J.: Prentice-Hall, 1969.
53. Eron, L. D., Huesmann, L. R., Lefkowitz, M. M., & Walder, L. O. Does television violence cause aggression? *American Psychologist,* 1972, *27,* 253–263.
54. Eysenck, H. J. *The IQ argument.* New York: Library Press, 1971.
55. Festinger, L., Reicken, H. W., & Schachter, S. *When prophecy fails.* Minneapolis: University of Minnesota Press, 1956.
56. Finder, M. Teaching English to slum-dwelling pupils. In D. L. Burton & J. S. Simmons (Eds.), *Teaching English in today's schools: Selected readings.* New York: Holt, Rinehart & Winston, 1965.
57. Finn, J. O. Expectations and the educational environment. *Review of Educational Research,* 1972, *42,* 387–410.
58. Flavell, J. H. *Developmental psychology of Jean Piaget.* New York: Van Nostrand Reinhold, 1963.
59. Flowers, C. E. Effects of arbitrary accelerated group placement on the tested academic achievement of educationally disadvantaged students. *Dissertation Abstracts,* 1966, *27,* 991-A. (Abstract)
60. Fuller, R. B. *Utopia or oblivion: The prospects for mankind.* Toronto: Bantam, 1969.
61. Furth, H. G. *Thinking without language: The psychological implications of deafness.* New York: Free Press, 1966.
62. Furth, H. G. *Piaget for teachers.* Englewood Cliffs, N.J.: Prentice-Hall, 1970.
63. Furth, H. G., & Wachs, H. *Thinking goes to school: Piaget's theory in practice.* New York: Oxford University Press, 1974.
64. Gage, N. L. (Ed.). *Handbook of research on teaching.* Chicago: Rand McNally, 1963.
65. Gage, N. L., & Berliner, D. C. *Educational psychology.* Chicago: Rand McNally, 1975.
66. Gagné, R. M. *The conditions of learning* (2nd ed.). New York: Holt, Rinehart & Winston, 1970.
67. Gagné, R. M. & Rohwer, W. D., Jr. Instructional psychology. *Annual Review of Psychology,* 1969, *20,* 381–418.
68. Galton, F. *Hereditary genius.* New York: World, 1962. (Originally published, 1869.)
69. Gardiner, W. L. An investigation of the understanding of the meaning of the logical operators in propositional reasoning (Doctoral dissertation, Cornell University, 1966). (University Microfilms No. 66-4109)
70. Gardner, J. W. *Excellence.* New York: Harper & Row, 1961.
71. Garfield, J. A. Address to Williams College Alumni. New York, December 28, 1871.
72. Gartner, A., Kohler, M. C., & Reissman, F. *Children teach children: Learning by teaching.* New York: Harper & Row, 1971.
73. Gesell, A., & Thompson, H. Learning and growth in identical twin infants. In R. G. Barker, J. S. Kounin, & H. F. Wright (Eds.), *Child behavior and development.* New York: McGraw-Hill, 1943.
74. Getzels, J. W., & Jackson, P. W. *Creativity and intelligence.* New York: Wiley, 1962.
75. Gibson, E. J., & Lewin, H. *The psychology of reading.* Cambridge: MIT Press, 1975.
76. Gibson, E. J., & Yonas, P. A new theory of scribbling and drawing in children. In *The analysis of reading skill.* Final Report, Project Number 5-12-3. Cornell University and U.S. Office of Education, December 1968.
77. Gibson, J. J. *The perception of the visual world.* Boston: Houghton Mifflin, 1950.
78. Gibson, J. J. *The senses considered as perceptual systems.* Boston: Houghton Mifflin, 1966.

79. Glaser, R., & Resnick, L. B. Instructional psychology. *Annual Review of Psychology*, 1972, *23*, 207–276.

80. Goertzel, V., & Goertzel, M. G. *Cradles of eminence.* Boston: Little, Brown, 1962.

81. Goldfried, M. R., & Merbaum, M. (Eds.). *Behavior change through self-control.* New York: Holt, Rinehart & Winston, 1973.

82. Guilford, J. P. Three faces of intellect. *American Psychologist*, 1959, *14*, 469–479.

83. Guilford, J. P. *Intelligence, creativity, and their educational implications.* San Diego: Robert R. Knapp, 1968.

84. Hadamard, J. S. *An essay on the psychology of invention in the mathematical field.* Princeton: Princeton University Press, 1945.

85. Haddon, F. A., & Lytton, H. Teaching approach and the development of divergent thinking abilities in primary schools. *The British Journal of Educational Psychology*, 1968, *38*, 171–180.

86. Haefele, J. W. *Creativity and innovation.* New York: Reinhold, 1962.

87. Hall, C. V. Does entrance age affect achievement? *Elementary School Journal*, 1963, *63*, 391–396.

88. Hardy, D. E. *On having no head: A contribution to Zen in the West.* London: The Buddhist Society, 1971.

89. Harlow, H. F. The formation of learning sets. *Psychological Review*, 1949, *56*, 51–65.

90. Harlow, H. F. The nature of love. *American Psychologist*, 1958, *13*, 673–685.

91. Harvey, O. J., White, B. J., Prather, M. S., Alter, R. D., & Hoffmeister, J. K. Teachers' belief systems and preschool atmosphere. *Journal of Educational Psychology*, 1966, *57*, 373–381.

92. Heron, W. The pathology of boredom. *Scientific American*, 1957, *195*(1), 52–56.

93. Herrnstein, R. IQ. *Atlantic Monthly*, September 1971, pp. 43–64.

94. Holt, J. *How children learn.* New York: Pitman, 1967.

95. Holt, J. *The underachieving school.* New York: Dell, 1969.

96. Hunt, J. McV. Toward a theory of guided learning in development. In R. H. Ojemann & K. Pritchett (Eds.), *Giving emphasis to guided learning.* Cleveland: Educational Research Council, 1966.

97. Illich, I. *De-schooling society.* New York: Harper & Row, 1971.

98. Itard, J. M. G. [*The wild boy of Aveyron*] (G. & M. Humphrey, trans.). New York: Appleton-Century-Crofts, 1962. (Originally published, 1932.)

99. Jackson, P. W. *Life in classrooms.* New York: Holt, Rinehart & Winston, 1968.

100. Jackson, P. W. *The teacher and the machine: Observations on the impact of educational technology.* Pittsburgh: University of Pittsburgh Press, 1968.

101. James, W. *Talks to teachers.* New York: Norton, 1958.

102. Jencks, C., Smith, M., Acland, H., Bane, M. J., Cohen, D., Gintis, H., Heyns, B., & Michelson, S. *Inequality: A reassessment of the effect of family and schooling in America.* New York: Basic Books, 1972.

103. Jensen, A. R. How much can we boost IQ and scholastic achievement? *Harvard Educational Review*, 1969, *39*, 1–123.

104. Jensen, A. R. Environment, heredity and intelligence. *Harvard Educational Review*, Reprint Ser. No. 2, 1970.

105. Jonas, G. *Visceral learning: Toward a science of self-control.* New York: Viking, 1972.

106. Jones, R. M. *Fantasy and feeling in education.* New York: Harper & Row, 1968.

107. Kamii, C., & Dermon, L. The Englemann approach to teaching logical thinking: Findings from the administration of some Piagetian tasks. In D. R. Green, M. P. Ford, & G. Flamer (Eds.), *Piaget and measurement.* New York: McGraw-Hill, 1972.

108. Kamin, L. J. *The science and politics of IQ.* Potomac, Md.: Erlbaum, 1974.

109. Karier, C. J. Testing for order and control in the corporate liberal state. In N. J. Block & G. Dworkin (Eds.), *The IQ controversy.* New York: Random House, 1976.
110. Kash, M. M., & Borich, G. D. *Teacher behavior and pupil self-concept.* Reading, Mass.: Addison-Wesley, 1978.
111. Keller, H. *Teacher: Anne Sullivan Macy.* New York: Doubleday, 1955.
112. Kleitman, N. Patterns of dreaming. *Scientific American,* 1960, *203*(5), 82–88.
113. Koestler, A. *The sleepwalkers: A history of man's changing vision of the universe.* London: Hutchinson, 1959.
114. Koestler, A. *The act of creation.* London: Hutchinson, 1964.
115. Kohler, W. [*The mentality of apes*] (E. Winter, trans.). New York: Harcourt, Brace, 1925.
116. Krathwohl, D. R., Bloom, B. S., & Masia, B. B. *Taxonomy of educational objectives, the classification of educational goals. Handbook II: Affective domain.* New York: David McKay, 1964.
117. Kuhn, T. S. *The structure of scientific revolutions* (2nd ed.). Chicago: University of Chicago Press, 1970.
118. Lefrancois, G. R. *Developing creativity in high school students.* Unpublished M. Ed. thesis, University of Saskatchewan, 1965.
119. Lefrancois, G. R. *Psychology for teaching: A bear always faces the front* (2nd ed.). Belmont, Calif.: Wadsworth, 1975.
120. Lepper, M. R., Greene, D., & Nisbett, R. E. Undermining children's intrinsic interest with extrinsic rewards: A test of the "overjustification hypothesis." *Journal of Personality and Social Psychology,* 1973, *28,* 129–137.
121. Lévi-Strauss, C. *The savage mind.* Chicago: University of Chicago Press, 1966.
122. Lewin, K., Lippitt, R., & White, R. K. Patterns of aggressive behavior in experimentally created "social climates." *Journal of Social Psychology,* 1939, *10,* 271–299.
123. Lorenz, K. [*King Solomon's ring*] (M. K. Wilson, trans.). London: Methuen, 1952.
124. Lortie, D. C. *School-teacher: A sociological study.* Chicago: University of Chicago Press, 1975.
125. Luria, A. [*The mind of a mnemonist*] (L. Solotaroff, trans.). New York: Basic Books, 1967.
126. Lyons, G. The higher illiteracy. *Harper's,* September 1976, pp. 33–40.
127. Maddi, S. R. The search for meaning. In W. J. Arnold & M. M. Page (Eds.), *Nebraska Symposium on Motivation* (Vol. 18). Lincoln: University of Nebraska Press, 1970.
128. Maddi, S. R., & Costa, P. T. *Humanism in personology: Allport, Maslow and Murphy.* Chicago: Aldine, 1972.
129. Mager, R. F. *Preparing instructional objectives* (2nd ed.). Palo Alto, Calif.: Fearon, 1975.
130. Mahoney, M. J., & Thoresen, C. E. *Self-control: Power to the person.* Monterey, Calif.: Brooks/Cole, 1974.
131. Maier, N. R. F. *Problem-solving discussions and conferences.* New York: McGraw-Hill, 1963.
132. Maltz, M. *Psychocybernetics.* New York: Pocket Books, 1969.
133. Mansfield, T. Great expectations: An interview with Thomas Mansfield. In "Institutionalization of expectancy: A special issue." *Urban Review,* September 1968, *3*(1).
134. Martin, J. R. *Explaining, understanding and teaching.* New York: McGraw-Hill, 1970.
135. Maslow, A. H. *Motivation and personality.* New York: Harper & Row, 1954.
136. Maslow, A. H. Creativity in self-actualizing people. In H. H. Anderson (Ed.), *Creativity and its cultivation.* New York: Harper & Row, 1959.

137. Maslow, A. H. The need to know and the fear of knowing. *The Journal of General Psychology*, 1963, *68*, 111–125.

138. Maslow, A. H. Synergy in the society and in the individual. *Journal of Individual Psychology*, 1964, *20*, 153–164.

139. Maslow, A. H. *The psychology of science: A reconnaissance.* Chicago: Henry Regnery, 1966.

140. Maslow, A. H. *Toward a psychology of being* (2nd ed.). Princeton: Van Nostrand, 1968.

141. Mathews, M. M. *Teaching to read: Historically considered.* Chicago: University of Chicago Press, 1966.

142. May, R. *The courage to create.* New York: Norton, 1975.

143. Mayer, M. *The schools.* Garden City, N.Y.: Doubleday, 1963.

144. McGuire, T. *The tooth trip: An oral experience.* New York: Random House, 1972.

145. McKeachie, W. J. *Teaching tips: A guide-book for the beginning college teacher* (5th ed.). Ann Arbor: George Wahr, 1965.

146. McKeachie, W. J. Instructional psychology. *Annual Review of Psychology*, 1974, *25*, 161–193.

147. McKim, R. H. *Experiences in visual thinking.* Monterey, Calif.: Brooks/Cole, 1972.

148. McLuhan, M. *The Gutenberg galaxy.* Toronto: University of Toronto Press, 1962.

149. Mead, M. *Culture and commitment: A study of the generation gap.* Garden City, N.Y.: American Museum of Natural History, 1970.

150. Merleau-Ponty, M. *The primacy of perception and other essays* (J. M. Edie, ed.). Evanston, Ill.: Northwestern University Press, 1964.

151. Merton, R. K. The self-fulfilling prophecy. In *Social theory and social practice.* Glencoe, Ill.: Free Press, 1949.

152. Milgram, S. Behavioral studies of obedience. *Journal of Abnormal and Social Psychology*, 1963, *67*(4), 371–378.

153. Miltz, R. J. *Development and evaluation of a manual for improving teachers' explanations.* Unpublished doctoral dissertation, Stanford University, 1971.

154. Montagu, A. (Ed.). *Race and IQ.* London: Oxford University Press, 1975.

155. Moore, O. K. Autotelic responsive environments and exceptional children. In O. J. Harvey (Ed.), *Experience, structure and adaptability.* New York: Springer, 1966.

156. Moore, O. K., & Anderson, A. R. The responsive environment project. In R. D. Hess & R. M. Bear (Eds.), *Early education.* Chicago: Aldine, 1968.

157. Mosteller, F., & Moynihan, D. P. (Eds.). *On equality of educational opportunity.* New York: Vintage, 1972.

158. Murphy, M. *Golf in the kingdom.* New York: Dell, 1972.

159. Mussen, P., & Eisenberg-Berg, N. *Roots of caring, sharing and helping: The development of prosocial behavior in children.* San Francisco: W. H. Freeman, 1977.

160. Oettinger, A., & Marks, S. *Run, computer, run.* Cambridge: Harvard University Press, 1969.

161. Ojemann, R. H., & Pritchett, K. Piaget and the role of guided experience in human development. *Perceptual and Motor Skills*, 1963, *17*, 927–940.

162. Osgood, C. E., Suci, G. J., & Tannenbaum, P. H. *The measurement of meaning.* Urbana: University of Illinois Press, 1957.

163. Parsons, T. The school class as a social system: Some of its functions in American society. *Harvard Educational Review*, 1959, *29*, 297–318.

164. Pavlov, I. P. [*Conditioned reflexes: An investigation of the physiological activity of the cerebral cortex*] (G. V. Anrep, ed. and trans.). London: Oxford University Press, 1927.

165. Peal, E., & Lambert, W. E. The relation of bilingualism to intelligence. *Psychological Monographs*, 1962, *76*(27, Whole No. 546).

166. Penfield, W., & Rasmussen, T. *The cerebral cortex of man: A clinical study of localization of function.* New York: Macmillan, 1950.
167. Phillips, J. L., Jr. *The origins of intellect: Piaget's theory.* San Francisco: Freeman, 1969.
168. Piaget, J. *The child's conception of the world.* New York: Harcourt, Brace, 1929.
169. Piaget, J. *The child's conception of physical causality.* London: Kegan Paul, 1930.
170. Piaget, J. *Play, dreams and imitation in childhood.* New York: Norton, 1951.
171. Piaget, J. *The child's conception of number.* New York: Humanities Press, 1952.
172. Piaget, J. *The construction of reality in the child.* New York: Basic Books, 1954.
173. Piaget, J. *Science of education and the psychology of the child.* New York: Grossman, 1970.
174. Piaget, J. *The child and reality: Problems of genetic psychology.* New York: Grossman, 1973.
175. Piaget, J. *To understand is to invent: The future of education.* New York: Grossman, 1973.
176. Pidgeon, D. A. *Expectations and pupil performance.* Stockholm: Almquist & Wiksell, 1973.
177. Poincaré, H. *The foundations of science.* New York: Science Press, 1913.
178. Ramírez, M. III, & Castañeda, A. *Cultural democracy, bicognitive development, and education.* New York: Academic Press, 1974.
179. Richards, A. Hunger and work in a savage tribe. Reported in M. Bates, *Gluttons and libertines: Human problems of being natural.* New York: Random House, 1958.
180. Richardson, K., & Spears, D. (Eds.). *Race and intelligence: The fallacies behind the race-IQ controversy.* Baltimore: Penguin, 1972.
181. Ripple, R. E., & Rockcastle, V. N. *Piaget rediscovered.* Ithaca: Cornell University Press, 1964.
182. Roethlisberger, F. J., & Dickson, W. J. *Management and the worker.* Cambridge: Harvard University Press, 1939.
183. Rogers, C. R. Toward a theory of creativity. In H. H. Anderson (Ed.), *Creativity and its cultivation.* New York: Harper & Row, 1959.
184. Rogers, C. R. *Freedom to learn: A view of what education might become.* Columbus, Ohio: Merrill, 1969.
185. Romanes, G. J. *Animal intelligence.* New York: Appleton-Century-Crofts, 1912. (Originally published, 1882.)
186. Rose, J. E., & Woolsey, C. N. The relation of thalamic connections, cellular structure, and evokable electrical activity in the auditory regions of the cat. *Journal of Comparative Neurology,* 1949, *91,* 441–466.
187. Rosenberg, S. The streetcar named Paradise Lost. In *The come as you are masquerade party.* Englewood Cliffs, N.J.: Prentice-Hall, 1970.
188. Rosenshine, B. To explain: A review of research. *Educational Leadership,* 1968, *26,* 303–309.
189. Rosenthal, R. *Experimenter effects in behavioral research.* New York: Appleton-Century-Crofts, 1966.
190. Rosenthal, R. Experimenter expectancy and the reassuring nature of the null hypothesis decision procedure. *Psychological Bulletin Monographs Supplement,* 1968, *70,* 30–47.
191. Rosenthal, R. The Pygmalion effect lives. *Psychology Today,* September 1973, pp. 56–63.
192. Rosenthal, R. The Pygmalion effect: What you expect is what you get. *Psychology Today Interview Tape.* Del Mar, Calif., 1974.
193. Rosenthal, R., & Jacobson, L. *Pygmalion in the classroom: Teacher expectation and pupils' intellectual development.* New York: Holt, Rinehart & Winston, 1968.

194. Rowe, M. B. *Teaching science as continuous inquiry.* New York: McGraw-Hill, 1973.
195. Samuels, M., & Bennett, H. *The well body book.* New York: Random House, 1973.
196. Sexton, P. *The feminized male.* New York: Random House, 1969.
197. Shannon, C. E., & Weaver, W. *The mathematical theory of communication.* Urbana: University of Illinois Press, 1949.
198. Shockley, W. Negro IQ deficit: Failure of a "malicious coincidence" model warrants new research proposals. *Review of Educational Research,* 1971, *41*(3), 227–248.
199. Shulman, L. S., & Keisler, E. R. *Learning by discovery: A critical appraisal.* Chicago: Rand McNally, 1966.
200. Simeons, A. T. W. *Man's presumptuous brain.* New York: E. P. Dutton, 1962.
201. Simon, J. Teacher, heal thyself. *Esquire,* March 1, 1978, pp. 37–39.
202. Singh, J. A., & Zingg, R. N. *Wolf-children and feral man.* New York: Harper, 1942.
203. Skinner, B. F. *Verbal behavior.* New York: Appleton-Century-Crofts, 1957.
204. Skinner, B. F. *Walden two.* New York: Macmillan, 1960.
205. Skinner, B. F. *The technology of teaching.* New York: Appleton-Century-Crofts, 1968.
206. Slater, P. *Earthwalk.* New York: Doubleday, 1974.
207. Sluckin, W. *Early learning in man and animal.* London: Allen & Unwin, 1970.
208. Smedlund, J. The acquisition of conservation of substance and weight in children. *Scandinavian Journal of Psychology,* 1961, 2, 11–20; 71–87; 153–160; 203–210.
209. Snow, C. P. *The two cultures: And a second look.* New York: New American Library, 1964.
210. Sommer, R. Classroom ecology. *Journal of Applied Behavioral Science,* 1967, *3*(4), 489–503.
211. Spalding, D. A. Instinct, with original observations on young animals. *British Journal of Animal Behavior,* 1954, *2,* 2–11.
212. Spitz, R. A. Hospitalism: An inquiry into the genesis of psychiatric conditions in early childhood. In O. Fenichel et al. (Eds.), *The psychoanalytical study of the child* (Vol. 1). New York: International Universities Press, 1945.
213. Stephens, J. M. *The process of schooling.* New York: Holt, Rinehart & Winston, 1967.
214. Taylor, C., & Barron, F. (Eds.). *Scientific creativity: Its recognition and development.* New York: Wiley, 1963.
215. Teitelbaum, P. Disturbances in feeding and drinking behavior after hypothalamic lesions. In M. R. Jones (Ed.), *Nebraska Symposium on Motivation* (Vol. 19). Lincoln: University of Nebraska Press, 1961.
216. Thistlewaite, D. L. *College press and changes in study plans of talented students.* Evanston, Ill.: National Merit Scholarship Corporation, 1960.
217. Thorndike, E. L. *Animal intelligence.* New York: Macmillan, 1911.
218. Thurstone, L. L. Primary mental abilities. *Psychometric Monographs,* 1938, *1.*
219. Thyne, J. M. *The psychology of learning and techniques of teaching.* London: University of London Press, 1963.
220. Toffler, A. (Ed.). *Learning for tomorrow.* New York: Random House, 1974.
221. Torrance, E. P. *Status of knowledge concerning education and creative science talent.* Minneapolis: University of Minnesota Press, 1960.
222. Torrance, E. P. *Guiding creative talent.* Englewood Cliffs, N.J.: Prentice-Hall, 1962.
223. Trungpa, C. *Meditation in action.* Berkeley, Calif.: Shambala, 1970.
224. Turner, R. L., & Denny, D. A. Teacher characteristics, teacher behavior, and changes in pupil creativity. *The Elementary School Journal,* 1969, *69,* 265–270.

225. Von Bertalanffy, L. *General systems theory: Foundations, development, applications.* New York: Braziller, 1968.
226. Walker, E. L. *Psychological complexity and preference theory: A hedgehog theory of behavior.* Monterey, Calif.: Brooks/Cole, in press.
227. Wallas, G. *The act of thought.* New York: Harcourt, Brace & World, 1921.
228. Watson, J. B. *Behaviorism.* Chicago: University of Chicago Press, 1924.
229. Watson, J. B., & Rayner, R. Conditioned emotional reactions. *Journal of Experimental Psychology,* 1920, 3, 1–14.
230. Watson, J. D. *The double helix.* New York: Atheneum, 1968.
231. Wertheimer, M. *Productive thinking* (2nd ed.). New York: Harper, 1959.
232. White, R. W. Motivation reconsidered: The concept of competence. *Psychological Review,* 1959, 66, 297–333.
233. Winn, M. *The plug-in drug: Television, children and the family.* New York: Viking, 1977.
234. Wittrock, M. C., & Lumsdaine, A. A. Instructional psychology. *Annual Review of Psychology,* 1977, 28, 417–459.
235. Young, J. Z. Visual response by octopus to crabs and other figures before and after training. *Journal of Experimental Biology,* 1956, 33, 709–729.

INDEX